A HISTORY

of

CAMBODIA

Fourth Edition

DAVID CHANDLER
Monash University

Westview
PRESS
A Member of the Perseus Books Group

Copyright © 2008 by Westview Press
Published by Westview Press,
A Member of the Perseus Books Group

Westview Press books are available at special discounts for bulk
purchases in the United States by corporations, institutions, and other
organizations. For more information, please contact the Special Markets
Department at the Perseus Books Group, 2300 Chestnut St.,
Philadelphia, PA 19103, or call (800) 255-1514, or e-mail
special.markets@perseusbooks.com.

Designed by Timm Bryson

Library of Congress Cataloging-in-Publication Data
Chandler, David.
  A history of Cambodia / David Chandler. — 4th ed.
      p. cm.
  Previously published: 3rd ed. 2000.
  Includes bibliographical references and index.
  ISBN-13: 978-0-8133-4363-1
  ISBN-10: 0-8133-4363-1
  1. Cambodia--History. I. Title.
  DS554.5.C46 2007
  959.6--dc22

                                        2007009971

10 9 8 7 6 5 4 3 2 1

For Liz, Maggie and Tom

CONTENTS

ILLUSTRATIONS

PREFACE TO THE
FOURTH EDITION

I'm grateful to Steve Catalano of Westview Press for encouraging me to prepare this edition of a book that was first published in 1983. Mr. Catalano is the latest in a series of talented and helpful editors at Westview who have worked with me on this book. I'm also grateful to Kay Mareia, the project editor, and to Tom Lacey for his assiduous and helpful copyediting. Like the previous editions, this one is dedicated to my children.

The structure and the general approach of the book remain unchanged, but I have revised Chapters 2, 3, 4, and 5 to reflect the valuable research that has been published since the 3rd edition appeared in 2000. I refer especially to the pioneering work of the Greater Angkor Project, Claude Jacques, Christophe Pottier, Ashley Thompson, and Michael Vickery. In the rest of the book I have tried to keep abreast of significant new scholarship. The closing pages, which deal with events since 2000, benefit from several visits to Cambodia and from discussions with many people including Erik Davis, Youk Chhang, Penny Edwards, Kate Frieson, Steve Heder, Don Jameson, John Marston, Un Kheang, and Kim Sedara.

After almost a half-century of being interested in Cambodia, I have contracted many other intellectual debts which it's a pleasure to acknowledge. The deepest ones are to my wife, Susan, who first encouraged me to write this book, and to the late Paul Mus, who inspired my first two years of graduate study. I'm grateful also to my former students

Ben Kiernan and John Tully, and to a multitude of colleagues and friends, including Joyce Clark, Christopher Goscha, Anne Hansen, Alexander Hinton, Helen Jessup, Alexandra Kent, Charles Keyes, Judy Ledgerwood, Ian Mabbett, Milton Osborne, Saveros Pou, Lionel Vairon, John Weeks, and Hiram Woodward. The list could be much longer. As Paul Mus has tellingly written, "People build themselves out of what is brought to them by friends."

In 2005 the third edition was ably translated into Khmer under the auspices of the Center for Khmer Studies. The interest that the translation aroused among Cambodians has been very gratifying to me, and I hope that some of the men and women who read the translation will become historians of Cambodia themselves.

Finally, these lines provide a sad but suitable occasion for me to mourn the recent loss of five amiable and talented *compagnons de route*: May Ebihara, Richard Melville, Ingrid Muan, Jacques Népote, and David Wyatt. I miss their friendship, their company, and their insights into Cambodia's history and culture.

Melbourne, Australia
February 2007
David Chandler

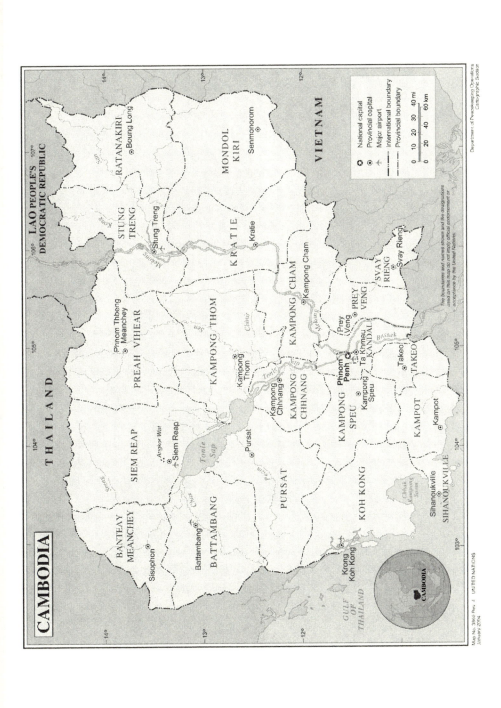

CAMBODIA

THAILAND

LAO PEOPLE'S DEMOCRATIC REPUBLIC

VIETNAM

BANTEAY MEANCHEY
Sisophon

BATTAMBANG
Battambang

SIEM REAP
Siem Reap
Angkor Wat

PREAH VIHEAR
Phnom Thbeng Meanchey

STUNG TRENG
Stung Treng

RATANAKIRI
Boung Long

KAMPONG THOM
Kampong Thom

KRATIE
Kratie

MONDOL KIRI
Senmonorom

PURSAT
Pursat

Tonle Sap

KAMPONG CHHNANG
Kampong Chhnang

KAMPONG CHAM
Kampong Cham

KOH KONG
Krong Koh Kong

KAMPONG SPEU
Kampong Speu

Phnom Penh
Ta Khmau
KANDAL

PREY VENG
Prey Veng

SVAY RIENG
Svay Rieng

TAKEO
Takeo

KAMPOT
Kampot

Sihanoukville
SIHANOUKVILLE

GULF OF THAILAND

Mekong
Tonle Sap
Sen
Srepok
Sekong
Se San
Bassac
Chinit

National capital
Provincial capital
Major airport
international boundary
Provincial boundary

0 10 20 30 40 mi
0   20   40   60 km

The boundaries and names shown and the designations used on this map do not imply official endorsement or acceptance by the United Nations.

Map No. 3860 Rev. 4   UNITED NATIONS
January 2004

Department of Peacekeeping Operations
Cartographic Section

1

INTRODUCTION

This book will examine roughly two thousand years of Cambodian history. Chapters 2 through 5 carry the story up to the end of the eighteenth century; the remaining chapters deal with the period between 1794 and 2007.

One reason for writing the book has been to close a gap in the historiography of Southeast Asia. No lengthy history of Cambodia has appeared since the publication of Adhémard Leclère's *Histoire du Cambodge* in 1914.[1] Subsequent surveys, in French and English, have limited themselves to the study of particular eras or have relied primarily on secondary sources.[2] Over the last sixty years or so, moreover, many of Leclère's hypotheses and much of his periodization—to say nothing of his style of approach—have been revised by other scholars, weakened by new documents, or altered by archaeological findings. The colonial era ended in 1953 and needs examination in terms of preceding history; moreover, the so-called middle period discussed in Chapters 5 through 7 has often been ignored even though it clearly forms a bridge between Angkor and the present.

The time has come, in other words, to reexamine primary sources, to synthesize other people's scholarly work, and to place my own research, concerned mainly with the nineteenth and twentieth centuries, into the framework of a general history, with a nonspecialist audience, as well as undergraduates, in mind.

As it stands the book examines several themes. One of these has to do with the effects on Cambodian politics and society of the country's location between Thailand and Vietnam. This theme, which is discussed in detail in Chapters 6 and 7, has been crucial since the second half of the eighteenth century and has recently faded in importance. For over two hundred years, beginning in the 1780s, the presence of two powerful, antagonistic neighbors forced the contentious Cambodian elite either to prefer one or the other or to attempt to neutralize them by appealing to an outside power. Cambodian kings tried both alternatives in the nineteenth century. Later on, Norodom Sihanouk, Lon Nol, and Pol Pot all attempted the second; the regime of the State of Cambodia (SOC), formerly the People's Republic of Kampuchea, which lasted from 1979 until 1991, committed itself to the patronage of Vietnam. A UN protectorate (1991–93) neutralized the contending foreign patrons of Cambodia by removing it from Cold War rivalries. In the late 1990s Cambodia and Vietnam joined the Association of Southeast Asian Nations (ASEAN), and the Kingdom of Cambodia, established under that name in 1993, has so far avoided seeking a dominant foreign patron, although in recent years China has emerged as an increasingly important ally and benefactor of the regime.

Another theme, really a present-day one, has to do with the relationship of contemporary Cambodians to their past. The history of Angkor, after all, was deciphered, restored, and bequeathed to them by their French colonial masters. Why had so many Cambodians forgotten it, or remembered it primarily as myth? What did it mean to have the memories and the grandeur brought back to life, in times of dependence? What happened to the "times between" Angkor and the modern era? And in what ways are the post-Angkorean years, the colonial era, and what has happened since 1954 connected to these earlier periods? How are the revolutionary events of the 1970s to be remembered, taught, and internalized? There has even been pressure from the government to play down the teaching of Cambodian history as too controversial.

A third theme arises from the pervasiveness of patronage and hierarchies in Cambodian thinking, politics, and social relations. For most of Cambodian history, it seems, people in power were thought (by themselves and nearly everyone else) to be more meritorious than others. Older people were also ideologically privileged. Despite some alterations these arrangements remained unchanged between Cambodia's so-called Indianized phase in the early years if the present era and the onset of Theravada Buddhism in the fourteenth century, when some egalitarianism, but not much, seeped into Cambodian social relations.[3] The widespread acceptance of an often demeaning status quo meant that in Marxist terms Cambodians went through centuries of mystification. If this is so, and one's identity was so frequently related to subordination, what did political independence mean?

A final theme, related to the third, springs from the inertia that seems to be characteristic of many rural societies like Cambodia. Until very recently, alternatives to subsistence agriculture and incremental social improvements of any kind were rarely available to most Cambodians and were in any case rarely sought, as the outcome could be starvation or punishment at the hands of those in power. In the meantime, crops had to be harvested and families raised, as they had been harvested and raised before. The way things had always been done in the village, the family, and the palace was seen as the way things *should* be done. Clearly, this attitude suited elite interests and kept the rest of society in line, but the process may well have been less cynical than we might wish to think. After all, how else was stability to be maintained? Throughout Cambodian history, in any case, governance (or *rajakar,* literally "royal work") was the privilege enjoyed by people freed in some way from the obligation of growing their own food. The governed grew food for those above them in exchange for their protection.

This conservative cast of mind has led some writers to suggest that, at least until the 1970s, Cambodia and its people were unchanging and asleep. The notion of changelessness suited the French colonial administration, as it implied docility. For later observers there has been something "un-Cambodian" about revolutionary efforts, however misguided and inept, to break into a new kind of life and something un-Cambodian about the country becoming a player on the global scene.

The notion of changelessness, of course, is an oversimplification of events, but it has persisted for a long time among students of Cambodian history and among Cambodians with a conservative point of view. The notion will be undermined in this book, for each of the chapters that follow records a major transformation in Cambodian life. The first perceptible one came with the mobilization of population and resources to form a somewhat Indianized polity at the start of the Christian era, discussed in Chapter 2. Another followed the concentration of power at Angkor in the ninth and tenth centuries, which is described in Chapter 3. A state emerged at Angkor that some scholars have seen as a classic example of Karl Wittfogel's notion of oriental despotism or of Marx's concept of an Asiatic mode of production and which has bequeathed an extraordinary legacy of religious monuments and sculpture.[4] Still another transformation, discussed in Chapter 4, overtook the Khmer when their capital was damaged by Cham invaders in 1177 and was rebuilt into a Buddhist city by the Khmer monarch Jayavarman VII, who was a Mahayana Buddhist. In the century following his death in 1220, still another transformation occurred: the conversion of most Cambodians from a loose-fitting form of Shaivistic Hinduism, with perhaps some Mahayana overtones, to Theravada Buddhism, the religion of the new kingdoms that were coming into being in what is now central Thailand. These changes are discussed in Chapter 5. The abandonment of Angkor in the fifteenth and sixteenth centuries and the southward drift of Cambodia's demographic center of gravity in this period probably had even more profound effects.

Because the sources are so thin and unreliable, the middle period of Cambodian history, extending from the abandonment of Angkor to the imposition of French control, is difficult to study, but it is clear that it was very different from its Angkorean forebear. For one thing, the spread of Theravada Buddhism (and its corollary, Thai cultural influence) diminished the importance of priestly families close to the king who had crowded around the throne looking for preferment. In Angkorean times, these families had controlled much of the land and manpower around Angkor through their connections with royally sponsored religious foundations. As these foundations were replaced by *wats* (Theravada Buddhist temples), the forms of social mobilization that had been in effect at Angkor broke down, and so did the massive and complicated irrigation system that had allowed Angkorean populations to harvest two or sometimes three crops of rice per year. The elite grew less numerous as a result of these changes and out-migration, while its interests became more commercial.

Unfortunately for us, these transformations occurred in a very poorly documented era. Through documents, we can examine Cambodian society before and after the transformations, but not while they were taking place. We have no clear idea, for example, why so many people changed religions when they did or how the process played out. Although there were clearly some economic incentives involved, it is hard to say why (and when) a landholding Angkorean elite transformed itself into, or was replaced by, an elite more interested in trade.

In the seventeenth and eighteenth centuries, Cambodia became a victim of its location. Its capital region (Phnom Penh/Udong/Lovek) lay at the eastern edge of the Theravada cultural zone that included Burma and Siam, and it was very close to the expanding southern frontier of Sinicized Vietnam. The region, in other words, lay along a cultural fault line. This fact affected the thinking and behavior of Cambodia's leaders, drawn into games of realpolitik that they could never expect to win. By the end of the eighteenth century, Cambodia had been devastated by civil wars and invasions from both sides; it was even without a monarch for several years. The early 1800s, discussed in Chapters 6 and 7, formed perhaps the darkest portion of the post-Angkorean era. By the mid-nineteenth century, Cambodia was almost a failed state. After a brief taste of independence under King Duang (r. 1848–60), the kingdom succumbed to French protection. Its rulers probably preferred this state of affairs to continuing Thai hegemony, but French rule soon came to resemble the "civilizing mission" imposed upon Cambodia earlier by the Vietnamese when the monarch's autonomy had also been sharply reduced.

The economic, social, and cultural changes of the colonial period in Cambodia resembled those that occurred elsewhere in Southeast Asia, but they were less intense than those that affected Java, Burma, and the Philippines under systematic colonial rule. As in these other colonies, however, the changes that swept through Cambodia helped to put together the framework for the Cambodian nation-state that emerged very briefly in 1945 and again in 1953.[5]

The three most obvious transformations in the colonial era discussed in Chapters 8 and 9, were in foreign trade, communications, and demography. Rice and corn, grown for the first time in large quantities for export, and rubber, grown for the first time altogether, now linked Cambodia with the world outside Southeast Asia. Its economy, never especially strong, became partially dependent on this outside world. Nothing altered with political independence; most of Cambodia's foreign exchange throughout the 1950s and 1960s came from earnings on the export of rice, rubber, and corn.

Perhaps the most visible difference between colonial and precolonial Cambodia, however, had to do with communications. By the 1920s, one could travel across Cambodia by car in a couple of days—a journey that had taken months just fifty years before. Cambodians began moving around the country by road and rail and found markets for their products opening up. The social changes that accompanied this new freedom of movement were obviously important, but they are hard to document precisely.

Finally, for every Cambodian who had greeted the French (if the image is appropriate) in 1863, there were four to say good-bye. Cambodia's population, estimated at slightly less than a million when the protectorate was declared, had risen to more than four million by the early 1950s. By keeping the kingdom at peace and by introducing some improvements in hygiene, the French presided over a demographic revolution that, when it intensified in the 1960s, soon put serious pressures on Cambodian resources. Since the 1980s these pressures have become even more severe, and Cambodia now has thirteen million people.[6]

It is difficult to say how decisive the Japanese occupation of Cambodia in World War II was, particularly as the French remained in nominal control until March 1945. With hindsight, however, it is clear that the summer of 1945, when Japan granted Cambodia its independence, had a profound effect on many Cambodian young people. In the late 1940s after the French returned, a new political ideology based on resistance rather than cooperation and on independence rather than subordination also took hold among many rural Cambodians, as well as in sectors of the Buddhist clergy and the educated elite. Some of these people opted for a revolutionary alternative to the status quo, occasionally with disastrous effects. These developments in the 1940s and early 1950s, discussed in Chapter 10, continued as an undertone to Cambodian political ideology ever since.

Cambodia gained its independence in 1953, but its economy remained much as it had been under the French. Under the relatively benign dictatorship of the former king, now titled Prince Norodom Sihanouk, which lasted from 1955 to 1970, education expanded, the economy flourished, and the country enjoyed a period now regarded by most Cambodians over fifty as a kind of golden age. By the mid-1960s, however, as the Vietnam War intensified and as Sihanouk's ability to control Cambodia's politics diminished, new forces came into play, including a revolutionary movement dominated from the shadows by the Communist Party of Kampuchea (CPK) led by a former schoolteacher, Saloth Sar, who later took the name Pol Pot.

In March 1970 Cambodia's National Assembly voted to remove the prince from power. Soon afterward the new, pro-American government declared that Cambodia had become a republic. This move, which ended over a thousand years of Cambodian kingship, which was restored in 1993, occurred in the context of a Vietnamese Communist invasion, U.S. involvement in the Vietnam War, and a burgeoning civil war inside Cambodia between the government and forces allegedly loyal to Sihanouk. The latter were soon controlled by the CPK, and a brutal civil war lasted until April 1975, when the Communists, known popularly in the West as the Khmer Rouge, were victorious.

Over the next three years, many of Cambodia's institutions were destroyed or overturned, and the urban population, forcibly exiled from towns and cities, was put to work alongside everybody else (except for soldiers and CPK cadres) as agricultural laborers. The new regime abolished money, markets, formal schooling, Buddhist practices, and private property. In a headlong rush toward a socialist Utopia, nearly two million Cambodians, or one in four, died of overwork, malnutrition, and misdiagnosed diseases or were executed.

The regime of Democratic Kampuchea (DK) effectively destroyed itself when its leaders decided in 1977, with Chinese encouragement, to wage war on the Socialist Republic of Vietnam. By that time, economic disaster in the countryside and uncertainty about the loyalty of high-ranking CPK members had led Pol Pot and his colleagues to set purges of the CPK in motion, during which at least fifteen thousand people were executed at the regime's secret prison after interrogation and after providing detailed, but often spurious, confessions.[7] Tens of thousands of others, especially in the eastern part of the country, were later killed for allegedly supporting the Vietnamese incursions of 1977 and 1978. These men and women were said to have Cambodian bodies and Vietnamese minds. Such actions hastened the collapse of DK and paved the way for a Vietnamese invasion. After 1979, Cambodia, known as the People's Republic of Kampuchea (PRK) and later as the State of Cambodia (SOC), struggled to its feet under Vietnamese protection. For several years, the regime submitted to Vietnamese guidance and control, particularly in the realms of defense, internal security, and foreign relations.

Throughout the 1980s, repeated votes in the United Nations condemned Vietnam's invasion of Cambodia and allowed DK representatives to occupy Cambodia's UN seat. Lacking diplomatic recognition (aside from allies of Vietnam), the PRK was unable to obtain development assistance, so the country's economic recovery was slow. Resistance forces, claiming loyalty to Sihanouk, the CPK, and an amorphous middle-class grouping, found sanctuary in Thailand and received political support from the United Nations that was spearheaded by the United States and China. Throughout the 1980s, Pol Pot's forces, estimated at between twenty thousand and forty thousand armed men and women, also benefited from extensive Chinese military aid.

The process of rediscovering and reshaping Cambodia's identity, which is not the same as reconstructing its prerevolutionary appearance, continued through the 1990s and beyond, as did yet another transformation whereby Cambodia today has become part of the wider community of Southeast Asian nations and moved into the global marketplace.

Given the importance of these successive transformations and because coherent economic data about Cambodia are so scarce, this book says very little about Cambodia's resources or its economy, except in passing. Aside from recent and sizable discoveries of oil offshore, as discussed in the final chapter, these have been remarkably consistent over the two millennia to be examined in the book. Developments in the manufacturing sector have also been significant since the early 1990s.

In early times, as discussed in Chapter 2, the cultivation of grain, probably wet rice for the most part, supported the people of the Mekong Delta in the region known to the Chinese as Funan. Chinese accounts tell us that farmers stored water in small, man-made ponds (*tra-peang* in Khmer) which they used for bathing and perhaps for irrigation, much as they were to do until the upheavals of the 1970s, when Cambodia's rural economy expanded rapidly and to a large extent broke down. The extensive hydraulic works at Angkor, discussed in Chapter 3, amplified this earlier technology. The relationships among the seasons, water, rice, and subsistence agriculture have remained crucial throughout Cambodian history. Supplements to the diet, however, may have changed somewhat. The amount of wild game has undoubtedly decreased, and in recent times imported and processed items have become available. The mainstay supplements, however—fish, roots, locally grown spices—appear to have changed very little from one century to the next. The economy of Angkor, now receiving detailed scholarly attention, is somewhat peculiar because, unlike most neighboring states, the empire never used money of any kind.

Until very recently, Cambodia's rural technology generally stayed the same. Pots, sickles, oxcarts, unglazed pottery, and cotton cloth, to name only five, appear to have changed little between the twelfth century, when they appeared on bas-reliefs at Angkor, and the present day.

A third consistency in the Cambodian economy lies in the field of exports. Until the colonial era when plantation crops that were grown for export (primarily rubber, corn, pepper, and rice) transformed Cambodia's national economy, the goods Cambodia exported were, for the most part, ones that grew wild in the woods. These included rhinoceros horns, hides, ivory, cardamom, lacquer, and perfumed wood. Because these exports paid for the luxuries imported by the Cambodian elite, it is important to note the symbiosis that existed between woodland populations responsible for gathering these products and the people who had settled in the agricultural plains. This relationship is examined in a nineteenth-century context in Chapter 6.

Another theme of the Cambodian economy is the country's annual victimization by monsoons. Like many other countries of Southeast Asia, Cambodia has two distinct seasons rather than four. The rainy season, dominated by the southeasterly monsoon, lasts from May to November. The rest of the year is dry. Over the years, rice farmers and administrators have calibrated their activities to the ebb and flow of these conditions. In the wet season much of Cambodia is under water. As a result, in precolonial times at least, military campaigns almost never began in wet weather; at the same time, because there was little for farmers to do in the fields once the rains had started, these months came to be favored by young men who wanted to spend short periods on the move or in monasteries as Buddhist monks.

Unlike the other countries of mainland Southeast Asia, Cambodia has no mountain ranges running north to south that might provide barriers to military penetration. Low ranges of hills mark off its northern frontier and parts of Cambodia's frontier with Vietnam. These have never posed serious problems for invaders, either from Champa in Angkorean times or more recently from Vietnam. Cambodia's vulnerability to attack, especially after the decline of Angkor, is a recurrent feature of its history and a theme of its more recent foreign relations. Conversely, in its periods of greatness, Cambodia expanded easily into the plains of eastern and central Thailand and extended its authority into the Mekong Delta, not yet occupied to any great extent by ethnic Vietnamese.

On the one hand, because Cambodia had no deep-water port of its own until the 1950s, most overseas commerce reached the Cambodian capital by coming upriver from the China Sea. On the other hand, foreign influences like foreign armies tended to come overland. The conversion of the kingdom to Theravada Buddhism discussed in Chapter 4 is an example of this process of infiltration and osmosis.

The transformations and continuities I have listed came under attack in 1975, when Cambodia's historical experience was challenged and discredited by Democratic Kampuchea, which worked hard to dissolve continuities, real and imagined, between revolutionary Cambodia and anything that had happened in earlier times.[8] We also have little idea how severe the damage was to rural Cambodian society during 1973 when U.S. B-52 bombers from Guam and Thailand dropped nearly twice as many tons of bombs on rural Cambodia as the United States had dropped on Japan in World War II.

The damage to the countryside and the Communists' repudiation of the past had important effects on people's memories and behavior. In the twenty-first century, Cambodia is a country that has been scarred by its recent past and identifies itself closely with more distant periods. It is the only country in the world that boasts a ruin on its national flag.

The complexity of Cambodia's past should encourage historians to refrain from making rash predictions. It may still be too soon, and it is certainly very difficult, to speak with assurance about the prospects for Cambodian society in its partially globalized, postrevolutionary phase. But the times that DK spokespersons were accustomed to call two thousand years of history still remain relevant to recent events and to Cambodians today. For these reasons, they deserve the sustained attention that the following pages hope to provide.

2

THE BEGINNINGS OF CAMBODIAN HISTORY

No one knows for certain how long people have lived in what is now Cambodia, where they came from, or what languages they spoke before writing was introduced, using an Indian-style alphabet, around the third century CE. Carbon 14 dates from a cave at Laang Spean in northwestern Cambodia, however, suggest that people who knew how to make pots lived in the cave as early as 4200 BCE. Another cave, near the ocean, was inhabited about a thousand years later. Presumably the first Cambodians arrived long before either of these dates; evidence of a more primitive, pebble-working culture has been found in the eastern parts of the country. Skulls and human bones found at Samrong Sen, inhabited since around 1500 BCE suggest that these prehistoric Cambodians physically resembled Cambodians today.[1]

Whether the early people came originally from what are now China and India and from elsewhere in Southeast Asia is still debated by scholars, as are theories that waves of different peoples moved through the region in prehistoric times. But recent finds suggest that mainland Southeast Asia had a comparatively sophisticated culture in the prehistoric era; some scholars even attribute the first cultivation of rice and the first bronze-casting to the region. In any case, it is likely that by the beginning of the Christian era the inhabitants of what is now Cambodia spoke languages related to present-day Cambodian, or Khmer. Languages belonging to the Mon-Khmer family are found widely scattered over mainland Southeast Asia as well as in some of the islands and in parts of India. Modern Vietnamese, although heavily influenced by Chinese, is a distant cousin. It is impossible to say when these languages split off from one another; some linguists believe that the split took place several thousand years ago. Khmer, then, unlike the other national languages of mainland Southeast Asia—aside from Vietnamese—is not a newcomer to the area. This continuity is one of many that strike students of Cambodia's past. What is interesting about the cave at Laang Spean is not merely that it was inhabited, on and off, for so long—the most recent carbon 14 date from the cave is from the ninth century CE—but that the methods used to make pottery found at the earliest level, and the patterns incised on them, have remained unchanged for perhaps six thousand years.

The "changelessness" of Cambodian history was often singled out by the French, who in the nineteenth and twentieth centuries saw themselves as introducing change and civilization to the region. Ironically, this theme was picked up by Pol Pot's revolutionary regime, which claimed that Cambodians were asleep or enslaved for two thousand years. Both points of view ignore a great deal of evidence; arguably, the revolution of the 1970s was the fifth major one that Cambodia has undergone since prehistoric times. But prerevolutionary Cambodians were less contemptuous of tradition than Pol Pot was. "Don't choose a straight path," a Cambodian proverb tells us. "And don't reject a winding one. Choose the path your ancestors have trod." Part of this conservatism, perhaps, is characteristic of a subsistence-oriented society in which experimentation can lead to famine and in which techniques of getting enough to eat are passed from one generation to the next.

We know very little about the daily lives of Cambodians in prehistoric times. We do know that their diet, like that of Cambodians today, included a good deal of fish. It seems likely that their houses, from an early date, were raised above the ground and made accessible by means of ladders. Clothing was not especially important; early Chinese accounts refer to the Cambodians as naked. After about 1000 BCE perhaps, they lived in fortified villages, often circular in form, similar to those inhabited nowadays by some tribal peoples in Cambodia, Laos, and Vietnam. Sites of such villages have been excavated in eastern Cambodia.[2] The Cambodians, like other early inhabitants of the region, had domesticated pigs and water buffalo fairly early, and they grew varieties of rice and root crops by the so-called slash-and-burn method common throughout the tropics as well as in medieval Europe. These early people probably passed on many of their customs and beliefs to later inhabitants of the region, although we cannot be sure of this, and there are dangers of reading back into prehistoric and early Cambodia what we can see among so-called primitive tribes or twenty-first-century peasants. We cannot be sure that these modern customs have not changed over time. Hairstyles, for example, changed dramatically in Cambodia as recently as the early eighteenth century, and in the 1970s they were changed again by the revolutionary regime.

All the same, it is unlikely that certain elements of Cambodian life and thinking, especially in the countryside, have changed a great deal since Angkorean times (from the ninth to the mid-fifteenth centuries) or even over the last few thousand years. These elements might include the village games played at the lunar new year; the association of ancestor spirits (*nak ta*) with stones, the calendar, and the soil; the belief in water spirits or dragons; the idea that tattoos protect the wearer; and the custom of chewing betel, to name a few.

INDIANIZATION

The notion of changelessness dissolves, however, when we discuss the revolutionary changes that suffused Cambodia at the beginning of the Christian era. This was the centuries-long phenomenon known as Indianization, whereby elements of Indian culture were absorbed or chosen by the Cambodian people in a process that lasted more than a thousand years.[3] No one knows precisely when the process began or how it worked at different times. All-inclusive theories about it advanced by French and Dutch scholars usually put too little emphasis on the element of local choice; a few writers, on the other hand, may have tended to exaggerate the importance of local elements. Generally, as George Coedes has remarked, scholars with training in Indian culture emphasize India's "civilizing mission," while those trained in the social sciences stress the indigenous response.[4]

Historians must deal with both sides of the exchange. The process by which a culture changes is complex. When and why did Indian cultural elements come to be preferred to local ones? Which ones were absorbed, revised, or rejected? In discussing Indianization, we encounter the categories that some anthropologists have called the Great and others, the Little traditions, the first connected with India, Sanskrit, the courts, and Hinduism, and the other with Cambodia, Khmer, villages, and folk religion. In the Cambodian case, these categories are not especially useful. We cannot play down the Great Tradition in Cambodian village life. Where does monastic Buddhism fit in, for example, or Little Tradition activities, like ancestor worship and folk stories, at the court? Village wisdom always penetrated the court, and princely values enshrined in Hindu epics and Buddhist legends, or *jataka* tales, penetrated village life. Nowadays, urban and rural cultural traditions interact in Cambodia in a similar fashion.

Nevertheless, the process of Indianization made Cambodia an Indian-seeming place. In the nineteenth century, for example, Cambodian peasants still wore recognizably Indian costumes, and in many ways they behaved more like Indians than like their closest neighbors, the Vietnamese. Cambodians ate with spoons and fingers, for example, and carried goods on their heads; they wore turbans rather than straw hats and skirts rather than trousers. Musical instruments, jewelry, the alphabet, and manuscripts were also Indian in style. It is possible also that Indians had introduced cattle raising in Cambodia at a relatively early date; it is unknown, to a great extent, in the rest of mainland Southeast Asia.

Trade between prehistoric India and Cambodia probably began long before India itself was Sanskritized. In fact, as Paul Mus has suggested, Cambodia and southern India, as well as what is now Bengal, probably shared the culture of "monsoon Asia," which emphasized the role played by ancestral, tutelary deities in the agricultural cycle.[5] These were often located for ritual purposes in stones that naturally resembled phalluses or were carved to look like them. Sacrifices to the stones, it was thought, ensured the fertility of the soil. Cults like this were not confined to Asia, but it is useful to see, as Mus has, that an Indian traveler coming across them in Cambodia would "recognize" them as Indian cults honoring the god Siva or one of his consorts. Similarly, a Cambodian visiting India, or hearing about it, would see some of his own cults in those that honored the Indian god.

During the first five hundred years or so of the current era, India provided Cambodia with a writing system, a pantheon, meters for poetry, a language (Sanskrit) to write it in, a vocabulary of social hierarchies (not the same as a caste system), Buddhism, the idea of universal kingship, and new ways of looking at politics, sociology, architecture, iconography, astronomy, and aesthetics. Without India, Angkor would never have been built; yet, Angkor was never an Indian city any more than medieval Paris was a Roman one.

Indian influence in Cambodia was not imposed by colonization or by force. Indian troops never invaded Cambodia, and if individual Indians enjoyed high status, as they often did, it was partly by convincing local people that they deserved it. When Indians came, at first as adventurers, perhaps, or as traders, they were absorbed into the local population. Perhaps just as often, news from India came via Cambodian traders who had visited the subcontinent. Indianization never produced the identity crisis among Cambodians that Chinese colonization and cultural imperialism produced among the Vietnamese. Cambodia never resisted India, which was not, in any case, a unified state. Moreover, unlike Vietnam vis-à-vis Han China, Cambodia never looked to India—after the fourteenth century or so—for ideas, approval, or advice. Indianization gave a format and a language to elite Cambodian life, but it was not narrowly political. Moreover, the hierarchical arrangements that came to characterize the language and behavior of the Cambodian elite, although owing something to Indian models, never sprang from a recognizable caste system affecting Cambodian society as a whole. At the village level, caste considerations never took root; what resembled a caste system at the medieval Cambodian court, moreover, probably was little more than a set of ritual procedures that showed respect for Indian traditions.[6] Another by-product of Indianization in Cambodia is that Cambodian nationalism, unlike its Vietnamese counterpart, has not generally pictured itself as the product of a struggle against foreign invaders and advice. Instead, national identity, until recent times, was seen as the sum of social arrangements in effect inside Cambodia. Indianization and elements of life that may be traceable to India were merely components of the sum. The fact that they came from India (just as our polysyllables so often come from Greece and Rome) was not considered a reason for alarm.

Like many Southeast Asian countries, Cambodia has a legend that originates with the marriage of a foreigner and a dragon princess, or *nagi*, whose father was the king of a waterlogged country. According to one version of the myth, a brahman named Kaundinya, armed with a magical bow, appeared one day off the shore of Cambodia. The dragon-princess paddled out to meet him. Kaundinya shot an arrow into her boat, frightening the princess into marrying him. Before the marriage, Kaundinya gave her clothes to wear, and in exchange her father, the dragon king, "enlarged the possessions of his son-in-law by drinking up the water that covered the country. He later built them a capital, and changed the name of the country to 'Kambuja.'"[7]

This myth is of Indian origin, as is the name Kambuja, and perhaps it describes some obscure confrontation that had occurred during the Aryanization of southern India rather than an event in Southeast Asia. But if it is useless as a fact, it offers us an interesting starting point for Cambodian history. In the myth, Cambodians see themselves as the off-spring of a marriage between culture and nature. Kaundinya's acceptance by his father-in-law, who drains the kingdom for him, is crucial to his success. This idea would have been familiar to Cambodians, for until recently a prospective bridegroom often had to gain his in-laws' approval by living with them before his marriage. In the myth, the local people (i.e., the dragons) respect the brahman and, in his honor, give the kingdom an Indian name (which first appears in a Cambodian inscription in the ninth century CE).[8] Later on, many Cambodian monarchs would trace their ancestry to this mythical pair, who represented, among other things, a marriage between the sun and the moon. To be a legitimate king, it seems, one had to be Cambodian and Indian at the same time.

FUNAN

Chinese officials recorded the Kaundinya myth; indeed, for the first few centuries of the Christian era, written sources for Cambodian history are almost entirely Chinese. These are supplemented by archaeological findings, especially from the remains of an ancient trading city located near the modern Vietnamese village of Oc-Eo in the Mekong Delta, excavated during World War II by an archaeological team supervised by Louis Malleret.[9]

Roman coins found at the site and at Angkor Borei date from the second and third centuries, and some Indian artifacts, including seals and jewelry, can be dated to the same period. Malleret believed that the port declined in importance in the fourth century. No contemporary records about it have survived, however, and we do not know what it was called by its inhabitants.[10] Because of its location, and some of the artifacts found at the site, Malleret concluded that the port was used by pilgrims and traders moving between India and China in the first centuries of the Christian era. The size of the city suggests that it played an important part in this trade, and its location was ideal for ships hugging the coast and "turning the corner" from or into the South China Sea.[11] The city probably provided warehousing for goods in transit between India and China and was an outlet for products collected from the forested interior of Cambodia and Vietnam.

Until the twentieth century, forest products and precious metals made up the bulk of Cambodia's export trade. These included gold, elephants, ivory, rhinoceros horn, kingfisher feathers, wild spices like cardamom, and forest products such as lacquer, hides, and aromatic wood. Plantation exports like rubber and pepper were developed in the colonial era; rice exports, which made up the bulk of twentieth-century Cambodian foreign trade, were also of little use in early times, when nearly everyone in the region produced enough to feed themselves. The point to make about these high-value, low-bulk goods is that they were cultivated or caught by forest people rather than by the inhabitants of towns. Many of them probably traveled considerable distances before they reached Oc-Eo, and so did the goods or coins that traders used to pay for them.

Until very recently, many scholars believed that Oc-Eo was the seaport for an important kingdom identified by Chinese sources as Funan and located by George Coedes (using linguistic evidence rather than archaeological findings) near the small hillock known as Ba Phnom, in southeastern Cambodia, east of the Mekong. According to Coedes, the word Funan derives from the old Khmer word for mountain (*bnam*), and he located the ritual center of the kingdom at Ba Phnom. A cult to Siva as a mountain deity existed in Cambodia as early as the fifth century CE and may well have been enacted on Ba Phnom. An Indian traveler to China reported that "it is the custom of the country to worship the celestial god Mahesvara Siva. This deity regularly descends on Mt. Mo-Tam so that the climate is constantly mild and herbs and trees do not wither."[12]

Paul Wheatley has suggested that the cult originated in southern India and that the mountain was not Ba Phnom but another hillock not far away, in what is now Vietnam.[13] The evidence that either mountain was a cult site is stronger than the evidence that Funan was a major, unified kingdom or that its political center was associated with either hill. What made the place important to the Chinese was that a principality dubbed Funan by the Chinese offered tribute to the Chinese emperor, on an irregular basis, between 253 and 519. Stone inscriptions in Sanskrit and Khmer from a century later are available for study; they do not provide evidence for a major kingdom.[14] It is possible, nonetheless, that small chiefdoms in Cambodia occasionally banded together and called themselves a kingdom for the purposes of sending tributary goods to China (an ideal occasion for encouraging trade) or of seeking Chinese help against their neighbors. It is also possible that Funan was thought to be a major kingdom because the Chinese wanted it to be one and, later, because French scholars were eager to find a predecessor for the more centralized kingdom of Angkor, which developed in northwestern Cambodia in the ninth century.

Despite their usefulness in many ways, Chinese sources for this period present peculiar problems for the historian, as many of them uncritically repeat data from previous compilations as if they were still true. Nonetheless, Chinese descriptions are often as vivid as this one about Funan:

> The King's dwelling has a double terrace on it. Palisades take the place of walls in fortified places. The houses are covered with leaves of a plant which grows on the edge of the sea. These leaves are six to seven feet long, and take the form of a fish. The king

rides mounted on an elephant. His subjects are ugly and black; their hair is frizzy; they wear neither clothing nor shoes. For living, they cultivate the soil; they sow one year, and reap for three. . . . These barbarians are not without their own history books; they even have archives for their texts.[15]

There is evidence that the major step during the Funan period toward the integration of the small, dry-rice-growing and root-cultivating principalities, whose people worshipped Siva, with hunting and gathering societies inland from Oc-Eo was the introduction, perhaps as late as 500, of systematic irrigation; drainage probably came earlier. We have seen in the Kaundinya myth that drainage was attributed to the good offices of a dragon king, but the most important passage related to this innovation, and to Indianization, is Chinese, one which appears at first to be a garbled version of the original myth:

> Then a Brahman named Kaundinya ruled the kingdom. A spirit announced to him that he would be called upon to govern Funan, so he traveled there . . . and the people of Funan came out to meet him, and proclaimed him king. He changed the institutions to follow Indian models. He wanted his subjects to stop digging wells, and to dig reservoirs in the future; several dozen families could then unite and use one of these in common.[16]

Seventh- and eighth-century inscriptions refer to rice fields adjacent to religious foundations that are suggestive of irrigated rice, and aerial photographs of the Mekong Delta show silted-over canals, which may have been used for drainage as well as transport.[17] If irrigation was widely used before the ninth century, it was not on an especially large scale and, with the exception of the seventh-century agglomeration of Isanapura (now known as Sambor Prei Kuk, near Kompong Thom), the village was the most characteristic unit of pre-Angkorean Cambodia. Indeed, Isanapura probably consisted of villages grouped around a common ritual center, whose stone buildings have survived. Even after the introduction of wet-rice technology, perhaps in the fourth or fifth century, the area under irrigation, which is to say, under the control of supravillage organizations, was never very great. Moreover, it seems likely that most villagers in the hinterland continued to grow dry rice and to cultivate roots, supplementing their diet by hunting and gathering, long after irrigation and wet-rice cultivation had taken hold in comparatively Hinduized communities.

People, rather than land per se, are needed to cultivate wet rice. Keeping in mind this fact, as well as the low density of the population in the entire area (always excepting Java, Bali, and the Red River delta in Vietnam), it is easy to see why, throughout Southeast Asian history, overlordship and power were so often thought of and pursued in terms of controlling people rather than land. Population pressure, of course, probably impelled some Cambodian rulers, perhaps including Jayavarman II, to take control over new territory where the population could be deployed to grow rice. There were periods of Cambodian history, under Jayavarman VII in the twelfth century, for example, when far-flung territorial control was an important part of a king's prestige. Nonetheless, control over territory per se (mere forest in most cases) was rarely as important as controlling people.

Indeed, the notion of alienable ownership of land, as distinct from land use, does not seem to have developed in pre-Angkorean Cambodia. Land left fallow for three years reverted to state control. The king, theoretically at least, was the lord of all the land in the kingdom, which meant that he could reward people with the right to use it. Many of the Cambodian-language inscriptions from the Angkorean period, as we shall see, dealt with complicated disputes about access to land and labor resources. The record of inscriptions and, by inference, of architectural remains from the first eight centuries of the Christian era fails to provide evidence of large-scale unified kingdoms on Cambodian soil and aside from Angkor Borei very little evidence of the development of urban centers. There seems to have been some continuity among members of the elite, traceable in part to their tendency to marry among themselves, as we learn from surviving inscriptions.

At the same time, it seems likely that the territory we now call Cambodia, like much of the rest of early Southeast Asia, contained a collection of small states, each equipped with a court and an elite, and that these segments had entourages, or "strengths," of people growing food for them who could also be called upon to fight. Presumably, these chiefdoms traded among themselves and raided each other, particularly for slaves. It also seems likely that each king, when undisturbed (or when disturbing others), thought of himself as a universal monarch, benefiting from Indian teachings, as well as a local chieftain, performing identifiable Cambodian tasks.

Leadership was measured to a large extent by prowess, which was measured by success in battle, by the ability to attract a large following, and by demonstrated skill at performing religious rituals and providing protection. As J.D.M. Derrett has pointed out, protection, along with rainfall, is the sine qua non of peasant society: protection from enemies, from rival overlords, from the forces of nature.[18] In recognition of this necessity, overlords in the time of Funan and throughout Cambodian history often included in their reign-names the suffix *varman* (originally "armor"; hence, "protection").

The overlords themselves thought that they could not live without supernatural protection, and most of them sought this, in part, through their devotion to Siva. Here they were assisted, for a time at least, by a group of Indian brahmans, the so-called *pasuputa,* who enjoyed a vogue in India and elsewhere in Southeast Asia around the fifth and sixth centuries.[19] These wandering ascetics preached that personal devotions to Siva were more rewarding than meticulous attention to brahmanical rituals or to the law of destiny, or karma. Technically, an overlord's devotion did not require the intercession of the *pasuputa,* and some of them presumably did without it. In any case, these self-made Hindus were perceived, and saw themselves, as superior men, vehicles of Siva, the god who "ceaselessly descended" onto a holy mountain. The transmission of Siva's potency via the overlord and his ritual acts to the people and the soil was an important source of cohesiveness in Cambodian society.[20] It has also been a source of continuity. As late as 1877, human sacrifices to a consort of Siva were conducted at Ba Phnom at the beginning of the agricultural year. Like those described in fifth-century Chinese sources, these had the objective of transmitting fertility to the region and, like the Chinese rituals, they were sponsored by local officials.[21]

In the Funan era, Buddhism also flourished in Cambodia, and the Buddhist concept of merit, which still suffuses much Cambodian thinking about society, resembles, in some ways, the notions of prowess and salvation just discussed. In both schemes of thought, power and ability were seen—especially by those who did not have them—as rewards for virtuous behavior in previous lives. The loss, diminution, or absence of power, moreover, revealed to people that a previous existence had been in some way flawed. A person's status in society, therefore, was programmed by someone else's performance in the past, and one's behavior here and now determined where one would stand when one returned to life. To improve personal status, then, one could accumulate merit by performing virtuous acts, like subsidizing a temple or being generous to monks, donating a gilded image of a god, or sponsoring religious festivals. Acts like these were thought to redeem the person performing them. As we shall see, the great temples at Angkor were also thought of as redemptive gestures of this kind, as bargains struck by kings with their immediate ancestors and, through them, with the gods. No one at the time or later could see if the bargains were a success, but the thought of neglecting to make them, especially when the afterlife meant a return to earth, occurred seldom if at all.

The notions of *patron, client,* and *entourage* become important during later stages of Cambodian history—they are certainly useful keys to nineteenth-century Cambodian society, and to some extent Cambodian political life today—but it would be dangerous to assume that precisely similar arrangements were in effect in Cambodia in the sixth and seventh centuries. We seldom know how overlords came to power, for example, or how they recruited followers. We do not know what made followers linger in their service, or often what the services entailed. The evidence suggests that we can describe pre-Angkorean society in Cambodia as an aggregation of leaders and followers, occupying spaces of territory and spaces in society that were thought about in terms of centers and peripheries, corresponding to the Indian concept of mandalas although the term itself was not used in a political sense in Cambodia at the time. With a multiplicity of centers, Cambodia was decentralized; segments of what we would call "society" (i.e., the total of the aggregations) acted independently of each other or were related in sporadic ways.

Things were not quite as simple, however. Localized religious cults, like the ones Evéline Porée-Maspero and others examined in Cambodia in the 1940s and 1950s,[22] generally stressed the welfare of the community rather than that of the individual, for without communities to perform the work, irrigated rice cannot be grown. Rural life requires alliances. The human sacrifices at Ba Phnom were one example of this communal orientation. Others included the complex of rituals still ushering in the agricultural year today—the sacred furrow, the towers of sand, and so forth; the royal cults that in effect negotiate with the dead for the welfare of the kingdom; and the boat races that take place in flooded rivers at the end of planting. Although these cults at first appear to be antagonistic to each other (the Great and Little traditions once again), in fact they are complementary.

Because genealogies were not maintained in Cambodia, except among the elite, the *nak ta,* or ancestor people, had no family names. They thus became the symbolic ancestors of people in a particular place, or by dying in a place they came to patronize its soil. *Nak ta* in inhabited sites could be spoken to and tamed; those in the forest or in abandoned places were thought to be more powerful and more malignant. As a place was inhabited, ancestral traditions over the years gathered around it, although seldom to the same extent as in China or Vietnam.[23] The pre-Angkorean record is almost silent about *nak ta,* but we can assert, by reading back from modern data, that a confrontation between Hindu and local beliefs was less frequent than was a blending of the two.

The tendency to syncretize, in fact, was noted by early Chinese visitors. The passage that refers to Siva's continuous descent onto Mt. Motan, for example, also mentions a bodhisattva, or Buddha-to-be, that was held in reverence at the time. Occasionally, two Indian gods were blended with each other, as Siva did with Vishnu to form Harihara, a composite deity much favored by Angkorean kings. By combining the attributes of Siva, the creator and destroyer of worlds, with those of Vishnu, the preserver, Harihara provided a range of inspiration, and displayed an ideal monarch's ability to hold contradictory forces in balance.[24]

The process of blending different religions meant that here and there local spirits received the names of Indian gods, just as localized Greek and Roman deities were renamed in the early years of Christianity. Hindu temples also were often built near sites favored by pre-Indian celebrations; there are Neolithic remains underneath the palace at

Angkor.[25] What was being stressed at times like this was the continuity of habitation and a continuity of sacredness—ideas in themselves that had deep roots in Cambodian culture. If ancestors became Indian gods in times of centralization and prosperity, the gods became ancestors again when the rationale for Hinduism and its priestly supporters diminished or disappeared. Thus, at Angkor, and in Cham sites in Vietnam studied in the 1930s by Paul Mus, Indian images and temples were worshiped in quite recent times not as emanations from India but as mysterious products of the *nak ta*.[26] This is partly because the literature of the Cham and Cambodian elites, which was used to explain and justify the images and temples, had disappeared or could no longer be deciphered, while the language village people used in their religious lives remained to a large extent unchanged from the pre-Indian era to colonial times.

The most enduring cult, as Paul Mus has shown, was the cult of the lingam, or stone phallus. This widely diffused motif, and the cults associated with it, exemplified links between ancestor spirits, the soil where they and the lingam "grew," and the fertility of nearby soil for agricultural use. Because of the territorial aspect of the cult (a lingam could be moved from place to place, ceremoniously, but was only potent in one place at a time) and the notion that the lingam was a patron of a community, it was closely supervised by local overlords and by the king in the Angkorean era. As early as the fifth century according to Chinese sources, a cult honoring a mountain god at the hill of Lingaparvata in southern Laos—nowadays known as Wat Ph'u—involved human sacrifices; the site was notable because it contained an enormous natural lingam, some eighteen meters (fifty-nine feet) high.[27] Lingaparvata, like Ba Phnom, was patronized as an ancestral site by several Angkorean kings.

The period of Funan, then, which lasted until the sixth century, was one in which Cambodia's political center of gravity was located south and east of present-day Phnom Penh. During this period, trade between India and China was intense, and one of the principal components of this trade was Buddhist religious objects. Local religious practices emphasized devotion to Siva, Vishnu, and the Buddha as well as to minor and local Hindu deities, particularly female ones, known as *kpoñ*.[28] Politics centered on villages and groups of villages, rather than on a tightly organized kingdom; irrigated rice allowed for surpluses and for some social differentiation, as Michael Vickery has argued, but not as much as developed later on. The main point to stress about the period, from a historian's point of view, is that we know about it from Chinese sources, which tell about local customs, centralization, and commodities for trade. We hear no Cambodian voices, as we do from the seventh century onward in the form of stone inscriptions. After the waning of Funan, in fact, our sources become richer and harder to use.

GOVERNMENT AND SOCIETY IN EARLY CAMBODIA

The first dated Khmer-language inscription from Cambodia was incised in 611, and the earliest Sanskrit inscription was carved two years later.[29] There are some two hundred datable inscriptions, in both languages, from the seventh century, and these give us a picture of the way Cambodian society was put together. According to the inscriptions, Cambodian society was divided, informally at least, into those who understood Sanskrit and those who understood only Khmer. For several hundred years, Sanskrit was used in inscriptions that supposedly addressed the gods. Khmer, on the other hand, was the predominant language of Cambodian men and women, those who were protected by the gods and descended, as gods did not, from their ancestors and the highly localized *nak ta*. Sanskrit inscriptions, in verse, praise the actions of kings and the elite, such as building Hindu temples, sponsoring Buddhist monasteries, winning wars, and offering gifts to monks and brahmans. Some of the speakers trace or doctor their genealogies, as if to cash in on or invent ancestral merit; many praise brahmans at the expense of other segments of the society; and all are fulsome in praise of those in power, who have, after all, allowed the temples to be built and the stone inscriptions to be incised. Much of the verse, according to Indianists, is highly polished, subtly worded, and well composed, comparing favorably with Sanskrit poetry composed in India at the time.

Khmer inscriptions, on the other hand, are all in prose. They record the founding of temples and the details of temple administration, such as the numbers and names of people attached to a particular foundation. They also give inventories of temple treasures and list the dimensions of rice fields, orchards, and ponds (*trapeang*) in a temple's jurisdiction. Many of them outline the duties of slaves and set the amount of taxes, payable in labor or in kind, levied to support the temple priests. Many of them close with a curse—always in Khmer—threatening people who neglect, rob, or disrupt the temple in question with punishment over many generations.

A little too neatly, perhaps, the line between Sanskrit and Khmer separates the so-called Great and Little traditions. On the one hand, there are wealth, poetry, intricacy, wordplay, priests, and access to the gods, i.e., a language that protects. On the other, there are poverty, prose, straightforward catalogs, slaves, and the world of ordinary people, i.e., a language about what receives protection. Both sets of inscriptions used the same sort of alphabet derived from India and, as a rule, were carved by the same masons. Presumably poets and priests, if they wanted to do so, could read them both. But were they intended to be read? In general, they were accessible enough, carved on temple door posts or on free-standing steles; probably the texts were also kept on perishable material in archives somewhere else. The reason they were carved at all may have been that writing on stone, the medium of the gods, served a special purpose. Stone was not used in secular sites; these, including palaces and ordinary dwellings, were built of wood, bamboo, and other perishable materials. Sanskrit, moreover, was said by the elite to be the language favored by the gods; stone was associated with permanence, which is to say, the dead. In incising the stones, Cambodians were speaking, collectively, to their ancestors; the inscriptions themselves, if in Sanskrit, spoke the language of the gods. A curse, or an oath of allegiance, inscribed on stone was thought to be stronger.

Moreover, the juridical aspect of the inscriptions should not be overlooked. By recording land grants on stone, for example, it was thought that beneficiaries would be recognized and protected; similarly, curses (in Khmer) might serve as burglar alarms and preserve the sites from depredations.

The division between Sanskrit and Khmer was also the division between those who grew rice and those who did not. It was everyone's ambition to be "rescued from the mud," but very few were. Most of those were placed, in Angkorean times, into various *varna*, or caste groupings, which made up perhaps a tenth of the society as a whole. These people included clerks, artisans, concubines, artists, high officials, and priests, as well as royal servants, relatives, and soldiers. Because they seldom served as slaves, and only a few of them were important enough to patronize a temple, these people appear rarely in Cambodian inscriptions. This omission means, among other things, that we never know the names of the people who designed and carved the magnificent statuary and temples of Angkor. By the seventh century, in fact, the city of Isana-pura was already the most extensive complex of stone buildings in all Southeast Asia, built a century ahead of similar constructions in Java. All the same the presence of these free people somewhere between the summit of society, as symbolized by the king's palace and his sacrificial mountain, and the rice fields that surrounded them should not encourage us to call them a bourgeoisie or even a middle class, because those terms are not transferable and our information about these people is too sparse.

The connotations of Western-oriented social terms like these bedevil us when we look to other Cambodian social groups. We have already noted that the term "king," or *raja*, probably meant less in Funan than it did in medieval Europe. Another important term, *knjom,* which can be translated as "slave," seems to have meant something more ambiguous to the Khmer than our word *slave.* For one thing, as Judith Jacob has shown, *knjom* was only one of some fourteen categories of slaves in pre-Angkorean Cambodia.[30] They had many levels of social status, different origins, and many kinds of duties. Those toiling in the fields resembled black slaves in the antebellum American South. Others, especially those attached to temples, may have seen themselves as enjoying quasi-clerical status. And yet, as all of these groups of people apparently could be bought, sold, and given away and had no freedom to escape, they were not servants either. Many of them were probably bondsmen working off debts contracted by themselves or by their parents. Were they serfs? The question should make us wary of the interchangeability of terms, and Communist statements in the 1970s that early Cambodia was feudal are inaccurate even when it is clear that the society was exploitative and divided sharply between haves and have-nots. The evidence that connects slaves to *places* is incomplete, although some of them appear to have been attached to certain places for several generations. This suggests hereditary servitude, or a liability to be called on, and being attached to a place rather than to a particular lord. Some villagers were free to grow their own rice but were not free to move, others appear to have been owned by temples, still others by members of the elite. Practice and theory seem to have varied from time to time and from place to place; generalizations about Cambodian society in this period are difficult to make.

Evidence from inscriptions suggests that slaves of various kinds may well have made up the majority of the Cambodian population at any given time. Free peasants were liable to calls on their time and energy to perform public works, favors for an overlord, or service to a temple or to serve in wars. Many of them, in fact, were either prisoners of war or their descendants.

The slaves themselves pass in and out of Cambodian history as mere names. These are a mélange of Sanskrit and Khmer words. From one inscription to another, they range from respectful references (some *knjom* are referred to by the equivalent of Mr. or Ms., for example) to derogatory ones, in which slaves have names like "dog," "imperfect," "red-in-the-face," and "bad-smelling." By and large, slaves with recognizably Sanskrit names (such as "loves justice," the "slaves of Siva," or, merely, Dharma) tended to have slightly higher status than the others, and many of them may have served as musicians and dancers. Many of their names would be recognizable in Cambodia today; the names of flowers, for instance, are still widely used for girls.

Another difference between pre-Angkorean slaves and those of the antebellum United States is that the villages they lived in, the food they ate, and the beliefs they shared were not very different from those found in times of freedom (whatever the term meant to a rice farmer at this time) or from those of the masters whom they served. If the *knjom* had been uprooted, they usually came from fairly similar cultures; the gap between the city and the countryside was not yet meaningful or wide. As servants of temples, moreover, many *knjom* participated in rituals that punctuated the year, such as the times when gilded images were washed,

A ninth-century statue buried in the forest near
Kompong Cham. Author's photo.

clothed, and paraded around a temple, or when the eyes of a Buddha-
image were ceremonially opened. They crowded around royal processions and made decorations for palanquins as these passed through. The
knjom lived in the vicinity of grandeur. Among themselves, they probably explained grandeur, in turn, in terms of merit and merit in terms of
protection. They saw themselves as engaged, like others in the society, in
plotting their own redemption. What better way to do this than to serve
the priests who served the temple gods?

We can come to these tentative conclusions by reading back from recent Cambodian life or by studying bas-reliefs, statues, artifacts, and inscriptions. But as almost always in Cambodian history, we write the
peasants' words, as it were, without having access to their voices. What
would they have said? It is difficult to imagine without asking a second
question: To whom would they be talking? Among themselves, of

Ninth-century statues abandoned in the forest near Kompong Cham. Author's photo, 1962.

course, most Cambodian peasants are frank and egalitarian, but they take few risks in the presence of outsiders. The peasants' apparent acceptance of superiors has led some scholars to argue for an essential harmoniousness in traditional Cambodian society. But Cambodian history is filled with rebellions and civil wars, and events since 1970 should make us wary of writers who insist on a natural passivity among Cambodian peasants. The absence of peasant voices makes it almost as hard, all the same, to make a case for persistent tumult as for harmony. Most of the time there was plenty of cause for both.

Yet, pre-Angkorean Cambodia, and perhaps even Angkor itself, was not an integrated despotic state. Instead, it was a collection and a sequence of principalities sharing a somewhat despotic language of politics and control. Because the rulers of these principalities, some of whom were women, saw themselves as absolute, they were rivals of each other and thus independent. And yet throughout the eighth century (a period about which Chinese sources are silent, for no tribute from Cambodia had arrived) Cambodia was becoming more politically coherent in a process masterfully described, using Khmer-language inscriptions, by Michael Vickery. Integration involved increased population, increased wet-rice technology, alterations in patterns of local authority and apparently random inputs, like victories in war or protracted periods of peace. As Cambodia's center of gravity continued to shift northward, the area of Aninditapura, in the vicinity of present-day Angkor, grew in importance in relation to the principalities along the upper Mekong, at Sambor, and elsewhere. The distribution of pre-Angkorean inscriptions indicates that the more populated sections of Cambodia—as in the twentieth century, but not in the Angkorean era—were along the banks of the Mekong and lower Tonle Sap, particularly to the south of present-day Phnom Penh, with other settlements along the upper Mekong near present-day Kratie.

Until quite recently, scholars sought to consolidate this assortment of small kingdoms under the name Chenla, which was given to one of them by the Chinese and preserved in nineteenth-century Vietnamese as a name for Cambodia. The Chinese, in fact, distinguished between two Chenlas, one associated with the Mekong Delta (and known as "water Chenla") and the other ("land Chenla") apparently located somewhere on the upper reaches of the Mekong, perhaps near present-day Wat Ph'u in southern Laos. The Chinese were not averse to exaggerating the importance of the so-called barbarian states from which they received tribute. European scholars in the nineteenth and twentieth centuries, perhaps forgetting the multiplicity of kingdoms that had characterized medieval Europe or precolonial Africa, also chose to see Chenla as a centralized successor state to Funan, thus making a neat progression from the earliest of these "mighty" kingdoms to the one concentrated at Angkor.[31]

In a brief and persuasive essay, however, Claude Jacques has crippled the usefulness of this interpretation:

> Inscriptions give evidence in the Khmer country of a multitude of little realms and princedoms; those which the Chinese called Funan and Chenla, on grounds unknown so far, were among them and may have been the most important. It seems that some princes managed, sometimes, to take the leadership of a more or less large collection of realms; but this situation was to all appearances only temporary.[32]

It is clear nonetheless that by the seventh and eighth centuries, coastal trading states in Cambodia like Funan (and others like it elsewhere in Southeast Asia) had faded or changed into polities farther inland, known in the Cambodian case by the collective term Chenla. The wealth of these new kingdoms derived primarily from extensive wet-rice agriculture and the mobilization of manpower rather than from subsistence agriculture and trade. Ideologies from India, which survive today in architecture, sculpture, and inscriptions, seem to have played a prominent role in molding and directing these societies, perhaps because ideas of this hierarchical kind were useful in legitimizing the extraction of surpluses more or less by force. Rituals may have become associated with wealth as time went on, and wealth may have become tied to supernatural skills, in a process of state formation ably discussed by Vickery and Jonathan Friedman among others.[33] It is impossible, however, to recapture the process from the documents that have survived. What is important in terms of the sweep of Cambodian history is that the geographical and economic shifts of the seventh and eighth centuries reversed themselves in the fourteenth and fifteenth centuries and that, just as the first set of changes can be associated with the formation of Angkor in the ninth and tenth centuries, the second set can be associated with the establishment of a less monumental, less ambitious, and somewhat more outward-looking state centered in the area of present-day Phnom Penh.

3

KINGSHIP AND SOCIETY
AT ANGKOR

Scholars usually place the Angkorean period of Cambodian history between 802 and 1431. In fact, these years mark neither a beginning nor
an end. The northwestern part of Cambodia, where the state we know
as Angkor (the name derives from the Sanskrit word *nagara,* meaning
"city") sprang up in the ninth century, had been inhabited by Khmer-
speaking peoples for several hundred years. Moreover, although much
of the city was abandoned in the fifteenth century, it remained an inhabited site and was restored as a royal city briefly in the 1570s. More important, one of its major temples, Angkor Wat (i.e., the city-temple),
was probably never abandoned by the Khmer, for it contains Buddhist
statuary from every century between the fifteenth and the nineteenth
and inscriptions on its walls from as late as 1747.[1] When the Angkor
complex was "discovered" by French missionaries and explorers in the
1850s, Angkor Wat contained a prosperous Buddhist monastery inside
its walls, tended by several hundred hereditary slaves.

These dates 802 and 1431 are useful all the same, for they mark off
Cambodia's period of greatness. At various times in these six hundred
years, Cambodia—known in its own inscriptions as Kambuja-desa—
was the mightiest kingdom in Southeast Asia, drawing visitors and tribute from as far away as present-day Burma and Malaysia as well as
from what were later to be Thai kingdoms to the west.

SOURCES FOR ANGKOREAN HISTORY

At the same time, these periods of systematic domination were infrequent and relatively short. We know too little about social conditions at this time, moreover, to classify all Cambodian kings as despots. Some of them, as far as we can tell, accomplished little or nothing; others left scores of inscriptions, temples, statues, and public works. Some kings ruled over a centralized, multileveled administration; others seem to have controlled only a few hundred followers. One fact that emerges from studying the kings in order—as L.P. Briggs, George Coedes and Claude Jacques have done—is that they were able to command a variety of people.[2] Seen from the top, where written records emerge, the Angkorean period is easy to generalize about but hard to penetrate. Seen in terms of artistic styles, media, and motifs—including the facility of Cambodian poets in Sanskrit—it is possible to talk about progress, development, and decline without being able to say why some periods were supposedly progressive and others decadent. Seen from the bottom, it is easy to generalize again about continuity between that era and much more recent times, but we are still handicapped by the poverty of our sources.

Sources, indeed, pose major problems. Those connected with inscriptions written in Sanskrit or in Khmer have been discussed in Chapter 2, but it is important to see how the biases of these documents produce a skewed picture of Cambodian society at Angkor. The Sanskrit poems proclaim the grandeur of kings; the Khmer inscriptions exhibit the precision with which jurisdictional squabbles were prosecuted and slaves registered. Here and there, we can use inscriptions to cross-reference official careers; here and there—especially when they provide inventories of temple treasures and personnel—they give us a glimpse of material culture. But it is as if U.S. history had to be reconstructed from obituary notices, wills, deeds, Fourth of July orations, and little else.

These kinds of documents, of course, are meticulously dated. With some exceptions, therefore, the chronological framework of Angkor, particularly for the monarchs who reigned there, has been reconstructed after having been forgotten by the Cambodians themselves. The job of chronological reconstruction was never easy; it occupied much of the career of perhaps the greatest scholar associated with early Southeast Asian history, the French savant George Coedes (1886–1968). Coedes was unwilling to speculate about matters not dealt with by inscriptions, and he left his successors with a variety of tasks concerning the corpus of Cambodian inscriptions he established.[3]

The inscriptions themselves, being dated, are rooted in time. Being parts of permanent buildings, some of which have all but disappeared, they are rooted in the landscape too. In spite of this, with rare exceptions, the inscriptions are not the place to look for details of life among Cambodia's rural population, or for clear statements of the political process as it operated at Angkor and elsewhere in the empire. Instead, they usually refer to extraordinary events—contracts entered into by people and gods—observed from "above" in poetry or from "below" in prose. The *history* they give us is comparable, in a way, to the lighting and extinction of hundreds of torches, here and there, now and then, over the landscape of mainland Southeast Asia. As each is lighted, we can look around and discern a few details of historical fact: Temple X was dedicated to such and such an Indian god, by so and so, on such and such a date. It had a particular number of slaves attached to it, identified by name and sex, and with children identified in terms of whether they could walk or not. The temple lands stretched east to a stream, south to a small hill, west and north to other landmarks, and then the light goes out. We know little about the way this temple fitted into the context of its time, whether its patrons enjoyed official status, or whether the temple remained in use for months or centuries. In some inscriptions, descendants return to the site to restore it in honor of their ancestors; other temples seem to have lasted only as long as individual patrons did.

The other sources we have for the study of Cambodian history are the temples themselves, and the statues and bas-reliefs they contain, as well as artifacts dating from Angkorean times that have been unearthed throughout Cambodia. These tell us a good deal about the sequence and priorities of Cambodian elite religion, about the popularity of certain Indian myths, and about ways in which they reflect the preoccupations

A Cambodian inscription, ninth century CE. Photo by Claude Jacques.

of the elite. They also tell us about fashions in hemlines, hairstyles, and jewelry; these have been used to arrange a chronology of artistic styles. The bas-reliefs are informative about weapons, armor, and battle tactics; those from the thirteenth-century temple-mountain, the Bayon, are a rich source for details about everyday Cambodian life.

So in addition to deeds, obituary notices, and orations, we can work with tableaux showing the people of Angkor for the most part disguised as mythical figures and with bas-reliefs showing them going about their daily business. What is missing from our sources are documents that stand above the others, giving an overall view of the society, or those that in a sense come from underneath it, providing details about taxes, land ownership, life stories, and folk beliefs.

JAYAVARMAN II AND THE FOUNDING OF ANGKOR

What happened in 802? The Sdok Kak Thom inscription, incised in 1050 in what is now southeastern Thailand, has been for many years a major source for Cambodian chronology and religious history, but some of its assertions have recently been called into question by several scholars. The inscription tells us that in 802 the monarch we call Jayavarman II came to the Kulen hills to the north of what was to become the Angkor complex and participated in a ritual whereby he somehow became a "universal monarch."[4] The ceremonies also celebrated a cult with which the inscription is particularly concerned, that of the *devaraja,* a Sanskrit term that translates as "king of the gods," unquestionably a cult linking the monarch with Siva. The ceremony had apparently been preceded some years earlier by an "auspicious magic rite" celebrated by Jayavarman at the cult site of Ba Phnom in the southeast.[5]

Jayavarman II and his son, Jayavarman III, left no inscriptions of their own, thereby encouraging scholars to suggest that the importance granted to these kings as founders of Angkor has been exaggerated. The Sdok Kak Thom inscription is primarily concerned with the sacerdotal family that, for more than two hundred years, officiated at the *devaraja* celebrations. And yet the biographical details that the inscription provides are very useful. Jayavarman II apparently resided in five parts of Cambodia at different times in his career. He appears to have moved from the southeast, near Ba Phnom, to the upper Mekong Basin, near Sambor, before moving west to occupy Aninditapura, to the north and east of the Tonle Sap, where he may have presided over a city and the construction of several small brick temples.

What was Jayavarman doing in these places? Even with all the facts we know about him—they are more extensive than for many later kings—there is still something mysterious about him. Who was he? Where did he come from? In a persuasive essay, Claude Jacques has argued that he arrived (or returned) from a place called Java (perhaps the island of that name, perhaps a kingdom in Sumatra, or even someplace else) around 770 when he was about twenty years old.[6] One of his first actions, according to a tenth-century inscription found in the area of Ba Phnom, was to perform a ceremony that "made it impossible for Java to control holy Cambodia." We do not know what the ceremony involved or why Jayavarman II was impelled to declare his independence at this time and in this way. Coedes has pointed out that although the ceremony clearly preceded the one performed on Mt. Kulen, it could easily have been one of several, in many parts of the kingdom, as Jayavarman moved through them over the next thirty years.

The references are tantalizing and incomplete. Was the ceremony performed at Ba Phnom imported from Java? Or was it one that linked Jayavarman II with ancestral spirits at Funan? The ceremony was important enough to be noted in an inscription concerned primarily with other things two centuries later. Given Ba Phnom's enduring importance as a cult site, as recently as the 1940s, the second explanation is tempting, but evidence to support it is lacking.

The rest of Jayavarman's early career has been traced by Jacques, Michael Vickery, and Oliver Wolters.[7] It primarily involved a series of military campaigns and the formation of alliances, through marriages and grants of land, with locally powerful people willing to transfer some of their allegiance to a newcomer claiming to be a universal monarch. An undated inscription gives the borders of Jayavarman II's kingdom as being "China, Champa, the ocean, and the land of cardamoms and mangoes"—a land perhaps located in the west.[8]

The assimilation of the Angkorean region into Kambuja-desa occupied more than twenty years. No inscriptions have survived from this period, and temples appear to have been small or made of perishable materials. These undocumented years are crucial all the same, for at this time the related notions of nationhood and kingship, remolded to fit the Cambodian scene, appear to have been gathering force. Both terms should be used with caution. Nationhood may have meant little more than having a name (Kambuja-desa) with which to contrast one's fellows with outsiders. Cambodians were insiders, owing their allegiance to a particular "universal" king, whose relation to them resembled Siva's relationship with the other gods. Perhaps both these ideas came in from Java, but they were probably already known from the Indian literature of statecraft, familiar to brahmans known to have been in Cambodia at this time.

The evidence for these suggestions springs from inscriptions carved long after Jayavarman's death. But Wolters, Vickery, and Jacques have argued convincingly that in his progress through Cambodia the future king welded together an assortment of disparate regions into some sort of self-aware community. Whether or not Jayavarman II succeeded in this task (or even if the task was what he had in mind) is open to question because of the obscurity that surrounds his reign. But it is clear that the kings who came after him honored him as the founder of a kingdom and as the instigator of a particular way of looking at Cambodia unlike what their own, perhaps more provincial ancestors had been able to achieve. Jayavarman II also served a more practical purpose. Cambodian folk thinking has always placed great emphasis on the veneration of ancestors, or *nak ta*, associated with particular places. Once the royal capital of Cambodia came to be at Hariharalaya (present-day Roluos), where Jayavarman II finally settled, subsequent kings came to honor him as a kind of ancestral founder-spirit of the sort that every Cambodian village possessed until recently.

Although it is no longer tenable to say that the cult of the *devaraja* was in some way a ritual process by which a king *became* a god, or a god-king, the evidence of ritual and ideological connections between almost all Cambodian kings and the god Siva is extensive, even if the *devaraja* cult as such may not have been as important as the authors of the

Sdok Kak Thom inscription and many subsequent scholars would like us to believe. The cult, in other words, was *a* royal cult, rather than *the* definitive one. Hermann Kulke has argued that the cult involved a statue of Siva, himself *devaraja,* or king of the gods, that was paraded through the streets of Angkor—and other royal capitals at festivals—in remembrance, perhaps, of the role the cult had played at the beginning of the Angkorean period, when Jayavarman II freed Cambodia from Java. Other scholars have different opinions.[9]

YASOVARMAN AND HIS SUCCESSORS

Jayavarman II's son, Jayavarman III, came to the throne young, hunted elephants, and died after ruling "wisely" in 877.[10] The writer who provided this information had a special interest in continuity, after all, with regard to the *devaraja* cult, for the Sdok Kak Thom inscription presumes, perhaps mistakenly, that the rulers who patronized the *devaraja* cult were the legitimate and unique rulers of Cambodia. This may have become the case, especially after the middle of the tenth century, but it is interesting that Jayavarman III's successor, the first to embark on a systematic program of temples and inscriptions at Hariharalaya, made only one muted reference to this predecessor, tracing his own legitimacy to relatives of a wife of Jayavarman II (not Jayavarman III's mother) and to a pair of "kings" about whom nothing else has come to light. Presumably, this was a way of casting his genealogy far beyond Jayavarman's usurpation, thus connecting him with the pre-Angkorean rulers.

In fact it was this very king, Indravarman (r. 877–89) who himself was a usurper, which may account for his muddled genealogy. His reign is important because it was the first of many to be marked by a triadic pattern of royal behavior described in the 1930s by the art historian Philippe Stern.[11]

The first phase was to sponsor irrigation works in honor of his subjects and the watery divinities of the soil. During Indravarman's reign, a large reservoir was constructed at Hariharalaya to trap rainwater. It was known as the Indratataka and covered three hundred hectares (approximately 650 acres). An inscription tells us that as soon as Indravarman became king, he made this promise: "In five days, I will begin to dig."[12]

Another purpose of such reservoirs was to indicate the extent of a king's power, and of his alliances with the gods, by re-creating the geographical features associated in people's minds with Mt. Meru, the mythical home of the gods, where lakes surround the central mountain. This north Indian fantasy, translated to waterlogged Cambodia, is not devoid of irony; but neither are Gothic towers in many U.S. college towns.

The second phase was for a monarch to honor his parents and his other ancestors by installing statues of them, usually in the guise of gods. Indravarman sponsored statues of his parents (as well as of others, including his mother's parents and Jayavarman II and his wife, all depicted as embodiments of Siva and his consort) in the stuccoed brick temple complex known today as Preah Ko (Sacred Cow).

This charming temple, completed in 879, inaugurated what is now called the Roluos style of Cambodian architecture.[13] In this style, several features that were to become important later—including the custom of enclosing temples in a series of concentric moats and walls—appeared for the first time. The sophistication of the carving and the predominance of floral motifs suggest that these skills had been developed earlier by carving wood. Although of modest size in comparison with later temples, Indravarman's monuments of Preah Ko and Bakong, his temple-mountain, were far more grandiose, in conception and appearance, than anything that had preceded them and hint at developments in religious ideology and social mobilization for which other evidence is lacking.

An inscription from Preah Ko ("In battle, which is like a difficult ocean to cross, he raised a pathway, made up of the heads of his arrogant enemies; his own troops passed over on it") indicates that Indravarman had become a universal monarch by subduing unspecified contenders. As the inscription also tells us, "It seems that the creator, Indra, tired of making so many kings, had fashioned this king named Indravarman, [literally, 'protected by Indra'] to form the joy of the three worlds, uniquely."[14]

Inscriptions far from Roluos suggest that Indravarman at least briefly commanded loyalties in northeastern Thailand and the Mekong Delta. One inscription, carved in honor of one of his teachers (himself a cousin of Jayavarman II) extends the earlier rhetoric:

Ruler of the entire world which he had conquered, established on the slopes of Mt. Meru, he was even steadier than the sun, which occasionally was distant.

Atop the lordly heads of the kings of China, Champa and Yavadvipa [Java?] his reign was like a flawless crown, made from a garland of jasmine flowers.[15]

Statements like this about kings, which may strike us as flowery, were circumscribed by the traditional characteristics of the gods which the kings were being made to resemble. The poet's skill was thought to consist of piling up these characteristics and half concealing some of them behind metaphors, similes, and puns. Just as the verses enumerated ways in which a king was like the god, the temples were catalogs and pictures of the world of the gods, a sort of mirror image. In this sense, the temples can be seen as puns, or plays on words, and mirror images of another world.

The final phase of Indravarman's program, as detected by Philippe Stern, was to erect a temple-mountain. This is now known as the Bakong, and it took the form of a stepped pyramid. Unlike the reservoir, or the Preah Ko, the Bakong was dedicated to the king himself and was to serve, after his death, as his sarcophagus. Coedes estimated that thirteen Angkorean kings, beginning with Jayavarman II, built such temple mountains.[16] Not all of them have survived, and those that have can be read in different ways. First, they were planned as duplicates of the mythical mountain, Mt. Meru, which stood north of the Himalayas at the center of the universe. Like Mt. Meru, they were homes for the gods and for deceased worthies, not only kings, who had been assimilated into heaven. They were also tombs, housing the ashes of the king. In some cases, particularly Angkor Wat, they were astronomical observatories as well.[17]

Bakong was the first Cambodian temple to be built primarily of stone rather than brick; it was also the first, with the possible exception of the eighth-century temple of Ak Yom, to have a pyramidal shape. The temple was reconstructed by French archaeologists in the 1930s, but by then nearly all of its bas-reliefs had disappeared.

Indravarman's son, Yasovarman, who reigned from 889 to about 910, was an important king. His inscriptions and his buildings suggest that he wanted to do more than his father did and to focus Cambodia around a royal *city*. Yasodharapura, the "city" of Angkor, bore his name until it was abandoned in the 1500s.

Yasovarman's first official action appears to have been to endow "a hundred" religious hermitages, equipping each with a royal rest house and a set of regulations.[18] Twelve nearly identical inscriptions related to these hermitages have been discovered. Two are near Roluos. Six of the others are from southeastern Cambodia, where Yasovarman, through his mother, claimed family connections from pre-Angkorean times. The spread of the inscriptions suggests that Kambuja-desa was becoming a recognized concept as well as an ideal.

Soon after this, Yasovarman honored his parents by building four brick temples, now known as Lolei, on an island he built in the middle of his father's reservoir. At the northeast corner of the reservoir—a time-honored direction in Cambodian religious thinking[19]—he built a raised highway running northwest toward the area sixteen kilometers (ten miles) away where he planned to establish his capital city. This area now houses the Angkor complex.

Yasovarman's choice of Angkor was probably influenced by his plan to build his own temple-mountain there on the summit of a natural hill. The choices available to him included a hill (Phnom Krom) that was too close to the Tonle Sap and another (Phnom Bok) that was too far away.[20] He constructed small temples on these two hills, however, and built his main temple on the hill known today as Phnom Bakheng and then as *phnom kandal* ("central mountain"), which still lies close to the center of the Angkor complex.

The Sdok Kak Thom inscription tells us that Yasovarman "established the royal city of Sri Yasodharapura and brought the *devaraja* from Hariharalaya to this city. Then he erected a central mountain (*phnom kandal*)."[21] Yasovarman's mountain was not identified as Phnom Bakheng until the 1930s. In conception and execution, it is far more grandiose than any of his father's monuments. Its symbolism has been studied in detail by Jean Filliozat, who has shown that the number of levels, statues, towers, and stairways, when read separately and together, correspond to various numbers, particularly 33 and 108, endowed by Indian religion with metaphysical significance. In some cases, pilgrims approaching the monument would be able to catch this allusion by counting the number of towers they could see.[22]

To the east of Phnom Bakheng, Yasovarman built a reservoir, the Yasodharatataka, roughly 6.5 kilometers (four miles) long and three kilometers (two miles) wide. Along its southern shore he had monasteries built for sects that honored Siva, Vishnu, and the Buddha. Elsewhere throughout his kingdom, he ordered temples built on natural hills, the most notable being Preah Vihear, on the edge of the precipice that nowadays forms part of the frontier between Cambodia and Thailand.[23]

These activities suggest that Yasovarman was able to command a far larger pool of manpower than his predecessors had. Yasovarman's inscriptions show him to have been a cosmopolitan monarch, aware of the grandeur of Indian civilization and tolerant of different religious beliefs. As usual, however, the sources reveal very little about his political activities, his alliances, or his idiosyncratic ideology. We have tantalizing glimpses of administrative reforms, including evidence that, in Yasovarman's legal code, fines were levied in relation to one's ability to pay and a suggestion that taxes were efficiently collected, in kind, throughout the kingdom. But for the most part we must settle for proclamations of his greatness, such as "He was a lion-man; he tore the enemy with the claws of his grandeur; his teeth were his policies; his eyes were the Veda. His glory was like a roar in all directions; his virtues made up his name."[24] Here, as so often in Sanskrit versification, many of the words are deliberate double entendres; the phrase "his eyes were the Veda," for example, plays on the similarity between the verb *to see* and the noun *sacred teaching*. These double meanings, as we have seen, appear at many points in Angkorean verse, as well as in the architecture of the temples.

Yasovarman died around 910. He was succeeded in turn by two of his sons. Little is known about them, and by 921 a brother of one of Yasovarman's wives was established in a rival city at Koh Ker, in an inhospitable area about one hundred kilometers (sixty-two miles) north of Angkor. The rival soon began to perform kingly actions, such as building a reservoir and beginning work on a temple-mountain. In 928, when the reigning king died at Yasodharapura, the Koh Ker ruler proclaimed himself king with the title Jayavarman IV. Work continued on his temple-mountain, known today as Prasat Thom, until about 930. The temple itself, housing a lingam estimated to have been eighteen meters (fifty-nine feet) high and about five meters (sixteen feet) in diameter (and probably made of metal, or encased in metal, for it has disappeared), was in fact the highest of the temples erected in Cambodia, with the exception of Angkor Wat.[25] Jayavarman IV's inscriptions boasted that the construction surpassed those of previous kings.

We do not know the basis of his colossal self-esteem, the nature of his following, or what prompted him to shift the capital from Yasodharapura. Although Jayavarman IV's extravagant claims may seem hollow or pompous to us, it is clear that, by force or persuasion, he was able to rule at Koh Ker over large numbers of people and in considerable splendor for twenty years. The site contains over forty temples constructed in this short period. His influence may well have extended into what is now northeastern Thailand where several temples in the Koh Ker style have survived. After his death in 942, one of his sons reigned briefly, and in 944 one of his nephews (on his mother's side, a nephew of Yasovarman as well), returned to Yasodharapura as King Rajendravarman II. In the words of a later inscription, this king "restored the holy city of Yasodharapura, long deserted, and rendered it superb and charming by erecting houses there that were ornamented with shining gold, palaces glittering with precious stones, like the palace of Indra on earth."[26]

Although little is known about Rajendravarman's reign, his imitation of procedures enacted by Yasovarman, such as building a temple honoring his ancestors in the middle of a lake, indicates that he wished to restore Angkorean kingship rather than to start a dynasty of his own or to connect himself with Jayavarman's brief dynasty at Koh Ker. Under Rajendravarman, two elegant temple-mountains, the Mebon and Pre Rup, were built as well as numerous other temples, especially in the north. His reign appears to have been peaceful, except for a successful campaign against Champa, and it ushered in a period of prosperity at Angkor that lasted for almost a hundred years. One aspect of this prosperity is the literary polish of Rajendravarman's Sanskrit inscriptions. One of these, the Pre Rup stele, runs to almost three hundred stanzas, glorifying Rajendravarman's genealogy, his learning, and his performance as king.[27] Another aspect of his reign was the commercial expansion of the Khmer kingdom westward into what is now northeastern Thailand; a third was his public tolerance of Buddhism. Rajendravarman appears to have studied Buddhism himself, and the minister in charge of public works throughout his reign was a prominent Buddhist.

Rajendravarman died in 968 and was succeeded by his son Jayavarman V, who was still a boy and appears to have spent several years under the close supervision of relatives and high officials. These men and their families figure largely in the highly polished inscriptions that have come down to us from his reign. One of the loveliest of the temples in the Angkor region, now known as Banteay Srei (Fortress of Women), was dedicated at the beginning of the reign by an official who was later Jayavarman's guru or tutor.[28] There is evidence that this delicate, small-scale temple, carved of pinkish sandstone, once served an important urban area, about sixteen kilometers (ten miles) north of the main Angkor complex. In 1916, when the region was heavily wooded, the temple was discovered by a French surveying party.

Although Shaivite like his father and many of the brahmans at the court, Jayavarman V was tolerant of Buddhism, and Buddhist scholarship flourished during his reign. An elegantly written inscription from Wat Sithor in Kompong Cham dating from this period shows how syncretic Buddhist thinking inside Cambodia had become, fusing elements of Buddhism and Shaivism in a way that led the nineteenth-century scholar Emile Senart to note, "Everywhere one senses a manifest preoccupation to disturb people's habits as little as possible, and to submerge deep differences inside surface similarities."[29] Inscriptions play down Jayavarman V's role as a builder of temple-mountains. His own, the Takeo temple, appears to be unfinished.

Jayavarman V's death in 1001 ushered in a turbulent and destructive period, but by 1003, another king, whose origins are unknown, was reigning at Angkor although the rest of the kingdom was not under his control. In the north, a prince calling himself Suryavarman, later to be king as Suryavarman I, was mentioned in several inscriptions.[30]

Some scholars have argued that neither of these kings was Cambodian by blood. As Michael Vickery has recently shown, however,

Suryavarman was almost certainly a Cambodian member of an elite family with links to the northeastern part of the kingdom.[31] It is intriguing that the blueprint used by Suryavarman to take power in the first decade of the eleventh century so closely resembles the one followed two centuries before by Jayavarman II. The process involved sporadic warfare as well as the formation of coalitions—by force, marriage, and cajolery—that enabled the pretender to reduce or buy off the power of local chiefs. Vickery suggested that Suryavarman had powerful allies among the priestly families that dominated the government at Angkor, and inscriptions of the time show him moving slowly westward, toward a partly depopulated capital, over a period of years—in itself an indication of the intricacy of his alliances.

Suryavarman won his final battle, an inscription tells us, "from a king surrounded by other kings." One new element in his rise to power is his patronage of Buddhism, although he apparently was not a Buddhist himself. There is evidence from hostile inscriptions that as he rose to power he destroyed *vrah,* or religious images,[32] but the meaning of this charge is unclear. Had Suryavarman been a Buddhist, the destruction might represent iconoclasm pure and simple. It is more likely that it was connected with the delegitimation of certain religious foundations whose patrons had been slow or unwilling to cooperate with him. Another inscription, in fact, suggests that during his reign the king deliberately impoverished members of the elite who had amassed great fortunes and thus represented distinct political threats.

One of Suryavarman's first actions in reaching Yasodharapura was to arrange that an oath of loyalty be sworn to him publicly by as many as four thousand officials, known as *tamvrac,* at the newly constructed royal palace. The oath has survived in a lengthy inscription, the only one of its kind, that states that the officials will be loyal to the king, and adds:

> If all of us who are here in person do not keep this oath with regard to His Majesty, may he still reign long, we ask that he inflict on us royal punishment of all sorts. If we hide ourselves in order not to keep this oath . . . may we be reborn in the thirty-second hell as long as the sun and moon shall last.[33]

The oath ends by asking that those who keep it be awarded religious foundations to administer as well as food for their families as "recompense due to people who are devoted to their master." Loyalty, in other words, was to be rewarded by the right to extract surpluses from regions under some sort of control by *tamvracs,* who were linked together by their allegiance to the king. The oath marks an intensification of royal power and also the imposition of a newly constituted, or reconstituted, elite connected to the control of land.

Suryavarman's reign, in fact, was characterized by the intensification of several aspects of kingship, coming at a time when bureaucratic power rivaled or even surpassed the power of the king. Suryavarman expanded the territory under Angkorean control, colonizing the western end of the Tonle Sap with new religious foundations. Further away, in the same direction, he annexed the Theravada Buddhist kingdom of Louvo, centered on present-day Lopburi in central Thailand. He also expanded the hydraulic works at Angkor, in a move that suggests that his other policies had increased the population of the city.

Under Suryavarman, priestly and bureaucratic functions seldom separate in practice were institutionalized. Government-sponsored religious foundations became conduits for government revenue and largesse in ways that remain obscure but that probably were connected with the power of priestly-bureaucratic families around the king.

His administration was an urbanizing one. A French scholar, Henri Mestrier du Bourg, has shown that, whereas for the preceding three reigns roughly twenty toponyms contained in inscriptions end with the suffix *pura,* or "city" (cf. Singapore, the "lion city"), under Suryavarman the number jumped to forty-seven, further evidence that his rise to power involved herding people into conglomerations from less tightly administered rural areas. Perhaps some of these *pura* were cities in name only, to enhance the prestige of locally based elites, but the evidence for urbanization coincides with other things we know about Suryavarman's reign.[34]

There is also evidence that merchants engaged in local and overseas trade became more active while Suryavarman was king. Throughout Cambodian history, the majority of such people appear to have been, in ethnic terms, outsiders—Chams, Chinese, or Vietnamese—but references to merchants as a group are more frequent in inscriptions dating from Suryavarman's reign. As usual, foreign trade involved the exchange of wild goods from forested areas for civilized ones, such as cloth or porcelain, but as Kenneth Hall has shown, commodities such as land, rice, buffalo, and slaves were also traded by Cambodians at this time for manufactured or exotic goods from other countries. Interestingly, this economic activity occurred without any consistent units of value or any official currency, a fact that persisted well into Cambodia's middle period.[35]

The extent to which Suryavarman's reign mobilized bureaucratic and coercive talents to concentrate people at Yasodharapura marked a departure from the past, and the success of his tactics showed subsequent kings that the kingdom could be organized and expanded by forcing its cultivators to work throughout the year. The food needed to support the apparatus (priests, kings, bureaucrats, and armies) could not be supplied by the single annual harvests that previously had sufficed for ordinary people to survive.

In extending his power in this way, Suryavarman enjoyed the advantages of a usurper. He was free to choose and reward his trusted followers, rather than finding himself hemmed in at the beginning of his reign by hangers-on from other courts. At first, governing the country with new officials probably meant that more attention was paid to local issues, for the new officials would still have debts to their clients in the countryside that their successors could ignore.

Suryavarman's successor, Utyadityavarman II (r. 1050–66) was a devotee of Siva. Guided by a powerful guru, he revived interest in the *devaraja* cult and also revived the custom of building a massive temple-mountain, the Bapuon, to house the lingam associated with his reign. As an inscription carved under his successor tells us:

> Seeing that in the middle of Jambudvipa, the home of the gods, there rose up a golden mountain, he made a golden mountain in the center of his city, out of emulation. On the summit of this mountain, in a golden temple, shining with celestial brilliance, he set up a Sivalinga made of gold.[36]

Guardian spirit, Preah Ko, ninth century. Photo by Walter Veit.

ANGKOREAN KINGSHIP

There are three ways of looking at Cambodian kingship in its heyday at Angkor. One is to study the king's relationship with Siva. Paul Mus, in a brilliant essay written in 1933, has argued that Siva's popularity in classical Southeast Asia may be traced in large part to his role as a spirit of the earth and also as an ancestral spirit, emerging from the earth (and thus from the ancestors) at first "accidentally," in the form of an outcrop of stone; later, purposefully, carved into the shape of a lingam representing the ancestors; and later still, as representing the rulers *and* ancestors of a particular place.[37] Siva in this sense was a literary form of an ancestor spirit held responsible for fertilizing the soil by inducing rain to fall on the region under his jurisdiction. This aspect of Cambodian kingship (found elsewhere in Southeast Asia, particularly in Vietnam) endured into the 1960s in the countryside. Siva and his consort, Uma, were gods to whom sacrifices, buffalo or human beings, were addressed because they were thought of as divinization of what lay under the earth. Intriguingly, when looked at in this way, the Cambodian king, as a patron of agriculture, resembles a Chinese emperor far more than a *raja* of traditional India.

The role of a Cambodian king was not merely to bring rain or to keep everyone's ancestors contentedly at bay. A second way of looking at Cambodian kingship, through the eyes of the people, is to see it in terms of the king's repeated and ritual enactment of lordliness and superiority in battle, sexuality, poetry, possessions, ceremony, and so forth. Seen in this way, the king was not an earth spirit or a priest but the hero of an Indian epic. This is the view taken in most of the Sanskrit-language inscriptions of Cambodia that praised kings as embodiments of virtue, actors living *above* society, associated with the sky, the sun, Indra, Vishnu, and Rama rather than with earthly or ancestral forces. As living superlatives (for each king was seen as the greatest, rather than one of many), kings provided the poets with a point of comparison, a kind of polestar from which society, flowing outward and downward, metaphorically organized itself, first through the *varnas* near the king and then on to free people, rice-growing villagers, and slaves. The king was superhuman without being helpful in any practical sense. He was a hero, occupying the top of society because of his merit and his power.

To members of the Angkorean elite, this reenactment of lordliness had at least two purposes. The first was to present godlike behavior (e.g., building a temple-mountain in imitation of Mt. Meru or defeating hordes of enemies) in order to obtain blessings for the king and the kingdom. The correct performance of rituals, especially exacting with regard to timing, was crucial to their efficacy. In this context, the word *symbol* is rather empty. The king believed in the rituals. So did his advisers. Ceremonies were the vehicles through which his lordliness, in which he also believed, was acted out.

A third way of looking at kingship is in terms of everyday Cambodian life. Sanskrit inscriptions are far less useful here than the Cambodian ones. Although society at Angkor, at first glance, appears to have been almost mechanically organized into strata, the inscriptions point to webs of relationships, responsibilities and expectations within which everyone who is mentioned appears to have been entangled. Seen in this way, the king, as a polygamist, a patron, and a giver of names, was perhaps the most entangled of them all. Ian Mabbett's thoughtful study of Angkorean kingship shows the range of things a king was expected to do, approve, and know about.[38] These included bestowing titles and emblems on his high officials; granting land and slaves to numerous religious foundations; constructing and maintaining irrigation works; constructing, decorating, and staffing temples; and conducting foreign relations, particularly in this era, with Champa to the east of the capital and with various tributary states to the north and west. The king was also the court of last appeal, and the inscriptions tell us how seemingly obscure squabbles involving landholdings often floated up through the judicial system to reach him—a feature of kingship that endured into the 1960s.[19]

At the same time, although the inscriptions tell us little about it, a king had to be a political operator to survive. As Mabbett has pointed out, many Sanskrit inscriptions praise the acumen of kings in terms of their resemblances to Rama or their knowledge of Indian political texts. As political manuals these learned writings certainly gave Cambodian kings plenty of room for maneuver, but it is in just this area, the day-today preferments, quarrels, and decisions, that the inscriptions are of so little help. The *flavor* of life at court in Angkorean times is inaccessible.

The Khmer inscriptions are of more assistance in telling us about the other levels of Cambodian society, the free people and the slaves, but again only at the moments described, recalled, or honored by an inscription. Mabbett's study of slavery at Angkor, which builds on earlier ones by Y. Bongert and A. Chakravarti, shows the bewildering complexity of categories in use for what we would call slaves and the bewildering number of tasks that were assigned to them.[40] As suggested in Chapter 2, it is still impossible to sort the terms out either diachronically or across the corpus of inscriptions. There are cases, for example, of slaves who owned slaves, slaves who married members of the royal family, and free people who were disposed of by others, just like slaves. Working back from later periods, one gets the impression that most of the people at Angkor were subjects (*reas*) rather than objects, or free people. They were at the disposition of patrons, who had the right to sell them to other people and, in many cases, they disposed of "lower" people themselves. In the inscriptions, slaves are listed as commodities.

These people were certainly the giants who were once thought to have built Angkor. Bas-reliefs on the Bayon show us that their tools, clothing, and houses changed little between Angkorean times and the period of the French protectorate. The bas-reliefs also depict their domestic animals, games, and marketing and clowns, shamans, ascetics, and peddlers. We are on less firm ground, however, when we seek to reconstitute their beliefs or the stories they told each other. No popular literature can be traced back to Angkor. This absence of written sources makes it difficult to bring the ordinary people of Angkor to life, except through the things they made, the reservoirs, temples, statues of stone and bronze, tools, pottery, and so on. What did a slave at Angkor think about his master? Was a master to be imitated, hated, avoided, or revered? How far down into the society or into a person's mind—did recognizably Indian ideas, gods, and vocabulary penetrate? The population was certainly more literate in Khmer than it was in Sanskrit, but nothing is known about the way literacy in either language was taught. The picture that emerges is one of familiarity with Indian culture (and perhaps knowledge of occasional Indian visitors as well) among the elite, thinning out in the rest of the society, until in the villages, as in the nineteenth century, we find ancestral spirits given Hindu names and Hindu statues treated as ancestral gods.

As we have seen, Cambodia's imitation of India stopped short of importing the Indian caste system. As Mabbett has shown in another penetrating essay, however, a set of ritual orders using *varna* nomenclature formed part of the king's repertoire of patronage, for caste standing was occasionally bestowed by the monarch on his own clients or on the clients of his associates.[41] Except at the beginning of a dynasty, a Cambodian king, like most Chinese emperors, could rule only by extending networks of patronage and mutual obligations outward from his palace, at first through close associates and family members but becoming diffuse, and more dependent on local power-holders, at the edges of the kingdom. Villagers far from Angkor would probably seldom have known the king's name any more than they did in the early twentieth century, when the following passage was recorded by French ethnographers working among the Cambodian population of southern Vietnam:

> In former times there were no canals, and no paths; there were only forests, with tigers, elephants, and wild buffaloes; no people dared to leave their villages.
>
> For this reason, hardly anyone ever went to the royal city. If anyone ever reached it, by poling his canoe, the others would ask him about it. "What is the king's appearance like? Is he like an ordinary man?" And the traveler, seeing all these ignorant people asking questions, would reply: "The king has an elegant, beautiful appearance, unstained by dust or sweat; he has no scars. . . ." But of course often he had never seen the king at all.[42]

ANGKOR WAT

The last years of the eleventh century in Cambodia were ones of turmoil and fragmentation. At different times, two or even three monarchs contended for the title of absolute ruler. At the end of the century, however, a new dynasty, which was to last for more than a hundred years, began to rule at Angkor. Little is known about the first two of its kings,

Jayavarman VI and his brother, Dharanindravarman I, but their nephew, Suryavarman II, under whom Angkor Wat was built, was, like Yasovarman II and Suryavarman I, another unifying monarch. If his inscriptions are to be believed, he gained power while still young after winning a battle against a rival prince: "Leaving the ocean of his army on the field of combat . . . he bounded to the head of the elephant of the enemy king, and killed [him] as a *garuda* on the slope of a mountain might kill a snake."[43]

Suryavarman II was the first king to rule over a unified Cambodian kingdom since Utyadityavarman II's death in the 1060s. The parallels with Suryavarman I, who was probably no relation, are numerous and instructive. Both kings came to power following periods of fragmentation and disorder. They responded to this, once Yasodharapura was in their hands, with vigorous administrative policies, with a pragmatic style of kingship, and by expanding the territory and manpower under their control. Suryavarman II campaigned in the east, against Vietnam (perhaps with encouragement from China) and Champa, using mercenaries drawn primarily from tributary areas to the west and using Chams in expeditions against Vietnam. He established diplomatic relations with China—the first Angkorean king to do so—and during his reign some impressive temples were built in what is now northeastern Thailand, including Pimai and Phnom Rung. Like Suryavarman I, he also sought to separate himself in religious terms from his immediate predecessors. Suryavarman I had done this by his patronage to Buddhism, whereas his namesake chose to exhibit a devotion, unusual for a Cambodian king, to Vishnu. In both cases, innovative or personal policies went along with a legitimizing cluster of actions, which linked the kings with pre-Angkorean pilgrimage sites like Wat Ph'u, with *gurus* associated with previous kings, and with artistic styles extending back into the reigns of the people they had managed to overthrow.

Suryavarman II's devotion to Vishnu led him to commission the largest, perhaps the most beautiful, and certainly one of the most mysterious of all the monuments of Angkor—the temple, tomb, and observatory now known as Angkor Wat.[44] The temple covers an area of two hundred hectares (almost five hundred acres). It was begun at the start of Suryavarman II's reign, and it was not completed until after his death, which occurred in about 1150, i.e., almost a century after the previous temple-mountain, the Bapuon. There is striking evidence, recently uncovered, that its central statue of Vishnu, long since vanished, was dedicated in July 1131, which was probably Suryavarman's thirty-third birthday—a number with important cosmic significance in Indian religion.

What is so mysterious about the temple? First, it opens to the west, the only major building at Yasodharapura to do so. In addition, its bas-reliefs, more than a mile of them around the outer galleries of the temple, are to be followed by moving in a counterclockwise direction, starting from the northwest quarter. The customary way of reading a bas-relief or of walking around a temple was to keep it all on one's right by moving in a clockwise direction, known by the Sanskrit term *pradaksina*. The reverse direction was usually associated with the dead; so was the west, for obvious meteorological reasons. (The word for *west* in modern Khmer also means "sink" or "drown.") Some French scholars have argued, therefore, that Angkor Wat, unlike the other temples at Angkor, was primarily a tomb.[45]

The arguments raged in learned journals until 1940, when Coedes proposed that Angkor Wat, like fifteen other royally sponsored Cambodian monuments, be thought of as a temple *and* a tomb. He cited stone receptacles, perhaps sarcophagi, that held part of the treasure of these other temples. As for the unusual orientation of Angkor Wat, Coedes suggested that this may have been in honor of Vishnu, Suryavarman's patron-deity, often associated with the west. Angkor Wat is the only temple at Angkor that we know to have been dedicated to him. The twelfth century, in fact, saw a vigorous revival of Vaisnavism, associated with popular religion, on the Indian subcontinent. This revival, it seems, like earlier ones in Indian religion, had repercussions at Angkor.

Between 1940 and the 1970s, little scholarly work was done on Angkor Wat. Scholars and tourists were content to marvel at the artistry of its bas-reliefs (many of them concerned with the prowess of Rama), the delicate and yet overwhelming proportions of the temple, and its continued hold on the imagination of ordinary Cambodians. In the mid-1970s, however, Eleanor Moron began studying the dimensions of the temple in detail, convinced that these might contain the key to the way the temple had been encoded by the learned men who designed it.[46]

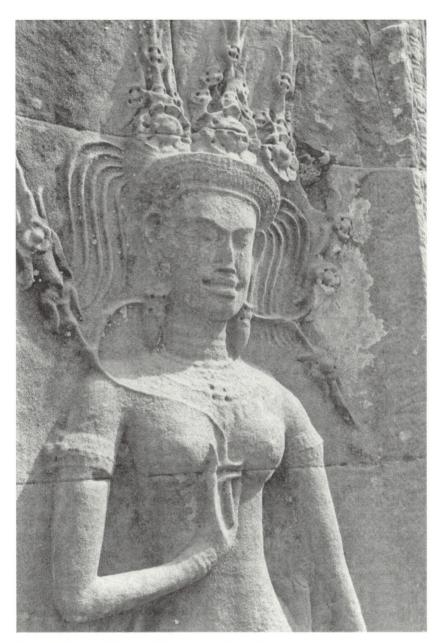

A heavenly angel (*thevoda*) from an eleventh-century temple, Thommanon. Author's photo.

After determining that the Cambodian measurement used at Angkor, the *hat,* was equivalent to approximately 0.4 meters (1.3 feet), Moron went on to ask how many *hat* were involved in significant dimensions of the temple, such as the distance between the western entrance (the only one equipped with its own causeway) and the central tower. The distance came to 1,728 *hat,* and three other components of this axis measured, respectively, 1,296, 867, and 439 *hat.* Moron then argued that these figures correlated to the four ages, or *yuga,* of Indian thought. The first of these, the Krita Yuga, was a supposedly golden age, lasting 1.728 million years. The next three ages lasted for 1.296 million, 864,000, and 432,000 years, respectively. The earliest age, therefore, was four times longer than the latest; the second earliest, three times longer; and the third earliest, twice as long. The last age is the Kali Yuga, in which we are living today. At the end of this era, it is believed, the universe will be destroyed, to be rebuilt by Brahma along similar lines, beginning with another golden age.

The fact that the length of these four eras correlates exactly with particular distances along the east-west axis of Angkor Wat suggests that the code for the temple is in fact a kind of pun that can be read in terms of time and space. The distances that a person entering the temple will traverse coincide with the eras that the visitor is metaphorically living through en route to the statue of Vishnu that was housed in the central tower. Walking forward and away from the west, which is the direction of death, the visitor moves backward into time, approaching the moment when the Indians proposed that time began.

In her research, Moron also discovered astronomical correlations for ten of the most frequently recurring distances at Angkor Wat. Astronomers working with her found that the siting of the temple was related to the fact that its western gate aligned at sunrise with a small hill to the northeast, Phnom Bok. Moreover, at the summer solstice "an observer . . . standing just in front of the western entrance can see the sunrise directly over the central tower of Angkor Wat."[47] This day, June 21, marked the beginning of the solar year for Indian astronomers and was sacred to a king whose name, Suryavarman, means "protected by the sun" and who was a devotee of Vishnu.

The close fit of these spatial relationships to notions of cosmic time, and the extraordinary accuracy and symmetry of all the measurements at Angkor, combine to confirm the notion that the temple was in fact a coded religious text that could be read by experts moving along its walkways from one dimension to the next. The learned people that determined the dimensions of Angkor Wat would have been aware of and would have reveled in its multiplicity of meanings. To those lower down in the society, perhaps, fewer meanings would be clear. We can assume, however, that even the poorest slaves were astounded and pleased to see this enormous temple, probably with gilded towers rising sixty meters (two hundred feet) above the ground, above its glittering moat and above the thatched huts of the people who had built it.

Although Suryavarman II may have led a campaign against Vietnam as late as 1150, the date of his death is unknown. In fact, the period 1145–82 produced almost no inscriptions, and its history must be recreated from later sources. Suryavarman's successor, perhaps a cousin, reached the throne under mysterious circumstances, probably in a coup d'état. This new king, Dharanindravarman, appears to have been a fervent Buddhist, although there is a possibility that he never reined as king at Yasodharapura. Around 1150, Yasovarman II, whose reign is mentioned in one of Jayavarman VII's inscriptions, succeeded him. In the inscription, Yasovarman is given credit for putting down a mysterious revolt in the northwest. The people who led this revolt, according to the inscription, were neither foreigners nor members of the elite; in bas-reliefs at the temple of Banteay Chhmar, they are depicted as people with animal heads.[48] Perhaps the revolt, like the Communist insurgency in the 1970s, was a supposedly unthinkable one, organized by the downtrodden segments of the society and by "forest people" against an allegedly unassailable elite.[49]

Instability continued in the 1160s. Yasovarman was assassinated by one of his subordinates, who then declared himself to be king. At this time also, the tributary state of Louvo sent tributary missions to China, suggesting at least partial independence from Angkor. The absence of inscriptions and the questionable legitimacy of rulers reinforce the impression of rapid change.

Angkor Wat, twelfth-century temple dedicated to Vishnu. The largest religious building in the world, its image has appeared on five successive Cambodian flags since 1953. Photo by Roger M. Smith.

Perhaps, as B.P. Groslier has suggested, the hydraulic organization of the kingdom had already begun to falter during the reign of Suryavarman II.[50] This system of reservoirs and canals, which guaranteed one harvest a year in dry times and two with adequate rainfall, was the basis of Angkor's rice-oriented agricultural economy and allowed the low-density concentration of large populations—perhaps as many as six hundred thousand.[51] Groslier has suggested that the system reached peak efficiency in the mid-eleventh century, as the hydraulic components of Angkor Wat a hundred years later were much smaller than those around earlier temple-mountains. Indeed, Groslier goes on, under Suryavarman II, for the first time in Cambodian history, hydraulically based cities were built at considerable distances from Angkor, at Beng Mealea and Kompong Svay. Perhaps this was done because the water resources in the Angkor region, which had lasted so long, had now been tapped to the limit although it is more likely, as recent research as revealed, that this peak was reached in the thirteenth century. Water came from a network of small streams, running south from the Kulen hills to the north along the slight slope that extended to the shores of the Tonle Sap. As demands for water increased, these streams were diverted closer and closer to their sources. This process reduced the nutrients that the streams brought to fertilize the Angkorean plain.

Because the slope of the plain is so slight, in dry periods the canals would probably have been nearly stagnant, especially if unstable political conditions, warfare, or epidemics had drawn off the labor normally used to maintain them. Groslier has suggested, as other scholars have done, that this increasing stagnation may well have coincided with the appearance of malaria on the Southeast Asian mainland, accelerating the process.[52] Here, as so often, we lack generalized statements about conditions at Angkor or any reliable statistics that might tell us about the size and composition of the population at a given time, the condition of the hydraulic network at particular times, and the relationship, or lack of it, between particular kings and productive agricultural life.

The close relationships among water management, grain production, priesthood, and temple foundations that characterized Angkor somewhat resembles the social organization of ancient Egypt and is similar also in some respects to the Maya civilization of medieval Guatemala.[53]

In all three cases, grain surpluses (of wheat, rice, or maize) were collected for the benefit of the state and its prevailing ideologues, the priests, who served as patrons of temples and advisers to the kings. Rice and other products produced by temple foundations formed the basis of the Angkorean economy, buttressed by whatever could be earned from trading forest products and minerals to other states. As Michael Coe has written, "There seem to have been taxes on everything—on land, on rice, salt, wax and honey. . . . Payments could be made in all kinds of goods, including . . . slaves, buffaloes, elephants and especially cloth."[54] The economy of Angkor is a promising field of research. Scholars concerned with the economy can build on Vickery's work on the preceding period, as well as on information gleaned by the ongoing Greater Angkor project, centered at the University of Sydney.[55]

4

JAYAVARMAN VII AND THE CRISIS OF THE THIRTEENTH CENTURY

From the time of Suryavarman II's death around 1150 until Jayavarman VII's coronation in 1182, only one dated Cambodian inscription has survived. Much of what we know about this period must be filtered through inscriptions carved at Jayavarman's behest, reflecting his view of the world as well as what he wanted people to believe about his early life. Because he was not, apparently, an entirely legitimate contender for the throne, his early years, like those of so many Cambodian founder-kings, are poorly documented.

Jayavarman's biography was pieced together by George Coedes, who saw him as a pinnacle of Cambodian history rather than as an aberration.[1] Jayavarman's inscriptions and what they tell us about his point of view make radical departures, in many ways, from what had gone before. Because of his radicalism and grandeur, Jayavarman VII has tended to dominate the historiography of Cambodia, particularly since Coedes's work in the 1930s. His reign, as we shall see, contained several mysteries and contradictions. Recent scholars have called Coedes's hagiography into question.

Jayavarman belonged to the so-called Mahiharapura dynasty. He appears to have been a first cousin of Suryavarman II and the son of a royal prince, Dharanindravarman, who may have reigned briefly as king and who was certainly a fervent Buddhist. B.P. Groslier has cast doubts on the first of these assertions because it is so poorly documented and because it places Jayavarman in the direct line of succession in a way that makes the facts we know about his life even more difficult to understand.[2]

It seems likely, all the same, that Jayavarman as a young man served in some capacity at Yasovarman's court. From 1166 to 1177, Jayavarman appears to have lived away from Angkor, perhaps in the vicinity of the temple now known as the Preah Khan in Kompong Svay, where Claude Jacques has located the city of Jayadityapura, and also in Champa. A portrait statue of him, manifestly earlier than others produced later in his reign, has been found at Preah Khan in Kompong Svay.[3] Was the city subservient to Angkor or a rival to it? How did Jayavarman relate to the usurper-king who followed Yasovarman to the throne? Even more important, what were his relationships with Champa to the east? We need to ask these partially unanswerable questions in order to place Jayavarman's reign, following his accession in 1178, in the context of his early life and in the framework of Cambodian foreign relations.

JAYAVARMAN VII AND BUDDHIST KINGSHIP

Throughout his life, it seems, Jayavarman immersed himself in the teachings of Mahayana Buddhism—the variant still followed in much of northern Asia. More than any other king, he labored to integrate Buddhist with Cambodian ideas of kingship. Buddhist kingship, as he practiced it, differed in several ways from the more eclectic Hindu model that had been followed for centuries at Angkor and was to form the ceremonial basis of Cambodian kingship until the institution was temporarily overturned in 1970. In the traditional version, a king was thought to enjoy, whether he was alive or not, a special relationship with a particular deity—usually Siva, more rarely Vishnu, occasionally the composite of them both known as Harihara—to whom his temple-mountain was eventually dedicated. The kings used this special relationship to explain their grandeur while their subjects assumed that the relationship had something to do with the provision of adequate rainfall.

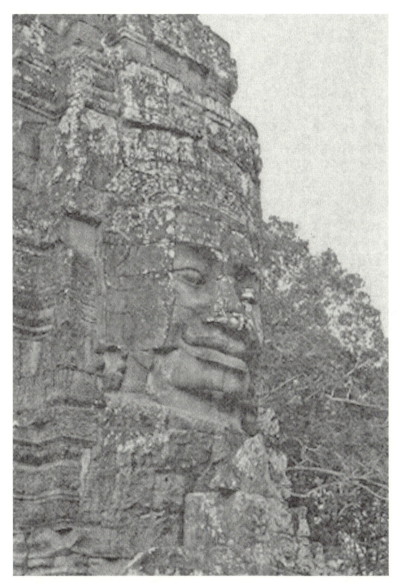

A tower at the Bayon, Jayavarman VII's temple-mountain, twelfth century CE. Photo by Walter Veit.

Because Cambodian society was organized hierarchically, and because the king was thought to centralize the kingdom, most Cambodians, like their contemporaries in medieval Europe, probably recognized the necessity for a king. Rare inscriptions, and perhaps the act of constructing reservoirs, indicated that an individual king occasionally had his subjects' general welfare on his mind. In human terms, however, the king was nearly always a distant, mysterious figure concealed inside an awesome palace. The notion that he was accountable to his people does not seem to have caught on. Inside his palace, and within the network of kinship and preferment relationships extending from it, the king was the master and the victim of a system whereby people clamored for his favors, for titles, for the right to own slaves or sumptuous possessions.

Buddhist kingship, of course, grew out of this Indian tradition (the Buddha had been an Indian prince), but in Jayavarman's reign these notions were modified in several ways. Jayavarman was no longer seen as the devotee of a divinity or as drawn up to the divinity in death. Instead, Jayavarman sought to redeem himself and his kingdom by his devotion to Buddhist teachings and by the performance of meritorious acts.[4]

Before examining how these ideas of kingship were acted out during his reign, we need to stress that his program was not aimed at reforming Cambodian society or at dismantling such Hinduized institutions as Brahmanism, slavery, and kingship. Far from it. In his conservatism, his ongoing tolerance of Hinduism, and his elitist frame of reference, Jayavarman VII was a recognizably twelfth-century king, although in Cambodian terms he was also perhaps a revolutionary one.

Put very starkly, the difference between a Hindu king and a Buddhist one is akin to the difference between a monologue that no one overhears and a soliloquy addressed to an audience of paid or invited guests. A Hindu king's rule was an aggregation of statements—rituals, temples, poems, marriages, inscriptions, and the like—that displayed his grandeur, acumen, and godliness. A Buddhist king made similar statements, but he addressed many of them, specifically, to an audience of his people. This made the people less an ingredient of the king's magnificence (as his thousands of followers had always been) than objects of his compassion, an audience for his merit-making and participants in *his* redemption. This, at least, is what many of Jayavarman VII's inscriptions and temples appear to have been saying.

Why did Jayavarman VII choose to break with the past? Scholars have several explanations. These include his apparent estrangement from the court at Angkor, combined with his resentment toward the usurper who had proclaimed himself king in 1167; and his having a "master plan" of buildings, ideology, and kingship that had been maturing in his mind after years of study and very possibly the influence of a scholarly, ambitious wife. These proposals are helpful, but they do not identify the real key to Jayavarman's reign—the Cham invasion of Angkor in 1177. Paul Mus and Jean Boisselier have argued that we can see Jayavarman's entire reign as a response to this traumatic event.[5]

Jayavarman's own links with Champa were close, and in the 1160s, he may have spent several years there. It's likely that his absence from Angkor was connected in some way with his being out of favor at the Cambodian court, for he returned home only after Yasovarman II had been deposed. As the sources of our uncertainty are Jayavarman's own inscriptions, all that is clear about the prelude to the Cham invasion of 1177—and indeed about Jayavarman's early career—is that later on he found little to boast about in these obviously formative years, some of which he may have spent in his mother's home city of Jayadityapura, east of Angkor.[6]

Because inscriptions tend to trace the causes of war to royal ambition, treachery, and revenge—that is, to the world of the *Ramayana*—it is difficult for us to determine exactly why Champa invaded Cambodia, by land certainly in 1177 and perhaps by water in 1178.[7] The prospects of booty and prisoners were certainly part of the Cham rationale; so were memories of earlier defeats. The expedition traveled to the Great Lake, and the Siem Reap River, taking the city of Yasodharapura by surprise: "With a powerful fleet, he pillaged it and put the king to death, without listening to any proposal of peace."[8]

Jayavarman appears to have been in Champa at the time of the 1177 invasion. In the following year he assembled a mixed Khmer-Cham army of supporters for a new campaign against the Chams at Angkor, defeating them in battle, although an inscription suggests that it was a Cambodian prince, not Jayavarman himself, who killed the Cham king "with a hundred million arrows." When Jayavarman arrived at Angkor after the invasion, he found the city "plunged into a sea of misfortune" and "heavy with crimes." Some of these troubles could be traced in his mind to the unmeritorious reigns of predecessors; others to the fractionalization of power inside the kingdom, referred to in an inscription written by his wife: "In the previous reign, the land, though shaded by many parasols, suffered from extremes of heat; under [Jayavarman] there remained but one parasol, and yet the land, remarkably, was delivered from suffering."[9]

Jayavarman VII was crowned in 1182–83, therefore, owing little to his predecessors and much, as his inscriptions tell us, to his acumen, his Buddhist faith, and his victories in battle. It's clear, however, that the period between victory and assuming power must have been filled with political negotiations and further conflicts—with the "many parasols," perhaps. Over the next thirty years or so (the precise date of his death is unknown), he stamped the kingdom with his personality and his ideas as no other ruler was able to do before Norodom Sihanouk in the 1960s and Pol Pot later on. Like these two figures, Jayavarman may have wanted to transform Cambodia and perceived himself as the instrument of that transformation.

Much of the interest in his reign springs from the tension inherent in the words *Buddha* and *king*. Using the Hinduized apparatus of kingship and the material grandeur associated with it, Jayavarman also sought in all humility, if his inscriptions are to be believed, to deliver himself and all his people from suffering. As a king he had roads built throughout his kingdom, perhaps to accelerate his military response to uprisings or invasions but also to facilitate access to areas rich in resources that could be exported to China via the Cham seaports that were now subservient to Angkor. This nationalization of kingship by a man who was arguably the most otherworldly of Cambodia's kings has given Jayavarman's reign a contradictory appearance. Sentences about the man soon fall into the pattern of "on the one hand" and "on the other."

For example, many of the bas-reliefs on the Bayon, depicting battles against the Chams, contain vivid scenes of cruelty. Similarly, some of Jayavarman's inscriptions praise his vengefulness and his skill at political infighting vis-à-vis the Chams. On the one hand, the portrait statues of

him that have come down to us depict him as an ascetic deep in medita-
tion.[10] From his so-called hospital inscriptions we learn that "he suffered
from the illnesses of his subjects more than from his own; the pain that
afflicted men's bodies was for him a spiritual pain, and thus more pierc-
ing."[11] Yet, on the other hand, his roads, temples, "houses of fire," reservoirs, and hospitals were thrown up with extraordinary haste between
his coronation in 1182–83 and the second decade of the thirteenth century; some were completed after his death. There were so many of these
projects, in fact, that workmanship was often sloppy, and by the end of
his reign local supplies of sandstone and limestone for use at Angkor
may have begun to run out.[12] Hundreds of thousands of ordinary
people, inscriptions tell us, labored to erect and maintain these constructions built, at the ideological level, to deliver them from pain. To a
twenty-first-century eye, this seems ironic, but we should remember that
suffering in Buddhist terms should not be taken merely in a physical
sense; it must also be related to the purposes of life and to the ways that
suffering of certain kinds can serve the teachings of the Buddha.

Why was Jayavarman's building program carried out with so much
haste? He was perhaps as old as sixty when he reached the throne; the
buildings may have constituted a race against time. The program may
have been part of a process of personal redemption, although the sins
for which he was atoning are not clarified by his inscriptions. What we
know about the first years of his reign comes from inscriptions written
at a later stage. These years were probably spent in deflecting yet another Cham attack, in quelling a rebellion in the northwest, and in re-
constituting Yasodharapura for the first time as a walled city. Major
shifts in population, as usual, followed these military campaigns, as the
Preah Khan inscription of 1191 suggests: "To the multitude of his war-
riors, he gave the capitals of enemy kings, with their shining palaces; to
the beasts roaming his forests, he gave the forests of the enemy; to prisoners of war, he gave his own forests, thus manifesting generosity and
justice."

As it would be with other Cambodian kings, making a sharp distinction
between Jayavarman's politics and his religion, between temporal and spiritual powers, and between his ideas about himself and his ideas about his
kingdom would be wrong. Before we dismiss him as a megalomaniac,

however, it is worth recalling that had no one shared his vision or believed in his merit, he would never have become king, especially starting out from such a weak position, and he certainly would not have been able to remain in power. Many high officials, brahmans, evangelical Buddhists, and military men probably saw advantages in the physical expansion of the kingdom, partly by means of royally subsidized religious foundations and partly through bringing previously hostile or indifferent populations under some form of control. By the beginning of the thirteenth century, in fact, Angkor was extracting tribute from much of what is now Thailand and southern Laos as well as from Champa, occupying the coastal areas of central Vietnam. To these corners of the known world the multiple half-smiling faces of Jayavarman's temple-mountain and his portrait statues addressed their benignly powerful glance.

At the same time, as Michael Vickery and others have suggested, considerable resentment must have built up against Jayavarman VII in the course of his reign among disaffected members of the elite, and among formerly privileged Hindu practitioners who resented the king's conversion. These elements of Khmer society, at the instigation of a later monarch (but which one?), probably were responsible for the anti-Buddhist iconoclasm that affected many of Jayavarman's major temples after his death.[13]

The art historian Philippe Stern, who studied Jayavarman's reign in detail, perceived three stages in the development of his iconography and architecture.[14] These coincide with the three phases of construction that Stern had noted for earlier Cambodian kings—namely, public works, temples in honor of parents, and the king's own temple-mountain.

The public works of earlier kings, as we have seen, usually took the form of reservoirs (baray). Other projects such as roads and bridges were also built, but they are seldom noted in inscriptions. But Jayavarman's program departed from the past. His hospitals, probably established early in his reign, were an important innovation, described in the stele of Ta Prohm. Four of them were located near the gateways to Angkor Thom. Others were built to the west of Angkor into what is now northeastern Thailand and as far north as central Laos. About twenty hospital sites have so far been identified. The Ta Prohm inscription says that the hospitals could call on the services of 838 villages, with adult populations totaling roughly eighty thousand people. The services demanded appear to have been to provide labor and rice for the staffs attached to each hospital, or approximately a hundred people, including dependents.[15] The hospital steles give details about the administration of the hospitals and about the provisions and staff allocated to them.

A second set of Jayavarman VII's public works consisted of "houses of fire" placed at approximately sixteen-kilometer (ten-mile) intervals along Cambodia's major roads. There were fifty-seven of these between Angkor and the Cham capital and seventeen more between Angkor and a Buddhist temple-site at P'imai in northeastern Thailand. The exact purpose of these buildings is unknown.[16]

Finally, there was Jayavarman's own reservoir, known now as the northern Baray and during his reign as the Jayatataka, located to the northeast of Yasodharapura.

These innovations stemmed from what Jayavarman saw as his mission to *rescue* his subjects, as the hospital inscription says:

> Filled with a deep sympathy for the good of the world, the king swore this oath: "All the beings who are plunged in the ocean of existence, may I draw them out by virtue of this good work. And may the kings of Cambodia who come after me, attached to goodness . . . attain with their wives, dignitaries, and friends the place of deliverance where there is no more illness."[17]

THE TEMPLES OF JAYAVARMAN VII

In the second stage of Jayavarman's reign he erected temples in honor of his parents. The first of these, now known as Ta Prohm ("Ancestor Brahma"), was dedicated in 1186. It honored Jayavarman's mother in the guise of Prajnaparamita, the goddess of wisdom, conceived metaphorically as the mother of all Buddhas. The temple also housed a portrait statue of Jayavarman's Buddhist teacher, or guru (the word *kru* means "teacher" in modern Khmer), surrounded in the temple by statues of more than six hundred dependent gods and bodhisattvas. The syncretism of Cambodian religion is shown by the fact that Shaivite and Vaisnavite ascetics were given cells on the temple grounds alongside Buddhist monks and learned men. The appearance of Ta Prohm today gives a poor idea of its original appearance, for unlike the other major temples at Angkor, it has never been restored; instead, it has been left to the mercy of the forest.

The next temple complex to be built by Jayavarman VII is known nowadays as the Preah Khan ("Sacred Sword"). Its inscription says that it was built on the site of an important Cambodian victory over the Chams, and its twelfth-century name, Jayasri ("Victory and Throne"), may echo this event. No other inscription mentions this battle, fought so close to Yasodharapura as to suggest a second Cham invasion of the city. Groslier, however, has argued that it took place and has proposed that it is depicted in bas-reliefs at the Bayon.[18]

Preah Khan was dedicated in 1191 and houses a portrait statue of Jayavarman's father, Dharanindravarman, with the traits of Lokesvara, the deity expressive of the compassionate aspects of the Buddha. The symbolism is relentlessly appropriate, for in Mahayana Buddhist thinking the marriage of wisdom (*prajna*) and compassion (*karuna*) gave birth to enlightenment, which is to say, to the Buddha himself, the Enlightened One.[19] In this stage of Jayavarman's artistic development, Lokesvara appears more and more frequently, and throughout his reign, the triad of Prajnaparamita (wisdom), the Buddha (enlightenment), and Lokesvara (compassion) was central to the king's religious thinking. The placement of the two temples southeast and northeast of the new center of Yasodharapura (later occupied by the Bayon) suggests that the three temples can be "read" together, with the dialectic of compassion and wisdom giving birth to enlightenment represented by the Buddha image that stood at the center of the Bayon, and thus at the heart of Jayavarman's temple-mountain.

The inscriptions from these two "parent temples" show us how highly developed the Cambodian bureaucracy had become, particularly in terms of its control over the placement and duties of the population, but also in terms of the sheer number of people in positions of authority who were entitled to deposit and endow images of deities inside the temple. Ta Prohm housed several thousand people, as its inscription attests:

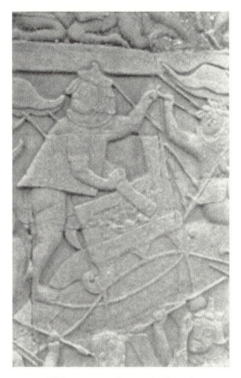

A twelfth-century bas-relief at the
Bayon depicting warfare between
Chams and Khmer. Photo by
Walter Veit.

There are here 400 men, 18 high priests, 2,740 other priests,
2,232 assistants, including 615 female dancers, a grand total of
12,640 people, including those entitled to stay. In addition, there
are 66,625 men and women who perform services for the gods,
making a grand total of 79,265 people, including the Burmese,
Chams, etc.[20]

Similarly, the people dependent on Preah Khan—that is, those obliged to
provide rice and other services—totaled nearly 100,000, drawn from
more than 5,300 villages. The inscription goes on to enumerate the men
and women who had been dependent on previous temple endowments.

Drawn from 13,500 villages, they numbered more than 300,000. The infrastructure needed to provide food and clothing for the temples— to name only two types of provision—must have been efficient and sophisticated.

Three interesting points emerge from the inscriptions. One is that outsiders—"Burmese, Chams, etc."—were accounted for in different ways than local people were, perhaps because they were prisoners of war without enduring ties to individual noblemen, priests, or religious foundations. Another is that the average size of the villages referred to in the inscriptions appears to have been about two hundred people, including dependents—still the median size of rice-growing villages in Cambodia in the 1960s. Finally, the inscriptions indicate that the temples, although dedicated to the Buddha and serving as residences for thousands of Buddhist monks, also housed statues and holy men associated with different Hindu sects. Jayavarman VII obviously approved of this arrangement, for we know that he also retained Hindu thinkers and bureaucrats at his court. Indeed, it is probably more useful to speak of the coexistence of Hinduism and Buddhism in Jayavarman VII's temples, and perhaps in his mind as well, than to propose a systematic process of syncretization.

The jewel-like temple known as Neak Po'n ("Twining Serpents") once formed an island in the Jayatataka and was probably completed by 1191, for it is mentioned in the inscription of Preah Khan:

> The king has placed the Jayatataka like a lucky mirror, colored by stones, gold, and garlands. In the middle, there is an island, drawing its charm from separate basins, washing the mud of sin from those coming in contact with it, serving as a boat in which they can cross the ocean of existences.[21]

The island with its enclosing wall, constructed in a lotus pattern, represented a mythical lake in the Himalayas, sacred to Buddhist thinking. Around the temple, as at the lake, four gargoyles spew water from the larger lake into the smaller ones. The temple itself, raised above the water by a series of steps, was probably dedicated, like Preah Khan, to Lokesvara, whose image appears repeatedly in high relief on its walls.

Groups of statues were also placed at the four sides of the temple. Unfortunately, only one of these, representing the horse Balaha, an aspect of Lokesvara, can be identified with certainty; two others are probably representations of Siva and Vishnu. Jean Boisselier has argued that the presence of these gods inside the enclosure can be read as a political statement, showing that the former gods of Angkor were now submitting to the Buddha. But why should they do so? Boisselier, following Mus, has suggested that Shaivism and Vaisnavism were seen to have failed the Cambodians when the Chams were able to capture and occupy Angkor in 1177. Lake Anavatapta, moreover, was sacred not only to all Buddhists but particularly to Buddhist rulers, or *chakravartin*, beginning, legend asserts, with the Emperor Asoka, who was able magically to draw water from the lake to enhance his own purity and power.[22]

In this second phase of his iconography, Jayavarman VII may also have sponsored additions to many earlier structures—notably the temples of P'imai in northeastern Thailand and Preah Khan in Kompong Svay.[23]

The sheer size of these foundations suggests a trend toward urbanization under Jayavarman VII, or at least a tendency to herd and collect large numbers of people from peripheral areas into the service of the state. It seems likely that Jayavarman VII, like Suryavarman II before him, was attracted to the idea of increasing centralization and the related idea of bureaucratic state control. Perhaps these ideas formed part of what he perceived as a mission to convert his subjects to Buddhism or were connected with organizing people to respond swiftly to foreign threats.

The second phase was marked by several stylistic innovations. These included the motif of multifaced towers inaugurated at the small temple of Prasat Preah Stung and carried to its apex in the entrance gates to the city of Angkor Thom and, ultimately, in the hundreds of faces that look down from the Bayon, the stone walls surrounding the entire city, apparently for the first time in Angkorean history, and the causeways of giants outside the gates of the city.

These constructions can be read in terms of both politics and religion. Boisselier, following Mus, has compared the wall-building at Angkor Thom to a fortified Maginot Line, supposedly offering an impenetrable defense against any Cham invasion. At the same time, the walls can be said to represent the ring of mountains that surround Mt. Meru or Jayavarman's temple-mountain, the Bayon.

After capturing the Cham capital in 1191, Jayavarman probably spent the rest of his reign at Yasodharapura. At this point, his buildings began to show signs of hasty construction and poor workmanship, as well as of a shifting ideology. The temple that was to become the Bayon, for example, was radically altered at several points in the 1190s and probably in the thirteenth century as well. [24]

An inscription from the end of Jayavarman's reign describes the city as his bride: "The town of Yasodharapura, decorated with powder and jewels, burning with desire, the daughter of a good family . . . was married by the king in the course of a festival that lacked nothing, under the spreading dais of his protection."[25] The object of the marriage, the inscription goes on to say, was "the procreation of happiness throughout the universe."

At the center of the city was the Bayon, a common folk-title for Angkorean monuments in the nineteenth century, when they were being named by the French,[26] with its hundreds of gigantic faces, carved in sets of four, and its captivating bas-reliefs depicting everyday life, wars with Champa, and the behavior of Indian gods. The temple at one time housed thousands of images. Its central image, discovered in the 1930s, was a statue of the Buddha sheltered by an enormous hooded snake, or *naga*. The statue had been forcibly removed from its honored position by iconoclasts, probably after Jayavarman VII's death, and had been thrown into an airshaft.

There has been considerable controversy about the symbolism of the temple and about what was meant by the causeways leading up to it, with giants (*asura*) and angels (*devata*) engaged in what looks like a tug of war, grasping the bodies of two gigantic snakes. Some have argued that the causeways represented the well-known Indian myth of the churning of the sea of milk. Others have agreed with Mus, who saw them as rainbows, leading people out of their world into the world of the gods. At another level, the *asuras* represented the Chams and the *devatas*, Cambodians. In this respect, it is tempting to perceive the city, and most of Jayavarman's works, in dialectical terms. For example, as we have seen, the pair of Lokesvara (compassion/father) and Prajnaparamita (intelligence/mother) give birth to the Buddha (enlightenment, thought to be the child of wisdom and compassion), i.e., Jayavarman VII himself. We have encountered this turn of mind before, in the cult of Harihara and in the opposition and synthesis in Cambodian popular thought of divinities associated respectively with water/moon/darkness and earth/sun/brightness. Similarly, the struggle between the Cambodians and the Chams, acted out along the causeways and in the bas-reliefs at the Bayon and at Banteay Chhmar, can be seen as bringing to birth the new, converted nation of Cambodia, in which the Buddha has won over the Hindu gods of Champa. This dialectic may well be the "message" of the Bayon, which Boisselier has called the "assembly hall of the city of the gods" because of the great number of images that had been sheltered there.[27] Once again, the message can also be read in terms of the civil polity, and so can the half-smiling faces that dominate the temple. As so often in Angkorean art, it would be narrow and inaccurate to interpret these haunting faces as representing only one kind of deity, performing one kind of task. In a way, for example, they serve as guardians of the Buddha and his teachings; in another, glancing out in the four directions, they oversee the kingdom and perhaps represent civil and military officials of the time. Boisselier, who has argued that they are princely manifestations of Brahma, has noticed also that their tiaras resemble those worn by the Cham *asuras* along the entrance causeways. None of the identifications so far has been completely persuasive.[28]

Another extraordinary feature of the Bayon, found also at Banteai Chhmar, is that its bas-reliefs depict historical Cambodian events rather than, say, incidents in the *Ramayana* or some other literary work that coincide with or resemble historical events.[29] Battles depicted on the Bayon and at Banteay Chhmar are fought with recognizable twelfth-century weapons, and other panels depict ordinary people buying and selling, eating, gambling, raising children, picking fruit, curing the sick, and traveling on foot or in ox-carts. Nearly all the customs, artifacts, and costumes depicted in the bas-reliefs could still be found in the Cambodian countryside at the end of the colonial era. Although the voices of these people are missing from Jayavarman's inscriptions, they move across his bas-reliefs with unaccustomed freedom, citizens at last of the country they inhabit, adorning a king's temple as they never had before.

Unless more inscriptions come to light from Jayavarman's reign, he will remain mysterious to us, because there are so many ambiguities about his personality, his reign, and his ideas. The mystery springs in part from the wide-ranging social and ideological changes that characterized thirteenth- and fourteenth-century Cambodia and may have been due in part to forces that Jayavarman or people near him set in motion.

Another source of ambiguity can be traced to the uneasy coexistence in Jayavarman's temples and inscriptions of an overwhelming compassion and an overwhelming will, of a detachment from things of the world—symbolized by the horse Balaha at the Neak Po'n—and a detailed program aimed at transforming the physical world of Angkor, which had been degraded, in Jayavarman VII's eyes by the Cham invasion. A third mystery is the silence, both in terms of buildings and inscriptions, that followed Jayavarman's reign and appears to have begun in his declining years. We have no way of telling if Jayavarman was in some sense to blame for this unusual silence, as in subsequent inscriptions he is hardly ever mentioned. The patterns of continuity, stressed so often in earlier inscriptions, seem to have been broken or damaged severely by his reign.

THERAVADA BUDDHISM AND THE CRISIS OF THE THIRTEENTH CENTURY

The largest change affecting Cambodia in the thirteenth century was the conversion of most of its people to the Theravada variant of Buddhism, discussed below.[30] What role Jayavarman VII played in this conversion or what his response to it may have been is impossible to judge. The history of his reign, from a personal perspective, seems to be the story of the imposition of one man's will on a population, a landscape, and a part of Asia ostensibly in the service of an ideal, Mahayana Buddhism. In its allegedly "liberating" fashion, it bears a fortuitous resemblance to the ideology of Democratic Kampuchea, which was also imposed from above. It is very doubtful that Jayavarman VII saw the Cambodian elite as his class enemies, as Pol Pot did, or that he preferred "forest people" to those living in Yasodharapura, but his selective break with the past, his wars with neighbors, the grandeur of his building program, and what appears to be his imposition of a new religion all have parallels with the 1970s. Interestingly, the only feature of Angkorean life singled out for praise by Democratic Kampuchea was precisely the full-scale mobilization of the people that Jayavarman VII, but very few other kings, managed to carry out.

Some writers have connected Cambodia's conversion to Theravada Buddhism to the upheaval that affected Southeast Asia in the wake of the Mongol invasions of China; others have seen it as evidence of the growing influence of Mon- and Thai-speaking peoples, who were already Theravada Buddhists, on the people of Angkor. We know that wandering missionaries from the Mon-language parts of Siam, from Burma, and from Ceylon (present-day Sri Lanka) played an important part in the process and that Cambodian pilgrims visited Ceylon to learn about Theravada Buddhism and to obtain clerical credentials. We also know some of the agents of the change, but it is difficult to say why conversion was so rapid and so widespread. Some scholars argue that the Theravada variant, unlike Brahmanism or Mahayana Buddhism, was oriented toward ordinary people. A more likely explanation, advanced by L.P. Briggs,[31] is that the increasing interaction between Khmer- and Mon-speaking residents of the Thai central plain, with the Mons being devotees of Theravada Buddhism, led gradually, over a half century or so, to the conversion of Khmer speakers farther east. We have no way of telling what aspects of the sect were more attractive than others, or which segments of society were drawn most rapidly to it. The conversion in any case was by no means total, for the Chinese envoy Zhou Daguan, who visited Angkor in 1296–97, noted that Brahmanism and Shaivism, as well as Theravada Buddhism, still enjoyed the status of approved religions.[32]

In other words, it is likely that the thirteenth century, one of the least-recorded of the Angkorean centuries in terms of datable inscriptions, was marked at Angkor by a serious religious upheaval or by a succession of upheavals, which had political causes and effects as well.

The end of Jayavarman VII's reign and the reign of his successor, Indravarman II (r. 1200–70), are obscure, although we know that Indravarman, like Jayavarman VII, was a Buddhist who may have extended some of his predecessors' works. Inscriptions found at the Bayon have little to say about the last phase of Jayavarman's life. Those at the four corners of his city, apparently all inscribed at the time of his death; however, provide helpful references to Jayavarman's wars against the Chams and the Vietnamese. These inscriptions are written, Coedes contended, in execrable Sanskrit. Several of them (like some of the bas-reliefs at the Bayon) are unfinished, almost as if the workmen had dropped their chisels on receiving news of the king's death.[33]

Surveying the art of the post-Angkorean era from another perspective, Ashley Thompson has written:

> The wild iconographic mingling of the vegetable, animal and human that announces the divine above each sanctuary threshold is gone. Images of fantastic creatures and powerful gods no longer populate the landscape. . . . The sensuality and majesty of the divine virtually disappear.[34]

This dearth of written information coincides with a critical period of Cambodian and Southeast Asian history. The thirteenth century was a period of crisis throughout the region—a time of rapid change, significant movements of population, foreign invasions, altered patterns of trade, the appearance of new religions, and shifts in the balance of power.[35] On the mainland a major change was the spread of Theravada Buddhism at the expense of state-sponsored and caste-enhancing Hindu cults. In the long run this change had several ramifications. In Cambodia and Thailand, brahmans retained their ceremonial positions at court but otherwise were diminished in importance. The rich mythical and literary bases of Indian literature and iconography, reflected up to now in bas-reliefs, sculpture, architecture, and inscriptions, narrowed perceptibly to satisfy the more austere requirements of Theravada aesthetics and Cambodian literature, like the local version of the *Ramayana,* came to be suffused with Buddhist values.

In terms of foreign relations, the two most important developments affecting Cambodia at this time were the weakening of its control over populations in present-day Thailand and the expansion of Chinese commercial activities in Southeast Asia under the Mongols and the early

Ming. Although Cambodian cultural influence remained strong in the central plain (where the Thai capital of Ayudhya was to be founded in the fourteenth century), Cambodian political control over the rest of the region diminished. Principalities that formerly sent tribute to Angkor, such as Sukot'ai and Louvo, now declared their independence symbolically by sending tribute to the Chinese court. So did principalities in Laos and others to the south. Angkor was once again vulnerable to invasion from every direction but the east, as Champa was no longer a power to be reckoned with. A Thai invasion, in fact, occurred toward the end of the thirteenth century and is recorded by Zhou Daguan.

ZHOU DAGUAN'S ACCOUNT OF ANGKOR, 1296–97

The record by Chinese envoy Zhou Daguan of his stay in Cambodia in 1296–97 is the most detailed account we have about everyday life and the appearance of Angkor.[36] Zhou's memoir is rich in circumstantial detail as he was not constrained by the Indian traditions that remove ordinary people from literary consideration. In his account, for example, we see Cambodians bathing, selling goods, and marching in processions. From our point of view, it is a shame that Zhou devoted so much of his short manuscript to exotic revelations of "barbarian" life. In fact, although he provided us with what amounts to a newsreel—or perhaps a home video—of his stay at Angkor, our appetites are whetted for the feature film he might have made had he known (or cared) about the gaps that have persisted ever since in the historical record.

The account, in translation, runs to fewer than forty pages, divided into forty sections. These range from a short paragraph to several pages and topically from religion, justice, kingship, and agriculture (to name only four) to birds, vegetables, bathing customs, and slaves. Many features of thirteenth-century Cambodian life that Zhou described—including tools, draft animals, and aspects of rural commerce—are still observable today, and others—such as slavery, sumptuary laws, and trial by ordeal— endured in modified form until the nineteenth century at least.

Five of Zhou's sections deal with religion, slaves, festivals, agriculture, and the king's excursions. Zhou found three religions enjoying official status at Angkor: they appear to have been Brahmanism, Theravada Buddhism, and Shaivism. The brahmans, Zhou noted, often attained high positions as officials, but he could find little else to say about them: "I don't know what the source of their doctrine is. They have nowhere that can be called an academy or place of learning, and it is hard to find out what books they study." The Theravada monks, known colloquially by a Thai phrase (*chao ku*), closely resembled their counterparts in Theravada Southeast Asia today: "They shave their heads and dress in yellow. They leave their right shoulder uncovered, and wrap themselves in a robe made of yellow cloth and go barefoot. And wear yellow robes, leaving the right shoulder bare. For the lower half of the body, they wear a yellow skirt. They are barefoot."

Like the palace and the houses of high officials, Zhou tells us, Buddhist monasteries could have tile roofs, but those of ordinary people had to be made of thatch. Zhou was impressed by the simplicity of the Theravada Buddhist *wats,* noting that (unlike Mahayana temples in China) they contained "no bells, cymbals, flags, or platforms," housing only an image of the Buddha made of gilded plaster. Finally, Zhou described the method used to inscribe palm leaf manuscripts, which persisted well into the twentieth century, particularly in the case of religious and historical texts.

The Shaivites, whom Zhou called "followers of the Dao," inhabited monasteries that were less prosperous than Buddhist ones. "They don't make offerings to an icon, only to a block of stone, like the altar stones of the gods of the earth in China." Although monastic Shaivism declined in importance after the abandonment of Angkor and soon disappeared altogether, Indianized cults, including the use of linga, continued into modern times, and officials calling themselves brahmans continued to work at the Cambodian court, where they were entrusted with the performance of royal rituals and with maintaining astronomical tables.

Zhou's account makes it clear that many of the people living at Angkor were in some sense slaves, for he tells us that "those who have many slaves have more than a hundred; those who have only a few have from ten to twenty; only the very poor have none at all." He went on to say that slaves were generally taken as captives from mountain tribes, a practice that persisted into the colonial era. It seems likely, in fact, that this is the way Cambodian society built itself up over time, gradually absorbing and socializing "barbarians," who figure in such large numbers in the inscriptions in Angkorean times. In Zhou's account, slaves were set apart from other people by several prohibitions: "They are only allowed to sit and sleep under the house. If they are carrying out their tasks then they can come up into the house, but they must kneel, join their hands in greeting and bow to the floor before they can venture forward." Slaves enjoyed no civil privileges; their marriages were not even recognized by the state. Forced to call their masters father and their mistresses mother, they tried frequently to escape and, when caught, were tattooed, mutilated, or chained.[37]

Although Zhou is informative about people at court and about slaves, he is vague about the proportion of society in the 1290s that was neither in bondage nor part of the elite. Clearly, the people with "a few" slaves would fall into this category; as would the private landowners, discussed in an earlier context by M.C. Ricklefs,[38] and the Sino-Cambodians who were active in local and international trade. Special privileges were extended to the elite and to religious sects and special prohibitions applied to slaves, but about those in between—the people, in fact, who probably made the kingdom prosper—we know far less than we would like.

When Zhou goes into detail, however, his account is often illuminating. His description of what he called a new year's festival, which occurred toward the end of November, is a good example of his narrative skill:

> A large stage is set up in front of the royal palace. There is room on it for a thousand or more people. It is hung everywhere with globe lanterns and flowers. Facing it on a bank more than two or three hundred feet away are some stall structures that are made of wood joined and bound together, like the scaffolding used to make a pagoda. Every night they put up three or four of these, or five or six of them, and set out fireworks and firecrackers on top of them. The various provincial officials and great houses take care of all the costs. When night comes the king is invited to come out and watch. He lights the fireworks and firecrackers which can be seen a hundred li [about a mile] away. The firecrackers are as

big as the rocks thrown by trebuchets and make enough noise to shake the entire city.

This ceremony, probably observed by Zhou himself, appears to have been celebrated at the end of the rainy season, when the waters of the Tonle Sap begin to subside, setting in motion the first stages of the agricultural year. After the move to Phnom Penh in the fifteenth century, the ceremony became known as the water festival and was similarly marked by fireworks, floats, and royal patronage until the monarchy was overthrown in 1970. The festival was revived, along with the monarchy, in 1993.

As to agriculture, Zhou noted that three or even four rice harvests a year were possible—a statistic singled out by Democratic Kampuchea in its efforts to revolutionize production. It is unlikely that this abundance applied throughout the country, for at Angkor several harvests were possible only because of the concentration of manpower there, the rich alluvial soil, and the water storage system perfected in the region over several hundred years. Another factor was the peculiarly helpful behavior of the Tonle Sap. According to Zhou's comments on the agricultural cycle's relationship to this beneficent body of water:

> For six months the land has rain, for six months no rain at all. From the fourth to the ninth month, it rains every day, with the rain falling in the afternoon. The high water mark around the Freshwater Sea Tonle Sap can reach some seventy or eighty feet, completely submerging even very tall trees except for the tips. Families living by the shire all move to the far side of the hills. From the tenth month to the third month there is not a drop of rain. Only small boats can cross the Tonle Sap.

The "miracle" of the Tonle Sap amazed many subsequent travelers to Angkor. As long as the region supported a large population, the deposits left by receding water provided useful nutrients for the soil. Even after Angkor was abandoned, the lake remained the most densely populated natural fishbowl in the world, providing generations of Cambodians with much of the protein for their diet.

We would welcome the chance to interrogate Zhou Daguan about the working of agriculture at this time. For example, how was the rice surplus handled? Were cultivators for the most part free people or some kind of slaves? Did agriculture differ markedly at Angkor from that in other parts of the kingdom? How much land was in the hands of members of the royal family and how much was controlled by Buddhist *wats*? What did this control imply?

As we have no answers to these questions, we must be grateful to Zhou for what he gives us. His description of rural marketing, for example, could easily have been written about rural markets in Cambodia today:

> The local people who know how to trade are all women. . . . There is a market every day from around six in the morning until mid-day. There are no stalls only a kind of tumbleweed mat laid out on the ground, each mat in its usual place. I gather there is also a rental fee to be paid to officials.

It seems likely, in view of Cambodia's trade with China, that many Chinese had by this time settled in Cambodia to engage in commerce. According to Zhou, the products exported by Cambodia in the thirteenth century were those that had been exported since the time of Funan; they were to form the bulk of Cambodian exports until the twentieth century. These were high-value, low-bulk items such as rhinoceros horns, ivory, beeswax, lacquer, pepper, feathers, and cardamom. Imported products included paper and metal goods, porcelain, silk, and wicker. It is unclear from Zhou's account how products were paid for although it seems unlikely that government-sponsored currency was in circulation. Zhou was fascinated by the king reigning at Angkor during his visit (Indravarman III, r. 1296–1308). The king had reached the throne, Zhou remarked, in a curious manner:

> The new king was the old king's (Jayavarman VIII's) son-in-law. When his father-in-law died, the new king's wife secretly stole the gold sword and gave it to him. The old king's own son was thus deprived of the succession. . . . The new king had a sacred piece of

iron embedded in his body, so that if anything like a knife or a arrow touched him he could not be injured. With this to rely on, he
ventured to come out of his palace.

These events, which had taken place just before the Chinese embassy's
arrival, are alluded to discreetly by some inscriptions that date from Indravarman's reign. One of them refers to the "old age" of Jayavarman
VIII and a "host of enemies" inside the kingdom. Another, echoing a
sentiment in one of Jayavarman VII's inscriptions, mentions that Indravarman shaded the country with his single umbrella, whereas no
shade had existed before, under "a crowd of [such] umbrellas."[39]

The transition between the reigns of Jayavarman VIII and Indravarman III, in fact, probably marked a sharp transition in Cambodian history, although we do not learn of it from Zhou Daguan. Under
Jayavarman VIII in 1285, the last stone temple, the Mangalartha, was
erected in the Angkor region. It was built by a high-ranking official and
dedicated to Siva; the "single umbrella" to which its inscription refers
may well have been Jayavarman's intolerant Hinduism. We know that
Indravarman III was careful to sponsor Theravada Buddhists as well as
brahmans, and it is tempting to speculate about a religious ingredient in
his apparently nonviolent coup d'état.

The king's procession, like so much else in Zhou's account, gains in
interest when compared with similar processions recorded in the colonial era.[40] It becomes clear in comparing the procession with the one
marking Sihanouk's coronation, or other twentieth-century processions
for which records have survived, that ceremonial Cambodian life and
the hierarchical arrangement of such events changed little between
Angkorean times and our own era. In Zhou's words:

> Each time he came out all his soldiers were gathered in front of
> him, with people bearing banners, musicians and drummers fol-
> lowing behind him. One contingent was made up of three to five
> hundred women of the palace. They wore clothes with a floral de-
> sign and flowers in their coiled-up hair, and carried huge candles,
> alight even though it was daylight. There were also women of the
> palace carrying gold and silver utensils from the palace and finely

decorated instruments made in exotic and unusual styles, for what purpose I do not know. . . . Palace women carrying lances and shields made up another contingent as the palace guard. . . . All the ministers, officials and relatives of the king were in front, riding elephants. Their red parasols, too many to number, were visible in the distance. . . . Late came the king, standing on an elephant, the gold sword in his hand and the tusks of his elephant encased in gold. He had more than twenty white parasols decorated with gold filigree, their handles all made of gold.

Zhou then described a royal audience of the sort that Indravarman conducted on a daily basis and closed his account by remarking superciliously, "We can see from this that although this is a country of barbarians, they know at first hand that they have a supreme ruler."

5

CAMBODIA AFTER ANGKOR

The least-recorded period of Cambodian history falls between Zhou
Daguan's visit to Angkor and the restoration of some of the temples
there by a Cambodian king named Chan in the 1550s and 1560s. The
intervening centuries witnessed major, permanent shifts in Cambodia's
economy, its foreign relations, its language, and probably, although this
is harder to verify, in the structure, values, and performance of Cambodian society. Evidence about these shifts that can be traced to the period
itself, however, is very thin. By the time the amount of evidence in-
creases and becomes reliable around 1550 or so, many of the shifts have
already taken place.

Evidence from the early decades of the period comes largely from
Chinese sources, for almost no inscriptions appear to have been carved
on stone inside the kingdom between the middle of the fourteenth century and the beginning of the sixteenth. Indeed, whereas over a thousand
inscriptions have been catalogued for the years prior to 1300, less than a
hundred more were carved in later centuries. Other sources include a
Cham inscription and some inscriptions from Thailand, while Thai
chronicles written in the seventeenth century, one of them very fragmentary, contain some accurate information about political and social events.
The Cambodian chronicles that purportedly deal with the period appear
to have been drawn from folklore and from Thai chronicle traditions,
and they are impossible to corroborate from other sources.[1]

THE SHIFT FROM ANGKOR TO PHNOM PENH

The Chinese evidence is important, for as Michael Vickery and Oliver Wolters have convincingly argued, the southward shifts in Cambodia's geographical and administrative center of gravity in the fourteenth and fifteenth centuries were probably connected with the rapid expansion of Chinese maritime trade with Southeast Asia under the Mongols and the early Ming. Twenty-one tributary missions were sent from Cambodia to the Ming court in China between 1371 and 1432—more, it seems, than throughout the entire Angkorean period—and although some of these missions may have been purely ceremonial, they must have come primarily to trade, to arrange for trade, and perhaps also to request Chinese support against the depredations of the Thai. The number of missions and the respect accorded them by the Chinese indicate not only that Cambodia remained active and powerful during this period but also that the Cambodian elite, less rigidly tied to religious foundations and the ceremonial duties of brahmanical bureaucracy, were eager to exploit the possibility of commercial relations with China. How and why this shift in their thinking and behavior occurred is impossible to ascertain, but several scholars have held that the shift should not be connected with the notion of decline for, as Wolters has remarked, "perhaps we have become too ready to regard the decline of Angkor in the fourteenth and fifteenth centuries as being on a catastrophic scale."[2] Indeed, throughout this period, rulers inside the present-day frontiers of Cambodia were able to compete for resources and trade with their new and prosperous neighbors in the recently established kingdom of Ayudhya to the west. The region of Angkor itself, as recent studies have revealed, was still quite heavily populated, and several buildings in the region were restored in these years. The Cambodians convinced the Chinese of their own continuing importance and were occasionally able, well into the seventeenth century, to attack Ayudhya and to defeat the Thai in war.

Because this shift of emphasis was accompanied by so few supposedly Angkorean activities (such as stone temple construction, grandiose inscriptions, and expanded irrigation works), authors have often spoken of decline or collapse where *change* or *transformation* would be more appropriate terms. *Decline*, for one thing, fails to explain Cambodia's enduring strength; for another, the word suggests that Jayavarman VII, for example, was in some ways a more authentically Cambodian king than the Theravada monarch observed in 1296 by Zhou Daguan. Some authors have connected the royal abandonment of Angkor—a historical event that may not even have taken place before the 1560s with a national failure of nerve and with major losses of population. Such losses, the argument runs, would have made it impossible to maintain irrigation works at Angkor, and the water, becoming stagnant, could have become a breeding place for malarial mosquitoes, further depleting the population in a spiraling process. Still others have argued that Theravada Buddhism was in some ways subversive of Angkorean cohesion while it invigorated the politics of Ayudhya and Pagan in Burma; the peaceable nature of this variant of the religion has been used to explain the defeats but not the Cambodian victories nor those of the Thai who shared the same beliefs.

What emerges from the evidence is that Cambodia was entering what Ashley Thompson has called its middle period well before the wholesale abandonment of Angkor. Angkorean institutions—inscriptions, stone temples, a Hindu-oriented royal family, and extensive hydraulic works, to name four traditions—seem to have stopped, faded, or been redirected soon after the conversion of the Cambodian elite and the general population to Theravada Buddhism, an event that probably took place not long after Jayavarman VII's death. It would be premature to see these social changes as springing uniquely or even primarily from the ideology or content of the new religion. It is more likely that they were related to the rise of the Theravada kingdom of Ayudhya to the west and to the entanglement, which was to last until the 1860s, between the Siamese and Cambodian courts. People, ideas, texts, and institutions migrated west from Angkor to Ayudhya, where they were modified and eventually reexported into Cambodia to survive as part of its genuine decline from the eighteenth century onward. The migration would have prisoners of war, including entire families, swept off to the west after successive Thai invasions of Angkor, the most important of these perhaps occurring in 1431. As this process was going on, other people and institutions were also migrating southward to the vicinity of Phnom Penh, where the capital of Cambodia was to remain for the next six hundred years.[3]

The suitability of Phnom Penh as a site for a Cambodian capital sprang in large part from its location at the confluence of the Mekong and the Tonle Sap. A fortified city at this point, the "four faces," could control the riverine trade coming down from Laos as well as trade in pottery, dried fish, and fish sauce from the Tonle Sap, to say nothing of incoming goods, primarily Chinese in origin, approaching Cambodia via the Mekong Delta, still largely inhabited by Khmer. Once the choice had been made to become a trading kingdom—and it is impossible to say when, how, or why this happened—locating the Cambodian capital at Phnom Penh made economic sense.

It is likely that the shift of the capital also represented a momentary triumph, later legitimized and prolonged, of regional interests and per-haps those of an individual overlord, at the expense of people lingering near Angkor or gathering strength in the Menam Basin to the west. These members of a southeastern Cambodian elite—for these interests were those of chiefs and their followings, rather than rice farmers singly or en masse—probably took advantage of their distance from Ayudhya to trade with China on their own account. It also seems likely that they could rely on support from overlords long entrenched in the region, which was the heartland of Funan, an area where Angkorean writ may often have been ignored.

But these are suppositions. It seems more certain that the myth con-nected with the founding of Phnom Penh, which tells of an old woman's discovery of a Buddha image floating miraculously downstream, was concocted after the city had come to life, under a name suggestive of its location at the crossroad of two rivers, a name that has survived into modern Khmer as Chatomuk, or "four faces," an interesting echo of the iconography of the Bayon.[4]

The role played by foreigners adept at trade in this new city is diffi-cult to assess, but influential figures probably included speakers of Malay, from Champa or the Indonesian islands who may have left be-hind in the Cambodian language words such as *kompong*, or "landing place," and *psar,* or "market," as well as several bureaucratic titles and administrative terms. The Malay legacy may have been deeper than this and needs to be explored, for seventeenth-century European descriptions of riverine Cambodia, and the way its politics were organized, strongly resemble descriptions from this era and later of riverine Malaya.[5] Other foreigners active in Phnom Penh at this time were the Chinese, already busily trading at Angkor in the thirteenth century; there were three thousand of them in Phnom Penh in the 1540s. It seems likely that Chinese and Malay traders and their descendants married into the Cambodian elite, just as the Chinese continued to do later on, tightening the relationships between the king, his entourage, and commercial profits.

By the late fifteenth century, it seems, the social organization, bureaucracy, and economic priorities of Angkor, based on heavy taxation, forced labor, and the primacy of a priestly caste, were no longer strong or relevant. New forms of organization, new settlement patterns, and new priorities based in part on foreign trade became feasible and attractive.

Some of the reasons for the changes that Cambodia underwent in this period have already been suggested. Another element conducive to change might be called the emulation factor, affecting both Phnom Penh (and other capitals nearby) and Ayudhya. These were newly established trading kingdoms, respectful but perhaps a little wary of the idea of Angkor. By the 1400s, Ayudhya and these Cambodian cities looked to each other rather than to a brahmanical past for exemplary behavior. Until the end of the sixteenth century, moreover, Phnom Penh (or Lovek or Udong) and Ayudhya considered themselves not separate polities but participants in a hybrid culture. The mixture contained elements of Hinduized kingship, traceable to Angkor, and Theravada monarchic accessibility, traceable to the Mon kingdom of Dvaravati perhaps, which had practiced Theravada Buddhism for almost a thousand years, as well as remnants of paternalistic, village-oriented leadership traceable to the ethnic forerunners of the Thai, the tribal peoples hailing originally from the mountains of southern China. Throughout the fourteenth century and much of the fifteenth, the official language common to both kingdoms was probably Khmer. In both societies the

Buddhist *sangha,* or monastic order, was accessible, in its lower reaches at least, to ordinary people. Brought into contact with each other through wars, immigration, and a shared religion, the newly established Thai and Khmer kingdoms blended with each other and developed differently from their separate forebears.

This hybrid blending was rarely peaceful. Both kingdoms estimated political strength in terms of controlling manpower rather than territory or resources and interpreted such strength (and tributary payments) as evidence of royal merit and prestige. The Thai would have learned from the Khmer, and vice versa, to a large extent via defectors and prisoners of war. Between the fourteenth and the nineteenth century there were frequent wars, generally west of the Mekong, between the Cambodians and the Thai. These laid waste the regions through which invading and retreating armies marched. The invasions usually coincided with periods of weakness in the areas that were invaded. In the 1570s, for example, after a Burmese army had sacked Ayudhya, several Cambodian expeditions were mounted against Siam. Invasion routes ran along the edges of the Tonle Sap, and this fact probably made the site of Yasodharapura unsuitable as a residential area for large numbers of unprotected people.

CAMBODIA IN THE FIFTEENTH AND SIXTEENTH CENTURIES

The narrative history of the fifteenth and sixteenth centuries, about which we know so little, can be disposed of fairly quickly. The Thai-oriented administration of the Angkor region, it seems, was overthrown by forces loyal to Phnom Penh toward the middle of the fifteenth century; that is, perhaps about twenty years after the last Thai attack on the old capital. During this period, a succession of kings, whose names and dates as reported in the chronicles are probably fictional, held power in Phnom Penh.

Chronicles suggest that by the end of the fifteenth century, conflict had developed between these new rulers as they renewed and formalized their relations with Ayudhya and with officials or chieftains with followings rooted in the southeastern *sruk,* or districts. A former slave, the chronicles state, led some of these forces, and Europeans writing somewhat later stated that this new king was in fact a relative of the monarch whom he had deposed.[6] What is important for later events is that the deposed king, Chan, took temporary refuge in Ayudhya before returning with an army to depose the usurper. His restoration under Thai patronage set a precedent that many Cambodian kings were to follow.

So did the fact that he was deposed by forces coming from the eastern portions of the kingdom. From the 1620s onward, these regions of dissidence could often rely on Vietnamese support. According to the Khmer chronicles, a Cambodian king married a Vietnamese princess in the 1630s and allowed Vietnamese authorities to set up customs posts in the Mekong Delta, then inhabited largely by Khmer but beyond the reach of Cambodian administrative control.[7] Over the next two hundred years, Vietnamese immigrants poured into the region, still known to many Khmer today as Lower Cambodia or Kampuchea Krom. When Cambodia gained its independence in 1953, some four hundred thousand Cambodians still lived in southern Vietnam, surrounded by more than ten times as many Vietnamese. The Khmer residents developed a distinctive culture, and many twentieth-century Cambodian political leaders, including Son Sen, Son Sann, Ieng Sary, and Son Ngoc Thanh, were born and raised as members of this minority. The presence of rival patrons to the west and east set in motion a whipsaw between Thai and Vietnamese influence over the Cambodian court, and between pro-Thai and pro-Vietnamese Cambodian factions in the provinces as well. Already severe in the 1680s,[8] this factionalism lasted until the 1860s, and arguably was revived under Democratic Kampuchea, where eastern-zone cadres were accused by Pol Pot and his colleagues of having "Cambodian bodies and Vietnamese minds."[9]

The first European to mention Cambodia was probably Tome Pires, whose *Suma Oriental* was written between 1512 and 1515. The kingdom he described was a warlike one, whose ruler "obeys no one," and Pires hinted at the richness of the products that could be obtained from it.[10] He was relying, however, on hearsay. The first eyewitness account comes from the Portuguese missionary Gaspar da Cruz, who visited Lovek toward the end of King Chan's reign in 1556. He left after about a year, disappointed by his inability to make converts, and chose to blame his failure on the superstitions of the people and their loyalty to

Buddhist monks. Cruz was impressed, indeed, by the solidarity of the Cambodians, and in an interesting passage he remarked that they

> dare do nothing of themselves, nor accept anything new without leave of the king, which is why Christians cannot be made without the king's approval. And if some of my readers should say that they could be converted without the king knowing it, to this I answer that the people of the country is of such a nature, that nothing is done that the king knoweth not; and anybody, be he never so simple may speak with the King, wherefore everyone seeketh news to carry unto him, to have an occasion for to speak with him; whereby without the king's good will nothing can be done.

He suggested that the *sangha* contained more than a third of the able-bodied men in Cambodia or, by his estimate, some hundred thousand, a fact with clear implications for politics and the economy. These monks commanded great loyalty from the population, and Cruz found them to be

> exceedingly proud and vain . . . alive they are worshipped for gods, in sort that the inferior among them do worship the superior like gods, praying unto them and prostrating themselves before them: and so the common people have great confidence in them, with a great reverence and worship: so that there is no person that dare contradict them in anything. . . . It happened sometimes that while I was preaching, many round me hearing me very well, and being very satisfied with what I told them, that if there come along any of these priests and said, "This is good, but ours is better," they would all depart and leave me alone.[11]

The absence of inherited riches cited by Cruz is a vivid example of royal interference in everyday life. When the owner of a house died, Cruz remarked, "All that is in it returneth to the king, and the wife and children hide what they can, and begin to seek a new life." Possessions, in other words, were held by people at the king's pleasure, as were ranks, land, and positions in society. This residual absolute power, it seems, gave the otherwise rickety institution of the monarchy great strength vis-à-vis the elite. One consequence of the arrangements cited by Cruz was that rich families could not, in theory at least, consolidate themselves into lasting antimonarchical alliances; the king's response to them (dispossessing a generation at a time) suggests that kings distrusted the elite.

Cruz said nothing about Angkor, although a later Portuguese writer, Diego do Couto, reported in 1599 that some forty years beforehand (in 1550 or 1551), a king of Cambodia had stumbled across the ruins while on an elephant hunt. The story is not confirmed by other sources, but several dated inscriptions at Angkor reappear in the 1560s, suggesting that the date of the rediscovery may be accurate, although it may have taken place during a military campaign instead of during a hunt, for the Angkor region was a logical staging area for Cambodian armies poised to invade Siam.

Couto wrote that when the king had been informed of the existence of ruins,

> he went to the place, and seeing the extent and the height of the exterior walls, and wanting to examine the interior as well, he ordered people then and there to cut and burn the undergrowth. And he remained there, beside a pretty river while this work was accomplished, by five or six thousand men, working for a few days. . . . And when everything had been carefully cleaned up, the king went inside, and . . . was filled with admiration for the extent of these constructions.[12]

He added that the king then decided to transfer his court to Angkor. Two inscriptions from Angkor Wat indicate that the temple was partially restored under royal patronage in 1577–78. Both of the inscriptions, and two more incised at Phnom Bakheng in 1583, honored the king's young son in whose favor he was to abdicate in 1584, possibly to delay a coup by his own ambitious and more popular brother.[13] The identically worded Phnom Bakheng inscriptions, in fact, may refer to this infighting by expressing the hope that the king would no longer be tormented by "royal enemies." It is equally possible, however, that the phrase refers to the Thai royal family, with whom the Cambodian elite had been quarreling throughout the 1570s.

Indeed, in spite of the apparent ideological solidarity noted by Cruz, and the florescence of Buddhism reflected in several inscriptions, the 1560–90 period was a turbulent one in which Cambodian troops took advantage of Thai weakness (brought on in part by the Burmese sacking of Ayudhya in 1569) to attack Thai territory several times. According to Europeans, the Cambodian king, worried by internal and external threats, changed his attitude toward Catholic missionaries, allowing them to preach and sending gifts of rice to the recently colonized centers of Malacca and Manila in exchange for promises of military help (which never arrived). Earlier, the king had apparently attempted to seek an alliance, or at least a nonaggression pact, with the Thai.

The flurry of contradictory activities in the field of foreign relations suggests instability at the court that is reflected in the frequent moves the king made, his premature abdication, and his unwillingness or inability to remain at peace with the Thai, who unsuccessfully laid siege to Lovek in 1587, a date confirmed by an inscription from southeastern Cambodia.[14] If subsequent Cambodian diplomatic maneuvering is a guide, it seems likely that these sixteenth-century moves were attempts by the king to remain in power despite the existence of heavily armed, more popular relatives and in the face of threats from Ayudhya and the surprisingly powerful Lao states to the north.

By 1593 Thai preparations for a new campaign against Lovek forced the Cambodian king to look overseas for help. He appealed to the Spanish governor-general of the Philippines, even promising to convert to Christianity if sufficient aid were forthcoming. Before his letter had been acted on, however, the king and his young son fled north to southern Laos, and another son was placed in charge of the defense of Lovek. The city fell in 1594.

Although Cambodian military forces were often as strong as those of the Thai throughout most of the seventeenth century, and although European traders were often attracted to Cambodia almost as strongly as they were to Ayudhya at this time, Thai and Cambodian historiography and Cambodian legend interpret the capture of Lovek as a turning point in Cambodian history, ushering in centuries of Cambodian weakness and intermittent Thai hegemony. The facts of the case as they appear in European sources are more nuanced than this, but the belief is still strong on both sides of the poorly demarcated border that a traumatic event (for the Cambodians) had taken place.

The popular legend of *preah ko preah kaev,* first published in fragmentary form by a French scholar in the 1860s, is helpful on this point and is worth examining in detail.[15] According to the legend, the citadel of Lovek was so large that no horse could gallop around it. Inside were two statues, *preah ko* ("sacred cow") and *preah kaev* ("sacred precious stone"). Inside the bellies of these statues, "there were sacred books, in gold, where one could learn formulae, and books where one could learn about anything in the world. . . . Now the king of Siam wanted to have the statues, so he raised an army and came to fight the Cambodian king."

The legend then relates an incident contained in the chronicles as well. Thai cannon fired silver coins, rather than shells, into the bamboo hedges that served as Lovek's fortifications. When the Thai retreated, the Cambodians cut down the hedges to get at the coins and thus had no defenses when the Thai returned in the following year to assault the city. When they had won, the Thai carried off the two statues to Siam. After opening up their bellies, the legend tells us,

> they were able to take the books which were hidden there and study their contents. *For this reason* [emphasis added] they have become superior in knowledge to the Cambodians, and for this reason the Cambodians are ignorant, and lack people to do what is necessary, unlike other countries.

Although keyed to the capture of Lovek, the legend may in fact be related to the long-term collapse of Angkor and perhaps to the relationships that had developed between Siam and Cambodia by the nineteenth century, when the legend emerged in the historical record. The temptation to prefer the earlier collapse as the source for the legend may spring from the fit between the legend's metaphors and what we know to have happened, i.e., the slow transfer of Cambodia's regalia, documents, customs, and learned men from Angkor to Ayudhya in the period between

Jayavarman VII's death and the Thai invasions of the fifteenth century. The statue of *preah ko* is a metaphor for Cambodia's Indian heritage and clearly represents Nandin, the mount of Siva. The less precisely described *preah kaev* is a metaphor for Buddhist legitimacy, embodied by a Buddha image like the one taken from Vientiane by the Thai in the 1820s (and known as a *preah kaev*) to be enshrined in the temple of that name in Bangkok; a replica is housed in the so-called Silver Pagoda in Phnom Penh. The seepage of literary skills from Cambodia to Siam and the increasing power of the Thai from the seventeenth century onward are ingredients in the legend which, like that of the leper king discussed in Chapter 4, may contain a collective memory of real occurrences half-hidden by a metaphorical frame of reference. The Cambodian scholar Ang Choulean, in his discussion of this legend, has called it "partially historic, mostly legend, but above all totally coherent."[16]

The myth, in other words, may have been used by many Cambodians to explain Cambodia's weakness vis-à-vis the Thai in terms of its unmeritorious behavior (chasing after the coins) and its former strength in terms of palladia that could be taken away.

The closing years of the sixteenth century, when the capture of Lovek took place, are well documented in European sources. These years were marked by Spanish imperialism in Cambodia, directed from the Philippines and orchestrated largely by two adventurers named Blas Ruiz and Diego de Veloso.[17] Their exploits illuminate three themes that were to remain important in Cambodian history. The first was the king's susceptibility to blandishments and promises on the part of visitors who came, as it were, from outer space. Both Spaniards were honored with bureaucratic titles and given *sruk* to govern and princesses for wives. The second theme was the revolution in warfare brought on by the introduction of firearms, particularly naval cannon, which played a major part in all subsequent Cambodian wars. Because they were masters of a new technology, Ruiz and Veloso were able to terrorize local people just as their contemporaries could in Spanish America, while accompanied by fewer than a hundred men.

The third theme was that by the end of the sixteenth century the Cambodian king and his courtiers had become entangled in the outside world, symbolized at the time by the multitude of foreign traders resident in Lovek and Phnom Penh. European writers emphasized the importance of these people and the foreign residential quarters at Lovek. These included separate quarters for Chinese, Japanese, Arabs, Spanish, and Portuguese as well as traders from the Indonesian archipelago; they were joined briefly in the seventeenth century by traders from Holland and Great Britain.[18] The traders worked through officials close to the king and members of the royal family, as well as through their compatriots. In the seventeenth century, according to Dutch sources, foreign traders were required to live in specific areas of the new capital, Udong, reserved for them and to deal with the Cambodian government only through appointed representatives, or *shabandar*. This pattern may have originated in China and also applied in Siam; its presence at Lovek in the depths of Cambodia's so-called decline, like other bits of data, suggests that the kingdom was by no means dead.

The Spanish missionary San Antonio also left an account of the closing years of the sixteenth century, which includes the adventures of Ruiz and Veloso. His account is often illuminating and occasionally comic, as when he attributes the construction of the temples at Angkor to the Jews, echoing local disbelief in Cambodian technology.[19] He was also convinced that Spain should colonize the kingdom for religious and commercial reasons, and this may have led him to exaggerate the value of its resources, as French visitors were to do in the 1860s. His impressions of prosperity may have sprung from the fact that visitors were forced by the absence of overland communication to limit their observations of Cambodia to the relatively rich and populated areas along the Mekong north of Phnom Penh, an area that was still one of the most prosperous in Cambodia when it was studied four hundred years later by Jean Delvert.[20] The goods that San Antonio saw included gold, silver, precious stones, silk and cotton cloth, incense, lacquer, ivory, rice, fruit, elephants, buffalo, and rhinoceros. The last was valued for its horns, skin, blood, and teeth as a "subtle antidote for a number of illnesses, particularly those of the heart," a reference to the Chinese belief that rhinoceros by-products were effective as aphrodisiacs. San Antonio stressed that Cambodia was prosperous because it was a gateway to Laos which, almost unknown to Europeans, was assumed to be some sort of El Dorado. He closed his discussion of Cambodia's prosperity with a passage that might seem to have been lifted from *Hansel and Gretel*, echoing the *preah ko preah keo* myth while altering the villains: "There are so many precious things in Cambodia that when the king [recently] fled to Laos, he scattered gold and silver coins, for a number of days, along the road so that the Siamese would be too busy gathering them up to capture him."[21]

San Antonio also remarked that the country contained only two classes of people, the rich and the poor:

> The Cambodians recognize only one king. Among them there are nobles and commoners. . . . All the nobles have several wives, the number depending on how rich they are. High ranking women are white and beautiful; those of the common people are brown. These women work the soil while their husbands make war. . . . The nobles dress in silk and fine cotton and gauze. Nobles travel in litters, which people carry on their shoulders, while the people travel by cart, on buffalo, and on horseback. They pay to the principal officials, and to the king, one-tenth of the value of all goods taken from the sea and land.

The slave-owning, nonmercantile middle class noted by Zhou Daguan seems to have diminished in importance, although there is evidence from legal codes and at least one chronicle that it continued to exist.[22] It is possible that its place was taken in Cambodian society to a large extent by foreign traders and semiurban hangers-on, while ethnic Khmer remained primarily rice farmers, officials, members of the *sangha,* and gatherers of primary produce. San Antonio's contempt for the *sangha* seems to have exceeded his curiosity.

As so often happens in Cambodian history, the rice farmers are omitted from the record. We see the people the visitors saw, the king, the elite, the foreign traders, and their slaves. Inland from the *kompong,* villages were linked to the trading capitals by economic relationships, by taxation, and by the social mobility provided by the *sangha;* the villagers were leading their lives. At least this is what we must suppose for without these people, kingship and other institutions in Cambodia would have withered on the vine. But like the particles of subatomic physics, in terms of which atomic behavior makes sense, these major actors are invisible and their voices are unheard.

In the early seventeenth century, Cambodia became a maritime kingdom, with the prosperity of its elite dependent on seaborne overseas trade conducted in large part by the European traders, Chinese, and ethnic Malays operating out of Sumatra and Sulawesi. Japanese and European visitors—Dutch, English, and Portuguese—left records of this period that are useful as they corroborate and supplement the Cambodian chronicles. These people were also involved in factionalism at the court and in plotting among themselves.

The period came to a climax of sorts in the 1640s when a Cambodian king married a Malay and converted to Islam.[23] He is known in chronicles as the "king who chose [a different] religion." In 1642 a Dutch naval force attacked Phnom Penh to avenge the murder of Dutch residents of the capital, but it was driven off. In the 1650s rival princes sought military help from Vietnam to overthrow the Muslim monarch, and when the troops came they were reinforced by local ones recruited in eastern Cambodia, a pattern followed in Vietnamese incursions in the nineteenth century and the 1970s. After a long campaign the Cambodian king was captured and taken off in a cage to Vietnam, where some sources assert he was killed and others that he died soon afterward of disease.

The remainder of the seventeenth century saw a decline in international trade as Cambodia's access to the sea was choked off by the Vietnamese and by coastal settlements controlled by Chinese merchants who had fled southern China with the advent of the Qing dynasty. The newcomers turned Saigon into an important, accessible trading center. Phnom Penh became a backwater, and by the eighteenth century Cambodia was a largely blank area on European maps. In the 1690s Chinese traders with Japan reported that Cambodia had suffered a sharp decline. One such trader wrote:

Cambodia is a poor country with a poorly organized government and armed forces. There are virtually no rich people. They do not produce raw silk. Their main products are deer hides, low quality brown sugar, lacquer . . . in small quantities.[24]

VALUES IN SEVENTEENTH-CENTURY CAMBODIA

It would be wrong to suggest that seventeenth-century Cambodian society can be best understood in terms of timelessness. In many ways it differed from its nineteenth-century counterpart. For example, nineteenth-century Cambodia had been brought to its knees by foreign powers; for most of the seventeenth century, Cambodia was still reasonably independent. Nineteenth-century Cambodia was isolated from the outside world by the same two powers, Siam and Vietnam, that dominated its internal politics; seventeenth-century Cambodia, on the other hand, traded freely with many countries until the 1680s. Also, the elite Cambodian literary tradition, enshrined in the local version of the *Ramayana*, the *Reamker*, as well as in the inscriptions at Angkor Wat and other works, was far more vigorous in the seventeenth century than in the nineteenth, as we shall see.

Saveros Pou has attributed these changes in part to Thai influence but more profoundly to what she referred to as a "slow degradation of values from the seventeenth century on."[25] It is easy to share her impression after reading the *Reamker* alongside some of the fatuous verse-novels composed in the 1880s or after comparing the seventeenth-century legal codes, translated by Adhémard Leclère and Gregory Mikaelian, with the scattered and often timorous documents left behind by nineteenth-century kings. Although the values she referred to emanated from the elite, Pou saw the decline as one that altered the collective acceptance of traditional values. She saw these values, in turn, as linked with Buddhist notions of the cosmos (enshrined in the long didactic poem known as the *Trai Phum*, "Three Worlds"), especially as these filtered into Buddhist teaching in oral form enshrined in the aphoristic collection of laws, or *chbab*, until very recently memorized by Cambodian schoolchildren. In other words she viewed seventeenth-century Cambodia as a nation abiding by rules that were later watered down, abused, or forgotten.

These values delineate proper conduct for the people. This conduct has to do in large part with one's position in society and governs the way that one relates to others. Everyone, of course, comes equipped with several positions, being at the same time older than some and younger than others, richer and poorer, wiser and more foolish, and so on. An elderly "inferior" is to be addressed with respect, for example; so is a younger monk, and a monk of peasant origin, in theory at least, is to be paid homage by a king. In many cases, moreover, one person's patron is someone else's client.

The *chbab* stress several normative relationships of this kind, the most important of which are probably those with parents and teachers. According to the *chbab*, these authority figures convey material to be memorized. There is nothing to discuss. The teacher's relation to his student, like so many relationships in traditional Cambodian society, was lopsided.[26]

The teacher, like a parent, bestows, transmits, and commands. The student, like the child, receives, accepts, and obeys. Nothing changes in the transmission process, except perhaps the diminishing ignorance of the student; knowledge is passed on by teachers who are former students over generations. If this involves little or no progress, we should recall that the idea of progress is not widespread and was not well known in precolonial Southeast Asia. What kept society coherent, Cambodians believed, was the proper observance of relationships among people as well as the shared acceptance of Buddhist ideology. The first of these involved proper language and appropriate behavior. The Khmer language, like many others in Southeast Asia (Javanese is perhaps the best example), displays differences between people in the pronouns they use in speaking to each other and, in exalted speech (used to describe royalty or monks, for example), in many verbs and nouns as well. Except among close friends not otherwise related (for relatives, family-oriented pronouns would normally be used), no word in traditional Khmer translated readily as *you* or *I*. Instead, words emphasized the status of the speaker in relation to the person addressed. Thus, *you* could be directed up, or down, as could *I* and the other personal pronouns.[27]

Cambodian thinkers also saw the universe in graded terms, with people inhabiting "middle earth." This is a familiar concept in many cultures, and so is its corollary, that behavior on Earth has been prescribed to an extent by heroes who have passed above or below us. To those of us accustomed to expanded (or fragmented) frames of reference, this picture of the world entails enslavement or mystification. To scholars like Saveros Pou, however, and, it would seem, to the poets who composed the *Reamker* ("the Glory of Rama"), the picture offered little to complain about in moral or aesthetic terms.[28] Perhaps there is a relationship between the day-to-day dangers of a society and the energy of belief that its thinkers invest in otherworldly or exceptionally beautiful alternatives. But to say this is to suggest that the *Reamker* is essentially a vehicle by which to escape society; its authors and many of its listeners, on the other hand, might say that the poem was an excellent vehicle for understanding it.

Egalitarian ideals and the related notion of class warfare have perhaps eroded our sympathies for hierarchical societies, which in twenty-first-century terms—themselves ephemeral, of course—appear to make no sense. We think of society as being at war with itself or at peace, brushing up against other societies with different interests, and so on. Seventeenth-century Cambodians had no word for society at all; the word *sangkum* appears to have entered the language via Pali, and Thailand, in the 1930s. They preferred to think of themselves in terms of a king and his subjects; in terms of a spectrum of relative merit; or as people, scattered over time and space, sharing recognizable ideals that sprang in turn from being farmers, being lowly, being Buddhists, and speaking Khmer.

An excellent way to enter the thought-world of seventeenth-century Cambodia is to look at the *Reamker* itself. The version that has survived contains only some of the events related in the Indian original, and many of these have been altered to fit into a Theravada Buddhist frame of reference and into Khmer. Although its characters inhabit a recognizably Indian, brahmanical world (as well as half-mythical kingdoms far away, it seems, from Southeast Asia), their behavior, language, and ideals are very much those of the Cambodian people who assembled to listen to the poem or to watch it enacted by dancers, poets, and musicians. These additional dimensions resemble the way in which medieval and Renaissance painters in Europe depicted Greek and Biblical figures wearing European clothes.

The plot of the *Reamker* can be easily summarized. Sent out in disgrace from the kingdom he was about to inherit, Prince Ream (Rama), accompanied by his wife, Sita, and his younger brother, Leak (Laksmana), travels in the forest and has many adventures until Sita is taken

Reenactment of the *Ramayana*, Battambang, 1966. Photo by Jacques Nepote.

away by the wicked Prince Reab (Ravana) who rules the city of Langka. Aided by Hanuman, the prince of the monkeys, Ream attacks Langka, hoping to regain his wife, and wins a series of battles. Here the Khmer version of the narrative breaks off. In terms of plot alone it is difficult to understand the hold the *Reamker* has had for so long on the Cambodian imagination. Its language is often terse, and the development of the action is occasionally obscure. This is partly because the poem has come down to us as a series of fairly brief episodes, each suitable for mime (with the verse to be recited) and geared to a performance by dancers or leather shadow puppets.

In modern times, episodes from the poem were often enacted by the palace dancers; in the countryside, they were acted out until recently as part of village festivals.[29] A complete oral version, somewhat different from the printed text, was recorded in Siem Reap in 1969.[30]

What probably captivated so many Cambodians about the *Reamker* was its combination of elegance and familiarity. Its subject, the conflict of good and evil, is the theme of much epic literature. On one level the poem is a statement of Theravada Buddhist values; on another, a defense of hierarchy and the status quo; and on a third, it is about the contrast between what is wild (*prei*) and what is civilized. The poem, in a sense, is itself a civilizing act, just as the Javanese word for "chronicle" (*babad*) is derived from one that means to "clear the forest."[31] Goodness in the poem and its three heroes are linked to meritorious action and elegance. Evil characters are unpredictable, passionate, in disarray.[32] The contrast is by no means mechanical, however, and is worked out in the course of the poem with considerable subtlety. The savage ruler of the forest, Kukham, for example, is filthy and spontaneous but is redeemed by his meritorious deference to Ream. On the other hand, Reab, the prince of Langka, consumed with passion and a slave to it, is almost as royal and at times nearly as elegant as Ream and Sita.

The role played by the *Reamker* in prerevolutionary Cambodia resembles the one enjoyed by the *wayang,* or shadow-puppet theater, in Java and Bali. Many Cambodians, in their encounters with the poem, found in it a completeness and balance that was probably missing from their everyday lives. Good and evil, as we all can see, are at war, and evil is often victorious. In the poem, however, the two are perpetually in balance, held in place as it were by almost equal quantities of ornamental verse. In the strophes that have survived, the major actors are never destroyed, perhaps because evil and good must survive in order to define each other. In the *Reamker,* as in many of the poems enacted in *wayang,* "nothing happens" in the sense that nothing changes or turns around.[33] The poem is useless as a revolutionary text, and it is also useless in a narrow sense as a historical document because we cannot locate it in a particular time and place. Its verbal elegance and its austerity, however, allow us a glimpse of the seventeenth-century Cambodian elite's range of values and of a high artistic polish that would be difficult to associate with a period of intellectual decline.

Placed against what we know of events in the seventeenth century, the gap between ideals and reality, as expressed in the poem, is wide and deep. Chronicles and European sources reveal a country whose capital was isolated from its hinterland, whose royal family was murderous, intriguing, and unstable, and which was at the mercy, much of the time, of elite factions, national catastrophes, and invaders. The persistence of Cambodian elites, however, and the continuity of overseas trade suggest that these crises, real enough at the time, were periodic rather than perpetual and affected the parts of the country that armies moved across rather than those outside their paths.

A revealing document from this period is a collection of fifty anecdotes, allegedly provided by an elderly female member of the royal family when a new set of Cambodian law codes was promulgated in the 1690s.[34] These deal with the notion of *lèse majesté* and thus concern the position of royalty in Cambodian society; they also reveal the strengths and weaknesses of Cambodian kingship at this time. The king's greatest strength, it seems, sprang from his capacity to assign and revoke titles, which were permissions to exploit people less fortunately endowed. Offenders against the king could be stripped of their possessions, and crimes of *lèse majesté,* even at several removes, were severely dealt with. One anecdote, for example, relates how a princess ordered her advisers to find her some fish. The officials encountered a fisherman, who muttered that they had no right to take his fish without paying for them. The officials took the fish and informed the princess about him, and he was fined for disrespect. Another anecdote relates that a king, out hunting, wandered from his entourage and encountered a buffalo tender who addressed him in ordinary language. Instead of punishing the man, the king returned to his followers to declare that he had increased his fund of merit, as he had obeyed the law that did not allow a king to punish subjects for disrespect outside the palace. "If I had shot the man when I was alone," he said, "I would have done a prohibited thing, and after my death I would have fallen into hell, because, after all, the man didn't know that I was the king." Other anecdotes reveal that the monarch was often used by ordinary citizens as the court of last resort, as Zhou Daguan had suggested in the thirteenth century.

These anecdotes differ from the chronicles and from the *Reamker* by providing day-to-day information about the king. They provide a picture of a variegated, conservative, and hierarchically organized society, consisting of a few thousand privileged men and women propped up by an almost invisible wall of rice farmers, in which great emphasis was placed on rank and privilege and on behavior thought to be appropriate to one's status. The texts also reveal how perilous it was to enjoy power in seventeenth-century Cambodia. The king, always fearful of being overthrown, ruled through changeable networks of favorites and relations, and he governed in many cases, it would seem, by pique. Officials rose into favor and fell from one day to the next. A chronicle from this period, for example, relates that a royal elephant trainer was named minister of war (*chakri*) after saving the king's life while he was hunting. Although the society was permanently ranked, change was possible and could rarely be predicted.

VIETNAMESE AND THAI ACTIVITIES IN CAMBODIA

The impression of instability was exacerbated by increasing foreign interference, particularly from the Vietnamese, whose "march to the south" (*nam tien*) once the Cham kingdoms had been subdued had carried colonists into the Mekong Delta by the 1620s. In 1626 the Nguyen overlords of the south broke off their ties with the northern Le dynasty and began governing the southern region on their own.[35] Although the area was lightly populated, Nguyen control eventually had the effect of sealing off Cambodia's southeastern frontier. The Vietnamese intrusion also had three long-term effects. First, the takeover of Saigon (known to Cambodians even today as Prey Nokor), meant that Cambodia was now cut off to a large extent from maritime access to the outside world, especially after other, smaller ports along the Gulf of Siam were occupied in the early eighteenth century by Chinese and Sino-Vietnamese entrepreneurs and Vietnamese troops.[36] Cambodian isolation, which lasted nearly two hundred years, was unique in precolonial Southeast Asia, with the exception of Laos. Second, the Nguyen institutionalization of control, a process that took more than two hundred years, eventually removed large portions of territory and tens of thousands of ethnic Khmer from Cambodian jurisdiction. This process produced a legacy of resentment and anti-Vietnamese feeling among Cambodians inside Cambodia. It fueled the collapse of Democratic Kampuchea and persists among many elite and émigré Cambodians today. Finally, by taking over the delta and extending de facto control over the Gulf of Siam (a state of affairs that lasted through the eighteenth century), the Nguyen placed Cambodia in a vise between two powerful neighbors; its capital region, moreover, was more accessible to Saigon than to Ayudhya or Bangkok.

A side effect of the advent of Vietnamese power was that the Cambodian royal family and its elite supporters were now liable to split along pro-Thai and pro-Vietnamese lines. Depending on which power supported an incumbent, his rivals would seek support from the other to overthrow him. The history of Cambodia in the eighteenth and nineteenth centuries is one of repeated invasions from Vietnam and Siam, usually preceded and followed by ruinous civil wars. Instability at the center extended into the *sruk*. Because loyalty to the throne was costly, perilous, and easy to avoid, by the end of the eighteenth century large areas of the kingdom were under only nominal control from Udong, and this state of affairs, in turn, decreased the king's ability to respond to foreign invasions. The king's power to reward his friends and punish dissidents had also been weakened by the rapid succession of monarchs, communication difficulties, and the need to withstand foreign attacks.

At the same time, it seems likely that certain continuity persisted at the capital among the bureaucratic elite who, along with the Buddhist sangha, were the curators of Cambodia's literate traditions. Several inscriptions at Angkor from the late seventeenth and early eighteenth centuries record the careers of important officials whose graceful rise to increasing responsibility contrasts sharply with the jagged sequence of events related by the chronicles.[37] Moreover, Vietnamese and Thai accounts agree that at several points in the eighteenth century (when it would be tempting to assert that Cambodia had already been bled white), Cambodian forces managed to repel their invading armies. This suggests, at the very least, that some regional leaders, nominally officials of the crown, were able in a crisis to mobilize enough supporters to harass and defeat a foreign expeditionary force, especially when the defenders were skilled in guerrilla warfare.

Evidence from the chronicles suggests, nonetheless, that one of the darkest periods of Cambodian history came in the last few decades of the eighteenth century. The ingredients, dynastic instability, foreign invasions, and civil wars, were familiar ones, but this time they were on a large scale.

The 1750s and 1760s were relatively calm as far as invasions from Siam and Vietnam were concerned, but they also saw a series of coups and countercoups by rivals in the royal family that involved assassinations and reprisals. In 1767 Ayudhya fell to a Burmese army. When a Thai prince and his entourage sought asylum in Cambodia and threatened to set up a legitimate kingdom there, a Thai regional overlord, Taksin, who had assumed royal power in Siam, launched a series of expeditions against Cambodia.[38] His aims were to reestablish Thai hegemony over the region and thus to backdate what he interpreted as his own enormous fund of merit. He also sought to avenge himself against the Cambodian king who, according to the chronicles, refused to send gifts to him because he was the "son of a Chinese merchant and a commoner," charges that appear to have been true. There is some evidence also that he wanted to put his own son on the Cambodian throne.

Thai pressure on the kingdom persisted into the 1770s, when the Nguyen were distracted by a populist rebellion led by the so-called Tay Son brothers, which threatened to overturn institutions throughout Vietnam. Sensing weaknesses in northern Vietnam, Thai armies attacked overland via Angkor, and their naval expeditions laid waste several small ports along the Gulf of Siam, partly in order to divert Chinese traders from this region to the vicinity of Bangkok and partly to avenge an earlier expedition financed by Chinese merchants from these coastal enclaves that had almost succeeded in capturing the new Thai capital, Thonburi. In 1772 the Thai burned down Phnom Penh. Seven years later a Thai protégé, Prince Eng, then only seven years old, was placed on the Cambodian throne at Udong under the regency of a pro-Thai official. In 1782 Taksin himself was deposed and was replaced by his minister of war (*chakri*), then campaigning in Cambodia. Later known in the West as Rama I, this man founded the dynasty that holds constitutional power in Thailand today.

By the 1780s the heir to the Nguyen throne, fleeing the Tay Son, had taken refuge in Bangkok, providing the basis for a rapprochement between the two nations when and if the prince assumed control of all Vietnam, as he did in 1802.

Prince Eng was taken off to Bangkok in 1790 and was anointed there by the Thai before being sent back to Cambodia four years later. His reign, which opened up a cycle of nineteenth-century history, is discussed in Chapter 6; the fact that he was crowned in Bangkok is symbolic of his dependence on the Thai.

CONCLUSIONS

The two main features of the post-Angkorean era were the shift of the capital from the rice-growing hinterlands of northwestern Cambodia to the trade-oriented riverbanks in the vicinity of Phnom Penh on the one hand and the increasing importance of foreign powers in Cambodian internal affairs on the other. It seems clear that the apparent self-sufficiency of Angkor was as much related to the absence of military rivals as to inherent strength or flexibility in Angkorean institutions. Many of these institutions, in fact, persisted into the middle period, both in Cambodia and in Thailand and got in the way of rapid bureaucratic responses (supposing that this was psychologically possible or culturally rewarding) in the face of foreign and domestic pressure.

Because of a shortage of data, it is impossible to enter the thought world of Cambodian villagers or to compare their responses to experiences at different stages of Cambodian history. How much difference did it make for them to become Theravada Buddhists, for example? What were the effects on daily life of the commercialization of the elite and the economy after 1500—to say nothing of the other changes noted in this chapter? Did the Europeans they saw have any effect on them? And what differences did they perceive, aside from linguistic ones, in being Cambodian instead of Thai?

There were several important changes between the fourteenth century and the beginning of the nineteenth, and the most important of these, perhaps, was the decline in the importance of a priestly class that for several hundred years had effectively linked landholdings, control of slaves, religious practices, education, and the throne. Another change was in the declining power of the royal family to influence events, although periods of relative weakness in the Angkor era, which must have occurred, are difficult to pin down. Perhaps equally important, but even harder to confirm, was the widespread and apparently increasing influence of the Thai on Cambodian life. Saveros Pou regarded this process as inimical to Cambodian identity, especially in terms of its effects on literary style, but recognized its importance in the history of the period.

Another important change—the intrusion of the Vietnamese into the official levels of Cambodian life—came later on, reaching peaks in the nineteenth and twentieth centuries. Even in the eighteenth century, however, Vietnamese activities had the effect of sealing off Cambodia from the outside world at exactly the point when other Southeast Asian countries, especially Siam, were opening up.

A final change was the decline in the popularity of kingship. Of all the post-Angkorean kings of Cambodia, only Duang (r. 1848–60) and Norodom Sihanouk seem to have struck a sustained chord of popular approval. The disjuncture between the palace and the people that is noticeable in the legal anecdotes of the 1690s probably widened in the following century. But this so-called decline, like many notions put forward about Cambodian history, is impossible to verify. After all, during the heyday of Angkor, we have only the kings' own words to support the notion that they were popular. Like the *Ramayana,* the king and his entourage had roles to play in people's thinking, but they played *central* roles only in their own. Although Clifford Geertz's phrase "theater state," originally applied to pre-colonial Java and more recently to nineteenth-century Bali, can be used with caution to describe Cambodian court life in this period, most Cambodian people probably knew and cared less about it than some scholars, entranced perhaps by the exoticism of the "theatrical" arrangements, might prefer. In periods of stability, of course, Cambodians probably had more time for ceremony and more surpluses to pay for ceremonies than in periods of warfare, famine, or distress.[39]

Between 1750 and 1850, however, the failure of successive kings to deliver protection and stability may well have undermined the relevance of the monarchy in the eyes of the rural population. But the texts that have survived are ambiguous and inconclusive and, as we shall see, when popular monarchs like Duang or Norodom Sihanouk came onto the scene they were revered more than ever. In any case, the rural poor could imagine no alternative set of political or patronage arrangements outside of easily snuffed-out millenarian rebellions that could grant them the protection they needed to plant, harvest, and survive.

6

STATE, SOCIETY, AND FOREIGN RELATIONS, 1794–1848

In the half century or so before the arrival of the French, who established a protectorate over Cambodia in 1863, Cambodian ideas about political geography did not include the notion that the country was defined primarily by the lines enclosing it on a map.[1] Maps were rarely used, and no locally drawn map of Cambodia in the early nineteenth century appears to have survived.[2] Instead, to the people who lived there, Cambodia probably meant the *sruk* where Cambodian was spoken and, more narrowly, those whose leaders (*chaovay sruk*) had received their official titles and seals of office from a Cambodian king.

Cambodians also thought of their country as a walled city with several imaginary gates. One chronicle places these at Sambor on the upper Mekong, Kompong Svay north of the Tonle Sap, Pursat in the northwest, Kampot on the coast, and Chaudoc, technically across the frontier in Vietnam on the Mekong Delta.[3] Fittingly, these gates were the places where invading armies traditionally swept into Cambodia. The territory they enclosed, in the form of a gigantic letter C (there was no eastern gate, for armies did not cross the Annamite cordillera), covered roughly half the area of Cambodia today.

Inside this imaginary wall, *sruk* varied in size and importance. Although boundaries were generally vague, some, like Pursat and Kompong

Svay, extended over several hundred square miles; others, like Koh Chan or Lovea Em, were islands in the Mekong or short stretches of cultivated land along the river.

SOCIETY AND ECONOMY

Little information about the size and composition of Cambodia's population in this period has survived. Under Vietnamese suzerainty in the 1830s, a census was taken, but the Vietnamese dismissed its figures as deflated.[4] French administrators in the 1860s, working from roughly compiled tax rolls, estimated Cambodia's population at slightly less than a million.[5] The area between Cambodia's imaginary gates, therefore, may have supported about three-quarters of a million people in the 1840s, but probably fewer, for the records are filled with accounts of regions being depopulated by famine, flight, and invading armies.

This population was overwhelmingly rural. The largest town, Phnom Penh, probably never held more than twenty-five thousand people.[6] The royal capital at Udong and the villages around it supported a population of ten thousand or so in the late 1850s; the Khmer-speaking city of Battambang, rebuilt by the Thai in the late 1830s, had three thousand inhabitants in 1839.[7] The only parts of the kingdom that were relatively densely settled before the 1860s were those to the south and east of Phnom Penh, like Ba Phnom and Bati, and to the north along the Mekong River south of Chhlong. Significantly, these relatively wealthy *sruk* were often located outside the routes of invasion and retreat chosen by the Thai and the Vietnamese.

Nearly all the people in Cambodia were ethnic Khmer, who occupied themselves with rice farming and with monastic and official life. Commercial and industrial tasks were handled by minority groups. Marketing, garden farming, and foreign trade, for example, were handled by Chinese or by people of Chinese descent.[8] Cattle trading, weaving, and commercial fisheries were controlled by a Muslim minority composed partly of immigrants from the Malay archipelago—known as *chvea,* or Javanese, in Khmer—but largely of immigrants from Champa known as Cham. The Kui people in the northern part of the country smelted Cambodia's small deposits of iron ore (and had done so at least since Angko-rean times). In the capital, a handful of descendants of Portuguese set-tlers who had arrived in the sixteenth and seventeenth centuries served as translators for the king and were in charge of his artillery pieces.[9] Be-fore the 1830s there seem to have been few Vietnamese residents in the kingdom. Indeed, even without accurate statistics, it seems likely that there were proportionately fewer of these various groups in the king-dom until the arrival of the French. In the colonial era the numbers of Chinese and Vietnamese residents increased enormously.[10]

Near the imaginary gates, in thinly populated *sruk* like Kratie, Pursat, and Kompong Svay, tribal groups, such as the Porr, Stieng, and Samre lived in isolated villages and collected the forest products that formed a major source of a monarch's income and the bulk of the goods that Cambodia sent abroad.

By the standards of other states in Southeast Asia at the time, Cam-bodia was poor. Unlike Burma and Laos, its soil contained few gems or precious metals. Unlike Siam, its manufacturing, trade, and commerce were underdeveloped, and finished goods, like brassware, porcelain, and firearms all came from abroad. Unlike Vietnam, Cambodia's com-munications were poor and its internal markets undeveloped. Agricul-tural surpluses were rare, savings were low, and money was used only at the palace and by minority groups. Rural trade was in barter, as it had been in Angkorean times, and was handled to a large extent by women. Cambodia had a subsistence economy; most of its people spent most of their time growing rice, with men and women working side by side. Landholdings tended to be small (even high officials seldom had access to more than a few hectares), yields were low, and irrigation works, which might have increased production, were rare.

To the Vietnamese emperor Minh Mang, writing in 1834, Cambodia was truly a "barbarian" country because "the people do not know the proper way to grow food. They use mattocks and hoes, but no oxen. They grow enough rice to have two meals a day, but they do not know how to store rice for an emergency."[11] Villagers often maintained a com-mon pond, or *trapeang*, to water their rice, as they had done at least since the days of Chenla, but there were no longer any of the dams and canals that had characterized Angkorean civilization. This was partly because there were now so few mouths to feed and partly because the mechanisms of state control were so much weaker. There were no incentives and little technology for farmers to vary their crops, market their surpluses, or increase their holdings. Communications between the *sruk* were poor, there were no roads to speak of until the 1830s, and bandits, invading armies, and the followers of local officials carried off what surpluses they could find.

Foreign trade was restricted because the potentially important entrepôt of Phnom Penh was cut off from the outside world for most of this period by the authorities in southern Vietnam. After 1808, in fact, visitors to Phnom Penh needed Vietnamese permission to go there. Ports on the Gulf of Siam, like Kampot, engaged in some coastal and peninsular trade, but they were more closely integrated into the Vietnamese and Thai economies than into the Cambodian one.[12]

A few ships traded with central Cambodia every year. Cargo lists from two of these, bound for China and Japan respectively in about 1810, have survived.[13] Their cargoes consisted of relatively small amounts of several different products. Three hundred pounds of ivory and two hundred pounds of pepper, for example, were among the goods exported to Japan while those going to China included small consignments of cardamom, hides, feathers, tortoise shells, and aromatic wood. Exports to Vietnam in the 1820s—trade with Vietnam was conducted partly in a tributary framework—included such goods as ivory, gutta percha, cardamom, dried fish, and elephant hides.

These were all traditional exports. The lists are like others that have come down from the seventeenth and early eighteenth centuries, particularly concerning junk trade with Japan and, via Chinese sources, from the Angkorean period.[14] External trade, including tribute, as we shall see, was an important source of the king's revenues and probably was important to the Chinese community in Phnom Penh and to privileged members of the king's entourage. But it was insignificant as far as the rest of the country was concerned.

Most Cambodians lived in villages. These can be divided, for the early nineteenth century at least, into three broad types. The first can be

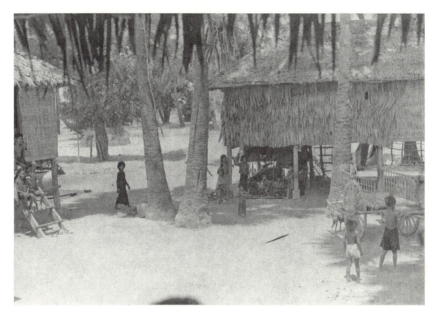

A rice-growing village in Kompong Speu, 1961. Author's photo.

called *kompong* after the Malay word meaning "landing-place," which often formed part of their names, as in Kompong Svay and Kompong Som.[15] These were located along navigable bodies of water and could support populations of several hundred people. Often they would include a *chaovay sruk* and his assistants; the *kompong* was usually enclosed in a stockade. Some of the inhabitants were likely to be Chinese or Sino-Khmer, Malay, and Cham, although minorities tended to keep to themselves in separate hamlets that formed elements of the *kompong*. *Kompong* were in touch with others on the same body of water, with rice-growing villages around them, and indirectly with the capital and the court. Through trading, travel, hearsay, and invasions, people in the *kompong* had some awareness of events elsewhere.

Rice-growing villages, the second category, enclosed the *kompong*, ideally in a broken arc. Poorer and smaller than *kompong*, rice-growing villages were numerous and more likely to be populated entirely by ethnic Khmer. Houses were scattered around in no special order, often near a Buddhist monastery, or *wat*, and also near the pond or stream that provided water for the village. Rice-growing villages were linked to the *kompong* and the world beyond in irregular ways—through incursions of officials looking for recruits or rice; through the *wat,* whose monks were encouraged to travel about in the dry season; through festivals at the new year and at other points in the calendar; and through trade with the *kompong,* exchanging rice and forest products for metal, cloth, and salt.

Rice-growing villages were unstable because they lacked means of defense and because, unlike rice growing villages in Vietnam, no institutionalized ancestor cult anchored people to one place rather than another. The chronicles are filled with references to villagers running off into the forest in times of crisis. In times of peace, their lives were shaped by the contours of the agricultural year and the ceremonies—Buddhist, animist, and vestigially Hindu—that marked off one stage of the rice-growing cycle from another.[16]

The opposition between wild and civilized, noted in the discussion of the *Reamker* in Chapter 5, persisted in the literature of the nineteenth century. A verse chronicle from Wat Baray, in the north-central part of the kingdom, deals with this theme repeatedly while offering a chronological treatment of nineteenth-century events. The chronicle relates the fortunes of a bureaucratic family caught up in the turmoil of Vietnamese occupation and civil war. Driven into the forest, they lose their identity, regaining it only when new titles are bestowed on male members, first by a Thai monarch and later by a Cambodian one. The chronicle was composed to celebrate the restoration of Wat Baray in 1856, and the audience to whom it was recited would for the most part have recognized the events related in it as true. What gives the chronicle its literary resonance is the way in which the lives of the characters follow patterns laid down for them by the *Reamker* and Buddhist ideology. The restoration of their status accompanied the restoration of the king; demerit was seen, in some way, as associated with the forest, a lack of official titles, and misbehavior impossible to trace.[17]

Similarly, in a poignant Cambodian folktale probably well known in the 1800s, three girls who are abandoned by their mother become wild and turn into birds, happily crossing the border between forest and field where, as it turns out, the birds they have become are most frequently to be found.[18] Because people's grip on the things we take for granted was so precarious in nineteenth-century Cambodia—dependent on the goodwill of foreigners and overlords, on rainfall, and on health in a tropical climate—it is understandable that "civilization," or the art of remaining outside the forest, was taken so seriously by poets and audience alike.[19]

The third type of village lay hidden in the *prei,* or wilderness, that made up most of Cambodia at this time. Here the people were illiterate and usually non-Buddhist; they spoke languages related to Khmer but owed no loyalties to the *kompong* or the capital unless these had been forced from them. The villages were frequently raided for slaves, and they were economically important because their populations were able to exploit forest resources that were valued in the capital and abroad. Their political loyalties, however, were to other villages in the *prei,* where people spoke the same dialect and performed similar religious rites.

PATRONAGE AND GOVERNMENT

How were Cambodian villages governed in the early nineteenth century? Some French writers have asserted that at this time they had no government at all,[20] and in most of them relations with outsiders and with the state were indeed sporadic and unfriendly. Quarrels within a village or between neighboring villages were settled by conciliation rather than by law, and often smoldered on for years. Villages were usually ruled, for ceremonial purposes and for the purposes of relations with higher authorities, by elderly men chosen by the villagers for their agricultural skill, literacy, good conduct, and fair-mindedness. Taxes in rice and labor seem to have been paid, irregularly, on demand. Village government was perhaps more noticeable in the *kompong,* where there were more officials and hangers-on, but there is no evidence that any villages in Cambodia were governed by formally constituted councils of elders, as was the case in nineteenth-century Vietnam.[21]

Rice-growing villages and those in the *prei* could be days apart from each other and from the nearest representative of authority. In their isolation the villagers faced inward, toward the lives and traditions they shared with one another. They identified themselves and saw their history in terms of localized religious traditions passed on from one generation to the next. Outside the villages, just past the fields in most cases, lay the *prei*, crowded with wild animals, malarial mosquitoes, and the spirits of the dead. Beyond the *prei*, where villagers seldom ventured, lay the world of the *kompong*, the capital, and the court.

French writers in the nineteenth century often denigrated Cambodian society (one of them referred to its institutions as "worm-eaten débris")[22] and compared it unfavorably with their own "rational," centralized one or with that of the Vietnamese. The trend has continued among some anthropologists concerned with Thailand, who have referred to Thai peasant society as "loosely structured."[23] The phrase is helpful, whether or not one attaches values to tight structure, in the sense that in Thai and Cambodian villages, in the nineteenth century at least, there were no "durable, functionally important groups" or voluntary associations aside from the family and the Buddhist monastic order, or *sangha*. When a village organized itself for defense, for instance, or for a Buddhist festival, it did so for a short time in response to a specific need.

Despite the apparent informality of these arrangements, there was considerable structural consistency in each Cambodian village and family. This arose from the fact that Cambodians always identified themselves in terms of their status relative to the person being addressed. This identification located them for the moment at a particular, but by no means fixed point in a flexible set of dyadic relationships extending downward from the king and the *sangha* through the graded bureaucracy of the capital and *kompong* to the villages and past them to the landless debt-slaves and minority peoples living literally at the edges of the state. As with most systematic social arrangements, what mattered to the people who used the system was the place they occupied inside it. If a person's place was relatively secure, people in weaker positions sought him out and offered homage in exchange for protection. The society, in a sense, was fueled by the exchange of protection and service implied in these "lopsided friendships," as they have been called.[24] In a village context these links might be with older or more fortunate members of one's family, monks in the local *wat*, bandit leaders, government officials, or holy men (*nak sell*) who appeared from time to time, promising their followers invulnerability and riches.

In the *kompong* and the capital, where people no longer grew their own food, patronage and clientship became more important and more complex. Having a patron and having clients were connected with one's chances to survive. People with access to power accepted as many followers or slaves as they could. In many cases, these men and women had contracted debts to their patrons, which they then spent their lifetimes working off. The widespread presence of slavery in nineteenth-century Cambodia should cloud over, to an extent, the sunny notion that clients entered their "lopsided friendships" as volunteers with a variety of choices. But it is also true that many people enslaved themselves to a patron, or *me* (the word can also mean "mother"), to protect themselves against the rapacity of others.

The rectitude and permanence of these relationships had been drummed into everyone from birth. Cambodian proverbs and didactic literature are filled with references to the helplessness of the individual and to the importance that everyone accept power relationships as they are. Both sides of the patron-client equation, in theory at least, saw their relationships as natural, even obligatory. "The rich must protect the poor," a Cambodian proverb runs, "just as clothing protects the body."[25]

The relationships in fact were seldom that genteel. Throughout Southeast Asia, patrons, like kings, spoke of "consuming" the territory and people they controlled, and there are few just officials in Cambodian folklore, in which officials are compared to tigers, crocodiles, and venomous snakes. Rural government was seen as an adversary proceeding. In one *sruk* at least, when a new *chaovay sruk* took office, a cockfight was held. One bird represented the newly arrived official; the other, the people of the *sruk*. The outcome of the fight supposedly gave both sponsors a hint about the balance of power that was expected to ensue.[26]

Why did the people accept these demeaning arrangements? Partly it was a case of force majeure. The alternatives of individual flight or organized resistance were usually impossible. Moreover, a man without a patron was fair game, and an unknown patron, like a foreigner, was more of a threat than one who lived nearby. Although the *chaovay sruk* often "ate" what little material wealth he could get his hands on, the social distance between him and the rest of the *kompong* was not especially great. His wives, for example, were local women. He lived in a simple house, chewed betel, and sponsored festivals at the *wat* and ceremonies to propitiate the *nak ta*. These officials shared their clients' food, their belief in magic, their vigorous sense of the absurd, and their distrust of other officials and outsiders. Probably because they lived among the people they supposedly controlled, *chaovay sruk* were more responsive to local issues than were authorities in the capital. The fact that all these "lopsided friendships" could be renegotiated in times of stress added to the instability of the system and perhaps to its attractiveness in the eyes of villagers and slaves.

For most Cambodians, these shifting networks of subordination and control, chosen or imposed, benevolent or otherwise, marked the limits of their experience and of their social expectations. Their ideas about the king, on the other hand, and about the Buddhist *sangha* took a different form and were expressed in a different language. Although it is useful to place the king and the *sangha* at the end of imaginary chains of local and spiritual authority extending down through the officials to the people, the people saw them as operating on a different plane and on a different set of assumptions. Little is known about the *sangha* in mid-nineteenth-century Cambodia, and it could be misleading to assert that conditions were the same as those in Siam or Burma. There is no evidence, for example, that the *sangha* played a political role vis-à-vis the royal family, although monks and ex-monks were active in the anti-Vietnamese rebellion of 1821.[27] By and large, monks were widely respected as repositories of merit, as sources of spiritual patronage, and as curators of Cambodia's literary culture. They occupied a unique, mysterious place in Cambodian life because they had abandoned—temporarily at least—agriculture, politics, and marriage.

People's ideas about the king tended to be grounded in mythology rather than their own experience. The relationship of the king to most of his subjects was not negotiated, rarely enforced, and was seldom face to face. For most of the early nineteenth century, by choice or by circumstance, the monarch was confined to his palace or lived in exile in

Casting a net on the Mekong, 1988, a technique that has remained unchanged for several hundred years. Photo by Christine Drummond.

Siam or Vietnam. Given the weight of traditional and popular literature about him and because they never saw him, views of the king held by villagers tended to be vaguer and more approving than their views of each other, their patrons, or even the *nak ta*. The king was at once as real and as unreal as the Lord Buddha. People would have accepted the *Ramayana*'s description of royal duties; they were "to be consecrated, to sacrifice, and to protect the people."[28] Many of them believed that the king could influence the weather. Unlike the *sauphea*, or judges, he could dispense true justice, and he was often the only political source of hope among peasants. This cluster of ideas persisted into the colonial era and beyond.

The king, of course, was not always or even often in the villagers' thoughts, but when he appeared in his capital after years of exile, as Eng did in 1794, Duang nearly half a century later, or Norodom Sihanouk 1991, the event ignited widespread rejoicing.

Several other segments of Cambodian society affected people's lives in the villages and the outcome of Cambodian politics. These included minor *sruk* officials and hangers-on, who were appointed in some cases from the capital and in others by the *chaovay sruk;* ex-monks, or *achar,* who acted as religious spokesmen and millenarian leaders, often in opposition to the *chaovay sruk;* itinerant traders, actors, and musicians; and poor relations of the rich, who were able to act as go-betweens. Unfortunately, the elite-centered chronicles usually devote little space to these categories of people so it is difficult to assess their power, except indirectly. A rice-growing village going into revolt against the Vietnamese, as many did in 1820 and 1841, for example, was unlikely to have done so merely through the exhortations of a high official.

THE *OKYA*

Historical records, on the other hand, have left a good picture of Cambodia's high-ranking officials, or *okya.*[29] Included in their number were the *chaovay sruk* and the officials surrounding the king. It is impossible to say how many *okya* there were at any given time. Lists of officials assembled in the 1860s and 1870s for the French are full of gaps and contradictions. Many of the titles in these lists do not appear to have been used, and titles occur in other sources that do not appear in the lists. Roughly, however, there seem to have been about two hundred *okya* in the capital and the countryside throughout most of the nineteenth century. The number was probably smaller after defections to the Thai in the 1830s and larger after Duang's accession in 1848. For these two hundred men, about seven hundred titles were available for use. Some of these, like those carried by the king's highest advisers and by most of the *chaovay sruk,* were always used. Others seem to have lapsed, for a while at least, after having been used by one or several incumbents.

Everything about the titles and the work associated with them, except the fact that they were conferred on the incumbent by the king, was subject to adjustment. Sometimes a title carried a rank. Sometimes it was associated with a job, such as maintaining the king's elephants, guarding his regalia, or collecting taxes. Certain titles were reserved for certain *sruk,* and the word *sauphea* when it occurred in a title often implied judicial functions. But none of these rules was rigorously applied. Favorites or people out of favor were given jobs to do or removed from them on an ad hoc basis. People went up the ladder (or fell off) quickly.

For example, one official whose function was to be in charge of the throne room of the second king (hardly an arduous calling) was named to head a diplomatic mission to Bangkok in 1819. Another, whose duties were to survey the levels of rice in the royal storehouses, led an army against the Thai in Battambang in 1818.

The titles that *okya* carried usually consisted of two or three honorific words, like *ratna* ("jewel") or *verocana* ("splendor"), drawn from Pali or Sanskrit. The *okya* received their titles along with the seals of office and insignia of rank (which included tiered umbrellas, betel containers, court costumes, and the like) from the king's hands in an intentionally awesome ceremony built around an oath of allegiance that had been in effect in more or less the same form for at least eight hundred years. At that time, and at regular intervals, the *okya* were expected to give presents to the king. French writers equated this exchange of titles and gifts with the notion that the Cambodian government was corrupt because jobs were available only to the highest bidder. At one level of thinking this was true, but little ethical weight was given to the transaction. High bidders, after all, were people whose power had to be reckoned with. Twice a year the *okya* assembled at the royal *wat* near the palace where they drank the "water of allegiance"—water brought to the capital, in theory, from streams throughout the kingdom—and renewed their oaths of allegiance to the king. Failure to attend this ceremony was tantamount to treason.

Once in office, an *okya* became part of the *komlang,* or strength (i.e., entourage) of some higher-ranking person. This might be one of the king's advisers, a member of the royal family, or the king himself. A similar system was in effect in Siam. It is not clear whether these alliances were meant to check or to enhance the power of the *okya* in question. Probably they served both purposes at once. The interconnections between certain regions, official posts, family ties, and particular jobs in this period remain obscure. One manuscript chronicle, dating from the early nineteenth century, suggests that the landholdings of *okya* in certain regions persisted from one generation to the next, even when the titles of one *okya* were not passed along to his son.[30] Titles in Cambodia, in any case, were not hereditary. Even the successor to the throne was chosen after a monarch's death from among several eligible candidates. A similar fluidity affected *okya* families, although high status seems to have run in particular families whose members enjoyed access to the king.

Despite these continuities, there were few certainties in Cambodian political life. Theoretically, the survival of an *okya* depended on the king. Akin Rabibhadana has cited a 1740 Thai decree that "a king can turn a superior person into a subordinate person, and vice-versa. When he gives an order, it is like an axe from heaven."[31] In reality, however, a king's power depended on how recently he had attained it and how many outstanding debts he had. It was hampered in any case by poor communications between the capital and the *sruk*.

A new king at the start of a dynasty, or after a period of exile, could often act like an "axe from heaven" and fill *okya* positions with men who had been loyal to him in his climb to power. King Duang rewarded his followers in this way in the 1840s, as we shall see, just as the first kings of the Chakri dynasty in Thailand (1782–) and Nguyen dynasty in Vietnam (1802–1945) rewarded theirs. Under a weak king, on the other hand, or one entangled in long-standing obligations, perhaps to older people, *okya* tended to root themselves in the *sruk*. In the process they became become more or less independent.

Uncertainty was an occupational hazard of Cambodian life. Everyone was on the lookout against everyone else. An *okya*'s obligations toward his king, his family, and his patrons sometimes overlapped and sometimes were in conflict. The other *okya* were potential allies and potential enemies; alliances and betrayals that took advantage of existing power balances occupied a good deal of an *okya*'s time.

Cambodia in the 1800s was not a bureaucratic society like China or Vietnam, and in times of peace an *okya*'s official duties were light. He had to wait upon his patron, there was little paperwork to do, and many tasks, like requisitioning supplies for the palace or raising armies for defense (Cambodia had no standing army), were farmed out among several *okya*. This was done perhaps to keep a single official from becoming too powerful and perhaps because there were no institutional mechanisms to prevent ambitious *okya* from shouldering each other aside in search of profit.

The judgment implied in these remarks may be too strong. Some *okya* were accomplished poets and musicians, and others were generous patrons of Buddhism and the arts. A few emerge from the chronicles as competent, innovative, or brave, but the uncertainty of favor, the ubiquity of rivals, and the unreliability of followers militated against an *okya*'s being active or even attracting official notice. The *okya* and the people, then, were tied to each other with bonds of terror, affection, duty, and contempt within the framework of a shared culture. In Cambodian terms the system worked, but when the Vietnamese tried to use the *okya* as their spokesmen in Cambodia in the 1830s and 1840s, they found them incapable of governing the country in a Vietnamese way— which is to say, of *administering* regions, conducting cadastral surveys, collecting taxes, and making detailed reports.

Aside from the king's five closest advisers, who formed a kind of cabinet, the most active and visible *okya* were the *chaovay sruk*. These men enjoyed considerable freedom and considerable power. They were authorized to collect taxes from their *sruk*, which meant that they had access to any surplus crops they could lay their hands on, and they were authorized to mobilize manpower for warfare or public works. In practice they maintained small private armies, as did their counterparts, the riverine chieftains of nineteenth-century Malaya. In populous *sruk*, these armies sometimes contained several thousand men; in others, they seem to have acted as bodyguards for the *chaovay sruk*. Access to manpower and rice meant that, in effect, the *chaovay sruk* controlled the balance of power in the kingdom. In fact, they more often acted individually than collectively, responding to local interests and dyadic arrangements. This meant that a king could count on some *chaovay sruk* but not on others and that invading armies might find some *chaovay* friendly and others opposed to them.

Some *chaovay sruk* were more important than others. Five of them, called *sdac tran*, or kings of the field, were the highest-ranking *okya* and were responsible, in an unspecified way, for the governance of several *sruk* at once.[32] Each of these groupings was known as a *dei*, or "earth." Unfortunately, nineteenth-century references to the phrase *sdac tran* occur only in French texts, and the meaning of *tran* itself is not clear. The officials seem to have acted as viceroys, or stand-ins for the king, in the performance of annual ceremonies in the five *dei* honoring the *nak ta*. They had the power to order executions, which the other *chaovay sruk* did not. In a functional sense they echoed the five high ministers around the king.

These five ministers in the capital were led by a first minister, sometimes referred to as the *ta-la-ha,* and included ministers of justice (*yomraj*), of the army (*chakrei*), of the navy and foreign trade (*kralahom*), and of the palace (*veang*). Each of these officials maintained his own *komlang* and probably had economic and patrimonial links with certain *sruk.* Loosely defined territorial responsibilities of these men overlapped or extended to those of the *sdac tran* and the *chaovay sruk,* as well as those of certain members of the royal family who were also entitled to "consume" particular regions. In times of stress, as several chronicles reveal, *okya* retreated to their villages, where they had relatives and land. Despite these regional links, however, the high-ranking *okya* spent their time close to the king, except in war, when some of them were called on to recruit troops and act as generals in the field. Their careers were tied to the fortunes of the king. Their effect on life in the countryside is not so clear. The palace-oriented chronicles probably exaggerate the importance of these men, and so did the Vietnamese when they looked for people to help them centralize and tidy up Cambodian government in the 1830s.

The last segment of Cambodian society that came between the villagers and their king consisted of other members of the royal family. In theory there could be hundreds of these, for kings were traditionally polygamous, but in the nineteenth century a series of deaths and coincidences sharply reduced their number. King Eng, who died in his twenties, had no surviving brothers and only five children. The oldest of these, Prince Chan, came to the throne when he was only six. When he died more than thirty years later, he left four daughters but no sons. His three brothers (the fourth had died as a child) went to Bangkok in 1812 and stayed there, with brief exceptions, until Chan's death in 1835. This meant that for most of his reign Chan was the only male member of the royal family living in Cambodia. The factionalism and jockeying for position, a conventional feature of Cambodian court life before and since, took place offstage, in Siam, and in the late 1830s in the Cambodian *sruk* under Thai control.

The Cambodian king, at the pinnacle of society, was remote from his subjects. Scholars have argued that this remoteness was expected of any Asian king. He was to rule by his largely invisible example, just as the sun shone, and he was to act as the custodian of a fund of merit and power—viewed perhaps as an interlocking, expendable commodity— that he had accumulated in previous existences en route to the throne. What has sometimes been called the purely religious or symbolic impor- tance of kingship in Southeast Asia, as transmitted in Indianized texts, has been overstressed. The frontiers between political and religious ac- tions and institutions were neither sharply delimited nor especially im- portant. In their daily lives, Cambodian kings were as concerned with mere survival as they were with their religious and ceremonial roles. Nonetheless, it would be incorrect to blot out the religious importance of kingship with evidence—however easy to assemble—of a given king's weakness or fallibility. Having a king was indispensable. According to the *Ramayana,* a country without a king enjoys "neither rain nor seed, neither wealth nor wife, neither sacrifices nor festivals,"[33] and the alarm of the *okya* in 1840–41 when Cambodia was briefly without a monarch shows how deeply ingrained these notions were. Only a king was em- powered to hand out the official titles, seals of office, and insignia of rank that held the Cambodian official class together. One Cambodian law even stated that an official without a seal did not need to be obeyed.[34]

In addition to setting Cambodia's official class in motion—an action that had no consistent effect on village life—the Cambodian monarch, like his counterparts elsewhere in Southeast Asia, presided over a series of partly brahmanical, partly Buddhist, and partly animistic ceremonies that, from the villagers' point of view, defined the boundaries of his merit and the limits of the agricultural year and were closely related to the success or failures of their harvests. The ceremonies included ones that honored the king's ancestors and the *nak ta,* ones that inaugurated and closed the rice-growing cycle, and ones that marked off stages of the Buddhist and solar calendars. In many of them the king was assisted by so-called court brahmans called *Baku* who also acted as guardians of his regalia—the sacred sword, arrows, and other objects that he handled only once in his lifetime, at his coronation. It is impossible to decide if the regalia were political or religious. Without them, a monarch could rule—handing out titles, raising armies, and so forth—but he could not reign. He had not been consecrated, as Prince Duang discovered in the 1840s when the Vietnamese withheld the regalia from him until they could extract favorable peace terms from the Thai.

The monarch's powers, then, although perhaps overstressed in the written record, remained considerable in the eyes of the *okya* and among the common people. The absence of a monarch was felt, at many points in the society, perhaps more acutely than his presence on the throne.

CAMBODIA'S RELATIONS WITH VIETNAM AND SIAM

As we have seen, the two most important characteristics of post-Angkorean Cambodia were the shift in the country's center of gravity from Angkor to Phnom Penh, with the commercial and demographic ramifications that the move implied and the roles played by the Thai and Vietnamese. Nineteenth-century Cambodia, therefore, must be seen in part against the background of its foreign relations.

These relations were carried out with two countries, Vietnam and Siam, and occurred within a framework of rivalry between the two larger kingdoms. Rivalry sprang from the unwillingness of either court to accept the other as its equal or its superior. This unwillingness, in turn, can be traced in part to the traditional language of tributary diplomacy, which stressed the inequality between the sender and the recipient of tribute.

A major objective of Southeast Asian diplomacy in the nineteenth century, indeed, was the ritualized expression of differential status through the ceremonial exchange of gifts. The rules for these tributary exchanges grew out of the particular system in which they occurred. The Thai and the Vietnamese, for example, had separate ones, which overlapped inside Cambodia.

Both systems owed a good deal to their counterpart in China,[35] which had been in effect since the third century BCE and was still in operation in the 1800s. From a Cambodian point of view, the Thai variant was looser and more idiosyncratic, for the Thai made allowances for local customs and local products while the Vietnamese did not. The latter were rigid in copying the Chinese model. In 1806, for example, Vietnamese Emperor Gia Long, in choosing gifts to send to the Cambodian king, transmitted facsimiles of the ones he had received, at the beginning of his own reign, from the Chinese emperor. Some of these, such as "golden dragon paper for imperial decrees" and Chinese bureaucratic costumes, were meaningless to the Khmer. The seals of investiture sent from Hué to Udong were irrelevant to Cambodians because they had camels carved on them, like the seals that the Chinese court sent to tributary states in central Asia and, incidentally, to Vietnam. One puzzled Cambodian chronicler referred to the animal as a "Chinese lion."[36]

From Vietnam's point of view, Vietnam was above Cambodia, just as China was above Vietnam. At the same time, of course, Cambodia was below Vietnam and Vietnam was below China. In other words, Vietnam was the master in one relationship and the servant in the other. As a by-product of this duality, the civilized goods sent from Hué to Udong were facsimiles of those sent from Beijing to Hué, while the so-called barbarian goods transmitted from Udong were the same sorts of products that Vietnam transmitted to China.[37]

In the matter of tributary gifts, the Thai were more flexible than the Vietnamese. The Chakri kings sent gifts to nineteenth-century Cambodian kings that the recipients could recognize and use. In exchange the Thai seem to have settled for whatever products they could get. Sometimes Cambodia sent pepper, at other times lacquer and cardamom. There is no evidence, however, that the Cambodians ever transmitted the gold and silver ornamental trees (*banga mas*) that were a feature of tribute to Bangkok from other dependent states.[38]

Similarly, the embassies that King Chan (r. 1797–1835) sent to Bangkok and Hué obeyed different sets of rules, as embassies to Bangkok were larger, more frequent, and more informal. The differences between the two diplomatic systems paralleled differences in Thai and Vietnamese official attitudes toward themselves, each other, and the Khmer. These differences became crucial and painful for the Khmer in the 1830s, when the Vietnamese emperor sought to administer Cambodia directly in a Vietnamese way. From a Cambodian point of view, how-ever, what mattered about the Thai and Vietnamese tributary systems and attitudes toward Cambodia was not that they were different and made different sorts of demands but, rather, that they were condescend-ing, overlapping, and expensive.

Thai and Vietnamese official relations with each other, until they soured in the 1820s, were marked by considerable informality.[39] This arose in part from a mutual unwillingness on the part of the Thai and the Vietnamese to accept or impose authority on each other because they en-joyed roughly similar power and prestige. The problem of hegemony did not yet arise in their relations with the Khmer, and notions about the roles both states should play in Cambodia were quite consistent. The barbarity of the Cambodian people and the subservience of their king, for example, were taken for granted, and so was the corollary that each superior state had a sort of civilizing mission to carry out inside Cambo-dia. The rulers saw themselves, in their official correspondence, as des-tined to supervise the Khmer. As one Thai diplomatic letter put it, "It is fitting for large countries to take care of smaller ones." Others referred to Chan as an "unruly child" and to the confluence of Thai and Vietnamese policies in Cambodia as "fruit and seeds forming a single unit."

Some of this language was a mask for realpolitik, but the images are nonetheless suggestive. The language of diplomatic correspondence, like the languages in everyday use in Southeast Asia, used pronouns that were hierarchical and family-oriented, and relationships between states were often described by using images of child rearing. In these the Thai and the Vietnamese became the "father" and the "mother" of the Khmer, whose king was referred to as their "child" or their "servant." In the 1860s a French official mused perceptively that Siam was Cambo-dia's father because its king gave names to the monarch, whereas Viet-nam was seen to be the mother because its rulers provided the Khmer with seals of office.[40] Whatever the reasons, Thai and Vietnamese state-ments, like those made later by the French, amounted to unilateral dec-larations of Cambodian dependence. The family-oriented images were unjustified and far-fetched, but they are a useful way of looking at the period—that is, as the continuing struggle between increasingly incom-patible parents for the custody of a weak and often disobedient child.

Although Thai political ideas were often couched in Buddhist terminology and Vietnamese ones in terms of a Sino-Vietnamese Confucian
tradition, Thai and Vietnamese objectives in Cambodia, seldom voiced
explicitly, were similar. Like the Nguyen, the Thai were eager to extend
their prestige along their frontiers and to amplify their self-images as
universally accepted kings. The Thai rulers also wanted to link themselves as patrons of Buddhism to the *chakravartin,* or wheel-turning
monarchs, who had reigned for so many centuries at Ayudhya. These
ambitions led the rulers of both states to expand the land and people
under their control.

After 1810 King Chan and his advisers were swept up into a game of
power politics that they had little chance to change and no opportunity
to win. They had no choice. In Vietnamese terms, Cambodia was a
fence, a buffer state, and a dumping ground for colonists. To the Thai,
the Cambodians were fellow Buddhist children basking in a fund of
Chakri merit who could provide cardamom for the court and manpower for Chakri wars. The Thai wanted the Cambodians to be loyal
while the Vietnamese wanted access to Cambodia's land and, incidentally, the king's recognition of their superiority. The Thai demanded service and friendship, but they were usually unable, given the way they
organized their armies and the distance between Bangkok and Phnom
Penh, to provide protection. The Vietnamese, on the other hand, provided protection of a sort, but their actions led for a time to the disappearance of Cambodia as an independent state. By different routes,
then, the Thai and the Vietnamese often accomplished the same things:
they took over certain *sruk,* they made hostages of the Cambodian ruler
and his relations, and they reduced the independence of the *okya.*

The outcome of this game was not obvious at first to Chan and his
advisers. In the early part of his reign, his alliance with Vietnam was
probably meant only to deflect some of the pressures on him from the
Thai. Letters between Bangkok, Udong, and Hué took so long that
Chan was able to buy time on several occasions by saying one thing to
the Thai and another to the Vietnamese. Moreover, for most of his reign
he kept his communications open with both capitals by means of the
embassies he sent them. In fact, Chan may well have been under the impression that the equilibrium that prevailed in the early years of his

reign was his own creation and that he had more bargaining power with his patrons than he really did. In this way, he resembled his younger brother's great grandson, Norodom Sihanouk, who ruled Cambodia in the 1950s and 1960s.

Even if the balance of forces and the inactivity of the Thai and the Vietnamese reflected Thai and Vietnamese choices dictated by their own perceptions of national interest, and even if Cambodia's independence reflected what were for the moment limited Thai and Vietnamese ambitions rather than Cambodian skill, there were still advantages to Chan in blurring the lines of his allegiance. One of the chronicles, allegedly quoting Emperor Gia Long, makes this point quite clearly:

> "Cambodia is a small country," the Emperor said. "And we should maintain it as a child. We will be its mother; its father will be Siam. When a child has trouble with its father, it can get rid of suffering by embracing its mother. When the child is unhappy with its mother, it can run to its father for support."[41]

Chan was not alone in playing this game. He was joined by his rivals in the Cambodian royal family whose alternating loyalties led King Rama III of Siam to write in the early 1840s, "The Cambodians always fight among themselves in the matter of succession. The losers in these fights go off to ask for help from a neighboring state; the winner must then ask for forces from the other."[42]

Chan's freedom of action was illusory. He survived as king only so long as one of his patrons and all of his rivals were inactive and so long as the relatively active patron provided him with military help. When either patron turned his attention fully to Cambodia, there was nothing Chan could do to deflect the destruction that ensued. Like Prince Sihanouk in the 1960s, or Pol Pot a decade later, Chan remained neutral as long as stronger powers allowed him to be so. Chan suffered an additional disadvantage in having no world leaders or world forums to turn to—no Mao Zedong, no Association of Southeast Asian Nations (ASEAN), and no United Nations.

7

THE CRISIS OF THE NINETEENTH CENTURY

The first sixty years of the nineteenth century form the darkest portion of Cambodia's recorded history prior to the Armageddon of the 1970s. Invaded and occupied repeatedly by Thai and Vietnamese forces, the kingdom also endured dynastic crises and demographic dislocations. For a time in the 1840s, it ceased to exist as a recognizable state. Just as Jayavarman VII's totalizing ideology can be compared in some ways to the ideology of Democratic Kampuchea, the first half of the nineteenth century bears some resemblance to the 1970s in terms of foreign intervention, chaos, and the sufferings of the Cambodian people.

Fortunately for historians, there is a wide range of sources to consult in Thai, Cambodian, and Vietnamese. The record that the sources reveal, however, is incomplete. For example, the ruler of Cambodia for much of this period, King Chan, is rarely quoted in surviving sources, and none of his own writings has survived; therefore, a crucial actor has no lines. Similarly, Thai-language sources often thin out just when we might wish to have more information about the politics of Thai foreign policy in the period.

The period opens and closes with Thai-sponsored coronations. Between these two events and particularly after 1810, invasions from Vietnam and Siam alternated with internal rebellions and court-sponsored resistance to invaders while the court, especially under Chan, pursued a policy apparently aimed at preserving independence (or merely staying

141

alive) by playing the Thai and the Vietnamese against each other. Although the political history of the period is reasonably clear, the politics leading up to the events, and people's motivations, are often difficult to discern. The pattern that emerges is one in which Cambodia drifted first away from Thai control then into the hands of the Vietnamese and finally back to Thai protection. By the early 1840s, much of its territory, the capital region in particular, was administered as a component of Vietnam. Three events in the drift can be singled out for study. These are the Thai absorption of northwestern Cambodia in the 1790s in exchange for putting Eng on the throne, the anti-Vietnamese millenarian rebellion that broke out in southeastern Cambodia in 1820, and the succession crisis of 1835 following a disastrous Thai military expedition. Each of these events marked a stage in the process of Cambodia's diminishing ability to control its own affairs.

THE IMPOSITION OF VIETNAMESE CONTROL

Eng's restoration in 1794 is treated in the Cambodian chronicles as an event of miraculous significance. When he left Bangkok, they assert, "the sky did not grow dark, nor did rain fall, but thunder boomed in the noon sky, making a noise like a mighty storm."[1] The restoration was indeed dramatic, for in the preceding fifteen years Cambodia had not been governed at all. A former official named Baen had been installed in Udong by the Thai, had been given the title of *ta-la-ha*, or first minister, and had busied himself with recruiting troops to fight the Tay Son Vietnamese regime inside Cambodia and in Vietnam. In 1794, after so many years of service, the Thai monarch Rama I seems to have felt obliged to reward him in some way.

The reward he chose to bestow, however, was hardly his to give, as it consisted of the large and prosperous *sruk* of Battambang and Mahanokor (or "great city," containing the ruins of Angkor). Baen had held power in this region for part of the 1780s and probably retained a personal following there, but in awarding the two *sruk* to him, Rama I removed them from Eng's jurisdiction without absorbing them into Siam. In the 1790s and for most of the nineteenth century, Thai suzerainty seems to have meant only that Baen and his successors were not obligated to provide laborers for Eng and had to transmit gifts, generally of wild cardamom, to Bangkok from time to time.

Details about the transfer are impossible to uncover, and perhaps documents were never drawn up. In the 1860s, in fact, a French official in Cambodia, seeking information about the Thai claims, reported to his superiors that "Siam is unable to present any documentation about the cession. The present king of Cambodia Eng's grandson Norodom, his officials, old men who have been consulted, and Eng's widow, who is still alive, are all of the opinion that none exists."[2]

In the twentieth century, however, the loss of the two *sruk* did much to poison Thai-Cambodian relations. Siam gave them up under pressure from France in 1907 but resumed control over most of their territory from 1941 to 1946. In the context of the 1790s, however, it is unlikely that Rama I was pursuing a long-range plan, and his grandson, Rama IV, put the matter succinctly when he wrote that "the Thai kingdom was able to enlarge itself [at this time] because it had the greater power."[3]

After building himself a palace in Udong and visiting Bangkok with a tributary mission in 1796, Eng died at the beginning of 1797. His reign seems to have been been uneventful, and his contributions to Cambodian history were almost inadvertent. By returning to Udong, which had been without a king for so long, he brought Cambodia back to life. By fathering four sons, he founded a dynasty that was to reign in Udong and Phnom Penh until 1970 and which was revived in 1992. These two contributions, rather than specific actions on his part, probably account for the reverence with which he is treated in Cambodian chronicles compiled for his descendants.

The next ten years, until his son Chan's coronation in 1806, are poorly documented. But for reasons that remain unclear, the young prince became alienated from the Thai court at some point and seems to have begun to formulate a pro-Vietnamese foreign policy. Whatever its causes—Thai sources hint at a feud between the young prince and Rama I—Chan's anti-Thai orientation is a persistent theme of his long reign.[4]

As soon as he had been crowned, for example, he hastened to strengthen Cambodia's tributary connections with Vietnam while maintaining his subservience to Bangkok, becoming in the words of the

Vietnamese emperor "an independent country that is the slave of two."[5] The process was even more complicated, for Chan's increasing animosity toward the Thai alienated some of his own *chaovay sruk*, especially in the northwest, and his personal insecurity is indicated by his request to the Vietnamese emperor at about this time that he be allowed to recruit Vietnamese residents of Cambodia to form his personal bodyguard. The pace of his alienation from Bangkok accelerated after Rama I's death in 1809. Chan refused to attend the cremation, and when two officials who had attended the ceremony showed signs of being pro-Thai, Chan had them put to death.

In 1811–12, conflict broke out inside Cambodia between Thai and Vietnamese expeditionary forces. The Thai supported one of Chan's dissident brothers; the Vietnamese responded to Chan's requests for help. All three of Chan's brothers fled to Bangkok at this time, leaving him free for the rest of his reign to pursue a pro-Vietnamese policy, even though the campaigns of 1811–12 were indecisive. Their net effect was to reduce Chan's freedom of action, as his growing dependence on the Vietnamese was greater than his former allegiance, so reluctantly given, to Bangkok. Twice a month, wearing Vietnamese bureaucratic costumes supplied from the Vietnamese capital at Hué, the king and his entourage had to visit a Vietnamese temple near Phnom Penh, where the capital had been moved in 1812, and bow before a tablet bearing the Vietnamese emperor's name. Over the next twenty years, Chan fought with decreasing success to achieve a measure of independence.

Three events stand out from these early years of relatively loose Vietnamese control. These are the unsuccessful Cambodian attack on the northwestern *sruk* in 1816; the excavation of the Vinh Te Canal in southern Vietnam, using Cambodian labor, around 1820; and the anti-Vietnamese uprising that broke out soon afterward in southeastern Cambodia and in Khmer-populated portions of Vietnam.

The military expedition of 1816 was the last attempt before the 1970s by a formally constituted Cambodian army to take the offensive against foreign troops, and it was a failure. Perhaps to placate the Thai, or merely because the campaign had failed, Vietnamese authorities in Phnom Penh asked Chan to discipline the *okya* who had led the expedition. Taken to Saigon afterward, the official was reprimanded and fined.

The sequence of events, insignificant in itself, epitomizes Chan's help-lessness in the face of Vietnamese pressure.

The Vinh Te Canal, in turn, later became a symbol of Vietnamese mistreatment of the Khmer, and the rebellion that followed its excavation revealed the depth of anti-Vietnamese feeling in the *sruk*, the persistence of millenarianism, and perhaps the ambiguities in Chan's subservience to the Vietnamese.[6] In 1817, Vietnamese officials in Saigon recruited several thousand Vietnamese and a thousand Cambodian workers to excavate, or perhaps merely to restore, the Vinh Te Canal that ran between the Gulf of Siam and the fortified citadel of Chaudoc, a distance of perhaps forty kilometers (twenty-five miles). According to a Cambodian chronicle written in the 1850s, work on the canal was arduous in the extreme: "Workers were divided into groups. One Vietnamese marched at the head of each group, another at the back, and a third in the middle. The Vietnamese would beat the Cambodians on the back, to make them hurry. . . . Everyone was exhausted, and covered with mud."[7]

This account of the excavations is followed immediately in the text by an account of an anti-Vietnamese rebellion placed by other sources in 1820–21. This suggests a causal relationship between the two events, which is reinforced by the fact that the revolt broke out fairly close to the site of the canal. This site was Ba Phnom, the small mountain in southeastern Cambodia that has sometimes been identified with Jayavarman II's rise to power in the late eighth century. In the nineteenth century it was an important population center and also a religious site.[8] The Ba Phnom revolt was led by a former monk named Kai, who claimed to be a holy man capable of making predictions. As he gathered allegedly invulnerable supporters around him, he forged a political movement. Moving north and west from the vicinity of Ba Phnom, his followers attacked Vietnamese military posts. A mixed Khmer-Vietnamese force sent against him by Chan failed, one source asserts, because the *okya* in charge of it deserted with their troops and turned on the Vietnamese. A purely Vietnamese force sent from Saigon, however, eventually defeated the rebels near Kompong Cham. The leaders were executed in Saigon, and some of their followers were beheaded in Phnom Penh.

The differences between Cambodian and Vietnamese accounts of the rebellion pose interesting questions, such as where Chan's loyalties lay. Chan may have known Kai as a monk in Phnom Penh, and in any case the king, whom the Vietnamese were to find "extremely superstitious" toward the end of his reign, would probably not have moved vigorously against a Khmer believed to have supernatural powers. Whatever Chan's views might have been, his response to the rebellion had to be restricted and discreet. There are parallels here with the situation that faced his nephew, King Norodom, in 1884 when an anti-French rebellion led by *okya* broke out in the countryside while Norodom was under French protection in Phnom Penh. Similar problems confronted Norodom's great-grandson, Norodom Sihanouk, in turn, in the 1950s and confronted the successor regime again in 1970–75.[9]

It is unclear how large the rebellion was or how much of a threat it posed in military and territorial terms; we know little about its goals beyond the assassination of Vietnamese. Vietnamese records understandably play down its importance; the locally oriented *bangsavatar* probably exaggerates its extent, momentum, and success. All the sources agree, however, that it was directed against the Vietnamese rather than against Chan and his *okya* and that those monks, former monks, and local officials were active in its ranks.

The chronicle version composed in the 1850s tended to confirm its audience's ideas about themselves, the Vietnamese, and history. All Vietnamese were described as cruel, while "people of merit" (*nak sel*) were powerful, and Khmer could not (or at least should not) be made to fight against Khmer. The Buddhist orientation of the text can be seen when we learn that the *nak sel's* followers were rendered invincible by prayers and amulets but lost this invincibility when they acted contrary to Buddhist law by killing people themselves. Without the special powers connected with nonviolence, the rebels, including former monks, were all slaughtered. When they died, "Rain fell for seven days. It fell without stopping, night and day. The unimportant and the mighty were forced to run for shelter. In the cold air, everybody shook. There was no way of knowing when the sun set or when it rose. The nation was unhappy."[10]

It would be difficult to exaggerate the atmosphere of threat, physical danger, and random violence that pervades primary sources like this one

Cambodian landscape, 2006.
Photograph by Tom Chandler.

and perhaps much of everyday life in nineteenth-century Cambodia. The sources are filled with references to torture, executions, ambushes, massacres, village burnings, and the forced movement of populations. The wars of the time were localized rather than national in scope, and expeditionary forces, which usually numbered only a few thousand men, were small by twentieth-century standards. At the same time, invaders and defenders destroyed the villages they came to, killed or uprooted anyone they met, and ruined the landscape that they moved across. Very few prisoners of war were taken or kept alive. A seventeenth-century Cambodian law, translated by Adhémard Leclère, stated that an expeditionary force needed only three days' supply of food because unfriendly populations that could be robbed were thought to be never more than three days' march away.[11] Parallels to the civil war that devastated Cambodia in the 1970s, and to the behavior of both sides, are obvious.

One enigma in this period is Chan himself. We know very little about him except that he was timid. A Vietnamese text from 1822 states that he was ill much of the time and kept inside his palace.[12] The Vietnamese emperor wrote of him in 1834, just before his death, that a "fresh wind or the cry of a bird could make him flee."[13] At the same time, Chan retained considerable freedom of maneuver. All through the 1820s he kept his lines of communication with Bangkok open. Tributary missions went to Bangkok every year, and Chan may have used them to provide intelligence to Thai officials, to sound out Thai policies, and to remain in contact with his brothers.

Relations between the two kingdoms broke down in the late 1820s as a result of Vietnamese support for an anti-Thai rebellion that erupted in 1824–25 around Vientiane. The breakdown also sprang from the fact that the rulers in Hué and Bangkok in the 1830s, Rama III and Minh Mang, unlike their fathers, owed nothing to each other and were free to pursue vigorous foreign policies, one of which was to increase influence, and therefore to court conflict, over Cambodia. Minh Mang was also suspicious of the Vietnamese viceroy in Cambodia, Le Van Duyet, whom he believed—correctly, as things turned out—to be associated with breakaway sentiment in southern Vietnam.[14]

The Thai made some tentative military probes into western Cambodia in 1830–31, but Rama III saw no chance of success until Duyet's death in 1832. When Minh Mang attempted to replace the viceroy's entourage with officials loyal to Hué, his move ignited a full-scale rebellion that was centered on Saigon and led by Duyet's adopted son.

When news of the revolt reached Rama III, he decided to assemble an expeditionary force. He saw several advantages in doing so. He could humiliate Minh Mang, whose forces had been tangentially involved in the Vientiane rebellion and elsewhere in the Thai tributary states of Laos. By seeking to establish a new tributary state in southern Vietnam, moreover, Rama III may have been planning to extend Thai and Sino-Thai commercial interests and to profit directly from trade between Saigon/Cholon and southern China, for Chinese merchants in Vietnam had supported the rebellion and had informed their counterparts in Bangkok. Finally, the Thai king may have been impressed by reports reaching him from Cambodia that many okya would now welcome the return of Chan's two brothers, Im and Duang (the third brother had died in Bangkok in 1825).

The time was ripe, in Rama III's own words, "to restore the kingdom of Cambodia and to punish the insolence of Vietnam."[15]

In the short run the campaign was a success. The Vietnamese quickly abandoned Phnom Penh and took Chan into exile in Vietnam. The Thai commander, Chaophraya (roughly, "Lord") Bodin, then occupied the capital, but poor communications with the naval forces attached to the expedition, which were supposed to attack the Vietnamese coast, combined with Vietnamese attacks soon forced him to withdraw in early 1834.[16]

The Thai political strategy of placing Im and Duang in power also failed because the two were unable to attract support. One chronicle, in fact, describes popular confusion early in the war, as Bodin's forces entered the kingdom:

> The people were surprised to see such a large army, and they shook with fear. The head of the army shouted at them: "Don't be afraid! His royal highness the king [sic] has arrived to rule over you." The people murmured about this, and sent messengers off to inform the king [i.e., Chan] in Phnom Penh.[17]

In Bodin's retreat from Phnom Penh, approximately four thousand local people were carried off. Of these, perhaps a thousand managed to escape as the overburdened Thai column reached Udong. These people then "wandered trembling and afraid in the deep woods."[18] As the Thai columns moved north and west, they disintegrated, and at about this time the rebellion in Saigon was finally suppressed.

THE VIETNAMIZATION OF CAMBODIA, 1835–40

When Chan returned to his battered, abandoned capital early in 1834, he found himself under more stringent Vietnamese control. Thai successes in their overland offensive had shown Minh Mang that he could not rely on the Khmer to provide a fence for his southern and western borders, and with the defeat of the rebellion he now moved to intensify and consolidate his control. To head this civilizing mission, he named the general who had crushed the rebellion in Saigon, Truong Minh Giang.

Giang needed Chan and his officials to provide the Vietnamese with labor, rice, and soldiers. Chan seems to have needed the Vietnamese somewhat less in material terms, but probably counted on them to protect him from assassination and revolt. Like later outsiders operating in Cambodia, Giang probably expected too much from the king and *okya*. Before 1834 was over, he reported pessimistically to Hué that

> we have tried to punish and reward the Cambodian officials according to their merits and demerits. We have asked the king to help us, but he has hesitated to do so. After studying the situation, we have decided that Cambodian officials only know how to bribe and be bribed. Offices are sold; nobody carries out orders; everyone works for his own account. When we tried to recruit soldiers, the king was perfectly willing, but the officials concealed great numbers of people. When we wanted to compile a list of meritorious officials, [the officials were willing, but] the king was unwilling, because he was jealous. For the last four months, nothing has been accomplished.[19]

Giang's impatience was understandable, for Cambodian politics at the time (and perhaps through much of its history, as we have seen) was characterized by a diffusion of power, a shortage of resources, and a negotiability of position that effectively kept anyone from becoming powerful for very long. That Cambodians should hesitate to accomplish tasks for the Vietnamese struck Giang as insulting, even treacherous, but Minh Mang urged him to do the best he could with the human materials at hand.

Bodin, in the meantime, had settled his forces in the Siamese-administered northwest. As the 1830s wore on, the Thai increased their military presence in Battambang and Siem Reap, placing Im and Duang in ambiguous administrative control, presumably to attract indigenous support against the Vietnamese. This program was matched to the south and east by an intensive program of Vietnamization, which affected many aspects of Cambodian life. The program was set in motion in 1834 and played itself out under the threat of Thai invasions for the rest of the 1830s, the last years of Minh Mang's reign.

An early victim of Vietnamization was Chan himself. Toward the end of 1834, according to the Vietnamese annals, he came under the influence of "magicians" who allegedly encouraged him to accept bribes and "let criminals out of jail."[20] In a sense, the so-called magicians were merely asking Chan to act like a traditional king, but their influence distressed Truong Minh Giang, who had them arrested and shot. For Chan himself, the end of his struggle to stay alive and to provide for himself and his people a measure of independence had arrived. In early 1835, after a month's illness, he died aboard his royal barge, moored opposite his ruined palace in Phnom Penh. He was forty-four years old, and he had reigned, in one way or another, for nearly forty years.

Chan's death posed problems for the Vietnamese for he had no sons and his eldest daughter, Princess Baen, was suspected of being pro-Thai. Soon after his death, the *okya* agreed to a Vietnamese suggestion that Chan's second daughter, Princess Mei, be named queen. To officiate at her investiture, Minh Mang sent a Vietnamese official from Saigon, and in a hall built specially for the purpose, Mei and her sisters faced north, toward the emperor's letter authorizing her to reign, while the Vietnamese delegate and other officials faced south, as the emperor always did in his palace in Hué.[21]

The ceremony bore no resemblance to a traditional Cambodian coronation, but from the Cambodians' point of view, the queen's ability to grant titles and bestow official seals (as well as to officiate at royal ceremonies) meant that she *was* their queen.[22] To the Vietnamese, who treated her as the ceremonial leader of a protectorate, these aspects of the question were unimportant when compared to the administrative reforms that Truong Minh Giang, at the emperor's request, was now ready to impose. Whereas previously the Vietnamese fort at Phnom Penh had been called Annam, or "Pacified South," the city itself and the surrounding countryside were now renamed Tran Tay, or "Western Commandery,"and Sino-Vietnamese names were given to all of Cambodia's *sruk*. Day-to-day administrative decisions, including personnel postings, salaries, military affairs, and the control of rice surpluses, were placed in Vietnamese hands, and some sixteen officials, seventy clerks, and ten schoolmasters were sent to Phnom Penh to form the core of an infrastructure for the administration. Until 1839–40, however, the administration of the *sruk,* including the all-important matter of labor mobilization, was left to the *okya,* who still operated with royal seals even though their appointments were cleared through the Vietnamese.

Minh Mang's policy of Vietnamizing Cambodia had several facets. He sought to mobilize and arm the Khmer, to colonize the region with Vietnamese, and to reform the habits of the people. He also tried for military reasons to standardize patterns of measurement, mobilization, and food supply. Control of the adult male population and the formation of a standing army, if possible, to resist the Thai was the essential ingredient of all the Vietnamese programs. Problems of recruitment arose because many of the *okya* were unwilling to relinquish control over their followers. The Vietnamese soon found, in fact, that Cham mercenaries were the only troops they could recruit.

Because ethnic Khmer caused so many problems for administration, Minh Mang sought to colonize the region with Vietnamese. He justified this policy on the grounds that "military convicts and ordinary prisoners, if kept in jail, would prove useless. Therefore, it would be better for them to be sent to Cambodia and live among the people there, who would benefit from their teaching." The idea that Vietnamese criminals were superior to innocent Khmer was another aspect of Vietnam's "civilizing mission" in Cambodia.[23]

Indeed, Vietnamese policies toward Cambodia in the 1830s foreshadowed the French *mission civilisatrice* ("civilizing mission") that was, during the colonial era, to weaken and dismantle so many Vietnamese institutions. In a lengthy memorial to Truong Minh Giang, the emperor outlined his policy:

> The barbarians [in Cambodia] have become my children now, and you should help them, and teach them our customs. . . . I have heard, for example, that the land is plentiful and fertile, and that there are plenty of oxen [for plowing] . . . but the people have no knowledge of [advanced] agriculture, using picks and hoes, rather than oxen. They grow enough rice for two meals a day, but they don't store any surplus. Daily necessities like cloth, silk, ducks and

pork are very expensive. . . . Now all these shortcomings stem
from the laziness of the Cambodians . . . and my instructions to
you are these; teach them to use oxen, teach them to grow more
rice, teach them to raise mulberry trees, pigs and ducks. . . . As for
language, they should be taught to speak Vietnamese. [Our habits
of] dress and table manners must also be followed. If there is any
out-dated or barbarous custom that can be simplified, or re-
pressed, then do so.[24]

The emperor closed by advising Giang to move cautiously in engineering social change. "Let the good ideas seep in," he wrote, "turning the
barbarians into civilized people."[25] Speed was not essential. "As for winning the hearts of the people, and teaching them, we plan to do this
rather slowly."[26] In a subsequent memorial, the emperor recognized that
even this slow process might never succeed, because "the customs of the
barbarians are so different from our own that even if we were to capture
all their territory, it would not be certain we could change them."[27]

There is no record of Vietnamese success in altering Cambodian agricultural techniques, although the need to do so was a recurrent theme in
their correspondence of the 1830s. Likewise, Vietnamese efforts to
quantify and systematize landholdings, tax payments, and irrigation
works came to little. What impressed the Khmer about the Vietnamese,
it seems, were their persistent demands for corvée labor and their cultural reforms, which struck at the root of Khmer notions of their own
identity. One of these was the order that Khmer put on trousers instead
of skirts and that they wear their hair long rather than close-cropped.
Other "barbarous" Cambodian customs, according to a Vietnamese
writer, included wearing robes without slits up the sides, using loin-
cloths, eating with the fingers, and greeting from a kneeling position
rather than from an upright one.[28] The two peoples lived on different
sides of a cultural divide, perhaps one of the most sharply defined of
those in effect in nineteenth-century Southeast Asia. This divide was to
be savagely exploited in the 1970s, first by Lon Nol and later by Pol
Pot.[29]

Within his own ideological framework, Minh Mang tried hard to be
informed about Cambodia, to be fair to its people, and to improve their

way of life. There are several references to rewards given Cambodian officials at his behest for meritorious service. On one occasion, he asked that a history of the country be sent to him, because, among other things, the Khmer "have been a nation for over 1,200 years, but we do not know precisely what year they began, in terms of the Vietnamese and Chinese dynasties that were then reigning."[30] Earlier, the emperor had asked Truong Minh Giang to send him detailed information about Cambodia's

customs, people, and agricultural produce. I want to know whether the people are prosperous, and whether or not the Cambodian militia has been trained. I also want to know if the barbarian people have learned Vietnamese ways, and if they are happy.[31]

In another memorial, Minh Mang outlined plans for replacing Cambodian *chaovay sruk* with Vietnamese, beginning with *sruk* close to Phnom Penh. In 1839 he was annoyed to hear that the *okya* continued to use Cambodian rather than Vietnamese official titles:

At Tran Tay [the emperor said] Cambodian officials have all been given titles from my court. However, I understand that in correspondence and conversation they still use Cambodian titles. . . . The Cambodians should be told that it is an honor to have titles bestowed on them by this court. In conversation, therefore, they should use our titles, rather than theirs.[32]

Chan's brother Duang had been living in Battambang for several years under Thai protection, and an obscure sequence of events in 1837 culminated in his arrest by the Thai and his return in chains to Bangkok. The sources suggest that Vietnamese emissaries from Phnom Penh had tried to lure him down to the capital with promises that he would be given the throne. Duang's replies to them were so ambiguous as to convince both the Thai and the Vietnamese that he intended to betray them, using *okya* in the capital region to gather supporters in an effort to regain Chan's somewhat dubious independence.[33]

In the meantime, the growing apprehension of the Vietnamese about Thai mobilization, and the slow progress of their own reforms, led them to tighten their administrative machinery in Cambodia. Anti-Vietnamese uprisings in 1837–39 were both a cause and an effect of these reforms. According to the Vietnamese annals, there were four parts to their revised strategy. The most innovative one was to redraw the *sruk* and to replace indigenous *chaovay* throughout the country with Vietnamese. In making selections for these posts (never actually filled, it seems), the Vietnamese ministries were urged to find "about twenty" low-ranking officials, whose educational attainments were less important than their agricultural experience and their talent as military leaders. The second element of the policy was to open more plantations, to train more indigenous soldiers, and to store more rice in an attempt to free the Vietnamese and mercenary garrisons from dependence on southern Vietnam. Third, the Cambodians were to be taught Vietnamese so as to "improve communications." Finally, the Vietnamese were to encourage further colonization of Cambodia by Chinese immigrants and Vietnamese convicts, even though Truong Minh Giang had pointed out the dangers of this policy at great length in a memorial to Minh Mang earlier in the year.

These reforms led the Thai chronicles to refer to Minh Mang's naming the Khmer "new Vietnamese."[34] The Vietnamese saw nothing harmful in this, any more than they did in the "civilizing" Cambodian weights, measures, fashions, and coiffures. Of the innovations, the one aimed at replacing the *chaovay sruk* probably had the most to do with the rebellion that broke out against the Vietnamese in 1840–41. It is significant that the *okya*, when attacked in this fashion, could easily rally followers to defend the status quo rather than what might well have been a more equitable and forward-looking Vietnamese administration. There are interesting parallels here with the opposition to the People's Republic of Kampuchea (PRK) administration in the 1980s.[35]

In December 1839, Prince Im, favored by the Thai since his brother's imprisonment, defected to Phnom Penh with several thousand men, mistakenly convinced that the Vietnamese intended to place him on the Cambodian throne. When he reached the capital, he was arrested by

Truong Minh Giang and taken off to Saigon and Hué, thus removing from the scene yet another contender for the throne.[36]

One Thai response to these events, when they heard of them in early 1840, was to install a military garrison in Battambang. When Chaophraya Bodin reached the city to investigate Im's defection, he found that of three hundred Cambodians with some sort of official standing in the *sruk*, nearly two hundred had fled. Uncertain about local support, he postponed his plans for a full-scale invasion of Cambodia.[37]

The rebellion against the Vietnamese that broke out in September and October 1840 had reached the planning stage in May. Intermittent uprisings, in fact, had broken out every year since 1836, and deteriorating conditions in Cambodia, as we have seen, had led Minh Mang to tighten Vietnamese administration. One of his steps was to improve the collection of taxes. Traditionally, these had been collected through the *okya*; however, the amount of tax, paid in rice and cloth, had never been sufficient to support the Vietnamese troops and officials in the country. In an 1840 decree, Minh Mang ordered that Cambodia's arable land be remeasured and that records be maintained concerning rainfall, granaries, and irrigation works so that Vietnamese operations in Cambodia could pay for themselves. He had been making similar demands for six years, he added, but little had been achieved.[38]

By June 1840, Minh Mang's patience was exhausted. He demoted Mei and her two sisters, giving them low ranks in the Vietnamese civil service. Following the demotion the six highest-ranking *okya*, including the *ta-la-ha*, were placed under arrest and taken off to Saigon, accused of falsifying census records and "hiding" some fifteen thousand people otherwise liable for militia duty and corvée.[39] This was done in secret, and their followers assumed that they were dead. Their disappearance was one of the most significant causes of the revolt.

Indeed, the failure of the Vietnamese to impose a workable pattern of administration in Cambodia was connected with their willingness, in the early years at least, to work through the *okya*, whose loyalty to them was intermittent at best and whose operating styles—based on fear, arrogance, patronage, local ties, and loyalties to relatives and other officials—were neither sympathetic nor conducive to a Vietnamese administration. Most of the *okya* were happy enough, it seems, to accept rewards occasionally from the Vietnamese. They showed no eagerness to become Confucian civil servants. By working with them, the Vietnamese accomplished few of their objectives, but as Vietnamese measures added up in large part to a policy of laissez-faire, most of the *okya* had no reason to take up arms against them.

When they took over the administration of the *sruk* themselves in 1840, however, the Vietnamese reached the point at which they could impose their will at the same time that their actions perhaps inevitably ignited a revolt. With a Thai invasion imminent, however, and the failure of the *okya* to perceive that Vietnamese economic and military interests in Cambodia overlapped their own, the Vietnamese had little choice, unless they were to abandon Cambodia altogether. Minh Mang's policies failed because he was unable to understand the intransigence or ingratitude of the "barbarians" in the face of paternally administered social change. In a decree to the Cambodian people in 1838, he had stressed the irrationality of this ingratitude:

> Thanks to . . . my generosity, imperial troops were dispatched to Cambodia, costing millions of coins, and brought you security by destroying the Thai. Troops were stationed [among you] to bring peace. This action was like bringing the Cambodian people out of the mud onto a warm feather bed, and was well-known by everyone. . . . Anyone who can think for himself should be grateful to the court; why are there people who hate us and believe the rebels?[40]

The situation became worse in September 1840, when a wide-ranging rebellion broke out. The uprising, which was centered in the eastern and southern *sruk*, is a rare example in prerevolutionary Cambodia of sustained and coordinated political action; the only others that spring to mind are the anti-French rebellion of 1885–86 and the so-called 1916 Affair (see Chapters 8 and 9). Smarting under Vietnam's civilizing mission, the *okya* had discussed the idea of rebellion among themselves for several months, in letters known today by their dates, addresses, and general contents; the letters themselves do not seem to have survived.[41] What set the rebellion in motion was an interlocking set of provocations by the Vietnamese together with Cambodian expectations of a Thai invasion and Thai support. The uprising collapsed in the early months of 1841, when a new emperor in Vietnam and the Thai invasion the insurgents had hoped for coincided with Vietnamese military successes and the rebel shortage of supplies. The rest of the early 1840s was filled with seesawing warfare and negotiations between the Thai and the Vietnamese and by a gradual shift in the balance of power in Cambodia in favor of the Thai.

The immediate cause of the rebellion, from the standpoint of the *okya*, was a sequence of Vietnamese actions that seemed to the *okya* to be aimed at extinguishing kingship, Buddhism, and the official class in Cambodia. The sequence began with the demotion of the princesses and the reshuffling of Vietnamese officials in Phnom Penh. It continued in June 1840 when Minh Mang instituted a Vietnamese taxation system. This made new demands on the *okya* by taxing additional products, such as fruit and vegetables, and by calling for a new census, cadastral surveys, and reports on water resources.

Another part of the Vietnamese program was to call in Cambodian seals of office in at least some of the *sruk*, replacing them with Vietnamese ones that carried no indication of rank. At least one rural official was dismissed at this time for corruption, and rumors spread among the *okya* that all officials would soon be arrested by the Vietnamese.

The climax came in August when the Vietnamese arrested Mei and her sisters in Phnom Penh. The women were lured aboard a barge after their immediate entourage had been softened up with liquor and a performance of Vietnamese opera; at this point, according to an eyewitness, "every time they talked they laughed and everyone was happy." The princesses were taken off to Vietnam, and Cambodia's regalia, which Mei had inherited from her father, accompanied them. At this time, the *okya* in Phnom Penh and the *sruk*, with rumors and the Vietnamese record toward Cambodians to rely on, assumed that *Ta-la-ha* Lung, his associates, and the four princesses had been killed, and they thought they were next.

To many Cambodians, the disappearance of their monarch, however restricted her authority and charisma might have been, signified the disappearance of the state. The absence of regalia with which to legitimize someone else made the situation worse. For the *okya*, the disappearance of their high-ranking patrons at court, the reformed tax system, the devaluation of seals of office, and the Vietnamese assault on their freedom of action were precipitants of revolt. Vietnamese "rational" actions, supposedly beneficial to the Khmer, struck at the roots of the identity of the *okya* and at their concepts of society as a whole. Vietnamese contempt for Theravada Buddhism and for Cambodia's language, culture, and institutions also hastened the decision of the *okya* to revolt.

The uprising was concentrated at first along the east bank of the Mekong but soon spread to Vietnamese settlements along the coast, like Ream and Kampot, to parts of southern Vietnam inhabited by Khmer, and to fortified villages inland. The news of the princesses' disappearance seems to have triggered the revolt, and the rebels' goal at this stage was the restoration of the status quo ante, personified by Mei and the exiled officials. Another objective, apparently, was the mere killing of Vietnamese. As one rebel wrote, "We are happy killing Vietnamese. We no longer fear them; in all our battles we are mindful of the three jewels [of Buddhism]: the Buddha, the law, and the monastic community."[42]

The Vietnamese were surprised by the level of coordination among the *okya* and blamed it on Thai influences, which Thai sources fail to confirm. They were also baffled by the absence of a single leader. Their estimate of rebel strength ran to thirty thousand men operating throughout the kingdom in "hundreds of" small bands and occasionally larger ones, usually in territory familiar to them and commanded by people they could trust. The formidable problems of counterguerrilla warfare were summed up in one Vietnamese report in 1841:

> The rebels have established posts along the riverbanks at strategic points. They appear and disappear at will. If our troops look to the east, the rebels escape to the west. . . . They concentrate their forces where the jungle is thick, and in swampy areas where our troops cannot maneuver. Other regions have tall grass at eye-level

and are very hot and dusty. One can march all day without finding potable water. Moreover, we have no intelligence about the
enemy, and no guides.[43]

The Vietnamese also had problems moving troops and supplies
against the river currents prevalent at that time of year, and the report
adds that "not even one" rebel had surrendered, despite the "tolerant"
policies of the Vietnamese court and even though the record is full of
references to the Khmer fleeing like "rats and mice," or attacking like
"swarms of mosquitoes." At the start of the rebellion, Minh Mang (who
was to die following an accident at the beginning of 1841) thought that
an adequate application of force, combined with rewards to loyal troops
and local officials, would be enough to put down the rebellion, which
angered him, he wrote, so much that his "hair stood on end."[44] He ordered *Ta-la-ha* Lung and others to write letters asking their relatives and
clients in Cambodia to surrender, thus misreading Cambodian loyalty to
unavailable and devalued patrons, and he also approved sending
"monks and magicians" into Phnom Penh to undermine morale. In the
last months of his reign, he demanded weekly reports from the front and
suggested that Cambodian crops and orchards be burned down as a preemptive measure. "The Cambodians are so stupid," he declared, "that
we must frighten them. Ordinary moral suasion has no effect."[45]

It is impossible to say what Minh Mang would have done had he survived the next seven years, but it is clear that the rebellion had begun to
lose momentum before his death and also that his successor, Thieu Tri,
was less committed than he had been to a victory in Cambodia.[46] The
new emperor began his reign looking for a solution that would be ac-
ceptable to his court and to the Cambodians, if not necessarily to the
Thai; at one stage, he brushed aside a suggestion that he negotiate directly with the Thai as being "wrong and foolish." Distance, distrust,
and the momentum of the war, however, as well as the ambiguity of
Thieu Tri's objectives in Cambodia, kept the conflict going until 1847.

Cambodian troops were often poorly supplied. At the end of 1840, a
rebel *okya* complained to the Thai that "we are unable to continue
fighting the Vietnamese. We lack the troops to do so, the rifles, the am-

munition, and the supplies. For weapons we have only knives, cross-bows, and clubs; we cannot continue to fight."[47]

SIAM AND THE RESTORATION OF CAMBODIAN INDEPENDENCE

As the Vietnamese court and its officials in Cambodia sought a solution to what they saw as an internal Vietnamese problem, Chaophraya Bodin's expeditionary force, numbering thirty-five thousand men, assembled near Battambang and then attacked and defeated the Vietnamese garrison at Pursat. Bodin was prepared to attack the capital but hesitated because he was short of supplies and lacked confidence in his troops. Instead he withdrew to Battambang, where he sought to consolidate his political position. During the siege of Pursat, eighteen rebellious *okya* had written him pleading for Thai support and for Duang's return from Bangkok.[48] The *okya* pledged allegiance to Rama III, complained about shortages of supplies, and asserted that Cambodians would be happy only if the political conditions of the early nineteenth century, before the Vietnamese had arrived, were reestablished.

Bodin transmitted the letter to Bangkok and added a recommendation for Duang's release from custody and his return to political power. In January 1841 Duang reached Battambang, accompanied by Thai and Cambodian advisers and carrying gifts for his supporters, including insignia of rank and royal accoutrements provided for him by Rama III.[49] According to one source, Bodin had urged Duang's release because "if there are no superior people to look after a population, the common people have no security."[50] The records also suggest that Bodin's motives included winning over the *okya* (he was eager that local Khmer, rather than his own inexperienced troops, should engage the Vietnamese) by promising them that Duang would rule over Cambodia. For the rest of the 1840s, Duang was to be closely watched and manipulated by Bodin. His return to Cambodia and Rama III's solicitude for him opened an era in Thai-Cambodian relations that lasted until French intervention in 1863.

While Duang was conferring with potential courtiers and Bodin was complaining that the newcomers were consuming Thai supplies, Thieu

Tri was attempting to understand and control Vietnamese policy toward Cambodia, with a view to thwarting a Thai invasion, pacifying rebellious provinces of southern Vietnam, and maintaining Vietnamese prestige. In late 1841 Truong Minh Giang attempted once again to bring Prince Im to power, but edicts issued in his name attracted no support. It was at this point, perhaps, that Truong Minh Giang realized that he had almost no chance of restoring a favorable political balance in Cambodia. He withdrew to Vietnam, taking with him Im, the princesses, and the population of the city, numbering some six thousand people. When he arrived in Vietnam, he sent a letter to Hué in which he took the blame for "losing" Cambodia, which he referred to as the emperor's "rightful property." He then took poison and died.[51]

The Vietnamese failure, however, did not mean that the Thai had succeeded, and by 1843 Cambodia had become a quagmire for Chaophraya Bodin. As he wrote Bangkok, "We have been in Cambodia for three years without accomplishing anything. We are short of supplies; people are going off into the forest to live on leaves and roots; and nearly a thousand men in our army have died from lack of food."[52] In 1844 he had to abandon Phnom Penh, where the Vietnamese soon reinstalled Princess Mei as Cambodia's "legitimate queen" while Thai forces congregated near Udong. The Vietnamese maneuver infuriated Bodin, who saw that many *okya* might now be unwilling to support the Thai. He complained to Bangkok that "all the Khmer leaders and nobles, all the district chiefs and all the common people are ignorant, stupid, foolish and gullible. They have no idea what is true and what is false."[53]

In spite of these difficulties, Vietnamese attempts to dislodge the Thai forces around Udong throughout 1845 were fruitless. By the end of the year the Thai and Vietnamese had opened negotiations for a cease-fire. The talks moved forward, for they were grounded in Thieu Tri's willingness to abandon his military positions in Cambodia and, by implication, his father's policies there. They moved slowly, however, in a context of military stalemate even though, in political terms, conditions were favorable to the Thai. In Prince Duang they had a seasoned, popular ruler, loyal to Bangkok and able to work through a well-established network of loyal officials in the *sruk*. But the Vietnamese still occupied a strong bargaining position, particularly as they retained Cambodia's regalia, without which Duang could not legitimately ascend the throne.

In a face-saving gesture, they demanded that a tributary mission headed by a Cambodian official travel to Hué in March 1846 and declare Cambodia's pro forma subservience to Vietnam.[54] When the embassy returned to Phnom Penh in June 1847, the Vietnamese handed over the Cambodian regalia and released several members of the Khmer royal family who had been in their custody, in some cases for many years. Soon afterward, they withdrew their forces from Cambodia. For the first time since 1811, there were no Vietnamese officials on Cambodian soil.

Over the next few months, in a series of ceremonial gestures, Duang reenacted the restoration of Thai-sponsored kingship that had been eclipsed for so many years. It would be a mistake to dismiss these ceremonial actions as mere protocol because Duang, like most Southeast Asian rulers at the time, did not disentangle what we would call the religious and political strands of his thinking, duties, and behavior. Kingly behavior, in other words, was thought to have political results, and political actions were thought to enhance or diminish a monarch's fund of merit.[55]

Many of these ceremonies had to do with the restoration of Theravada Buddhism as the state religion. One account relates that Duang

> leveled the [Vietnamese] fortifications at Phnom Penh, and hauled away the bricks to build and restore . . . [seven] Buddhist monasteries near Udong. Broken Buddha-images were recast, and new ones were carved. Monks were encouraged to live in monasteries again, and people were encouraged to respect them.[56]

To his subjects, Duang's return to Cambodia and the restoration of Buddhism there were ex post facto proofs of his kingliness, legitimacy, and merit. An inscription from 1851 describes the electric effect of this restoration in the 1840s:

> There was a mighty ruler, whose name was Duang. He came from the royal city [Bangkok] to Cambodia, and lived in the fortified

city of Udong. With merit, skill, and masterly intelligence, the
king scattered his enemies in terror; and soon the three warring
states were friends again.[57]

On an auspicious day in April 1848, Duang was anointed by Thai
and Cambodian brahmans in Udong and ascended the Cambodian
throne. He was fifty-two years old, and his reign, which lasted twelve
years, can be seen as something of a cultural renaissance. For most of
these years the kingdom was at peace, and although Thai political advisers and some Thai troops lingered at Udong, Duang was relatively free
to make political decisions, such as those connected with awarding titles
to *okya*. The chronicles of his reign emphasize its restorative aspects. A
wide range of institutions and relationships was involved. The chronicle
points to linguistic reforms, public works, sumptuary laws, and new sets
of royal titles. From other sources, we know that Duang was an accomplished poet and presided over the promulgation of a new law code and
the compilation of new chronicle histories.[58]

Chroniclers in the 1880s and the 1930s, looking back to those few
years of Cambodian independence prior to French control, seem to have
have considered Duang's reign to be a kind of golden age. The king himself was relatively cautious after so many years of semicaptivity in
Bangkok. His relations with Rama III and Rama IV (King Mongkut)
were dutiful and subservient, as his letters to these monarchs show.[59] He
made no attempt to improve relations with Vietnam in the hope of gaining some freedom of maneuver, perhaps because he was frightened by
the precedent of the 1830s and because from the Vietnamese point of
view any improvement in relations would only have intensified his dependency on them. Instead, in 1853 he somewhat clumsily sought
French protection by sending gifts and offering his "humble homage" to
the emperor of France, Napoleon III, via the French consulate in Singapore. Duang was probably put up to this by French Catholic missionaries who were active near Udong. His gifts included four elephant tusks,
two rhinoceros horns, and sizable quantities of sugar and white pepper.
A French diplomatic mission to his court, bearing a draft treaty of
friendship (see Chapter 8), was not allowed to proceed to Udong by the
Thai, who had swiftly brought their client monarch to heel.

Duang seems to have sought French help not so much to escape Thai protection, which would have been impossible to manage, as to defend himself against the Vietnamese. In letters to the French, he referred to them, as Pol Pot was to do in the 1970s, as Cambodia's "traditional enemies." Ironically, in the 1860s France took over Vietnam's patronage of Cambodia, eliminated Vietnamese influence, and then proceeded to encourage Vietnamese immigration into Cambodia. After his attempt to make friends with France had failed, Duang explained himself to a French missionary, saying, "What would you have me do? I have two masters who always have an eye fixed on me. They are my neighbors, and France is far away."[60] Clearly, many conditions had to change before Cambodia could emerge from this dual dependency, which had lasted with brief interludes for more than fifty years.

8

THE EARLY STAGES
OF THE FRENCH
PROTECTORATE

There are several ways of looking at the years of French hegemony over Cambodia. One is to break them into phases and to trace the extension and decline of French control. Another would examine the period and its ideology and practice—political, economic, educational, and so forth—from a French point of view. A third would treat the period as part of Cambodian history, connected to the times before and after French protection. Now that the French are gone, the third perspective seems the most attractive. Although there are serious gaps in the sources and although useful primary material in Khmer aside from royal chronicles is very scarce, in this chapter I attempt to see the French as often as possible through Cambodian eyes.

In the meantime, if we look at the colonial era in terms of the waxing and waning of French control (the first of the three perspectives), the years break fairly easily into phases. The first phase lasted from the establishment of the protectorate in 1863 to the outbreak of a national rebellion in 1884. The second phase would extend from the suppression of the rebellion in 1886 to King Norodom's death in 1904 when a more cooperative monarch, Norodom's half-brother, Sisowath, came to the throne. The third phase lasted until Norodom Sihanouk's coronation in 1941 and spans the reigns of Sisowath (r. 1904–27) and his eldest son,

Monivong (r. 1927–41). This period, it can be argued, was the only sys-
tematically *colonial* one in Cambodian history, for in the remainder of
the colonial era (1941–53) the French were concerned more with holding onto power than with systematizing their control.

From a Cambodian perspective, however, it is possible to take the
view that the colonial era falls into two periods rather than four, with
the break occurring at Sisowath's coronation in 1906. From that point
on, Cambodians stopped governing themselves, and the Westernization
of Cambodian life, especially in the towns, intensified. What would
have been recognizable in a *sruk* in 1904 to a Cambodian official of the
1840s had been modified sharply by 1920, when the French government, particularly at the local level, had been organized as part of a total
effort in Indochina.

But until the late 1940s, I suspect, few Cambodians would have considered these mechanical changes, or the French presence as a whole, as
having a deleterious effect on their lives or on their durable institutions
of subsistence farming, family life, Buddhism, and kingship. The political stability that characterized most of the colonial era can be traced in
part to French patronage of the king and the king's patronage of the
sangha, which tended to keep these two institutions aligned (politically,
at least) with French objectives—partly because kings, monks, and officials had no tradition of innovative behavior and partly because heresy
and rebellion, the popular methods of questioning their authority, had
been effectively smothered by the French since the 1880s. In terms of
economic transformations, the significant developments that occurred in
the technology of rice farming tended to be limited to the northwestern
part of the kingdom, where huge rice plantations had come into being.
In the rest of the country, as Jean Delvert has shown, the expanding
population tended to cultivate rice in small, family-oriented plots, as
they seem to have done since the times of Chenla.[1]

Because of this stability, perhaps, many French writers tended to ro-
manticize and favor the Cambodians at the expense of the Vietnamese.
At the same time, because in their terms so little was going on, they also
tended to look down on the Cambodians as "lazy" or "obedient." An
ambiguous romanticism suffuses many French-language sources on the
colonial era, especially in the twentieth century, when clichés about the

Prince Sisowath and his entourage, 1866. Courtesy of Bibliotheque Nationale, Paris.

people were passed along as heirlooms from one official (or one issue of a newspaper) to the next. At the same time, until the early 1940s, no Cambodian-language sources questioned the efficacy of French rule or Cambodia's traditional institutions.

For these reasons it is tempting to join some French authors and skip over an era when "nothing happened." But to do so would be a mistake because what was happening, especially after the economic boom of the 1920s, was that independent, prerevolutionary Cambodia (with all its shortcomings) was being built or foreshadowed despite large areas of life that remained, as many French writers would say, part of the "timeless" and "mysterious" Cambodia of Angkor.

It is tempting also to divide French behavior in Cambodia into such categories as political, economic, and social, terms that give the false impression that they are separable segments of reality. What the French meant by them in the context of the colonial situation tended to be idiosyncratic. *Politics*, for example, meant dissidence and manipulation rather than participation in an open political process. Ideally, in a colony there should be no politics at all. *Economics* meant budgets, taxes, and revenues—in other words, the economics of bureaucratic control. On the rare occasions when French writers looked at Cambodia's economy, they related it to the rest of Indochina, particularly in terms of export crops and colonial initiatives like public works, rather than to Cambodian needs and capabilities. By the 1920s, in the eyes of French officials, Cambodia had become a rice-making machine, producing revenue in exchange for "guidance." This meant that the essence of government—*rajakar*, or "royal work"—remained what it had always been, the extraction of revenue from the peasants. As for *social*, the word as the French used it did not refer to solidarity among people or relationships that added up to political cohesion. Instead, *society* meant a conglomeration of families, obediently at work.

The chronological perspective and the analytical ones just mentioned may be helpful in examining the colonial era because looking at these years in terms of Cambodian history means looking at them in terms of continuity and change. From this angle, the alterations to Cambodian society and the thinking of the Cambodian elite are as important as the apparently timeless life in the villages, which was also changing.

THE ESTABLISHMENT OF THE FRENCH PROTECTORATE

The beginnings of French involvement in Cambodia are to be found in the eighteenth century, when Catholic missionaries took up residence in the kingdom, especially in the vicinity of Udong. French involvement did not become political, however, before the 1850s, coincident with French involvement in Vietnam. In the mid-1850s King Duang sought French support in an attempt to play off the Thai against the Vietnamese, but a French diplomatic mission to Cambodia in 1856, armed with a draft treaty of cooperation, failed to reach the Cambodian court, which was frightened away from welcoming it by Thai political advisers. The draft treaty, incidentally, contained several clauses that passed into the operative one concluded in 1863. The French wanted teak for shipbuilding, for example, as well as freedom to move about the country and freedom to proselytize for the Roman Catholic faith.[2]

French interest in Cambodia deepened with their involvement in Vietnam and also after a French naturalist, Henri Mouhot (1826–61), visited Duang's court and then proceeded to Siem Reap, where he discovered the ruins of Angkor. Mouhot suggested in a posthumously published book about his travels that Cambodia was exceptionally rich and that its rulers were neglecting their patrimony.[3] Duang's openness to Mouhot and to other European visitors in this period stemmed in part from his friendship with a French missionary, Monseigneur Jean Claude Miche, whose mission headquarters was located near Udong and who had actively supported the 1856 diplomatic mission. Miche convinced the king that there could be advantages in being free from Thai control and Vietnamese threats. In the last two years of his reign, moreover, Duang also saw French expansion into Vietnam as an opportunity for him to regain territory and Khmer-speaking people lost to the Vietnamese over the preceding two hundred years.[4]

Bogged down in guerrilla warfare in Vietnam and unsure of support from Paris, the French administrators in Saigon were slow to respond to Cambodia's assertions of friendship. The matter lapsed when Duang died in 1860 and Cambodia was plunged into a series of civil wars. Duang's designated heir, Norodom, was unpopular in the eastern *sruk* and among Cham dissidents, who had almost captured Udong while Duang was alive. Norodom had spent much of his youth as a hostage at the Thai court. Unable to rule, he fled Cambodia in 1861, returning with Thai support at the end of the following year. But he returned on a probationary basis, for his royal regalia remained in Bangkok. Angered by Thai interference and attracted by French promises of gifts, Norodom reopened negotiations with the French. According to a contemporary, the French admiral in charge of southern Vietnam, "having no immediate war to fight, looked for a peaceful conquest and began dreaming about Cambodia."[5]

The colonial era began without a shot and in a tentative way. A delegation of French naval officers concluded a treaty with Norodom in Udong in August 1863, offering him protection at the hands of a French resident in exchange for timber concessions and mineral exploration rights. Norodom managed to keep the treaty secret from his Thai advisers for several months. When they found out about it and notified Bangkok, he quickly reasserted his dependence on the Thai king, declaring to his advisers, "I desire to remain the Thai king's servant, for his glory, until the end of my life. No change ever occurs in my heart." The Thai, in turn, kept Norodom's change of heart a secret from the French, who learned of it only after his earlier declaration of faith had been ratified in Paris in early 1864.[6]

What Norodom wanted from the French vis-à-vis the Thai is unclear. He seems to have been playing for time, and the method he chose resembled that of his uncle, King Chan, with the French in the role of the Vietnamese. He also wanted to be crowned, and by the middle of 1864, the Thai and the French had agreed to cosponsor his coronation. The unintentionally comical aspects of the ceremony are recounted by several French sources. Thai and French officials quarreled about precedent, protocol, and regalia while Norodom, using time-honored filial imagery, proclaimed his dependence on both courts. For the last time, the Cambodian king's titles were chosen and transmitted by Bangkok; for the last time, too, the Cambodian king claimed to draw legitimacy from two foreign courts. For the first time, a Cambodian king accepted his crown from a European. The next three Cambodian monarchs followed suit. From this point on, Thai influence in Cambodia began to wane, fading even more sharply and more or less for good after King Mongkut died in 1867.[7]

The imposition of French protection over Cambodia did not end the dynastic and millenarian rebellions that had plagued the beginning of Norodom's reign, although French military forces were helpful in quelling these rebellions by 1867. The most important of them was led by Pou Kombo, an ex-monk who claimed that that he had a better right than Norodom to be king. A year before, Norodom had shifted his palace to Phnom Penh. He had been urged to do so by the French, just as Chan had been encouraged to move by the Vietnamese earlier in the century, and for similar tactical reasons. In the French case, commercial motives were also at work, for Phnom Penh was more accessible from Saigon than an inland capital would have been, and it was hoped that the exploration of the Mekong River under Commandant E. Doudart de Lagrée (1823–68) would result in data about the river's northern reaches that would justify French pipe dreams of Phnom Penh as an important commercial city.[8]

For the French the 1860s and 1870s were a heroic period, partly because government remained largely in the hands of young naval officers hungry for glory, eager for promotion, and entranced by the exotic setting in which they found themselves. By and large, these omnicompetent pioneers of colonialism—Doudart de Lagrée, Francis Garnier, Jean Moura, and Etienne Aymonier, among others —possessed great energy, intellectual integrity, and sympathy for ordinary Khmer. They explored the Mekong, translated Cambodian chronicles, deciphered inscriptions, and arranged for the shipment of tons of Cambodian sculpture to museums in Paris, Saigon, and eventually Phnom Penh. The grandeur of their exploits and of Cambodia's distant past formed a sharp contrast in their minds with what they regarded as the decay of the Cambodian court and the helplessness of the Cambodian people. At the same time, as Gregor Muller has shown, the protectorate in its early years was plagued by unscrupulous French adventurers posing as entrepreneurs and eager to capitalize on royal cupidity and the ambiguities of French control.[9]

There was probably little difference, however, between the way Cambodia was governed in the 1860s and 1870s and the way Angkor had been governed almost a thousand years before. In both cases, perhaps, and certainly for most of the years between, government meant a network of status relationships and obligations whereby peasants paid in rice, forest products, or labor to support their officials in exchange for their protection. The officials, in turn, paid the king, using some of the rice, forest products, and peasant labor with which they had been paid. Entrepreneurs—often Chinese, occasionally French—paid the king for the right to market and export the products. The number of peasants one could exploit in this way depended on the positions granted by the throne, positions that were themselves for sale. Officeholders in such a system tended to be members of the elite with enough money or goods on hand to purchase and protect their positions.

THE TIGHTENING OF FRENCH CONTROL

Within the palace, Norodom governed Cambodia in what the French considered to be an arbitrary, authoritarian way. The French, however, offered him no alternative style, and throughout his reign Norodom was drawn less by the idea of a sound administration than by what he considered to be the imperatives of personal survival. Revolts against his rule (and implicitly against his acquiescence to the French) broke out in 1866–67 and in the 1870s. Both attracted considerable support, and the French put both down with difficulty. Unwilling to blame themselves for this state of affairs, the French blamed Norodom and were increasingly drawn to support his half-brother, Sisowath, who had led troops alongside the French in both rebellions.

Under French pressure and while another half-brother, Siwotha, was in revolt against him, Norodom agreed in 1877 to promulgate a series of reforms. Although these were never carried out, they are worth noting as precursors of more extensive French control and as indications of areas of French concern. The reforms sought to dismantle royal involvement in landownership, to reduce the number of *okya*, to rationalize tax collection, and to abolish slavery. Had they been enacted, they would have worn away the power bases of the Cambodian elite. Like Minh Mang in the 1830s, the French disliked the Cambodian way of doing things, which interfered with their ideas of rational, centralized control. Institutions like slavery and absolute monarchy, moreover, went down poorly with officials of the Third Republic, less charmed by the romantic operetta aspects of Cambodia than Napoleon III and his entourage had been.

In the early 1880s, as the French tightened their grip on Vietnam, it was only a matter of time before they solved what they saw as Cambodia's problems and imposed their will on the Cambodian court. The comedy in Phnom Penh had gone on too long and had cost the French too much. The Cambodians had not seen the importance of paying for French protection. The French became impatient and assumed for this reason that time was running out. The riches of Cambodia remained largely untapped. What had seemed exotic and quaint in Cambodian society in the 1860s and 1870s was now seen by a new generation of civilian officials as oppressive; it was time for protection to become control.

In 1884 the French succeeded in getting Norodom to agree to siphon off customs duties, especially on exports, to pay for French administrative costs. Norodom sent a cable to the president of France protesting French pressure and was chided for doing so by the governor-general of Cochin China, Charles Thomson, who had been negotiating secretly with Sisowath to arrange a transfer of power should Norodom prove resistant to the reforms.[10]

A few months later, Thomson sailed from Saigon to Phnom Penh and confronted Norodom with a wide-ranging set of reforms encased in a treaty that went further than previous documents had to establish de jure French control. Thomson arrived at the palace unannounced one day at 10 p.m., traveling aboard a gunboat that was anchored within sight of the palace. As Norodom reviewed the document, Thomson's armed bodyguards stood nearby. Aided by a complaisant interpreter, Son Diep, who rose to bureaucratic heights after Norodom's death, the king signed it because he saw that doing so was the only way to stay on the throne; he undoubtedly knew of Sisowath's machinations. Perhaps he thought that the document's provisions would dissolve when the French encountered opposition to the provisions from the Cambodian elite. This is, in fact, what happened almost at once, but Article 2 of the treaty nevertheless marked a substantial intensification of French control. As it read, "His Majesty the King of Cambodia accepts all the administrative, judicial, financial, and commercial reforms which the

French government shall judge, in future, useful to make their protectorate successful."[11]

It was not this provision, however, that enraged the Cambodian elite, who by that time probably viewed Norodom as a French puppet. The features they saw as revolutionary (and that the French saw as crucial to their program of reforms) were those that placed French *résidents* in provincial cities, abolished slavery, and institutionalized the ownership of land. These provisions struck at the heart of traditional Cambodian politics, which were built up out of entourages, exploitation of labor, and the taxation of harvests (rather than land) for the benefit of the elite, who were now to become paid civil servants of the French, administering rather than consuming the people under their control.

Although few French officials had taken the trouble to study what they referred to as slavery in Cambodia, and although their motives for abolishing it may have included a cynical attempt to disarm political opposition in France to their other reforms, it is clear that the deinstitutionalization of servitude was a more crucial reform, in Cambodian terms, than the placement of a few French officials in the countryside to oversee the behavior of Cambodian officials. Without this reform the French could not claim to be acting on behalf of ordinary people. More importantly, they could do nothing to curb the power of the perennially hostile Cambodian elite, which sprang from who controlled personnel. Without abolishing slavery, moreover, the French could not proceed with their vision—however misguided it may have been—of a liberated Cambodian yeomanry responding rationally to market pressures and the benefits of French protection.

By cutting the ties that bound masters and servants—or, more precisely, by saying that this was what they *hoped* to do—the French were now able to justify their interference at every level of Cambodian life. Their proposal effectively cut the king off from his entourage and this entourage, in turn, from its followers. The French wanted Cambodia to be an extension of Vietnam, with communal officials responding directly to the French, even though government of this sort and at this level was foreign to Cambodia, where no communal traditions—had they ever existed—survived into the nineteenth century.

In the short run the Cambodian reaction to the treaty was intense and costly to the French. In early 1885 a nationwide rebellion, under several leaders, broke out at various points.[12] It lasted a year and a half, tying down some four thousand French and Vietnamese troops at a time when French resources were stretched thin in Indochina. Unwilling to work through Norodom, whom they suspected of supporting the rebellion, the French relied increasingly on Sisowath, allowing him a free hand in appointing pro-French officials in the *sruk*, further undermining Norodom's authority. It seems likely that Sisowath expected to be rewarded with the throne while Norodom was still alive, but as the revolt wore on the French found that they had to turn back to Norodom to pacify the rebels. In July 1886 the king proclaimed that if the rebels laid down their arms, the French would continue to respect Cambodian customs and laws—in other words, the mixture as before. The rebellion taught the French to be cautious, but their goals remained the same— to make Cambodian governance more rational and to control the kingdom's economy. It was at this stage that the French began to surround Norodom with Cambodian advisers who were loyal to them rather than to the king. These were drawn, in large part, from the small corps of interpreters trained under the French in the 1870s. The most notable of them was a Sino-Khmer named Thiounn, who was to play an important role in Cambodian politics until the 1940s.

The issue at stake in the rebellion, as Norodom's chronicle points out, was that the "Cambodian people were fond of their own leaders," especially because alternatives to them were so uncertain. A French writer in the 1930s blamed the French for their hastiness in trying to impose "equality, property, and an electorate,"[13] because Cambodians were supposed to choose their own village leaders under an article of the treaty. He added that, in fact, "the masters wanted to keep their slaves and the slaves their masters"; people clung to the patron-client system that had been in effect in Cambodia for centuries.

Faced with the possibility of a drawn-out war, the French stepped back from their proposed reforms. Although the treaty was ratified in 1886, most of its provisions did not come into effect for nearly twenty years, after Norodom was dead.

At the same time, it would be wrong to exaggerate this Cambodian victory or to agree with some Cambodian writers in the early 1970s who saw the rebellion as a watershed of Cambodian nationalism, with Norodom cast as a courageous patriot cleverly opposing French control. The evidence for these assertions is ambiguous. Norodom, after all, accepted French protection in a general way but attacked it when he thought his own interests, especially financial ones, were at stake. There is little evidence that he viewed his people as anything other than objects to consume, and certainly the French distrusted him more than ever after 1886. They spent the rest of his reign reducing his privileges and independence. But it would be incorrect to endow Norodom or the rebellious *okya* with systematic ideas about the Cambodian nation (as opposed to particular, personal relationships).

With hindsight we can perceive two important lessons of the rebellion. One was that the regional elite, despite French intervention in Cambodia, was still able to organize sizable and efficient guerrilla forces, as it had done against the Thai in 1834 and the Vietnamese in 1841; it was to do so again in the more peaceable 1916 Affair discussed in Chapter 9. The second lesson was that guerrilla troops, especially when supported by much of the population, could hold a colonial army at bay.

The next ten years of Norodom's reign saw an inexorable increase in French control, with policies changing "from ones of sentiment . . . to a more egotistic, more personal policy of colonial expansion."[14] All that stood in the way of the French was the fact that Norodom still made the laws, appointed the officials, and controlled the national economy by farming out sources of revenue (such as the opium monopoly and gambling concessions), by demanding gifts from his officials, and by refusing to pay his bills. By 1892, however, the collection of direct taxes had come under French control; two years later, there were ten French *résidences* in the *sruk*. The 1890s, in fact, saw increasing French consolidation throughout Indochina, culminating in the governor-generalship of Paul Doumer (1897–1902).

In Cambodia this consolidation involved tinkering with fiscal procedures and favoring Sisowath rather than any of Norodom's children as the successor to the throne. French officials wanted Norodom to relinquish control but were frightened by the independent-mindedness of many of his sons, one of whom was exiled to Algeria in 1893 for anti-colonial agitation. The king's health was poor in any case and was made worse by his addiction to opium, which the French provided him in ornamental boxes free of charge. As French officials grew more impatient with Norodom and as he weakened, they became abusive. After all, there were fortunes to be made by colonists in Cambodia, or so they thought, and Norodom barred the way. The climax came in 1897 when the *résident supérieur*, Huynh de Verneville, cabled Paris that the king was incapable of ruling the country. Verneville asked to be granted executive authority, and Paris concurred. The *résident* was now free to issue royal decrees, appoint officials, and collect indirect taxes. As Milton Osborne has pointed out, high-ranking Cambodian officials, previously dependent on Norodom's approval, were quick to sense a shift in the balance of power.[15] By the end of the year, the king's advice—even though he had now regained his seals and Verneville had been dismissed—was heeded only as a matter of form; the new *résident supérieur* was in command, answerable to authorities in Saigon, Paris, and Hanoi. What was now protected after a thirty-year tug-of-war between Norodom and the French, was not Cambodia, its monarch, or its people, but French colonial interests.

In the meantime, long-postponed royal decrees, such as one that allowed French citizens to purchase land, had produced a real estate boom in Phnom Penh. The effect of the reforms in the *sruk*, as far as we can tell, was less far-reaching. Throughout the 1890s, French *résidents* complained officially about torpor, corruption, and timidity among local officials, although one of the latter, sensing the tune he was now expected to play, reported to his French superiors that "the population of all the villages in my province is happy; [the people] have not even the slightest complaint about the measures that have been taken."[16] The Cambodian countryside, however, as many French officials complained, remained a terra incognita. No one knew how many people it contained, what they thought, or who held titles to land. Although slavery had been abolished, servitude for debts—often lasting a lifetime—remained widespread. Millenarian leaders occasionally gathered credulous followers and led them into revolt; in the dry season, gangs of bandits roamed the countryside at will. At the village level, in fact, conditions were probably no more secure than they had ever been.

And yet, many high-ranking French officials still saw their role in the country in terms of a civilizing mission and of rationalizing their relationships with the court. In the countryside, ironically, Sisowath was more popular than Norodom, partly because the people had seen him more often, on ceremonial occasions, and partly because Norodom's rule had been for the most part rapacious and unjust. Sisowath, in fact, looked on approvingly at developments in the 1890s, and by 1897 or so French officials had formally promised him the throne.

Norodom took seven more years to die. The last years of his reign were marked by a scandal involving his favorite son, Prince Yukanthor, who sought to publicize French injustice in Cambodia when he was in France by hiring a French journalist to press his case with French officialdom. Officials paid slight attention, except to take offense. Yukanthor's accusations were largely true, if perhaps too zealous and wide-ranging, as when he declared to the people of France, "You have created property in Cambodia, and thus you have created the poor."[17]

Officials in Paris persuaded Norodom by cable to demand an apology from his son. It never came, for Yukanthor preferred to remain in exile. He died in Bangkok in 1934 and until then was viewed by French colonial officials with slight but unjustified apprehension.

The two last prerogatives that Norodom surrendered to the French were the authority to select his close advisers and the right to farm out gambling concessions to Chinese businessmen in Phnom Penh. Little by little, the French reduced his freedom of action. Osborne has recorded the battles that Norodom lost, but the last pages of the royal chronicle (compiled during the reign of Sisowath's son, King Monivong, in the 1930s) say almost nothing about the confrontation, leaving the impression that the reign was moving peacefully and ceremoniously toward its close.

SISOWATH'S EARLY YEARS

Norodom, like millions of people of his generation, was born in a village and died in a semimodern city, graced at the time of his death with a certain amount of electricity and running water. The modernization of the edges and surfaces of his kingdom, however, spread very slowly. Communications inside Cambodia remained poor; monks, royalty, and officials—the people held in most respect—resisted institutional change; and the so-called modernizing segment of the society was dominated by the French, aided by immigrants from China and Vietnam. The modernizers, interestingly, thought in Indochinese terms, or perhaps in capitalist ones, while members of the traditional elite saw no reason to widen their intellectual horizons or to tinker with their beliefs.

Norodom's death, nonetheless, was a watershed in French involvement and in Cambodian kingship as an institution, as the French handpicked the next three kings of the country. Until 1953, except for a few months in the summer of 1945, high-ranking Cambodian officials played a subordinate, ceremonial role, and those at lower levels of the administration were underpaid servants of a colonial power. At no point in the chain of command was initiative rewarded. While Norodom lived, the French encountered obstacles to their plans. After 1904, with some exceptions, Cambodia became a relatively efficient revenue-producing machine.

The change over the long term, which is easy to see from our perspective, was not immediately perceptible in the *sruk*, where French officials found old habits of patronage, dependence, violence, fatalism, and corruption largely unchanged from year to year. Offices were still for sale, tax rolls were falsified, and rice harvests were underestimated. Credulous people were still ready to follow sorcerers and mountebanks. As late as 1923 in Stung Treng, an ex-monk gathered a following by claiming to possess a "golden frog with a human voice."[18] Banditry was widespread, and there were frequent famines and epidemics of malaria and cholera. The contrast between the capital and the *sruk*, therefore, sharpened in the early twentieth century, without apparently producing audible resentment in the *sruk*, even though peasants in the long run paid with their labor and their rice for all the improvements in Phnom Penh and for the high salaries enjoyed by French officials, fueling the resentment of anti-French guerrillas in the early 1950s and Communist cadres later on.

When Sisowath succeeded his brother in 1904 he was sixty-four years old. Ever since the 1870s he had been an assiduous collaborator with the French. He was a more fervent Buddhist than Norodom and he was more popular among ordinary people, some of whom associated him with the Buddhist ceremonies that he had sponsored (and that they had paid for) rather than the taxes charged by his brother or by the French. According to one French writer, he was so frightened of his brother, even in death, that he refused to attend his cremation. The first two years of his reign, according to the chronicle, were devoted largely to ceremonial observances and to bureaucratic innovations (such as appointing an electrician for the palace and enjoining officials to wear stockings and shoes in Western style).[19] On another occasion, Sisowath harangued visiting officials—probably at French insistence—about the persistence of slavery in the *sruk*.[20] Throughout the year, like all Cambodian kings, he sponsored ceremonies meant to ensure good harvests and rainfall. Each year for the rest of his reign, the French provided Sisowath (as they had Norodom) with an allowance of high-grade opium totaling 113 kilograms (249 pounds) per year.[21]

This early stage of his reign culminated in Norodom's cremation in 1906, which was followed almost immediately by Sisowath's coronation. For the first time in Cambodian history, the ceremony is described in detail in the chronicle (as well as by French sources). It lasted for several days. One of its interesting features was that the French governor-general of Indochina was entrusted with giving Sisowath his titles and handing him his regalia. Another was that the *chaovay sruk*, summoned to the palace for the occasion, solemnly pledged to the king "all rice lands, vegetable fields, water, earth, forest and mountains, and the sacred boundaries of the great city, the kingdom of Kampuchea."[22]

Almost immediately after being crowned, Sisowath left Cambodia to visit the Colonial Exhibition at Marseilles, in the company of the royal ballet troupe.[23] His voyage is scrupulously recorded in the chronicle, which makes it sound like an episode in a Cambodian poem, and also in the account of a palace official who accompanied the king. Sisowath's progress through Singapore, Ceylon, and the Indian Ocean is reverently set down in both texts, and so are gnomic comments about the sights farther on (three-story buildings in Italy, the coastline of the Red Sea consisting of "nothing but sand and rock"). At Port Said, people eagerly came to pay homage to "the lord of life and master of lives in the south." In Marseilles, when the king made a speech, "All the French people who were present clapped their hands—men and women alike." The chronicle and the official's somewhat overlapping account gives the impression that the king *decided* to visit France; in fact, his visit was forced on him by the requirement of the exposition officials that the royal ballet perform at the Colonial Exhibition.[24] From the French point of view, unofficially at least, this visit by an aged potentate and his harem told them what they already "knew" about his exotic, loyal, and faintly comic little country.[25]

After exchanging visits and dinners with the president of the republic, and a trip to Nancy to observe "the 14th of July in a European way," the king returned to Cambodia. Although neither the chronicle nor the palace official's narrative of the voyage mentions discussions of substantive matters, Sisowath's visit to Paris coincided with Franco-Thai negotiations there that culminated, a few months later, in Siam's retrocession to Cambodia of the *sruk* of Battambang and Siem Reap.[26] The trip received little publicity at home and is mentioned in French reports from the *sruk* only in connection with a rumor that Sisowath had gone to France to plead with the French to legalize gambling in Cambodia.

The number of pages in Sisowath's chronicle devoted to the return of Battambang and Siem Reap suggests that the compilers, like the French, considered this to be the most important event of the reign, even though the king had little to do with it beyond providing the *résident supérieur*, in 1906, with a history of Thai occupation. The importance of the retrocession was probably connected with the importance that Angkor, and especially Angkor Wat, had retained for the Cambodian monarchy for several centuries.[27] In 1909 a copy of the Cambodian translation of sacred Buddhist writings, the *Tripitaka*, was deposited in a monastery on the grounds of Angkor Wat, and for another sixty years Cambodian monarchs frequently visited the site and sponsored ceremonies there.

As we have seen, the northwestern *sruk* had come under Thai control in 1794, apparently in exchange for Thai permission for Eng, Sisowath's grandfather, to rule at Udong. Over the next hundred years, except for a brief period in the 1830s, the Thai made little effort to colonize (or depopulate) the region, choosing to govern it at most levels with ethnic Khmer. Although they did nothing to restore the temples at Angkor, they

Entrance to the Royal Palace in Phnom Penh. Photo by Roger Smith.

left them intact. Revenue from the two *sruk*—in stipulated amounts of cardamom and other forest products—was not especially high, and the region was more defensible by water from Phnom Penh than overland from Bangkok.[28]

For these reasons, but primarily to avoid further friction along its border, the Thai decided in 1906 to cede the *sruk* to France. The French and the Thai signed the final agreement in April 1907, and the *sruk* came under French control toward the end of the year. Sisowath was not encouraged to visit the area, however, until 1909, for reasons that the chronicle fails to make clear.

And yet the king and his subjects were overjoyed at the restoration of Angkor. In the *tang tok* ceremonies of October 1907, when officials traditionally offered gifts to the monarch, widely attended celebrations occurred throughout the kingdom to "thank the angels" (*thevoda*) for the return of the *sruk*, and local officials assigned to the region came to Phnom Penh to pay homage to the king.

Over the next half century, French scholars and Cambodian workers restored the temples at Angkor. In the long run the restoration was probably France's most valuable legacy to Cambodia. Battambang, especially in the 1920s, developed into the country's most prosperous *sruk,* providing the bulk of Cambodia's rice exports and sheltering, idiosyncratically, the greatest number of landlords in the country as well as the highest number of immigrants from elsewhere in Cambodia and from the Cambodian-speaking portions of Cochin China.[29]

By 1909, typewriters had been installed in all the *résidences;* automobiles came into use on a national scale at about the same time. These two improvements in French administration had several unintentional effects. For one thing, the volume of reports required by *résidents,* and consumed by their superiors in Phnom Penh, Saigon, Hanoi, and Paris, increased dramatically. *Résidents,* more than ever, were tied down to their offices, presiding over a two-way flow of paper. They were seldom in contact, socially or professionally, with the people they were paid to supposedly civilize and protect. In automobiles, tours of inspection became speedier and more superficial, for *résidents,* and their aides were confined to passable roads. In fact, the intensification of French economic and political controls over Cambodia, noticeable throughout the 1920s and after, was accompanied, ironically, by the withdrawal of French officials from many levels of Cambodian life. The government that a Cambodian peasant might encounter in these years was composed of a minority of Cambodians and of a great many Vietnamese brought into the protectorate because they could prepare reports in French, and this interplay between Cambodians and Vietnamese had important effects on the development of Cambodian nationalism, especially after World War II.

9

CAMBODIA'S RESPONSE TO FRANCE, 1916–45

Two events of political importance stand out in the last ten years or so of Sisowath's reign. These are the so-called 1916 Affair and the murder of a French *résident*, Félix Louis Bardez, in rural Kompong Chnang in 1925. The first of these revealed how little the French knew about communications and social organization in Cambodia after more than fifty years of being in control. The second, perhaps because it was the only incident of its kind in the colonial era, shocked the regime and was blown out of proportion in postcolonial times by Cambodian nationalist writers.

THE 1916 AFFAIR

To understand the 1916 Affair, we must remember that the French financed almost all of their activities in Cambodia, including public works and the salaries of French officials, by a complex and onerous network of taxes on salt, alcohol, opium, rice, and other crops, as well as on exported and imported goods, and by levying extensive fees for all government services. Of those too poor to buy their way out of corvée labor assignments the French could require ninety days of labor. The cash to pay rice taxes came only when peasant householders had sold their harvests for cash or had been able to earn enough cash to pay the taxes by hiring themselves out in the off-season. There was a certain amount of flexibility in the system because tax records were poorly kept and local leaders tended to underestimate the number of people they controlled in order to spread the tax burden more evenly through the population and to increase their own opportunities for profit.

During World War I, the French increased this burden throughout Indochina by floating war loans to which local people, especially the leisure classes (presumably Chinese merchants), were forcefully urged to subscribe; by levying additional taxes; and by recruiting volunteers for military service abroad. In late November 1915, some three hundred peasants from the area northeast of Phnom Penh arrived in the capital with a petition to Sisowath asking him to reduce the taxes that were levied by the French but collected by Cambodian officials. The king met the delegation and ordered its members to go home, promising vaguely that some adjustments would be made.[1]

News of the confrontation apparently spread in the *sruk* to the east of Phnom Penh—long a hotbed of antidynastic sentiment—and larger and larger delegations, sometimes numbering as many as three thousand peasants, began walking into the capital and assembling outside the palace to place their grievances before the king. French *résidents,* reporting on these movements, registered their surprise not only at the size of the delegations but also, as one wrote, at the fact that they had "been set in motion with such disconcerting speed." Another mentioned that no one had predicted the affair, although "the entire population was involved." French police estimated that some forty thousand peasants passed through Phnom Penh in the early months of 1916 before being ordered back to their villages by the king. Other estimates run as high as a hundred thousand. Scattered incidents in the *sruk* later in the year claimed a half-dozen Cambodian lives; at the same time, Sisowath toured the eastern *sruk* by automobile, exhorting peasants to remain peacefully in their homes and canceling any further corvée for 1916.

In the long run, the 1916 Affair had little effect on the way the French ran Cambodia or on Cambodian responses to the French. In fact, it is unclear that the demonstrations opposed the French protectorate at all; French administrators were sidestepped by the petitioners, who sought justice directly from the king. What is extraordinary about the demonstrations is the speed and efficiency with which they were organized by provincial leaders whose identity and motives remain obscure. The incident undermined French mythology about lazy and individualistic Cambodians, who were supposedly impervious to leadership or ideology. Some French officials, panicked by the size of the delegations, blamed the affair on "German agents." Others saw evidence of deep-seated antimonarchic feeling, citing a manifesto that had circulated earlier in 1915, stating that "the French have made us very unhappy for many years by keeping bad people as the king and as officials while treating good people as bad."[2]

Interestingly, the 1916 Affair coincided with serious anti-French demonstrations in Cochin China. The possibility of links between the two was noted by some French officials, but the speed with which Cambodian disaffection died down suggests that people there had been demonstrating to relieve local wrongs.

In the nine years that passed before the assassination of *résident* Bardez, the French tightened and rationalized their control over Cambodia—and especially over the organization of revenue collection and day-to-day administration—so much so that some "aged" Cambodian officials complained that "too many changes" were taking place. In 1920, for example, the French arranged for rice taxes to be collected by local officials rather than by officials sent to the *sruk* from Phnom Penh. A year later, the French experimented with a "communal" reorganization of Cambodia along Vietnamese lines, only to drop the idea after a year or so. The French extended their supervisory role to cover local justice in 1923, expanded *wat* education from 1924 onward, and used corvée to build an impressive array of public works, particularly roads and a mountain resort at Bokor favored by the king, which was built by prisoners (with a tremendous loss of life) and opened in 1925. The first rice mills had opened in Cambodia in 1917—previously, unmilled rice had been shipped to Saigon—and the 1916–25 period (with the noticeable exception of 1918–19, a year of very poor harvests and, in some *sruk*, famine conditions) was one of increasing prosperity in Cambodia, especially for local Chinese merchants and the French.[3]

The gap in income between the French and the Cambodians—with the rare exceptions of a few favored officials and the royal family—was very wide. A French official could earn as much as twelve thousand piastres a year. With exemptions for a wife and two children, such an official would pay only thirty piastres in tax. Cambodian officials were paid less for similar jobs and were the first to have their wages cut during the depression of the 1930s. A Cambodian farmer, on the other hand, with no salary other than what he could earn (at thirty cents per day, or ninety piastres a year) or what he could sell his crops for (seldom more than forty piastres a year), was saddled with a range of taxes that totaled in the 1920s as much as twelve piastres per year. He was taxed individually and in cash payment in lieu of corvée, his rice was taxed at a fixed percentage, and he paid high prices for salt, opium, and alcohol and abattoir taxes when his livestock went to slaughter.

What did the peasant receive in exchange? Very little, despite French rhetoric to the contrary. Monthly reports from French *résidents* show that widespread rural violence and disorder, which made no direct challenge to French control, seldom rose into the political portions of the reports. It is clear, however, that to most villagers the perpetual harassment of bandit gangs, especially in the dry season, was far more real than any benefits brought to them by the French.[4]

Before the 1930s the French spent almost nothing on Cambodian education. A French official in 1922 accurately characterized efforts in this field as a mere façade. Medical services were also derisory, and electricity and running water were almost unknown outside Phnom Penh. Cambodia's money, in other words, went to finance French officials and the things they wanted to build. In exchange, Cambodia was protected from control by anyone else, as well as from the perils of independence. The French succeeded in keeping the nineteenth century from repeating itself while keeping the twentieth century at bay. The fear of modernity runs through a good deal of French writing about colonial Cambodia, even though the French in another context perceived their role as one of transmitting modernity to the Khmer. Because what they were supposed to be doing was not allowed to take place, the French took refuge in beliefs about the purportedly innate characteristics of the Cambodians, which supposedly kept them immune from modern ideas.

These beliefs were based less and less on direct experience with the Cambodians themselves. The most articulate critic of French colonialism at this time, the medical official André Pannetier, remarked that competence among Frenchmen in the Khmer language declined steadily as the twentieth century wore on.[5] Ironically, as the adventure and romance of serving in Cambodia wore thin, the clichés with which French bureaucrats described the Cambodian people became increasingly fuzzy and romantic. The process came to a climax of sorts in 1927, when former Governor-General Paul Doumer, by then president of France, unveiled a group of statues on the staircase that links the railroad station in Marseilles with the city below. One of these, entitled "Our Possessions in Asia," depicts a half-naked teenaged girl decked out in approximately Angkorean garb, lying on a divan and being waited on by smaller half-clad girls representing Laos and Vietnam. Considered the easiest and oldest of French protectorates in Indochina, Cambodia was rewarded by being portrayed as the oldest child and as receiving tribute of a kind from the other two. The notion that Cambodians lay around receiving tidbits, of course, may also have been at the back of the sculptor's mind.[6]

THE ASSASSINATION OF *RÉSIDENT* BARDEZ

In late 1923 the acting French *résident* in Prey Veng, a vigorous and ambitious official named Félix Louis Bardez, reported his belief that there were three reasons why tax receipts were so low: "the complete inactivity of Cambodian officials, the lack of supervision [over the officers expected to collect the taxes], and shortcomings in collection procedures."[7] During the course of 1924, Bardez improved the procedures for tax collection in the *sruk* to the extent that all eighteen categories of tax yielded more revenues than in 1923. He showed that the system could be made more productive by working harder himself. Indeed, the two categories of tax in which revenues rose the most—rice taxes and Chinese head taxes—were precisely those that could be increased on the spot by a vigorous *résident* eager to expose the compromises, doctored books, and exaggerations of local officials.

Bardez's success in Prey Veng attracted the attention of his superiors, and in late 1924 he was transferred ahead of many more senior officials to be *résident* in Kompong Chhnang, which had long been bedeviled by banditry and low tax revenues. Bardez's arrival coincided roughly with the promulgation of a supplementary tax to pay for the mountain resort of Bokor, but money was hard to come by, as Bardez admitted to a friend, and receipts from Cambodian officials were slow in coming. One official trying to collect the new taxes was severely beaten by villagers in the district in early 1925.

On April 18, angered by reports that another village, Krang Laav, was delinquent in its payments, Bardez visited the village himself, accompanied by an interpreter and a Cambodian militiaman.[8] Summoning delinquent taxpayers to the village hall, or *sala*, he had several of them handcuffed and he threatened to take them to prison, even though they would not be subject to fines for their delinquency for three months. His refusal to let the prisoners have lunch while he himself was eating destroyed the patience of the crowd of people looking on, who lacked food or shelter. In a confused mêlée, Bardez and his companions were set upon by twenty or thirty people. Within half an hour, Bardez, the interpreter, and the militiaman had been beaten to death with chairs, fence palings, ax handles, and the militiaman's rifle butt. The corpses were then mutilated; according to some witnesses, the murderers danced around them. Soon afterward, incited by local leaders who were never brought to trial, seven hundred Cambodians—the crowd that had gathered to listen to Bardez—began marching on Kompong Chhnang to demand remission of their taxes. After a few hours, however, their fervor died down, and the marchers broke up or were dispersed by an armed militia before they reached their destination.

News of Bardez's murder shocked the French community in Phnom Penh, largely because it was the first time villagers had killed a high-ranking French official on duty. Officials had been killed by bandits or by their servants, but none while collecting taxes. The precedent obviously was a dramatic one. Moving swiftly through their protégés in the royal family, the French saw to it that Sisowath sent his eldest son, Prince Monivong, to the area with a French political counselor to communicate his discontent. This took the form of a royal ordinance changing the name of the village from Krang Laav to Direchhan ("Bestiality").[9] The ordinance forced the villagers to conduct expiatory services for Bardez on the anniversary of his murder for the next ten years. A key feature of the ordinance was its insistence on collective guilt. This was the line pursued by the defense in the trial of the eighteen men arrested for Bardez's murder, but it was dismissed by the prosecution, which saw danger in linking the murder with any kind of political discontent. Interestingly, one of the men arrested for the murder was still alive in 1980, when he told an interviewer that "everyone in the village" had beaten Bardez and his companions.[10]

The trial of the men accused of the murders opened in Phnom Penh in December 1925 and was widely reported in the press, which fitted the case into a pattern of increasing anticolonial feeling elsewhere in Indochina. At the trial the prosecution tried to prove that the defendants were pirates from outside the village and that robbery had been their motive. In fact, although the taxes collected by Bardez disappeared in the mêlée, his own billfold was untouched. More to the point, his diary was confiscated by the prosecution and classified as confidential because of the "political" material it contained. Testimony by several of Bardez's friends suggested that the diary may have recorded his pessimism about collecting extra taxes. To one of them he had remarked shortly before his death that there was simply not enough money in the *sruk* to meet the newly imposed demands. High-ranking French officials interfered with witnesses for the defense. At one point, the defense attorney's tea was apparently poisoned by unknown hands, and a stenographer hired by the defense was forced by her former employers to return to her job in Saigon. What the French wanted to keep quiet, it seems, was the fact that emerged at the trial—on a per capita basis the Cambodian peasants paid the highest taxes in Indochina as a price for their docility.

The Bardez incident resembles the 1916 Affair and the 1942 monks demonstration, discussed below, in that nothing like it had happened previously in the colonial era. It exposed the mechanics of colonial rule and the unreality of French mythology about the Cambodian character. One aspect of the widening distance between the French and the Cambodians was the fact that Bardez, after fifteen years of conscientious service in Cambodia, was still unable to speak Khmer. Without knowing the language, how accurate could his assessments be of what ordinary people were thinking? It is as if a great deal of Cambodian life in the colonial period was carried out behind a screen, invisible and inaudible to the French. Another French *résident,* writing at about this time, made a perceptive comment in this regard: "It's permissible to ask if the unvarying calm which the [Cambodian] people continue to exhibit is not merely an external appearance, covering up vague, *unexpressed feelings* [emphasis added] . . . whose exact nature we cannot perceive."[11]

Résidents might justify their conduct by saying that they were paid to administer the population, not to understand it. Every month they were required to complete mountains of paperwork, to sit for days as referees in often inconclusive legal cases, and to supervise the extensive programs of public works, primarily roads, which the French used to perpetuate corvée, to modernize Cambodia, and to justify their presence in the kingdom.

THE BEGINNINGS OF NATIONALISM

The Bardez incident also offers us a glimpse of Cambodian peasants entering the historical record. Before 1927, in fact, there were no Khmer-language newspapers or journals in the kingdom, and Cambodian literature, when it was printed at all, consisted almost entirely of Buddhist texts and nineteenth-century verse epics. The first novel in Khmer, *Tonle Sap*, was published in 1938, two years after the appearance of the first Khmer newspaper, *Nagara Vatta* ("Angkor Wat").[12] Although these facts are not especially surprising in view of French inactivity in Cambodian education, they contrast sharply with the quantity of printed material produced in the Vietnamese components of Indochina. Literacy in Cambodia had been linked since Angkorean times with the study and promulgation of religious texts. In the colonial era, literacy in Khmer was almost entirely in the hands of the Buddhist monkhood. Before 1936, in fact, the only Khmer-language periodical, *Kambuja Surya* ("Cambodian Sun"), had been published on a monthly basis under the auspices of the French-funded Institut Bouddhique. With rare exceptions, the journal limited itself to printing folklore, Buddhist texts, and material concerned with the royal family. Even Cambodian chronicle histories in Khmer were not yet available in print.[13]

Because of these conditions, the picture that emerges from the 1930s is a peculiarly unbalanced one. The reading of French novels, official reports, and newspapers allows us to reconstruct Cambodian history with much of the population left out or merely acted upon by events. The manuscript chronicles of King Sisowath and his son, King Sisowath Monivong (r. 1927–41), are not especially helpful, for they limit themselves to a formulaic narration of events in which the king himself was involved, although Monivong's chronicle opens up a little to cover such events as the 1932 coup d'état in Siam, the Italo-Ethiopian war, and the French surrender to Germany in 1940. The requirements of the genre removed individual voices from the texts; even the kings are rarely quoted.[14] Because archival sources from the *sruk* themselves for the colonial era are not available for study, it is difficult to gauge the style and extent of social change and intellectual upheaval, the extent to which they can be traced to French initiatives, and Cambodian responses to them in the period before World War II. Arguably, modernizing change in Cambodia did not filter into the villages until the 1950s; yet the face of Cambodia was already very different in the 1930s from what it had been when the French arrived or even at the beginning of the century.

Overland communications had changed dramatically. From 1900 to 1930, some nine thousand kilometers (5,400 miles) of paved and graveled roads had been built by corvée throughout the kingdom. Between 1928 and 1932, moreover, a 500-kilometer (300-mile) stretch of railroad was built between Phnom Penh and Battambang, and it was later extended to the Thai border. These changes meant that thousands of rural Cambodians were now able to move rapidly around the country by bus, and visits to Phnom Penh and district capitals became easier and more frequent. These developments also favored French penetration and Chinese exploitation of the rural economy. The commercial development of Cambodia—especially in terms of rice exports and rubber plantations—benefited the French, the Chinese entrepreneurs who monopolized the export trade, and to a lesser extent the Vietnamese laborers who worked the rubber plantations. William E. Willmott has shown that Chinese immigration into Cambodia, which remained steady at around two thousand a year until the 1920s, rose to five thousand a year during the boom years.[15] The Chinese population of the kingdom rose accordingly—from perhaps one hundred seventy thousand in 1905 to three hundred thousand at the beginning of World War

II. Almost invariably, these immigrants went into petty commerce, already dominated by Chinese and Sino-Cambodians. Because many Vietnamese immigrants to Cambodia, aside from those recruited for the plantations, also preferred urban employment, cities in Cambodia, as so often in colonial Southeast Asia, became enclaves dominated by foreign bureaucrats, immigrants, and entrepreneurs. This fact was not lost on the Cambodian elite, but the elite was unable or unwilling to do anything about it.

And the elite itself, although relatively small, was gradually increasing in importance. An interesting coincidence occurred in 1930. As the first stretch of track on the railroad went into service, the first Cambodian students, including two princes and four men destined to be ministers in the 1940s and 1950s, graduated from a French lycée in Saigon. Cambodia had to wait until 1936 for a lycée of its own, which was named after Sisowath and occupied the site of his former palace. Primary education, for the most part, remained in the hands of the *sangha*, and the French sponsored, at very little cost, a network of some five thousand extant *wat* schools in which students learned traditional subjects in time-honored ways.[16]

These developments took place in the context of the economic boom that affected most of Indochina in the 1920s. In Cambodia the greatest beneficiaries were the firms engaged in the export of rice and in the newly opened rubber plantations near Kompong Cham. The plantations had little economic impact on the Cambodian countryside, but rice production rose sharply to meet international demands, and new funds generated by the widening tax base were diverted into even more extensive public works, including the beautification of Phnom Penh, the electrification of provincial towns, the road-building mentioned above, and the construction of seaside resorts and mountain hotels, which benefited the French and the embryonic tourist industry. Under such conditions the Bardez incident barely ruffled the surface of French complacency.

The world Depression of the 1930s, however, reversed or suspended many of these trends, as the local price of rice plummeted from three piastres to one piastre a *picul* (about 68 kilograms, or 150 pounds). The Cambodian peasants' reaction, insofar as it can be gauged from *résidents'* reports, was to reduce rice hectarage (which dropped by a third throughout the country from 1928 to 1933), to seek postponement or remission of taxes, and to find solace in some areas in millenarian religious cults, such as the recently inaugurated syncretic cult of Cao Dai in neighboring Cochin China.[17]

The period was marked by several uprisings against the French in the Vietnamese components of Indochina, but Cambodia remained quiet. In their reports, French *résidents* frequently complimented the Cambodian peasants for the "stoicism" with which they continued to react to the highest and most variegated tax burden in Indochina. One of them traced this obedience to the Cambodians' "reverence for authority." Nonetheless, the level of rural violence—with Khmer victimizing Khmer—appears to have risen slightly only to decline when the economic crisis faded in the mid-1930s. Tax delinquency in rural areas reached 45 percent in 1931 and more than 60 percent in the following year, when remissions were granted by the *résident supérieur*. As most Cambodians reverted to subsistence farming, Phnom Penh's population, unsurprisingly, rose only slightly—from ninety-six thousand in 1931 to barely one hundred thousand in 1936. Throughout this period, and indeed until the 1970s, the capital was informally divided into three residential zones, with Vietnamese and Cham to the north, Chinese and French in the commercial center, and Cambodians to the south and west of the royal palace, which faced the Mekong River.

In an effort to increase tax revenue, in 1931 the French encouraged King Monivong, who had succeeded his father five years earlier, to tour the *sruk,* where he admonished audiences supplied by local officials on the virtues of frugality and hard work. The king himself continued to live well, and his grandson, Norodom Sihanouk, later recalled that Monivong spent very little of his time attending to official business, preferring the company of his numerous wives and concubines.[18] One of his favorites was an elder sister of Saloth Sar, the man who was to emerge in the 1970s as Pol Pot, the secretary of the Cambodian Communist Party. In the midst of the Depression, the French built several new palace buildings for Monivong. In 1932 he entertained the French minister of colonies, Paul Reynaud, who had come to Indochina to investigate the effects of the Vietnamese uprisings of the previous year. In Cambodia the visit was entirely ceremonial and stage-managed by the powerful

Cambodian official Thiounn, who by now held the portfolios of finance, palace affairs, and fine arts. He had more or less governed the country under the French since the beginning of Sisowath's reign. Ironically, three of his highly educated grandsons were to become prominent members of the Cambodian Communist Party.

When the economy of Indochina recovered slowly in the mid-1930s, rice exports, particularly from Battambang, reached one hundred thousand metric tons a year, and new crops—especially maize—were grown in large quantities for export. Administratively, the last part of the decade saw increased Cambodian participation in administration, especially in the *sruk,* where many who became officials of independent Cambodia—including Nhek Tioulong, Lon Nol, and Sisowath Sirik Matak—were beginning their careers. In political terms the French were pleased to notice that disturbances in Cochin China, arising in part from conflicts between Trotskyite and Communist supporters of the Popular Front government in France, aroused no echoes in Cambodia, where a late but well-mannered "awakening" was the subject of a tendentious French brochure published on the occasion of a governor-general's visit in 1935.[19] By the word *awakening* the French meant economic advances and administrative participation by the Khmer rather than any increased autonomy or a sharpened awareness of the colonial situation. The roots of postwar Cambodian nationalism, nonetheless, can be found in the 1930s, at first in a cooperative and well-mannered guise, while the French were looking in vain for the sorts of revolutionary politics and violence that they were encountering at the time in Vietnam. Confidential French political reports throughout the decade registered "none" under the obligatory rubric of revolutionary activities, and latter-day Cambodian historians looking for the roots of the Cambodian Communist movement cannot find them in this period.[20]

And yet, an awakening of a sort *was* taking place, primarily among the Cambodian elite in Phnom Penh and especially among those educated at the kingdom's first high school, the Collège (and, after 1936, the Lycée) Sisowath, where the curriculum was entirely in French. Earlier in the decade, students at the collège had appealed to the king against the favoritism allegedly shown to students of Vietnamese heritage. By 1937 an association of graduates had more than five hundred members.

This association was the first of its kind in Cambodia, where voluntary associations along professional lines had always been slow to develop and had been discouraged by the French. For years the French had lamented the Cambodian aversion to solidarity while opposing any Cambodian attempts—by veterans of World War I, for example, or by adherents of the Cao Dai—to form associations. The fear of solidarity, in fact, appears to have dominated the French reaction to the Bardez affair, as we have seen. For administrative purposes the French preferred to deal with a society that was, theoretically at least, arranged vertically rather than horizontally. A similarly bureaucratic turn of mind, perhaps, made many French officials suspicious of new developments in the countryside—whether they were sponsored by Protestant missionaries, the Cao Dai, or any other external agent—while doing little themselves to change the status quo, characterized by widespread poverty, poor health, and no modern education.

The three key channels for Cambodian self-awareness in the 1930s, in fact, were the Lycée Sisowath, the Institut Bouddhique, and the newspaper *Nagara Vatta*, founded in 1936 by Pach Chhoeun and Sim Var. Both men, in their thirties, were soon joined by a young Cambodian judge, born in Vietnam and educated in France, named Son Ngoc Thanh.[21] The three, in turn, were closely associated with the Institut Bouddhique, to which Son Ngoc Thanh was later assigned as a librarian. This brought them into contact with the leaders of the Cambodian *sangha*, with Cambodian intellectuals, and also with a small group of French scholars and officials led by the imaginative and energetic secretary of the institute, Suzanne Karpelès, who were eager to help with Cambodia's intellectual renaissance.

The editorial stand of *Nagara Vatta* was pro-Cambodian without being anti-French. It objected to Vietnamese domination of the Cambodian civil service, Chinese domination of commerce, and the shortage of suitable employment for educated Khmer. Editorials also condemned the usury of Chinese rural merchants, French delays in modernizing the educational system, the shortage of credit for Cambodian farmers, and the low pay of Cambodian civil servants. The paper also sought to increase the distance between Cambodian history and aspirations on the one hand and those of the Vietnamese on the other. One editorial even went so far as to compare Hitler's territorial aggrandizement in Europe to that of Vietnam in nineteenth-century Cambodia. A thread of anti-Vietnamese feeling gradually emerged in the paper, a feeling that was to run through the ideology of every Cambodian government after independence until the Vietnamese invasion of 1978–79.

But in terms of its own historical context, what was important about *Nagara Vatta* was that for the first time since 1863 a conversation had opened up between the French and their allegedly dormant clientele, as well as among the Cambodian elite. The paper's circulation as early as 1937 rose to more than five thousand copies. Readership was undoubtedly far higher.

Who were its readers? Who were the new elite? Primarily, they seem to have been young Cambodian men in the lower ranks of the civil service, educated at least partially in the French educational system. Undoubtedly, they were concentrated in Phnom Penh. In his memoirs of this period, Bunchhan Muul, by the 1970s a high official in the ill-fated Khmer Republic, wrote that the paper saw as its mission the awakening of the Cambodian people—an image that persisted into the 1950s, when Son Ngoc Thanh returned from exile and founded another nationalist paper entitled *Khmer Krok* ("Cambodians Awake"). The *Nagara Vatta* was important because it gave thousands of Cambodians a chance for the first time to read about events in the outside world in their own language.

Nevertheless, the emerging Cambodian elite defined in terms of educational qualifications was very small. By 1939 the number of *bacheliers* graduated from the Lycée Sisowath was barely half a dozen, and perhaps a dozen Cambodians had been trained in tertiary institutions abroad. The gap between political awareness and technical proficiency, which persisted into the postcolonial period, can be blamed initially on French inertia in the field of indigenous education, itself traceable to French unwillingness to pay the bills.

Before the fall of France in June 1940, none of the officials in Indochina had openly voiced doubts about the permanence of the French presence in Asia. There were no moves in Cambodia, for example, to widen the electorate, to introduce representative government on anything other than a consultative basis, or to train Cambodians in a systematic way to replace Frenchmen in the administration. In the *sruk*, however, some devolution took place in the 1930s whereby experienced and senior local officials, rather than Frenchmen, were allowed to prepare local budgets and write periodic reports.[22] The sense of irony among French officials, it seems, was not highly developed. In 1939, elaborate ceremonies were sponsored in Phnom Penh to honor the 150th anniversary of the French Revolution, and the venue was the Place de la République.[23]

THE IMPACT OF WORLD WAR II

World War II—more precisely the period between June 1940 and October 1945—must be seen as a watershed in the history of Indochina. This is particularly true of Vietnam, but French policies in Cambodia, springing from weakness, and Cambodian responses to them differed sharply from what had gone before. By the end of 1945, Cambodian independence, impracticable and almost inconceivable in 1939, had become primarily a matter of time.

Much the same state of affairs applied throughout Southeast Asia and particularly in Burma and the Netherlands East Indies (now Indonesia). The development of nationalism in Indochina differed in that France was the only colonial power in the region to retain day-to-day control of its possessions for the greater part of World War II. The French managed to do so by making substantial concessions to the Japanese. Elsewhere in Southeast Asia between 1942 and 1945, the Japanese jailed colonial officials and ruled through local leaders, usually recruited from the ranks of opponents of colonial rule. In Indochina, on the other hand, the French sought to defuse nationalist thinking and activity by maintaining secret police surveillance, by opening up their administration to local people, and by liberalizing some of their policies. In the Cambodian case it can be argued that this liberalization, and several events associated with it, gave birth to elite Cambodian nationalism in the form it assumed until the 1970s.[24]

Phnom Penh, aerial view, 1970. Courtesy of Khmer Republic
Ministry of Information.

Five of these events are worth examining in detail: the Franco-
Siamese war of 1940–41; the coronation of Monivong's grandson,
Norodom Sihanouk, in 1941; the so-called monks demonstration of
July 1942; the Romanization crisis of the following year; and finally, the
Japanese *coup de force* of March 9, 1945, that dismantled French con-
trol throughout Indochina.

These events were played out against the background of Vichy rule in
Indochina, from July 1940 to March 1945, in the hands of Vice-Admiral
Jean Decoux.[25] Vichy rule in some ways was more flexible, in others
more repressive and certainly more ideological than the governments
provided by the Third Republic had ever been. This was partly because
officials, to appease the Japanese and following ideological preferences
of their own, tended to follow a pro-Axis, anti-British line and partly
because, perceiving their vulnerability in Southeast Asia, they sought to
retain control while using very little of their depleted military forces.

Examples of their flexibility in Cambodia included raising the salaries
and widening the responsibilities of indigenous officials; encouraging an

enhanced sense of national identity linked to an idealization of the Angkorean era and of Jayavarman VII in particular; and organizing paramilitary youth groups along Vichy lines. These groups gave thousands of young Cambodians their first taste, outside the *sangha,* of membership in an extrafamilial group.

The regime was repressive as well. In late 1940 elected bodies (of some importance in southern Vietnam especially) were abolished throughout Indochina. After the monks' demonstration, *Nagara Vatta* ceased publication in 1942, and more than thirty Cambodians were imprisoned for long terms following that demonstration. These moves had their greatest impact on the people who were to lead Cambodia's nationalist movement in the 1940s and 1950s. They had little effect in the countryside as far as we can tell.

What the French were trying to do in France and in Indochina in these years was to endure the war. They hoped to reemerge even after an Axis victory with some identity and much of the French empire intact. In Cambodia and Vietnam, part of the process involved harking back to better days and to warlike heroes and heroines like Joan of Arc, the Trung sisters, and Jayavarman VII. In Cambodia the French chose to work through the institutions of the monarchy, whereas those who opposed them became in the course of the war increasingly antimonarchic, setting the stage for factions that have endured in Cambodian politics ever since.

The Franco-Thai war broke out in late 1940 because the pro-Japanese Thai government of Phibul Songgram, aware of French military weakness, seized the opportunity to seek to regain territories in Cambodia and Laos that the Thai had ceded earlier in the century to the French. These actions fit their irredentist nationalism of the period. On land, poorly equipped French forces suffered a series of defeats. At sea, however, French aircraft and warships scored a major victory over the Thai fleet in January 1941.[26] Frightened by the possibility of further embarrassments to the Thai, the Japanese forced the French to negotiate in Tokyo. The upshot of these negotiations was that Battambang, most of Siem Reap, and parts of Laos—a total of slightly more than sixty-five thousand square kilometers (twenty-five thousand square miles)—were ceded to the Thai for the derisory sum of six million piastres.[27] The

French managed to retain Angkor for their Cambodian protégés, but the humiliating loss of territory so embittered King Monivong that for the remaining months of his life (he died in April 1941) he refused to meet with French officials or to converse with anyone in French.

Monivong's death posed a problem for French officials concerned with the possibility, however faint, of dynastic squabbling so soon after their military defeat.[28] Throughout the 1930s, Monivong's son, Prince Monireth (1909–75), had been favored for the throne although French officials had also proposed the candidacy of Prince Norodom Suramarit, a grandson of Norodom's who was married to Monivong's daughter. Rivalry between Norodom and Sisowath's descendants had surfaced occasionally in the colonial era, largely because many members of the royal family had little to do besides quarrel with each other. In the aftermath of the war with Thailand, the French governor-general, Jean Decoux, favored the selection of Suramarit's son, Norodom Sihanouk (b. 1922), then a student at a French lycée in Saigon. His ostensible rationale for preferring Sihanouk to Monireth was the need to heal the rift between the Norodom and Sisowath branches of the family. It is also likely that, of the two candidates, Sihanouk seemed more malleable and less independent.

The shy young man who came to the throne in April 1941 and was crowned in October seemed an unlikely candidate to dominate Cambodian politics for over sixty years. He was an only child whose parents were estranged; in his memoirs he has recalled his lonely, introverted childhood.[29] Although an excellent student and a good musician, he had received no training for the throne, and for the first few years of his reign he worked closely with his French advisers.

When he started out, Sihanouk made modest efforts at reform to bolster his image with the Cambodian people and to compensate for the reclusiveness of his grandfather's last months. The annual gift of opium from the French to the king was canceled, Palace Minister Thiounn was encouraged to retire, and the prince became active in Vichy-oriented youth groups.[30] His freedom of action was limited not only by French advisers but also by the fact that by August 1941 eight thousand Japanese troops had been posted to Cambodia. No one knew what the Japanese intended.

French military weakness and Japanese sympathy for certain anti-colonial movements evident throughout Southeast Asia by 1942 had not passed unnoticed among the intellectuals—many of the members of the *sangha*—who were associated with *Nagara Vatta* and the Institut Bouddhique. Between 1940 and 1942, the paper took an increasingly pro-Japanese, anticolonial line. During these years, at least thirty-two issues of the paper were censored by the French, and in ten issues the lead editorial was suppressed. Perhaps in some cases the censorship involved overreaction on the part of the French. Nothing has yet been published about Japanese financial support for the Cambodian nationalists at this early stage, but some collaboration can be assumed and was actively sought by Son Ngoc Thanh and his associates. The climax of the confrontation between this group of Cambodians and the French occurred in July 1942 in the monks demonstration.[31]

Throughout the twentieth century the French had looked somewhat warily at the Buddhist *sangha* in both Cambodia and Laos, noticing that it offered the Lao and Khmer an alternative value system to the colonial one. In Cambodia as in Thailand, the *sangha* was made up of two sects, the larger known as the Mahanikay and the smaller, which enjoyed royal patronage, as the Thammayut. Jurisdictional quarrels between the two, which differed on no doctrinal matters but on several procedural ones, were frequent, and because of the Thammayut's palace and elite connections, monks with antimonarchic ideas tended to gravitate to the Mahanikay.

One of these monks, Hem Chieu (1898–1943), a teacher at the advanced Pali school in Phnom Penh, was implicated in an anti-French plot when he proposed to several members of the Cambodian militia vague plans for a coup. A pro-French militiaman apparently informed on him, and he was arrested with a fellow monk on July 17, 1942. Hem Chieu was an important member of the *sangha,* and the manner of his arrest—by civil authorities who failed to allow him the ritual of leaving the monastic order—affronted his religious colleagues while handing nationalists of the *Nagara Vatta* clique a cause célèbre. Over the next three days, the nationalists engaged in secret conversations with the Japanese, seeking their cooperation in sponsoring an anti-French demonstration in support of the arrested monks. According to Son Ngoc

Thanh, Japanese authorities in Saigon (who had jurisdiction over their colleagues in Phnom Penh) agreed in some fashion to sponsor the Cambodian rally planned for July 20.[32]

On that morning more than a thousand people, perhaps half of them monks, marched along Phnom Penh's principal boulevard to the office of the French *résident supérieur,* Jean de Lens, demanding Hem Chieu's release. The demonstrators were trailed by French, Cambodian, and Vietnamese police agents who took photographs of them. The editor of *Nagara Vatta,* Pach Chhoeun, enthusiastically led the march and was arrested as he presented a petition to a French official inside the *résidence.* Along with other civilian demonstrators rounded up over the next few days, Chhoeun was quickly tried. The sentence of death imposed on him was commuted to life imprisonment by the Vichy government—the same sentence meted out to the murderers of Bardez seventeen years before. Son Ngoc Thanh, who later admitted his involvement in planning the demonstration, apparently hid in Phnom Penh for several days before escaping to the Thai-controlled city of Battambang. By early 1943 he had been offered asylum in Tokyo, where he remained for the next two years, writing forlorn, infrequent letters to nationalist colleagues in Battambang, pleading that they keep the nationalist flame alive and assuring them of continued discreet Japanese cooperation.

The collapse of the demonstration suggests that Thanh and his colleagues overestimated Japanese support and underestimated French severity. The French, in any case, were eager to demonstrate that they remained in charge. The march and Hem Chieu's name, like the 1916 Affair and the Bardez incident, passed into Cambodian anticolonial folklore, resurfacing in 1945 during the anti-French resistance and again, among different groups, following the anti-Sihanouk coup of 1970. In 1979 after the Vietnamese invasion, a boulevard in Phnom Penh, formerly named after King Monivong, was renamed in Hem Chieu's honor. The earlier name was restored in 1992. The ex-monk had died of illness on the French penal island of Poulo Condore in 1943.[33] In the short term the demonstration accomplished nothing, and Sihanouk in his memoirs dismissed it as "tragicomic." At the time, he apparently accepted the view of his French advisers that it was foolish and unjustified.

THE GROWTH OF NATIONALISM AND THE RETURN OF THE FRENCH

The remaining three years of World War II are important for Cambodian history, but they are difficult to study. French archives for the period remain closed for the most part, and the French-controlled press for the period, like Sihanouk's unpublished chronicle, is largely ceremonial and bureaucratic in emphasis. Nationalists fell silent, fled to Battambang, or spent the years in prison. For these reasons the so-called romanization crisis of 1943 is difficult to assess.

In 1943 the new French *résident*, Georges Gautier, announced his intention to replace Cambodia's forty-seven-letter alphabet, derived from medieval Indian models, with the roman one. The transliteration was worked out by the renowned philologist George Coedes; available samples show that the system retained the phonetics of spoken Khmer quite well. Gautier and his colleagues viewed the reform as a step toward modernization, which in turn was seen unequivocally as a good thing. In a pamphlet devoted to explaining the reform, Gautier attacked the "Cambodian attitude to the world" as "out of date" (*démodée*) and compared the Cambodian language to a "badly tailored suit."[34] The addition of a supposedly more rational French vocabulary to romanized Khmer, Gautier thought, would somehow improve Cambodian thought processes. Citing the example of romanization in Turkey, while remaining diplomatically silent about the romanization of Vietnamese, Gautier seems to have believed that the virtues of the reform were as self-evident as what he thought of as the primitiveness of the Cambodian mind.

Many Cambodians, however, and especially those in the *sangha*, saw the reform as an attack on traditional learning and on the high status enjoyed by traditional educators in Cambodian society. Cambodians in civil life were less affronted by the reform, although Sihanouk has claimed that he was on the point of abdicating over the issue. Despite these objections, the reform was pushed vigorously by the French in 1944–45, especially in government publications and in schools; the romanization decree did not apply to religious texts. Nonetheless, when the French were pushed aside by the Japanese in March 1945, one of the first actions of the newly independent Cambodian government was to rescind romanization; since then, no attempt has been made by any Cambodian government to romanize the language.[35] Once again, as was so often true in Cambodian history, what the French saw as a self-evident improvement in the status quo was seen by the Cambodians as an attack on the essential character of their civilization, defined in part as what Cambodians believed had been passed down from Angkorean times. Indeed, the decree abrogating the reform mentioned that for Cambodia to adopt the roman alphabet would mean the society would become "a society without history, without value, without mores, and without traditions."[36]

On March 9, 1945, romanization became, literally, a dead letter when the Japanese throughout Indochina disarmed French forces and removed French officials from their posts. The move was intended to forestall French armed resistance; it also fit into Japanese plans to equip local forces throughout Southeast Asia to resist the Allied landings that were expected later in the year. On March 13, in response to a formal Japanese request, King Sihanouk declared that Cambodia was independent and changed its name in French from Cambodge to Kampuchea, the Khmer pronunciation of the word.[37] Sihanouk's decree invalidated Franco-Cambodian agreements, declared Cambodia's independence, and pledged Cambodia's cooperation with the Japanese.

Two weeks after this declaration, Vietnamese residents of the city rioted against the French, on the basis of a rumor that the French intended to kill, or at least imprison, all Vietnamese residents in France. Disturbed by the violence of these demonstrations, the Japanese intervened on the side of the French, whom they herded into protective custody for the remainder of the war. In early April, speaking to the newly reinforced Cambodian militia, Sihanouk condemned French forces, which had been unwilling to help Japan defend Cambodia against an unspecified enemy. He urged Cambodians to "awaken." It is likely that the speech reflected the views of a Japanese political adviser, Lieutenant Tadakame, who was assigned to the palace at about this time.[38]

Other steps toward independence taken in this period included reinstituting the Buddhist lunar calendar at the expense of the Gregorian one and using Khmer instead of French to identify government ministries. Independence, of course, was relative; the Japanese remained in

Cambodia in force. At the same time, the summer of 1945—like the months of March 1970 and April 1975 in certain ways—allowed a clique of Cambodian intellectuals to interpose themselves between the monarchy and the colonial or neocolonial power.

The period represented the first time that Cambodian patriotic ideas could receive an open airing as well as the first time Cambodians were encouraged to form politically oriented groups. On July 20 Sihanouk presided over a rally commemorating the monks demonstration of 1942. He was joined on this occasion by Pach Chhoeun, just released from jail, and Son Ngoc Thanh, who had returned to Cambodia from Tokyo in April.[39] A speaker at the rally, not the king, regaled the crowd with a litany of Cambodian patriotism, citing antimonarchic rebellions in the 1860s, the 1884–86 revolt, the 1916 Affair, the Bardez incident, and the 1942 monks demonstration. The speaker failed to mention that on only one of these occasions, in 1884–86, had the Cambodian monarch chosen the "right side." But the message was not lost upon Sihanouk, and these examples of nationalism, suppressed for the rest of his reign, in the late 1940s and 1950s passed into the folklore of the Cambodian Communists and the antimonarchic wing of the Democratic Party.

Another strand of postwar Cambodian nationalism consisted of officially sponsored antipathy to the Vietnamese, and clashes took place in this stirring, disorderly summer between Khmer and Vietnamese inhabitants of southern Vietnam. At the same time, Sihanouk took few steps, other than that of forming a paper alliance with the Vietnamese regime in Saigon, to formulate a joint strategy to resist the French when they returned. Sihanouk's mind at this time is difficult to read. It is likely, however, that the obscure antiroyalist coup of August 9–10, 1945, sponsored by some hotheaded members of Cambodian youth groups, deepened the king's hostility toward such figures as Pach Chhoeun and Son Ngoc Thanh.

Of seven participants later arrested by the French, five became active in the anti-French guerrilla movement, and three of these joined the forerunner of the Cambodian Communist Party. At the end of August, after the Japanese surrender, Sihanouk's chronicle reports that a nationalist demonstration attracted thirty thousand people, including armed members of the militia and members of various youth groups. Four days later, a referendum engineered by Son Ngoc Thanh allegedly drew 541,470 votes in favor of independence, with only two opposed. There is no evidence that a full-scale referendum had taken place, although a proposal for one apparently circulated as a memorandum to officials for their approval. The figures represent an attempt by Son Ngoc Thanh to bolster his bargaining position vis-à-vis the French, who had begun to filter back into southern Indochina under British auspices at first. Throughout September, Thanh urged his colleagues to join him in an alliance with the Vietnamese to resist the French. Many of these men disagreed with Thanh and sought to gain Cambodia's independence separate from Vietnam's. Some even preferred the return of the French to Thanh's continuing in power. For these reasons, when French officials arrested Thanh on October 12, 1945, in Phnom Penh, no one objected. Thanh himself seems to have been taken completely by surprise. That very morning he had presided, as the prime minister of Kampuchea, at the reopening of the Lycée Sisowath. He had lunch in the Saigon central prison.[40]

With Thanh removed from the scene (he was to spend most of the next six years in comparatively comfortable exile in France), King Sihanouk opened negotiations with the French, who appeared to many to have been ready to reimpose their control as in 1940–41. The modus vivendi signed by French and Cambodian delegates in early 1946, however, was a vaguely promising document, diluting French control and offering Cambodia membership in two nonexistent confederations. One of these, the Indochinese Federation, seems to have been little more than Indochina with somewhat increased indigenous participation at the top. The other, the French Union, was a diffuse and ambiguous brotherhood of peoples who had been colonized by France, based on the shared experience of French civilization. The agreement promised Cambodia a constitution and the right to form political parties, but French control remained in such fields as finance, defense, and foreign affairs. In other words, the French of early 1946 had replaced the Japanese of the summer of 1945. They had not, however, reconstituted the previous status quo.

10

GAINING INDEPENDENCE

It is easy to argue that French rule in Indochina effectively came to an end in the summer of 1945. This did not appear to be the case, however, to the new breed of French officials sent out by General de Gaulle's government to replace the people who had looked after the region up to 1945. During the war, in fact, de Gaulle had made the recovery of the French empire, and Indochina in particular, an important goal of his government in exile.

In Cambodia the French were forced in October 1945 to make conciliatory gestures to the members of the indigenous elite whom they needed to run the kingdom's day-to-day affairs. These were the people whose awakening the French had celebrated in the 1930s. They had become patriots in the meantime and, from the French point of view, intellectually belligerent. Many of them interpreted the summer of 1945 less as a humiliation of the French that had to be avenged than as a victory for the Cambodians themselves. Cambodia, they argued, needed to *regain* its independence. A leading convert to the cause, although he was quieter than most, was King Norodom Sihanouk.

Once the modus vivendi had been signed in early 1946, the French began to tidy up their colony. In Phnom Penh they restored the street names honoring French colonial heroes and French events that had been changed to Cambodian ones in 1945.[1] Another step was to abolish the newly instituted national holidays that honored Sihanouk's declaration of independence in 1945 and the monks demonstration of 1942. A third was to place Son Ngoc Thanh on trial for treason, charging him with collaboration with the Japanese (against whom, incidentally, the French had only belatedly declared war).

THE DEVELOPMENT OF POLITICAL PARTIES

In this atmosphere of business as usual, the electoral act that came into effect in the summer of 1946 opened up deep and unexpected fissures in the Cambodian elite. For the first time in their history, Cambodians were allowed to form political parties, and three sprang rapidly to life. As V.M. Reddi has pointed out, all of these "were led by princes, all of them shared the fear of neighboring countries, and all professed loyalty to the monarchy."[2] The first and last of these characteristics should come as no surprise, but the phrase "fear of neighboring countries" needs an explanation.

In 1946–47 Thailand was still governed by the relatively radical civilian regime that had been financing anti-Japanese, and subsequently anti-French, guerrillas along the Cambodian frontier since the fall of the Phibul government in the summer of 1944. In 1945 these groups formed into the Khmer Issarak ("Free Khmer"), and a government in exile was hastily assembled in Bangkok. Throughout this period, moreover, the Thai retained control of the *sruk* in northwestern Cambodia that they had taken over in 1941. These regions offered sanctuary to four of the twelve persons implicated in the August 1945 coup, as well as to others, such as Bunchhan Muul, who had participated in the monks demonstration and were now unhappy with the return of the French. The new political parties in Phnom Penh were fearful of Thai intrusions into Cambodian politics. They were probably even more frightened, however, by developments inside Vietnam, where Communist guerrillas in the south were threatening French rule and a Communist government in the north enjoyed de facto independence.[3]

There were, all the same, significant differences between the two leading parties, the Democratic Party (Krom Pracheathipodei), led by Prince Sisowath Yuthevong, and the so-called Liberal Party (Kanaq Sereipheap; literally, "Freedom Group"), led by Prince Norodom Norindeth. The difference between these two princes encapsulated the differences between two wings of Cambodian opinion. Prince Yuthevong (1912–47) had just returned from nearly a decade of higher education in France, his wife was French, and he wanted Cambodia to practice the kind of democracy he had admired in France. His party's program called for negotiating Cambodia's independence as quickly as possible. Prince Norindeth, on the other hand, was a conservative. As one of Cambodia's largest landowners, he believed that Cambodian politics should involve educating the people—slowly—and maintaining a dependent relationship with France. This was a view shared by many other members of the royal family. The Liberals were clandestinely funded by the French, who were fearful of the Democrats' popularity. The third party, the Progressive Democrats, led by Prince Norodom Montana, was insignificant and quickly faded from the scene, but it was as conservative as the Liberal Party, and it may have enjoyed a measure of support from the king and his advisers.[4]

The Democratic Party attracted people who had been drawn in the early 1940s to *Nagara Vatta* and the ideas of Pach Chhoeun and Son Ngoc Thanh. Its strength came in large part from the Mahanikay sect of the *sangha,* from younger members of the bureaucracy, from supporters of the Issarak movement, and from Cambodia's intellectual class (*nak cheh dung* in Khmer). Some elements within the party favored violent action, an alliance with Issarak guerrillas and perhaps, at this early stage, with the Communist Viet Minh as well.[5]

The Liberal Party, on the other hand, sought to maintain the status quo. The party drew its strength from elderly members of the government, wealthy landowners, the Cham ethnic minority and the Sino-Cambodian commercial elite. The party had strong provincial roots, it seems, especially among *chamkar* (riverbank plantation) owners near Kompong Cham. Its strength could be traced in large part to patronage networks in particular regions.

Sihanouk in his memoirs related that he was drawn to neither of these groups, and that neither sought him out. Many Democrats, indeed, seem to have seen Sihanouk as a puppet of the French, and much of his conduct in the 1946–49 period appears to bear this out. At the very least, Sihanouk seems to have felt that the only way to regain his country's independence was by negotiating with the French in a friendly, diplomatic way. The king's distrust of the Democrats probably sprang from his generalized suspicion of ideology, his traumatic experiences in the summer of 1945, and perhaps the feeling that he was being disrespectfully upstaged.

In September 1946, soon after the parties had been formed, elections for the Consultative Assembly were held to form a group to advise the king about a constitution for the country. More than 60 percent of the newly enfranchised voters went to the polls (a far higher percentage than voted in elections in Thailand). The Democrats won fifty of the sixty-seven seats; the Liberals, fourteen; independent candidates, three.

These results revealed the popularity of the Democratic Party among Cambodian authority figures who were in a position to "deliver the vote." In this election, as in others over the next twenty years or so, many peasants voted as they were told by people whom they habitually obeyed.⁶ As in the 1916 Affair, moreover, Cambodians—in this case, the Democrats—showed a disconcerting ability to organize and inspire their followers. In the case of the Democrats, these patrons would be local officials, teachers, and members of the *sangha* while those who voted for Liberal candidates were often endorsing their traditional economic patrons. At the same time, the sub rosa connections between some Democrats and the Issarak, and the connections that others made between the party and earlier Cambodian patriots, such as Hem Chieu, probably appealed to many voters more strongly than the Liberals' program of supporting the landowning elite. Indeed, the effects in the countryside of the disappearance of French control between March and October 1945 have never been examined. It would seem likely that bandit gangs, the principal target of the French-controlled Cambodian police in the colonial era, grew in number and importance. Many of these by early 1946 were referring to themselves as Issarak, and many peasants, especially at a distance, probably thought of the bands as patriotic.⁷

Sihanouk was distressed by the Democrats' victory, which he interpreted as a rebuff. In his memoirs he is scathing about the party and particularly about Prince Yuthevong, suggesting that his own unformed political ideas were preferable, even in 1946, to Yuthevong's. After more than thirty years, he was still unable to respect Yuthevong, referring to him and his followers dismissively as "demos."

Because the Democrats now assumed that they had a mandate to impose a constitution on the kingdom, rather than merely to advise the king about one, and because the constitution they drafted in 1946–47 reduced the powers of the king, Sihanouk soon became even more estranged from the constitutional process. Indeed, the 1947 Constitution was modeled closely on the Constitution of the Fourth Republic in France. In this document, real power devolved to the National Assembly and thus to the Democrats, who held the majority of assembly seats.

But what did power amount to? The Democrats, like everyone else in the kingdom, were handicapped because independence could no longer be *declared*, as it had been in the summer of 1945. It had to be *granted* by the French. Before the middle of 1949, however, the French made few concessions to anyone in Indochina. Unable to deliver independence, the Democrats began to squabble among themselves. This trend was exacerbated by the death of Prince Yuthevong from tuberculosis in July 1947, the arrest of several high-ranking Democrats on spurious charges later in the year (the so-called Black Star affair), and the assassination of Yuthevong's successor, Ieu Koeuss, in 1950.[8] Even after the so-called treaty of 1949 (discussed below) French police arrested a dozen leaders of the party on charges, later dropped, that they were conspiring with Issarak forces. The Democrats could do nothing about it; Cambodia's independence, as many of them had maintained since 1946, was a façade.

The Issarak armed struggle against the French, which had caused serious disruptions to the Cambodian economy in 1946–47, slowed down after Battambang and Siem Reap were returned to Cambodian control in 1947, and a regime unsympathetic to Issarak aspirations soon afterward came to power in Bangkok. In 1949, moreover, several thousand Issarak, particularly those opposed to the Viet Minh, took advantage of an amnesty offered them by Prime Minister Yem Sambaur. As non-Communist resistance to the French decreased, moreover, the Democrats were in less of a position to reply to spurious French charges that they supported the Viet Minh.

Another factor that handicapped the Democrats was that the people who held economic power in the kingdom—the French, members of the royal family, Chinese, and Sino-Cambodians—opposed the kinds of disorder that a real struggle for independence would have entailed. Most of them were doing well. If they were involved in politics at all, they supported the Liberal Party, as did the French administration. This meant that the Democrats were short of funds with which to influence officials, win elections, or finance an armed insurrection. The Democrats, forming the majority of the National Assembly (and thus theoretically enjoying political power), were in fact powerless to impose their will on the elite, the French, or their electorate—whose views, in fact, were rarely sought.

Ensconced in the National Assembly and hampered by a constitution that encouraged factional splits, the Democrats were cut off intellectually, economically, and physically from most of Cambodia's ordinary people. The only weapon available to them was to impede the orderly procedures of government by refusing to pass bills or to ratify agreements. As cabinet followed cabinet through a series of revolving doors—for, unlike in the British system, no elections followed these parliamentary crises—Cambodia's government ironically came more and more to resemble the government of the Fourth Republic from which its members were so eager to liberate themselves. Moreover, governments in Paris often held power so tenuously and for such short periods that Cambodians of any political persuasion, as Sihanouk was to discover in 1953, seldom encountered coherent French policies to oppose or experienced ministers who were qualified to negotiate. In fact, for reasons that are not entirely clear (although financial motives were important), no French governments before 1953–54 showed any willingness to take France out of Indochina.

By the end of 1949, all the same, the French appeared to have partially caved in, creating fictive independent regimes in Indochina. The move enabled the United States to grant financial aid to these "governments" and indirectly to the French, who were bogged down in the First Indochina War. The treaty signed with Cambodia at that time granted what Sihanouk would later call "50 percent independence."[9] The treaty allowed Cambodia some freedom of maneuver in foreign affairs as well as an autonomous military zone embracing Battambang and Siem Reap. Control over finance, defense, customs, and political resistance re-

Cambodian classical dancer, Phnom Penh, 2003.
Photo by Douglas Niven.

mained in French hands, but as Sihanouk has asserted, a process had begun that would be difficult to reverse. The Democrats opposed the treaty as inadequate, but it came into force all the same.

The French had several reasons for compromising at this point with Cambodia. The war throughout Indochina had intensified, and the Communist victory in China now provided the Viet Minh with an arsenal, a sanctuary, and an ally. The Soviet acquisition of nuclear arms in 1949 was to be followed in early 1950 by the conclusion of a thirty-year pact with the People's Republic of China. Beginning in 1948–49, the

French sought increased military aid from the United States on the grounds that they were no longer engaged in a colonial war but were fighting a crusade against Communism. To many in the United States and France, the outbreak of the Korean War in June 1950 confirmed this line of argument, and U.S. aid flowed into Indochina in ever-increasing amounts.

THE GROWTH OF THE LEFT

The history of the next four years is crucial to an understanding of what has happened in Cambodia ever since. Three trends need to be discussed. The first is the waning of the Democratic Party and the eclipse of the National Assembly. The second, related to this, is the flowering of comparatively right-wing political groupings and anti-Communist military leaders, who often enjoyed the favor of the king. In fact, officials concerned with these groupings, including Nhek Tioulong and Lon Nol, reappeared in several of Sihanouk's cabinets in the independence period. More important, perhaps, the consolidation of left-wing resistance to the French inside Cambodia, a process that began in 1950 and concluded in 1951 with the foundation of a recognizably Cambodian Communist Party, also dates from this period. In a sense, these three pieces remained on the board throughout Sihanouk's rule.

The fading of the Democrats can be traced to French reluctance to negotiate with them, the king's perennial hostility, and a shift by some opportunistic members of the party to a more royalist stance in order to gain preferment. Moreover, even their traditional disruptive role in the assembly was curtailed for much of the period because Sihanouk saw to it that the assembly was almost never in session.

Nonetheless, in 1951 he yielded to pressure to elect a new assembly in accordance with the constitution. The Democrats, perhaps sensing a trap, said that they were unwilling to go to the polls because of increasing insecurity in the countryside. When the Liberals and several hastily formed right-wing parties (one led by a middle-echelon bureaucrat, Lon Nol) threatened to contest the elections with them, the Democrats changed their minds.

The results resembled those of 1947, at least on the surface, for the Democrats captured fifty-five of the seventy-eight contested seats. Ominously, from the Democrats' point of view, some 498 different candidates had presented themselves for these seats, with little hope of winning, and had siphoned off tens of thousands of votes. For this reason, as well as the persistent strength of Liberal candidates, the Democrats attracted less than half the total vote, polling 148,000 while the Liberals attracted 82,000 voters and the various new parties attracted nearly 100,000. It was clear, as Michael Vickery has pointed out, that "any movement which could unify the right could immediately cut the ground from under the Democrats."[10]

Soon after the victory, Sihanouk persuaded the French to permit Son Ngoc Thanh to return from exile in France. In his memoirs, Sihanouk explains the action by referring to Thanh's friendship with his father, Prince Suramarit, but he may have thought, along with his French advisers, that bringing Thanh back might divide the Democrats while neutralizing Thanh himself as political threat. In any case, Thanh's return to Cambodia on October 29, 1951, was melodramatic. Thousands of people greeted him when he arrived at Phnom Penh airport, and thousands more lined the route into the city. It took the 300-car cortege almost an hour to cover the ten kilometers (six miles) involved. French intelligence officials estimated the crowds at more than half a million—an almost incredible indication of the organizational capacities of the Democrats and of the extent of popular support, partly for Son Ngoc Thanh himself and partly for an early solution to the problem of continuing dependence.

On the very day of Thanh's return, the French commissioner, Jean de Raymond, was murdered by his Vietnamese houseboy. The two events have never been publicly linked by scholars of the period, although the coincidence is remarkable. A clandestine Communist broadcast, two weeks later, managed to touch all the bases by asserting:

> For the French, the death of Raymond means the loss of a precious collaborator. For the puppets, it means the loss of a generous master. For the Cambodian people, Raymond's death means

the end of a great enemy. For Buddhism, his death means that a devil, which can no longer harm religion, has been killed.[11]

Thanh was politically inactive for the remainder of 1951, refusing several cabinet posts. In January and February 1952, however, he tested the water by touring the provinces with his old friend, Pach Chhoeun, recently named minister of information by the Democrats. This tour, which played down Sihanouk's importance, infuriated the king and convinced the French that Thanh was being encouraged by the Americans, who had provided public address systems for Pach Chhoeun. Soon after returning to Phnom Penh, Thanh founded a newspaper called *Khmer Krok* ("Cambodians Awake"), explaining the title in his first issue: "We know that the Cambodian people, who have been anaesthetized for a long time, are now awake. . . . No obstacle can now stop this awakening from moving ahead."[12]

Soon afterward, on March 9, 1952, the seventh anniversary of the Japanese *coup de force,* Son Ngoc Thanh fled the capital with a radio transmitter and a handful of followers, the most eminent being a leftist intellectual named Ea Sichau. Within a month, Thanh had set up his headquarters along the Thai border in the northern part of Siem Reap, joining forces with an Issarak band under the leadership of Kao Tak. Between 1952 and the Geneva Conference in 1954, Thanh and his supporters were aided to an extent by Thai intelligence agencies. Within his own zone, he experimented with a loosely regimented ideology that he labeled national socialism, traceable in part to his admiration for the Japanese political institutions he had observed in exile during World War II.[13] It is unclear whether he believed that by going into exile in the Cambodian mountains he could remain in command of the independence movement, as he had seemed to be on his triumphal return to Phnom Penh, but his efforts to win over pro-Communist guerrillas were unsuccessful, and only a few hundred people—most of them idealistic high school students—followed him into the *maquis.* After independence Thanh's importance faded, and his following decreased. In the late 1950s and 1960s he eked out a shadowy existence working for the Thai and the Vietnamese in their efforts to destabilize Sihanouk's regime. His nationalistic fervor through 1957 or so is difficult to question, but his motives for abandoning Phnom Penh in 1952 are difficult to figure out. Perhaps he overestimated the extent of his support among the non-Communist Issarak (or, conversely, underestimated Communist support among the guerrillas). French intelligence reports assert that he still enjoyed the support of some of the older Democrats in Phnom Penh and perhaps he hoped for international support as well. After his exile, however, he was no longer a force to be reckoned with, either by Sihanouk or by the French.[14]

By the time of Thanh's defection in 1952, Communist-controlled guerrilla bands, operating in cooperation with the Viet Minh, occupied perhaps a sixth of Cambodia's territory and tied down several thousand French troops. Two years later, at the time of the Geneva Conference, some estimates suggested that Communist forces controlled more than half the kingdom.

Where had they come from? When the Indochinese Communist Party (ICP) was founded in Hong Kong in 1930, it included no Cambodian members, and indeed only a handful of ethnic Khmer had joined the party before the end of World War II.[15] In 1945–47, however, Viet Minh forces made an effort to support "liberation struggles" in Laos and Cambodia. At the same time, as we have seen, the Thai government had a policy of aiding all anti-French guerrillas in Indochina, and the Khmer Issarak, operating along the Thai frontier and in the Thai-controlled *sruk* of Battambang and Siem Reap, included men who later formed right-wing and left-wing factions. Left-wingers included the pseudonymous Son Ngoc Minh (in fact a former monk, Achar Mean), Sieu Heng, and Tou Samouth. On April 17, 1950, twenty-five years to the day before the Communist "liberation" of Phnom Penh, the First National Congress of the Khmer Resistance was held in the southwestern part of the kingdom under the leadership of Son Ngoc Minh. The congress, in turn, established the Unified Issarak Front, dominated by ethnic Cambodian members of the ICP. According to a history of the Cambodian Communist Party prepared in 1973, there were only forty of these at the time. As Ben Kiernan has pointed out, however, hundreds more had already been trained in Communist political schools set up under Vietnamese auspices as early as 1947. The most famous of these, founded in 1950, was named after the dissident monk Hem Chieu.[16]

The ICP claimed to have dissolved itself in early 1951, and separate Communist parties were soon formed in Laos, Cambodia, and Vietnam. The Khmer People's Revolutionary Party (KPRP) was founded in September 1951. Its statutes, translated from Vietnamese into Khmer, were drawn from those of the "newly constituted" party in Vietnam. According to party records, the KPRP at this stage had perhaps a thousand members; French intelligence in 1952 estimated Communist-controlled Issarak forces as numbering about five thousand.[17] This latter figure is probably an underestimate, because the French appear to have been unable to infiltrate the party and because it was in their interests, and in those of their client, King Sihanouk, to play down estimates of Communist popularity, especially in public statements. As impatience with French control increased among many segments of the population and as Vietnamese guerrillas elsewhere in Indochina moved from strength to strength, these pro-Vietnamese forces in Cambodia grew in numbers, efficiency, and cohesion. So did the KPRP. By July 1954, eight months after independence, the party had an estimated two thousand members, many of whom were to seek refuge in Vietnam following the Geneva accords. Another index of the party's growth was the fact that French authorities in 1952 believed that taxes and contributions levied by revolutionaries among the population amounted to the equivalent of half the national budget.

Although the Vietnamese cadres in these guerrilla units gradually relinquished their positions to ethnic Khmer, who were always in control of the KPRP, it is clear that these leaders in the anti-French resistance differed in several ways from their counterparts in the Democratic Party and elsewhere along the political spectrum. For one thing they had come to see their struggle as part of an international movement, connected with Marxist-Leninist laws of history. At another level the liberation of Cambodia from the French did not mean, for them, the continuation of the status quo among Cambodians or the intensification of a supposedly traditional animosity between Cambodians and Vietnamese. They saw liberation from the French, in other words, as a stage in the Cambodian revolution rather than a goal. Moreover, without being puppets of the Vietnamese, the KPRP's leaders in the early 1950s accepted Vietnam's leadership in the struggle to liberate Indochina from the French and in the formation of socialist parties throughout the region. In terms of relative power, such a policy made sense. Seen from another perspective, both the French and Sihanouk tried hard to equate anti-French resistance (as opposed to a policy of negotiated independence) with a pro-Vietnamese, pro-Communist, and therefore un-Cambodian betrayal. What was being betrayed, of course, were the hierarchical social arrangements that had characterized Cambodia throughout its history. In 1952–53, in fact, Sihanouk and his entourage frequently and absurdly labeled Son Ngoc Thanh a Communist. A decade later, he reached for the fascist label to describe his former prime minister, then allegedly on the payroll of the United States.

The interplay between nationalism and internationalism inside the Cambodian Communist movement, as in many others elsewhere in the world, plagued the party throughout its history. Should Cambodian interests (whatever they were) come first? What was Cambodian socialism? And how did this, in turn, fit into the history and the alignments of the Vietnamese? By denying any socialist or internationalist component in Cambodian nationalism, one could proclaim Cambodia's *intrinsic* greatness, refer repeatedly to Angkor, and make racist slurs against the Vietnamese. This was the route that Sihanouk chose to follow in the late 1960s, and it was also followed by Lon Nol and at several points by the Pol Pot regime. Radicals also employed it occasionally in the early 1950s to gain support. In a speech delivered in November 1951, for example, a Communist spokesman asserted that

> the Cambodian race is of noble origin. It is not afraid of death, when it is a question of fighting the enemy, of saving its religion, and of liberating its fatherland. The entire race follows the Buddhist doctrine [sic] which places death above slavery and religious persecution. King Yasovarman is a remarkable example.[18]

By seeking legitimacy in the Cambodian past, in antimonarchic heroes, and in aspects of the Buddhist religion, these radicals cast a wider net than the people around King Sihanouk were able or willing to do. They saw independence as a goal in itself, having little effect on the structure of Cambodian society or on their own place inside it. They saw little value in mobilizing the Cambodian people or in destabilizing the regime. For these reasons, heroes like Siwotha, Hem Chieu, and Pou Kombo—favored by the Issaraks, by some of the Democrats and by Communist propaganda at this early stage—quickly disappeared from textbooks and ideology. The fate of these heroes under successive regimes forms an interesting leitmotif in Cambodian history. After years of neglect they reemerged under the Khmer Republic, alongside many former Democrats, only to vanish again under Pol Pot, whose official ideology, while retaining a pro-Angkorean slant, also stressed the impersonality of the regime's organization. Heroes were ephemeral; the revolutionary organization (*angkar padevat*) endured. To complete the cycle, some of the discredited heroes reemerged in 1979 under the PRK, providing new names for Phnom Penh streets—names that were altered yet again when Sihanouk became king in 1993.[19] It was also in 1979 that a five-towered depiction of Angkor Wat on the Cambodian flag, favored by the Issarak in the 1950s, replaced the three-towered one favored by previous regimes and reinstated in 1993.

Cambodian university students in France were another source of recruits for Cambodia's Communist movement. Between 1945 and 1960, several hundred of these young men and women were exposed to an intoxicating mixture of radical politics, personal freedom, and anticolonial solidarity. Some were recruited into the French Communist Party; many more perceived a wide gap between French ideals, life in France and French colonial performance. Others, going further, saw clear connections between prerevolutionary France, prerevolutionary Russia, and twentieth-century Cambodia, ruled by what they saw as a feudal, reactionary elite. Sihanouk's suppression of the Democratic Party (discussed below) accelerated the radicalization of many young Khmers—including such future leaders of DK as Saloth Sar (Pol Pot), Ieng Sary, Son Sen, and Khieu Samphan.

SIHANOUK AND THE ACHIEVEMENT OF INDEPENDENCE

Throughout the first few months of 1952, the Democrats in the National Assembly continued as best they could to thwart Sihanouk's policies. Son Ngoc Thanh remained a distant threat. French intelligence sources estimated that almost two-thirds of the kingdom was no longer under the day-to-day control of the Phnom Penh government. To Sihanouk and his conservative advisers, the time had come for a dramatic series of gestures to gain the country's independence forcibly from France and to maintain themselves in power.

In a scathing speech to the assembly in early June 1952, Sihanouk declared, "All is in disorder. Hierarchy no longer exists. There is no rational employment of talent. . . . If it is right to be dissident, this means that all the best patriots will seek refuge in the forest."[20] Soon afterward, with the connivance of the French, Sihanouk staged a coup against his own government. Moroccan troops secretly brought up from Saigon for the purpose surrounded the National Assembly, and the king dismissed the Democrats from the cabinet. No shots were fired. Sihanouk assumed power as prime minister, appointing his own cabinet and leaving the Democratic-controlled assembly to wither on the vine. At this point, he demanded a mandate from his people, promising to deliver complete independence within three years, i.e., before June 1955. Although no referendum was carried out at this time, Sihanouk acted as if his mandate had been granted and began what he was later to call his crusade for independence.

Although the coup had been peaceful, demonstrations against it broke out in Cambodia's lycées, where antimonarchic, pro-Democrat sentiment was strong. Radical Cambodian students in France referred to Sihanouk as a traitor to the nation. In a vituperative manifesto issued to the king on July 6, 1952, the students called on him to abdicate, blaming him for recent French military attacks, for dissolving the assembly, and for negotiating with the French instead of fighting them.[21] The manifesto went on to accuse Sihanouk's ancestors Sisowath and Norodom of collaborating with the French against what they called national heroes. The remainder of 1952, it seems, was a trying time for Sihanouk, as the French in effect decided to call his bluff.

He was aided by the Democrats' intransigence. The assembly refused to approve his government's budget in January 1953. Declaring the nation to be in danger, Sihanouk dissolved the assembly, promulgated martial law, and ordered the arrest of several Democratic assemblymen, who were now deprived of parliamentary immunity. As V.M. Reddi asserted, Sihanouk was acting out a well-planned scenario. He justified it informally by telling a French correspondent, "I am the natural ruler of the country . . . and my authority has never been questioned."[22] He was appealing to the people over the heads of the elected officials, just as he now planned (without saying so at the time) to appeal directly to the French.

The king's newly acquired political energy and his insistence upon independence shocked many French and members of the royal family. Some journalists came to terms with the king's awakening by labeling him insane, perhaps because he had been what they called comical and exotic (i.e., cooperative) for so long.

In February 1953 Sihanouk announced that he was traveling to France for his health—a tactic he was often to employ during the remaining years of his reign. In fact, as he revealed in his memoirs, he departed with meticulously prepared dossiers listing outstanding matters to be discussed and negotiated with the French. His illness was political but the stakes were high. When he arrived in France, he wrote immediately to the aged and constitutionally powerless French president, Vincent Auriol, warning him that "I have based my future as king and that of my dynasty on the policy of adhesion to the French Union and collaboration with France, to which I am and shall be loyal."[23] He added that if the Communists invaded Cambodia, he could not guarantee that his subjects would act to defend French interests.

Auriol's advisers apparently thought that Sihanouk's long letter and another that arrived soon afterward were alarmist, and Auriol waited two weeks to answer them. When he did he said only that he had studied the letters with care and asked Sihanouk to lunch. At that point, officials in the French government concerned with Indochina respectfully told the king to return to Cambodia, hinting that he might even be replaced as king.[24]

For the next month or so, Sihanouk traveled slowly homeward, pausing to give press and radio interviews in Canada, the United States, and Japan in which he publicized Cambodia's plight and the intransigence of the French. He used this tactic of publicizing supposedly confidential discussions for the remainder of his life. In 1953, however, it was a bold course to follow, for he was gambling not only with the French and potential foreign allies but also with the opposition at home, with the Vietnamese, and with the KPRP.

He arrived back in Phnom Penh in May and dramatically offered his life in exchange for Cambodia's independence. Negotiations in Paris proceeded slowly, so in June the king went into voluntary exile, first to Thailand, where he was not made welcome, and then to the autonomous military region of Siem Reap, where he took up residence at his villa near Angkor Wat and refused to speak with French officials in Phnom Penh. In Vietnam the war was going badly for the French, and it had become increasingly unpopular at home. Sihanouk's increasing resistance to the French and the prospect of increased fighting in Cambodia caused them to consider his demands more seriously than they had planned.

In October 1953 the French caved in and granted the king authority over Cambodia's armed forces, judiciary, and foreign affairs. Their economic hold on the kingdom, however—particularly in the import-export sphere and in the highly profitable rubber plantations—remained intact. Despite these remnants of colonial rule, Sihanouk is correct, on balance, in interpreting the French collapse at this point as a personal victory. Using the same communications network that in 1916 and again in 1951 had frightened French authorities, Sihanouk now ordered officials in the *sruk* between Siem Reap and Phnom Penh to organize demonstrations in his favor. As he drove back to his capital on the second anniversary of Son Ngoc Thanh's return from exile, hundreds of thousands of people lined the road, uncertain perhaps what independence would mean but at this stage happy enough to applaud their king and what they hoped would be an end to fighting. Soon afterward, Sihanouk was officially proclaimed a national hero.[25]

In the short term, France's departure from the scene had three effects. In the first place, Cambodia's independence and the relatively low level of fighting in the kingdom between November 1953 and the middle of 1954 strengthened the hand of Sihanouk's delegation to the Geneva Conference in the summer of 1954. The delegation, led by Nhek Tioulong, took a stubborn view of indigenous Communists, who were allowed no part in the deliberations and were also frozen out by

Vietnamese Communist delegates eager to earn concessions for Vietnam and, to a lesser degree, for pro-Vietnamese Pathet Lao forces in Laos.[26] Surprisingly, perhaps, many Cambodian radicals continued to accept leadership from Vietnam throughout the 1950s and 1960s. For over a thousand of them, 1954 marked the beginning of a long march that would take them to exile in Hanoi, not to return to Cambodia until the early 1970s when most of them were killed by U.S. bombing, by Lon Nol's army, or by internal Communist purges at the instigation of Pol Pot, who by then was the leader of the Cambodian Communist Party. A few hardy survivors of this group were given cabinet positions in the post-1979 government of Cambodia, established by the Vietnamese in the wake of their invasion.[27]

Another consequence of Sihanouk's so-called crusade was that the Democratic Party and Son Ngoc Thanh, who had failed to deliver independence, lost much of their appeal. At the same time, figures further to the right who had remained loyal to the king, such as Lt. Col. Lon Nol, Nhek Tioulong, and Penn Nouth, now gained in stature and were favored for government posts.

Perhaps the most lasting consequence of independence in 1953 was that Sihanouk felt he had obtained a mandate to govern Cambodia as he saw fit. The subsequent decimation of the KPRP and the eclipse of the Democrats gave him the impression (encouraged by many foreign visitors and by his entourage) that his crusade had been not only successful but also astute and that the suffusion of Cambodia the state by Sihanouk the man was a salutary political development. A consequence of this, especially evident in the 1960s, was that Sihanouk felt no obligation to be at peace with Thailand and South Vietnam or to grant freedom of action to people he disliked. Just as he had gone it alone in 1953 and won, so Cambodia could be independent from its perennially hostile neighbors by courting the friendship of such faraway powers as China, France, and Yugoslavia.

While this was going on, the forces that had been unleashed in the summer of 1945 fell into disrepute. Sihanouk and his advisers, never partial to social change, correctly saw that these forces endangered the stability of the country. And, as we have seen, the inherent stability of Cambodia, often the subject of absurd romanticism among colonial writers, has rested throughout nearly all of Cambodian history on the acceptance of the status quo as defined by those in power.

What, then, did independence mean? The removal of the French probably meant little to most Cambodians, who continued to pay taxes to finance an unresponsive government in Phnom Penh (or Udong or Angkor) whose so-called royal work, almost by definition, removed it from contact with the people and made officials, for the most part, self-centered, concerned with status, and ill at ease with anyone else's aspirations. It was certainly just, in other words, to remove the Cambodian elite and the comparatively small intellectual class from French control. That removal left these people free not to govern themselves so much as to govern others without vigorously seeking their consent. Because the people in the countryside had never been asked to play a part in any government, they saw few short-term rewards in resisting those in power, who were now at least Cambodians rather than French or Vietnamese.[28] Although Cambodia celebrated its independence at the end of 1953 and gained military autonomy after the Geneva Conference in 1954 when Viet Minh troops and their Cambodian sympathizers took refuge in North Vietnam, it can be argued that the elections of 1955, and the emergence of Sihanouk as Cambodia's major political actor, marked a sharper turning point in Cambodia's political history.

The elections had been stipulated by the Geneva Conference as part of a healing process for the non-Communist segments of Indochina. The Democrats were weakened by factional quarrels and by nearly three years away from power, but they were still the best-organized political party, and their leaders looked forward to winning the elections. Many younger Democrats opposed the apparently pro-American policies Sihanouk had been following since Geneva and argued that Cambodia should be neutral in its alignments. They shared this line with a pro-Communist Party that had just taken shape in Cambodia, known as the Krom Pracheachon, or People's Group. Cambodia's hard-core Communist Party, founded in 1951, remained concealed from view. Younger Democrats moved their own party to the left in late 1954, pushing such stalwarts as Sims Var and Son Sann aside and replacing them with anti-monarchic neutralists like Keng Vannsak and Svay So and with even more radical figures including Thiounn Mumm, then a member of the

French Communist Party. Mumm cooperated with Saloth Sar, who had spent some months in the Vietnamese maquis in 1953–54, to coordinate the Democrats' tactics with those of the Pracheachon. Many observers in Cambodia at the beginning of 1955 expected the two parties to win a majority of seats in the assembly.

The revival of the Democrats and the popularity of the Pracheachon distressed conservative politicians in Phnom Penh and enraged the king who, as the self-proclaimed "father of Cambodian independence," had hoped to call the country's political shots. Outside the capital and intellectual circles his own popularity remained high. A referendum in February 1955 asked voters to choose between a white ballot with his picture on it and a black one inscribed with the Cambodian word for no. The vote was enhanced by the fact that discarding the king's picture was seen as disrespectful and grounds for arrest. Then and later, Sihanouk was adept at reinforcing his genuine popularity with bullying tactics so as to gain almost 100 percent approval.

Gambling that he was now more popular than the political parties, Sihanouk abdicated the throne in early March without warning and entered political life as a private citizen after designating his father, Prince Suramarit, as the new king. Soon afterward, Sihanouk founded a national political movement, the Sangkum Reastr Niyum, usually translated as People's Socialist Community. To be a member of the movement, one had to abjure membership in any other political group, as Sihanouk's intention was to smash the existing political parties. Several of these folded in the course of 1955, and their leaders rallied to the Sangkum. This left the Liberals, the Democrats, and the Pracheachon to contest the elections. The leader of the Liberals, Prince Norodom Norindeth, was offered a diplomatic post in Paris, which he accepted, leaving his party in disarray.

Shortly after founding the Sangkum, Prince Sihanouk, as he was now called, went to Bandung in Indonesia to attend a conference of African and Asian political leaders. Before he left he declared that he had abdicated so as to defeat the "politicians, the rich, and the educated, who are accustomed to using . . . their knowledge to deceive others and to place innumerable obstacles in the path over which I must lead the people."[29]

In his absence civil servants were bullied into joining the Sangkum in large numbers, a move which deprived the Democrats of several hundred registered members.

Sihanouk's tactics took the Democrats and Pracheachon by surprise, as did his decision at Bandung to co-opt their neutralist foreign policy while holding onto U.S. military and economic aid. At the conference, Sihanouk was lionized by many anti-Western heads of state, including Indonesia's Sukarno and China's Zhou Enlai. When he returned to Cambodia, he hastened to garnish his new importance with electoral approval.

The 1955 elections, the last before the 1990s to be freely contested by a range of political parties, also marked the first attempt of many to mobilize the security apparatus of the state in favor of one particular group. Between May and September 1955, several opposition newspapers were shut down and their editors were imprisoned without trial. Democrat and Pracheachon candidates were harassed, and some campaign workers were killed in a rough-and-tumble campaign waged against vaguely defined special interests on behalf of Cambodia's so-called little people. Voters were intimidated on polling day as well, and several ballot boxes thought to contain Democrat ballots conveniently disappeared. When the votes were counted, Sangkum candidates had won all the seats in the assembly and over three-quarters of the vote. The understaffed International Control Commission, set up by the Geneva Conference to oversee the elections, was unable or unwilling to sort out campaign offenses, perhaps because the generally pro-Western Indian and Canadian representatives outvoted the pro-Communist Poles on the commission.[30]

A new kind of politics had overtaken and replaced the less robust constitutional variety that had endured by fits and starts since 1947. Politics in Cambodia between 1955 and 1970 were characterized by Sihanouk's monopoly of political power and the emergence of Cambodia onto the international stage. Sihanouk's style was widely popular and the kingdom prospered. As in the past, however, this prosperity was to a large extent dependent on the behavior of Cambodia's neighbors and on the policies of larger, more distant powers. Cambodia was neutral and at peace, in other words, for as long as its neutrality served the interests of other states. Sihanouk's formidable political skills may have postponed the apocalypse that overtook his country in the 1970s, but they did not prevent it. In terms of what happened then and later, many Cambodians in recent years have seen his time in power as constituting a golden age. Others have come to perceive his ruling style as domineering and absurd, closing off any possibility of pluralism, political maturity, sound planning, or rational debate. By treating Cambodia as a personal fief, his subjects as children, and his opponents as traitors, Sihanouk did much to set the agenda, unwittingly, for the lackadaisical chaos of the Khmer Republic, the horrors of Democratic Kampuchea, and the single-party politics of the postrevolutionary era.

11

FROM INDEPENDENCE
TO CIVIL WAR

For fifteen years Prince Sihanouk and the Sangkum Reastr Niyum over-shadowed Cambodian life. Because Sihanouk was removed from office by his own National Assembly in 1970, it is convenient, but misleading, to interpret this period in terms of his decline, a process that few observers noted at the time. Nonetheless, by 1966, Sihanouk had reached a turning point in his political career and his grip on the political process had begun to weaken, along with his self-confidence. These changes can be linked to the intensification of the Vietnam War as well as to indigenous political factors. In any case, the assembly elected in 1966, although allegedly made up of loyal Sangkum members, was the first since 1951 whose members the prince had not handpicked himself. In 1970 these were the people who voted Sihanouk out of office.

THE ASSEMBLY ELECTION

The Democrats, Sihanouk's principal opponents in 1955, were driven from politics before the 1958 elections. Sihanouk's continuing vindictiveness toward this group is curious because by 1956 the party had virtually ceased to exist and nearly all its members had joined the Sangkum. Nonetheless, in September 1957, claiming that the Democrats were endangering his policies, Sihanouk summoned five leaders of the party to a debate on the grounds of the royal palace in Phnom Penh.

Large crowds were assembled nearby, and the proceedings were broadcast over loudspeakers. Intimidated by the crowds, the Democrats were unable to voice any clear opinions, and after three hours of bullying by Sihanouk and his associates, they were allowed to leave. On their way out of the palace enclosure they were beaten by soldiers and police, and one of them was hospitalized. Over the next few days, thirty or forty people suspected of Democrat leanings were beaten in Phnom Penh, and Sihanouk, before going overseas for a vacation, secretly decorated some of the soldiers involved in the palace beatings.[1] Soon afterward, the Democratic Party dissolved itself and disappeared from the political scene.

In 1958, therefore, the only opposition to the Sangkum was the left-wing Pracheachon, which had gathered over twenty thousand votes in 1955. In a foolhardy gesture, the group nominated a handful of candidates, but all but one withdrew before election day in the face of police repression. The remaining candidate, Keo Meas, earned 350 votes out of several thousand cast in his electoral district. After the election he went underground to avoid arrest. His candidacy marked the end of pluralistic electoral politics in Cambodia until the 1990s, aside from a brief interlude under Lon Nol.

Over the next two years, Sihanouk's government survived a series of plots against it that were hatched in Saigon and Bangkok with the knowledge of the United States.[2] The plots made the prince more suspicious than ever of his neighbors and their American patrons, whose cool behavior toward him contrasted sharply with the courtesy he was shown by leaders and diplomats from France, Indonesia, and the Communist bloc. In the Cold War atmosphere of the time, Sihanouk was labeled pro-Communist by the United States. For his part, the plots enabled Sihanouk to label his opponents un-Cambodian, a tactic followed by the next two governments in Phnom Penh.

By the early 1960s Sihanouk had forged a tactical alliance with elements of the Cambodian left as well as with Communist China. These alignments had four short-term effects. The first was a drift to the left of Cambodia's print media, which were mostly overseen by the prince himself. Related to this was a tolerance on the part of the government toward left-wing teachers in Cambodia's schools. Many of these men and women, in turn, were recruited into Cambodia's clandestine Communist movement in these years and drew some of their students along with them. The second effect was the election to the assembly in 1962 of several leftists educated in France, such as Khieu Samphan, Hou Yuon, and Hu Nim. Without admitting their Communist leanings, these men joined the Sangkum and were rewarded by the prince, as their colleagues in the Pracheachon were not.

A third effect was Sihanouk's decision in 1963 to cut off U.S. economic and military assistance. In a related move he nationalized Cambodia's banks and the country's export-import trade. The circumstances surrounding these decisions, which followed the assassination of Ngo Dinh Diem in Vietnam, are still unclear. It is possible that Sihanouk expected France and China to pick up where the Americans left off, but those two powers, although remaining friendly to Cambodia, were unwilling to make that kind of open-ended financial commitment. Nationalization, like many Cambodian policies, seems to have been decided on by Sihanouk on the spur of the moment, with the intention of making Cambodia a genuinely socialist state. The fourth effect of Sihanouk's tolerance of the Left was that nearly all of Cambodia's radicals were able to survive the 1950s and early 1960s without being shot or going to jail. Right-wing opponents of the prince, whom he perceived as working for foreign powers, were less fortunate.

In 1960 Sihanouk's father, King Suramarit, died. After a series of maneuvers, Sihanouk had himself named Cambodia's chief of state with his mother, Queen Kossamak, continuing to serve as a monarch for ceremonial purposes. This decision severely weakened the monarchy by which Cambodia had been governed continuously for over a thousand years.

For the newly elected assembly, Sihanouk sought candidates who were younger and better educated than those whom they replaced. Naturally distrustful of intellectuals, the prince was convinced that he could manipulate, cajole, and outmaneuver them once they were in the assembly or elsewhere in the government, as he viewed the assembly as a personal possession and a rubber stamp. The 1962 elections, which occurred soon after war broke out in South Vietnam between Vietnamese loyal to the pro-U.S. government of Ngo Dinh Diem and others who sought to unify the country under the Communist leadership in Hanoi, reflected the Prince's widespread popularity and bolstered his self-confidence.

As it did so often in Cambodia's recent history, the country soon became a hostage to Vietnamese events. Sihanouk's efforts to play both sides against each other and to keep Cambodia out of the war are reminiscent of King Chan's maneuvers in the nineteenth century. Between 1961 and 1970, Sihanouk's policies saved thousands of Cambodian lives. When he was overthrown, however, he broadcast an appeal to his "brothers and sisters" asking them to wage a civil war. Whether the three hundred thousand deaths that occurred after that—inflicted by North and South Vietnamese, U.S., and contending Cambodian forces—could have been avoided had he stepped aside is impossible to say.

The Vietnam War destabilized the Cambodian economy and eventually drove Sihanouk from office. Otherwise, he would probably not have been overthrown, and Cambodia's Communists would not have come to power. The Cold War tensions that were being played out in Vietnam, at enormous human cost, had little relevance in Cambodia, but this did not stop Cambodia from becoming engulfed in the conflict. In a sense Cambodian history between 1965 and 1993, if not beyond, was orchestrated from southern Vietnam and from such faraway cities as Hanoi, Washington, and Beijing.

In 1965 over two hundred thousand U.S. troops swarmed into South Vietnam to prop up the Saigon government and to prevent a Communist victory. Within a year the United States was exploding hundreds of thousands of tons of ordnance in Vietnam while absorbing and inflicting tens of thousands of casualties. In the meantime, North Vietnamese troops had moved into position in the south to reinforce locally recruited guerrillas. As the war intensified it threatened to spill over into Cambodia, as it had already spilled over into Laos.

Throughout 1965 Sihanouk repeatedly proclaimed Cambodia's neutrality and sought guarantees from outside powers for his country's frontiers. In 1964 he broke off diplomatic relations with the United States and sought without success to convene an international conference that would lead to the neutralization of Southeast Asia and the withdrawal of U.S. troops. By 1966 he had also allied himself secretly with the North Vietnamese, a decision, though probably impossible to avoid, that was a major reason for his being deposed four years later. Sihanouk felt certain that the Vietnamese Communists would win the war. He wanted to remain in power and to keep Cambodia independent; in the meantime, he wanted to prevent Cambodians from being killed. An alliance with the North Vietnamese, so long as it was kept secret, seemed a good way of accomplishing these objectives.

Under the terms of the alliance, the North Vietnamese were allowed to station troops in Cambodian territory and to receive arms and supplies funneled to them from North Vietnam and China via the Cambodian port of Sihanoukville. In exchange they recognized Cambodia's frontiers, promised to leave Cambodian civilians alone, and avoided contact with the Cambodian army. South Vietnamese and U.S. officials soon learned about the presence of North Vietnamese troops in Cambodia and the movements of weapons and supplies, without knowing the details of the agreement Sihanouk had reached. Sihanouk denied for several years that any Vietnamese troops were in Cambodia, which angered the United States and South Vietnam but enhanced the image of injured innocence that the prince projected to the outside world.

In September 1966, Sihanouk's political idol, Charles de Gaulle, then president of France and a supporter of neutralization in Southeast Asia agreed to make a three-day visit to Cambodia, shortly before the assembly elections were to take place. The prince had little time or energy to stage-manage both occasions, and he felt sure that de Gaulle's visit was the more important of the two. Positions in the assembly, however, were coveted by many middle-class Cambodians, partly because holding office offered them informal opportunities for making money. While making plans for de Gaulle's visit, Sihanouk was besieged with petitions for endorsement from hundreds of prospective candidates. Reluctant to antagonize some of his supporters, he threw the balloting open, and over 425 Sangkum candidates competed with each other for eighty-two assembly seats.

President de Gaulle's visit came to a climax with a floodlit performance by the Cambodian royal ballet on the terraces of Angkor Wat. The French president made a warm speech in which he praised his host and urged the neutralization of Southeast Asia. Sihanouk had worked hard to make the visit a success—it cost the equivalent of several million dollars, and the foreign media coverage was favorable and extensive— and it may have been the high-water mark of the prince's years in power. When the general left, however, Sihanouk was faced with a national election in which, for the first time since 1951, the candidates owed him nothing.

In the elections, candidates favoring local interests triumphed over those whose main credentials were based on their loyalty to Sihanouk. Some writers (including Sihanouk at the time) have called the results a triumph for reactionary forces, and certainly the elections were the first since 1951 in which candidates had to relate to the voters. To gain support, many candidates made unrealistic promises, like their counterparts in other countries, and spent large sums of money. Many candidates were ideologically conservative, but so were most Cambodians, particularly in rural areas. Interestingly, however, the three leftist candidates who had paid close attention to their constituents over the years were reelected in 1966 with increased majorities.

The new prime minister, General Lon Nol, the commander of Cambodia's army, was known for his loyalty to the prince, his aloofness, and the army's loyalty to him. He also attracted the support of middle-aged conservatives, particularly among the Sino-Cambodian commercial elite. These men thought Sihanouk's style embarrassing and his economic policies disastrous. Many of them, like most of the army officer corps, regretted Cambodia's break with the United States and objected to the fact that the nationalization of imports and exports had moved this profitable sector of the economy into the hands of often-incompetent government officials. As many members of the new assembly shared these feelings of impatience, the stage was set for a confrontation between Sihanouk on the one hand and the assembly and the commercial elite on the other.

SIHANOUK'S POLICIES

In the 1960s an American correspondent wrote that "Cambodia Is Sihanouk," and this view was echoed by a French writer, who entitled a chapter of her book about Cambodia "He Is the State," echoing the "I am the state" adage attributed to the seventeenth-century French monarch Louis XIV.[3] Both assertions were true up to a point. The prince's insistence that he was the embodiment of Cambodia, and that Cambodians were his children, made it hard for visitors, journalists, or diplomats to disentangle genuine national interests, problems, and priorities from those that Sihanouk proclaimed on a daily basis.

Given that situation and knowing what happened afterward, it is difficult to reconstruct Cambodian politics and society during the Sihanouk era without considering Sihanouk or lowering the volume of his voice. The prince's speeches, the journals he controlled, and the approving words of foreign writers often drown out other documents and speakers. So did his censorship. On the other hand, looking at the 1960s largely in terms of the prince's decline may encourage one to exaggerate the importance of his opposition (particularly among the Communists), to minimize his real accomplishments, and to blame the prince for the chaos that beset his country after he was overthrown.

To be fair to him, considering the choices he faced in the 1960s, his foreign policies now seem more defensible than his domestic ones. The key elements of these policies were his friendship with China, his search for as many foreign patrons as possible, and his secret alliance with North Vietnam. A corollary of these policies was his distrust of the United States, Thailand, and South Vietnam.

A formal alliance with North Vietnam, as I have suggested, was probably impossible to avoid. Had he forbidden the Vietnamese Communist forces to move across Cambodia, they would have done so anyway and would have decimated any Cambodian forces sent against them. They did just that in 1970–71, when the post-Sihanouk government tried to drive them out of the country. Had the prince allied himself with South Vietnam, the Vietnamese civil war would have spilled over into Cambodia, as it did in 1970 when thousands of Cambodians died or were wounded. Nor would an alliance with Thailand have protected his country against the North Vietnamese. Neither Thailand nor South Vietnam was prepared to make the promises to Cambodia that Sihanouk extracted from Hanoi. His friendship with China was an attempt to find a counterweight to his neighbors as well as a power capable of restraining the North Vietnamese in Cambodia. It was also a response to what Sihanouk interpreted as the genuine friendship and support offered him by the Chinese premier, Zhou Enlai.

Sihanouk's efforts to keep Cambodia independent and to avoid the Vietnam War were probably unrealistic, and his expectations of genuine friendship from Communist powers were naïve. But what choices did he have? In the late 1950s the United States had made it clear that its own policies, as far as Cambodia was concerned, would always favor Thailand and South Vietnam, a favoritism that included a tolerant attitude toward the anti-Cambodian policies of the two regimes. Sihanouk believed with some justification that he was surrounded by hostile powers and that the United States would never take him seriously. He was also motivated by a genuine patriotism and saw no future for his country if it were swept into the Vietnam War.[4]

The two most consistent aspects of Sihanouk's domestic policy were his intolerance of dissent and his tendency to identify his opponents with foreign powers. To be a Cambodian, in his view, meant being pro-Sihanouk, just as Sihanouk himself, the father of the Cambodian family, was pro-Cambodian. There was no real tradition of pluralist politics in the country, and throughout the Sihanouk era dissent was viewed as a mixture of treason and *lèse majesté*.

Sihanouk was a skillful politician, fond of keeping his opponents off balance by seeming to favor first one and then another. Campaigns targeting the Left followed campaigns launched against the Right, and rivals' suggestions were occasionally appropriated as his own—as in the choice of a neutralist foreign policy in 1955. Placing himself in the middle of the Cambodian political spectrum—envisioned as a tricolor with radical red Khmer *(Khmers rouges)* on one side and conservative blue Khmer on the other—Sihanouk, the white Khmer, refused to make formal alliances with any group. Technically neutral (and profoundly Francophile), he was totally in charge.

OPPOSITION TO SIHANOUK

Between 1955 and the late 1960s, opposition to Sihanouk's rule was poorly organized and ineffective. Except among a handful of radicals, segments of the elite, and parts of the monastic order, the prince was probably almost as popular as he claimed to be. His advisers told him, and he probably came to believe, that there was no basis for dissent in Cambodia. The visible alternatives, once the Democrats had been brushed aside, were the Pracheachon and the Khmer Serei, or Free Khmer, and neither was a formidable force.

The Khmer Serei comprised paramilitary units made up of ethnic Khmer who were recruited, paid, and armed by the Thai and the South Vietnamese and was more or less under the command of the discredited exile Son Ngoc Thanh. Physically on foreign soil and patronized by foreign powers, they were easy targets for Sihanouk's vituperation. When members of the movement were caught inside Cambodia, they were tried in secret and then executed by firing squads. Films of the executions were shown publicly for several weeks.

As for the Pracheachon, its members were often under surveillance, and its newspapers, even though they toed a pro-Sihanouk, anti-U.S. line, were frequently shut down. Several Pracheachon members were killed or put in prison between 1957 and 1963. The clandestine components of the Communist movement, led by Tou Samouth until his assassination by Sihanouk's police in 1962 and thereafter by Saloth Sar, had little success in maintaining the pre-1954 momentum they had commanded among rural people. In the cities, however, Sar and his colleagues, as well as the Communists in the assembly, were popular with intellectuals, monks, and students in their last years of school. To these people, Communist teachers like Saloth Sar and his wife, Khieu Ponnary, who never spoke of their party affiliations, offered an inspiring contrast, in terms of their firm ideology and correct behavior, to the lackadaisical and corrupt Cambodian elite. As teachers they were dedicated and strict, but it was their moral fervor, expressed primarily as a hatred of privilege, corruption, and injustice, that endeared them to their students and to many in the Buddhist monastic order.

In early 1963 Sihanouk launched an anti-Left campaign by broadcasting the names of thirty-four people who he claimed were plotting to overthrow his government. The list named several leftist schoolteachers in Phnom Penh (including Saloth Sar and Ieng Sary), leftists in the assembly, and some intellectuals recently favored by the prince. Melodramatically, Sihanouk summoned all of them to an audience and offered to turn the government over to them. When they refused the offer and pledged loyalty to him, he allowed most of them to resume their former jobs.[5]

Saloth Sar and Ieng Sary, however, were also members of the clandestine Communist Party's Central Committee, which until then had been safe from Sihanouk's police. It seems likely that Sihanouk knew nothing of their party affiliations, but they feared that he did and they fled to the Vietnamese border where they sought protection from Vietnamese Communist troops in an encampment they later referred to as Office 100. Left-wing teachers who remained behind became cautious about expressing their views, as did the members of the underground party in Phnom Penh, now headed by Nuon Chea and Von Vet. For the next three years, left-wing opposition to Sihanouk's rule made little headway.

A stronger restraint on Cambodia's Communists was imposed by the North Vietnamese, whose alliance with Sihanouk would have been threatened by indigenous resistance to his rule. They advised their Cambodian colleagues to wait for a Vietnamese victory and to wage a political as opposed to an armed struggle. This patronizing guidance gave the Cambodians the options of doing nothing or getting caught by the police; unsurprisingly, resentment began to build up among many of them. Some felt, perhaps naively, that they had the same right to a national revolution as did the Vietnamese. Their resentment, however, had a long fuse and exploded only after Communist military victories in 1975.

SIHANOUK'S RULE: A BALANCE SHEET

Between 1955 and 1970, Sihanouk's most positive contribution was to keep Cambodia from being swept into the firestorm in Vietnam. Doing so required skillful footwork, and he paid a price in the resulting animosity from the pro-U.S. regimes in Saigon and Bangkok, whose leaders would have been contemptuous of any Cambodian claims to genuine autonomy.

We can conclude that Sihanouk's domestic record is mixed. Perhaps the most positive aspect of the ramshackle ideology he called Buddhist socialism was his insistence on large expenditures for education (amounting in some years to over 20 percent of the national budget).

Unfortunately, the prince could not foresee the discontent that would affect tens of thousands of high school graduates and hundreds of university graduates in the late 1960s when they found it hard to obtain well-paid employment. Some of these young men and women drifted into the Communist movement, and many more blamed Sihanouk for their plight.

Sihanouk's identification with Cambodia's poor, however sentimental, did much to increase their feelings of self-worth and their identification with the Cambodian state. Ironically, by raising their political consciousness and their awareness of injustice, Sihanouk probably hastened his own demise. His repeated references to Cambodia's grandeur and uniqueness may have misled some younger Cambodians into thinking that they could successfully resist the Vietnamese and others, and that Cambodia's Communist revolution, when it occurred, would be purer and more far-reaching than any so far.

Sihanouk also encouraged a certain amount of political participation and debate by means of so-called national congresses held twice a year outside the royal palace. In theory, any member of the Sangkum was welcome to attend these meetings and express his or her political views. The congresses dealt with uncontroversial issues and, like so much else in Cambodian life, they were stage-managed by the prince, whose policies were voted on by a show of hands. After 1963 the caliber of the debates deteriorated, and Sihanouk used the meetings to abuse his enemies, to defend himself (and Cambodia) against criticism, and to assert that Cambodia was superior to its neighbors and, in ethical terms at least, to most larger powers.

Another positive aspect of Sihanouk's style was his capacity for hard work. He often spent eighteen hours a day reading government papers, and his energetic tours of the countryside put him in touch with literally hundreds of thousands of ordinary Khmer. These contacts almost satisfied his hunger for approval. His hyperactivity was a disadvantage, however, because he preferred talking to listening and was unwilling or unable to delegate authority, even on subjects he knew little about. He also perceived ordinary Cambodians as his children—a view inherited from the French—rather than as people capable of making choices or handling their own affairs.

Phnom Penh in the 1960s was the prettiest capital in Southeast Asia, and many Western journalists taking a break from the Vietnam War were intoxicated by Cambodia's charm. They wrote glowingly about Sihanouk's "island of peace," the contented, peaceable Khmer, and Sihanouk's "charisma." Culturally, life in the capital at least was very appealing.[6] The prince granted many of them interviews, which made excellent copy, but unsurprisingly they said little about the despotic aspects of his rule or the economic problems the country faced. Had they done so their visas would not have been renewed. Indeed, for several months in 1967–68, on Sihanouk's order no foreign journalists were allowed into the country.

Aligned with these more positive aspects of Sihanouk's ruling style, and affecting everything he did, were his vanity, his impatience with advice, and his unwillingness to face Cambodia's economic, infrastructural, and social problems. He rode roughshod over opposition. Hundreds of dissidents disappeared—and are presumed to have been assassinated—during his years in power, and several thousand peasants were killed in the aftermath of a Communist-led uprising in the northwest in 1967.

Like many of his ancestors, Sihanouk saw Cambodia as a family and as a personal possession. He also treated it as a theatrical troupe. Many of his subjects, particularly older people, agreed to play supporting roles and endowed him with supernatural powers. So did the courtesans who surrounded him and played roles in his films. Sihanouk's genuine patriotism and his capacity for hard work were marred by his narcissism and willfulness. Chosen by the French as an instrument for their policies, he was unable to withstand the pressures that built up against him and his country in the late 1960s, when his patrons and enemies overseas conspired to dismantle his neutral stance and when the people he had generously seen through school and college refused to be treated as his children forever.

SIHANOUK'S DECLINE

The first of several turning points in Sihanouk's rule probably came in November 1963 when he broke off the U.S. military aid program that had provided the pay for his armed forces and, in effect, a 15 percent subvention to the national budget. No similar patron stepped forward, although China provided some military equipment over the next few years, and the Cambodian army declined as an effective combat force. In related decisions Sihanouk nationalized the import-export sector of the economy and closed Cambodia's privately owned banks. His motives in cutting off U.S. aid were related to his desire to stay out of the Vietnam War and to maintain good relations with members of the Communist bloc. The other decisions were parts of an effort to gain control over the economy and to cripple the Chinese and Sino-Khmer business elite in Phnom Penh.[7]

The two decisions had unforeseen effects. Sihanouk's break with the United States made him vulnerable to pressures from the Right and lowered military morale. The nationalization of foreign trade soon encouraged the commercial elite to trade clandestinely with Communist insurgents in Vietnam. By 1967 over a quarter of Cambodia's rice harvest was being smuggled to these forces, which paid higher prices than the Cambodian government could afford. At the same time the government lost revenue from the export taxes it normally charged on rice. Foreign trade was also hampered by the loss of entrepreneurial skills and government ineptitude.

To stem the outflow of rice, a decision was made in early 1967 that army units should gather the rice surplus in several areas, pay government prices for it, and transport it to government warehouses. In western Battambang, near Samlaut, resentment against this decision flared into armed conflict. Tens of thousands of farmers fled or were herded into the forest, where they were pursued and wiped out by government forces and hastily assembled vigilante groups. Years later, Sihanouk remarked offhandedly that he had "read somewhere that ten thousand" people had been killed in this repression, and other sources confirm the figure. The killings, of course, had been carried out under his orders.[8]

The uprising unnerved the prince because one purpose of the alliance with North Vietnam, in his view, had been to bring Cambodian Communists under stricter Vietnamese control. Sihanouk found it inconceivable that his "children" could move against him because of genuine grievances connected with his policies—in this case the forced collection of rice. He suspected the Vietnamese of double crossing him but was in no position to do anything about it.

Increasingly suspicious of the Left, Sihanouk was too proud to make overtures to Cambodia's conservatives, whom he had vilified so often. His tactics after Samlaut were to maintain his attacks on the Left, to attempt to hold onto the middle ground, and to seek to renew diplomatic relations with the United States in the hope of reinstating economic and military aid. By then, however, most U.S. policymakers perceived Cambodia as a side issue to their country's involvement in Vietnam and wanted relations with Sihanouk only on their terms.

Because of losses of revenue as a result of clandestine trading, mismanagement of state-controlled industry, and extravagant expenditures, Cambodia's economy in 1967–68 was faltering. Agricultural problems had never attracted Sihanouk's sustained attention. These included low yields, poor irrigation, and excessive interest charged on loans to farmers, and they were being exacerbated by a rapidly increasing population and fluctuations in world prices. By 1967 these problems had become severe, yet Sihanouk's reaction was still to ignore them. Increasingly, he turned over political power to Lon Nol and Sirik Matak. He hoped that something would turn up to save the country's economy or that the people in charge would perform so badly as to again enhance his power. Sensing his vulnerability, however, his enemies gathered strength.

Between 1963 and the end of 1966, Cambodia's leading Communists were camped along the Vietnamese border under Vietnamese protection. Communists later took credit for Sihanouk's break with the United States, but in fact their influence on events in these years was close to zero, and Saloth Sar, the party's leader, spent more than twelve months in 1965–66 outside the country.

In 1965 Sar was summoned to North Vietnam for consultations. Walking north along the Ho Chi Minh Trail, he took two months to reach Hanoi, where he was taken to task for his party's nationalist agenda. The secretary of the Vietnamese Communist Party, Le Duan, told him to subordinate Cambodia's interests to Vietnam's, to help Vietnam defeat the United States, and to postpone armed struggle until the time was ripe.[9]

Bruised by these attacks, Sar said nothing to antagonize his patrons. Soon afterward, however, he traveled to China and was warmly welcomed by radical officials. Inspired by the early phases of the Cultural Revolution, Sar transferred his loyalties to a new set of patrons and a more vibrant revolutionary model. With hindsight, it is interesting to speculate about the effect of events in China at the time on the members of the Cambodian delegation. How did they react to Mao Zedong's flight to Shanghai, his swim in the Yangtze, and his inauguration of the Cultural Revolution? And how did they interpret Defense Minister Lin Biao's widely publicized speech emphasizing the importance of self-reliance in Communist revolutions? The speech must have worried the Vietnamese, for whom Chinese military aid was crucial in the war with the United States; on the other hand, it may have secretly pleased those Khmer who saw Vietnamese assistance as a form of suffocation.

In any event, the visit to China was a turning point in Sar's career and perhaps in the history of Cambodian Communism as well. Prudently, however, he said nothing to the Vietnamese about his change of heart. Back home, he established his headquarters in a remote, heavily wooded section of the country. For the next four years, with a group of like-minded colleagues, he lost touch with everyday Cambodian life, polished his Utopian ideas, nourished his hatreds, and thought about seizing power.

Over a year later, just before the Vietnamese Communists launched the Tet Offensive, the Communist Party of Kampuchea (CPK), as it now styled itself, inaugurated an armed struggle against Sihanouk, striking out from its bases in the northeast and the northwest. The struggle, insignificant at first, gathered momentum over the next two years, and by early 1970 insurgent forces had occupied, or rendered unsafe for others to occupy, nearly a fifth of Cambodia's territory. In the cities, meanwhile, many students and teachers who had been alienated by Sihanouk's narcissistic rule found themselves enthralled by the possibilities of the Cultural Revolution in China and the May 1968 uprisings in France. For many young Cambodians these movements seemed to offer viable alternatives to the perennial corruption and conservatism of Cambodian politics.

During this volatile time, Sihanouk busied himself with making feature films over which he exercised total control as writer, director, producer, and leading actor. Making them offered relief from a political game that had become too complex for him to win and too dangerous to play. The prince also scrambled to realign himself with the United States while reasserting his friendship with that country's enemies in Vietnam. These contradictory moves discredited him even further with his enemies inside the country, and by late 1969 high-ranking conservative officials had begun plotting against him. Whether or not they received encouragement from officers in the newly reopened U.S. embassy is a matter for speculation.[10]

The most prominent of the plotters was Sihanouk's cousin, Sisowath Sirik Matak, a career civil servant who had become deputy prime minister under Lon Nol. Matak had grown impatient with Sihanouk's mismanagement of the economy, and he was dismayed by the presence of Vietnamese bases on Cambodian soil and by his cousin's impulsive, contradictory foreign policy. Pro-Western himself, and with links to Phnom Penh's commercial elite, Matak was tired of playing a supporting role in Sihanouk's never-ending opera.

Lon Nol, the prime minister, was a more enigmatic figure. He is not known to have objected to the prince about the cutoff of U.S. aid, the alliance with the Communists, or the shipments of arms through Cambodian territory. Indeed, many of his officers became rich by dealing in arms, medicines, and supplies for which the Vietnamese paid generously. By 1969, however, Cambodian troops were under fire from Communist insurgents, and the Vietnamese administration of many base areas had drawn complaints from local people. Lon Nol was also under pressure from some of his officers who saw Cambodia's isolation from U.S. aid and, by implication, from the Vietnam War as impediments to their financial ambitions. Moreover, Lon Nol was not immune to flattery, and he came to see himself as uniquely capable of saving Cambodia from the *thmil*, or "unbelievers," as he called the Vietnamese hammering at his country's gates.

While pressures were mounting, Sihanouk's interest in governing declined. Years of overwork had worn him down, and his inability or unwillingness to attract and keep young, competent advisers had begun to tell. His decision to open a casino in Phnom Penh to raise revenue had disastrous results. In the last six months of 1969, thousands of Cambodians lost millions of dollars at its tables. Several prominent people, and dozens of impoverished ones, committed suicide after sustaining losses, and hundreds of families went bankrupt. Sihanouk, no gambler himself, was indifferent to the chaos he had caused, and his own expenditures continued to mount. A climax of sorts occurred in November, when an international film festival, stage-managed by the prince, ended with one of his own films, "Twilight," being awarded a solid-gold statue sculpted from ingots donated for the purpose by Cambodia's national bank. When Sihanouk left the country for his annual holiday in January 1970, many people who remained behind interpreted his departure as a flight.

THE COUP OF 1970

Over the next two months, Sisowath Sirik Matak and his colleagues struggled to put Cambodia's house in order, shutting down the casino and privatizing the banks. Matak traveled secretly to Hanoi to see what could be done to remove Vietnamese troops from Cambodian soil. Documents signed by Sihanouk agreeing to the Vietnamese bases infuriated him. Deliveries of supplies to Vietnamese forces inside the country were halted, and the stage was set for a full-scale confrontation with Vietnam—a scenario Sihanouk had struggled to avoid for fifteen years.

In early March, riots broke out in Phnom Penh against the embassies of North Vietnam and its surrogate in South Vietnam, the National Liberation Front. The riots got out of hand, and both buildings were badly damaged. From Paris, Sihanouk condemned the violence, although the riots had occurred with his permission. Conditions were ripening for the coup d'état that Matak had been considering for several months, and the timetable was accelerated because it was feared that Sihanouk might soon return. On the night of March 17, Matak and three army officers visited Lon Nol at his house, threatened him with a pistol, and made him sign a declaration supporting a vote against the prince scheduled for the following day in the National Assembly. When he signed the document, as if aware of the long-term consequences of his action, Lon Nol burst into tears.[11]

Sihanouk dismissed from office; graffito
in Phnom Penh, 1970. Author's photo.

What followed was an anticlimax and in sharp contrast to the oper-
atic style of Sihanouk's politics. The National Assembly, as it was entitled to do, voted 86–3 to remove its confidence from the prince and to
replace him as chief of state, pending elections, with the relatively color-
less president of the assembly, Cheng Heng. Lon Nol remained prime
minister with Matak as his assistant. The coup was popular among educated people in Phnom Penh and in the army, but rural Cambodians
were totally unprepared for it. Many of the plotters wanted to declare
Cambodia a republic but delayed doing so after pro-Sihanouk riots
broke out in several provinces.

Meanwhile, the prince, who learned of the coup while traveling home
via Moscow, was in Beijing. His first thought was to seek political asy-

lum in France, but after talks with Zhou Enlai and the Vietnamese premier, Pham Van Dong, he agreed to take command of a united front government allied to North Vietnam, whose Cambodian forces would consist largely of the Communists his army had been struggling to destroy only a month before. At the end of March the prince broadcast an appeal to his "brothers and sisters" (they were no longer his children, apparently) to take up arms against Lon Nol. Pro-Sihanouk riots broke out almost immediately in the eastern part of the country. Fueled by panic, arrogance, and racism, Cambodian army units massacred hundreds of unarmed Vietnamese civilians near Phnom Penh on the dubious grounds that they were allied with the Communists. They were certainly easier to locate than the North Vietnamese armed forces and easier to kill, but the viciousness of the massacre, and Lon Nol's failure to express regret, evaporated the goodwill the regime had earned overseas.

For most Cambodians, moreover, the idea that Vietnamese forces should leave Cambodia was more popular than the coup itself. After Lon Nol gave the Vietnamese Communists forty-eight hours to leave the country—probably the most unrealistic command in modern Cambodian history—many Cambodians were enraged to learn that the Vietnamese had ignored him, and tens of thousands poured into the armed forces to drive the "invaders" from the country. Thousands were killed or wounded over the next few weeks, picked off by Vietnamese soldiers who had been in combat in some cases for over twenty years. In May 1970, a joint U.S.–South Vietnamese invasion of eastern Cambodia drove the North Vietnamese forces farther west. The invasion protected the U.S. withdrawal from Vietnam, but it probably spelled the end of Cambodia as a sovereign state.[12]

THE KHMER REPUBLIC'S SLOW COLLAPSE

Lon Nol's two offensives against the Vietnamese in late 1970 and 1971 were named after the pre-Angkorean kingdom of Chenla. They were encouraged by the United States, but Lon Nol's troops were badly trained, poorly equipped, and often badly led. Experienced North Vietnamese forces cut them to pieces, and after 1971 Lon Nol's troops mounted no major offensive actions. After becoming a republic in October 1970, the government survived for four more years, largely because of U.S. military and economic assistance and heavy bombing.

The last four years of the Khmer Republic were violent and melancholy. Lon Nol suffered a stroke in early 1971. Although he recovered rapidly, he never regained full political control. Without strong leadership many politicians in Phnom Penh busied themselves with forming factions and amassing wealth. A leading actor was Lon Nol's younger brother, Lon Non, whose efforts were concentrated on keeping Sisowath Sirik Matak—or anyone else—from gaining power from Lon Nol.

In the countryside, republican army officers often falsified the numbers of soldiers under their command so as to pocket the salaries provided by the United States. Some officers also sold military equipment to the Communists; few were prepared to take offensive action. Lon Nol was reluctant to punish the malfeasance or corruption of officers who were loyal to him. Instead, he spent much of his time writing long letters to his friend, President Nixon, pleading for U.S. aid while listening to Buddhist mystics who promised magical solutions to the war. By the end of 1972 the Khmer Republic controlled Phnom Penh, a few provincial capitals, and much of Battambang. The rest of the country was either in Communist hands or unsafe for anyone to administer.

In the first half of 1973 the United States brutally postponed a Communist victory by conducting a bombing campaign on Cambodia that, in its intensity, was as far-reaching as any during World War II. Over a hundred thousand tons of bombs fell on the Cambodian countryside before the U.S. Congress prohibited further bombing. No reliable estimate of casualties has ever been made, but the campaign probably halted the Communist forces encircling Phnom Penh, even though some have argued that it hardened the will of the surviving Communist forces. The war dragged on for another year and a half, but President Nixon's reaction to the end of the bombing was to declare to an aide that, as a result, the United States had "lost" Southeast Asia—a section of the world it had never owned.[13]

The Communists' response to over twenty years of Vietnamese assistance to their movement was to massacre most of the Cambodians sent down from North Vietnam as soon as North Vietnamese troops withdrew

Young girls in revolutionary costume, 1972. Photo by Serge Thion.

from Cambodia at the end of 1972, following the cease-fire agreed upon by Vietnam and the United States. These killings occurred in secret. The Communists also experimented with programs of collectivization in the zones under their control, and in early 1973, during the U.S. bombing campaign, the CPK introduced compulsory cooperatives in some areas. By then, rumors were reaching Phnom Penh about the uncompromising conduct of the insurgents, who took no prisoners and who herded inhabitants into the forest whenever they captured a town or village. Many people in Phnom Penh dismissed these rumors as propaganda and continued to believe that the Khmer Rouge were puppets of the Vietnamese. At the same time they were exhausted by the war and ready for almost any alternative to the corrupt and inefficient Khmer Republic.

The end came in early 1975 when the Communists mined the riverine approaches to Phnom Penh and thus prevented shipments of rice and ammunition from reaching the capital. Airlifts arranged by the United States were unable to bring in enough rice to feed Phnom Penh or enough ammunition to defend it. For the next three months the Cambodian

Communists tightened their noose around the city, now swollen with perhaps two million refugees. In early March, Lon Nol flew out of the country taking along a million dollars awarded him by his government. Last-minute attempts to negotiate with Sihanouk, set in motion by the United States, came to nothing. At this point or shortly beforehand, and without waiting for approval from his Vietnamese allies, Saloth Sar and his colleagues decided to take Phnom Penh.

On the morning of April 17, 1975, columns of Communist troops dressed in peasant clothes or simple khaki uniforms, ominously silent and heavily armed, converged on Phnom Penh from three directions. Many of them were under fifteen years of age. Walking slowly down the capital's broad avenues, emptied of other traffic, they responded coldly to the people's welcome. Their arrival coincided roughly with the Cambodian new year and came two weeks before the Communist victory in South Vietnam. The coincidences were deliberate, for the Communists probably intended that the year to come, like year one of the French Revolution, would usher in an entirely new phase of Cambodian history, without any connections to the revolution in Vietnam.[14]

12

REVOLUTION IN CAMBODIA

It is uncertain whether historians of Cambodia a hundred years from now will devote as much space to the country's brief revolutionary period as to the much longer, more complex, and more mysterious Angkorean era. For nearly all mature Cambodians in the early twenty-first century, however, the three years, eight months, and twenty days that followed the capture of Phnom Penh in April 1975 were a traumatic and unforgettable period. Because of the ferocity with which Cambodia's revolution was waged, however, and the way it contrasted with many people's ideas about pre-1970 Cambodia, a chapter-length discussion of the period fits well in a narrative history of this kind.

The Communist regime that controlled Cambodia between April 17, 1975, and January 7, 1979, was known as Democratic Kampuchea (DK). Survivors remember the time as *vinh chu chot* (three words for the sharp tastes of unripe fruit). The bitter-tasting revolution that DK sponsored swept through the country like a forest fire or a typhoon, and its spokesmen claimed after the military victory that "over two thousand years of Cambodia history" had ended. So had money, markets, formal education, Buddhism, books, private property, diverse clothing styles, and freedom of movement. No Cambodian government had ever tried to change so many things so rapidly; none had been so relentlessly oriented toward the future or so biased in favor of the poor.

The leaders of DK, who were members of Cambodia's Communist Party (CPK) were for the most part hidden from view and called themselves the "revolutionary organization" (*angkar padevat*). They sought to transform Cambodia by replacing what they saw as impediments to national autonomy and social justice with revolutionary energy and incentives. They believed that family life, individualism, and an ingrained fondness for what they called feudal institutions, as well as the institutions themselves, stood in the way of the revolution. Cambodia's poor, they said, had always been exploited and enslaved. Liberated by the revolution and empowered by military victory, these men and women would now become the masters of their lives and, collectively, the masters of their country.

The CPK monitored every step of the revolution but concealed its existence from outsiders and did not reveal its socialist agenda or the names of its leaders. It said nothing of its long-standing alliance with the Communists in Vietnam and very little about the patronage of China and North Korea that the regime enjoyed. For several months the CPK's leaders even allowed foreigners to think that Sihanouk, who had served as a figurehead leader for the anti–Lon Nol resistance, was still Cambodia's chief of state. By concealing its alliances and agendas, the new government gave the impression that Cambodia and its revolution were genuinely independent. In 1978 Saloth Sar (Pol Pot) boasted to Yugoslavian visitors that Cambodia was "building socialism without a model." That process began in April 1975 and continued for the lifetime of DK, but by acknowledging that there were no precedents for what they were doing, Pol Pot and his colleagues had embarked on a perilous course.[1]

To transform the country thoroughly and at once, Communist cadres ordered everyone out of the cities and towns. In the week after April 17, 1975, over two million Cambodians were pushed into the countryside toward an uncertain fate. Only the families of top CPK officials and a few hundred Khmer Rouge soldiers were allowed to stay behind. This brutal order, never thoroughly explained, added several thousand deaths to what may have been five hundred thousand inflicted by the civil war. Reports reaching the West spoke of hospital patients driven from their beds, random executions, and sick and elderly people as well as small children dead or abandoned along the roads. The evacuation shocked its victims as well as observers in other countries, who had hoped that the new regime would try to govern through reconciliation. But these men and women may have forgotten the ferocity with which the civil war had been fought by both sides. Still other observers, more sympathetic to the idea of revolution, saw the evacuation of the cities as the only way Cambodia could grow enough food to survive, break down entrenched and supposedly backward-looking social hierarchies, loyalties, and arrangements and set its Utopian strategies in motion.[2]

The decision to evacuate the cities was made by the CPK's leaders shortly before the liberation of Phnom Penh, but it was a closely kept secret and took some Communist commanders by surprise. One reason for the decision was that the capital was genuinely short of food. Another was the difficulty of administering several million people who had failed to support the revolution. A third was that the CPK's leaders were fearful for their own security. Perhaps the overriding reason, however, was the desire to assert the victory of the CPK, the dominance of the countryside over the cities and the empowerment of the poor. Saloth Sar and his colleagues had not spent seven years in the forest and five years after that fighting a civil war to take office as city councilors. They saw the cities as breeding grounds for counterrevolution. Their economic priorities were based on the transformation of Cambodian agriculture, especially on increasing the national production of rice. By exporting the surplus, it was hoped that the government would earn hard currency with which to pay for imports and, eventually, to finance industrialization. To achieve such a surplus, the CPK needed all the agricultural workers it could find.

For the next six months, the people who had been driven out of the cities—known to the regime as "new people" or "April 17 people"—busied themselves with growing rice and other crops under the supervision of soldiers and CPK cadres. Conditions were severe, particularly for those unaccustomed to physical labor, but because in most districts there was enough to eat, many survivors of DK who had been evacuated from Phnom Penh came to look back on these months as a comparative golden age. For the first time in many years, Cambodia was not at war, and many so-called new people were eager to help to reconstruct their battered country. Perhaps, after all, Cambodia's problems were indeed so severe as to require revolutionary solutions. A former engineer has said, "At first, the ideas of the revolution were good." He added, however, that "they didn't work in practice."[3]

For many rural Cambodians, and especially those between fifteen and twenty-five, fighting against feudalism and the Americans in the early 1970s had provided beguiling glimpses of freedom, self-respect, and power—as well as access to weapons—that were unimaginable to their parents or to most Cambodians. These young people, to borrow a phrase from Mao Zedong, were "poor and blank" pages on which it was often easy to inscribe the teachings of the revolution. Owing everything to the revolutionary organization, which they referred to as their mother and father, and nothing to the past, it was thought that these young people would lead the way in transforming Cambodia into a socialist state and in moving the people toward independence, mastery, and self-reliance. To the alarm and confusion of many older people, these often violent young Cambodians became the revolution's cutting edge.

DK TAKES POWER, 1975–76

The DK period in Cambodia was characterized by regional and temporal variations. By and large, those parts of the country that had been under CPK control the longest tended to be the best equipped to deal with the programs set out by the party and the most accommodating to the new people. Cadres were better trained and more disciplined in the east, northeast, and southwest than they were in the northwest. Unfortunately for the new people, the northwest, centered on the provinces of Battambang and Pursat, had been the most productive agricultural area in prerevolutionary times. For this reason hundreds of thousands of new people were driven into the northwest in early 1976. The regime's demands for crop surpluses were heavier there than in other regions, and so were the sufferings that ensued.[4]

The CPK divided Cambodia into seven zones (*phumipheak*), which in turn were broken down into thirty-two administrative regions (*dombon*). In general, conditions were relatively tolerable through 1976 in the northeastern and eastern zones, somewhat worse in the southwest, central, and

Zones and administrative divisions of Democratic Kampuchea.

west, and worst of all in the northern and northwestern zones. Within the zones there was also considerable variation, reflecting differences in leadership, resources, and external factors such as the fighting with Vietnam that broke out in earnest in the east and the southwest in the middle of 1977.[5]

Life was hard everywhere. On a national scale it is estimated that over the lifetime of the regime nearly two million people—or one person in four—died as a result of DK policies and actions. These included overworking people, neglecting or mistreating the sick, and giving everyone less food than they needed to survive. Perhaps as many as four hundred thousand were killed outright as enemies of the revolution. Most of these people died in provincial prison. On a per capita basis, and considering the short life span of DK, the number of regime-related deaths in Cambodia is one of the highest in recorded world history.

Whether or not the death toll fits the terms of the UN genocide convention has been vigorously debated. Those who argue for the use of the term see close parallels in the Cambodian case to what happened during the Holocaust, in Armenia, and in Rwanda. Those arguing against the term suggest that racist motives were much lower on DK's agenda (except for the systematic execution of Vietnamese residents in 1978 and, in some cases, Muslim Cham) than was destroying the regime's political enemies, a category of victims purposely omitted from the UN genocide convention. For these critics the term *crimes against humanity* fits what happened in DK better than the highly charged and perhaps misleading *genocide*.[6]

The DK period can be divided into four phases. The first lasted from the capture of Phnom Penh until the beginning of 1976 when DK formally came into existence, a constitution was proclaimed, and a new wave of migration was set in motion from the center and southwest, which were heavily populated but relatively unproductive, to the rich rice-growing areas in the northwest. The southwest had been liberated early and contained many revolutionary bases. It was crowded with refugees from Phnom Penh. Most of the northwest on the other hand had remained under republican control until April 1975. The regime counted on this area to lead the way in expanding Cambodia's rice production, and the new people were the instruments chosen to achieve this goal. The fact that they were socially unredeemable was seen as an advantage because their deaths made no difference to the regime. In a chilling adage recalled by many survivors, they were often told, "Keeping you is no profit; losing you is no loss."[7]

During this period, Phnom Penh radio enjoined its listeners via anonymous speakers and revolutionary songs to "build and defend" Cambodia against unnamed enemies (*khmang*) and traitors (*kbot cheat*) outside and within the country in patterns reminiscent of Maoist China. In view of the regime's collapse in 1979, there was a poignant optimism built into these pronouncements, but in the early stages of the revolution many Cambodians seem to have believed that it would succeed. Moreover, from the perspective of the party's leaders, genuine or imagined enemies had not yet surfaced.

DK's second phase lasted until the end of September 1976 and marked the apogee of the regime, although conditions in most of the countryside deteriorated as the year progressed. It is uncertain why the leaders of the CPK waited so long to come into the open. They had managed to control the population without identifying themselves for nearly a year and a half. Perhaps this anonymity made them feel secure. China's continuing patronage of Sihanouk might also have been a factor in the CPK's postponing of its outright assumption of power. When the Chinese prime minister, Zhou Enlai, who was Prince Sihanouk's most important patron, died in January 1976, the leaders of the CPK were ready to brush the prince aside and to force him to retire as chief of state. A confidential party document of March 1976 stated that "Sihanouk has run out of breath. He cannot go forward. Therefore we have decided to retire him."[8] Sihanouk resigned three days later. In reports broadcast over Phnom Penh radio probably for foreign consumption, he was offered a pension that was never paid and a monument in his honor that was never erected. By April 1976 he was living under guard in a villa on the grounds of the royal palace with his wife and their son, Sihamoni, who became king of Cambodia when Sihanouk retired in 2004. The prince stayed there, in relative comfort but in fear of his life, until he was sent by DK on a diplomatic mission to the UN in January 1979. The March 1976 DK document also noted that the new government "must be purely a party organization" and stated that "Comrade Pol," a pseudonym for Saloth Sar who was not otherwise identified, would be prime minister.

The constitution of Democratic Kampuchea, promulgated in January 1976, guaranteed no human rights, defined few organs of government and, in effect, abolished private property, organized religion, and family-oriented agricultural production. The document acknowledged no foreign models, denied any foreign alliances or assistance, and said nothing about the CPK or Marxist-Leninist ideas. Instead, it made the revolution sound like a uniquely Cambodian affair with no connection to the outside world.[9]

When National Assembly elections were held in March, the CPK's candidates were voted in unopposed. They included members of the

CPK Central Committee, elected as peasants, rubber workers, and so on, as well as others harder to identify. Pol Pot, not otherwise identified, represented "rubber workers in the eastern zone." The candidates had no territorial constituencies, being seen instead as representatives of certain classes of Khmer. New people were not nominated or eligible to vote, and it seems that in much of the country no elections ever took place. The assembly met only once, to approve the constitution, and never played a significant role in DK. Like the elections themselves, the assembly seems to have been formed to placate foreign opinion.

The people who achieved a prominent place in the new government were a mixture of intellectuals who had studied in France, including Pol Pot, Ieng Sary, Sary's wife, Ieng Thirith, Hu Nim, Khieu Samphan, Thiounn Thioenn and Son Sen; older members of the Indochinese Communist Party like Nuon Chea, Nhek Ros, Chou Chet, Non Suon, Ta Mok, and Sao Phim; and younger militants who had never left Cambodia, such as Von Vet, Khek Pen, and Chhim Samauk. Those in charge of the zones did not include any ex-students from France; they were concentrated in the newly established ministries of Phnom Penh.

THE FOUR-YEAR PLAN

Over the next few months, Pol Pot and his colleagues drafted a four-year economic plan "to build socialism in all fields." The plan was to go into effect in September 1976, but it was never formally launched. It called for the collectivization of all Cambodian property and proposed ever-increasing levels of rice production throughout the country, with the aim of achieving an average national yield of three metric tons per hectare (1.4 tons per acre). The prerevolutionary national average, harvested under less stringent conditions and with monetary incentives, had been less than a ton per hectare, one of the lowest yields in Southeast Asia. The goal of tripling the average was to be achieved by extensive irrigation, double and triple cropping, longer working hours, and the release of revolutionary fervor supposedly derived from the people's liberation from exploitation and individual concerns. The plan was hastily written. No effort was made to see if its proposals were appropriate to soil and water conditions in particular areas or if the infrastructure with which to achieve its goals was in place. Instead, the plan called for an "all out, storming offensive" by everyone throughout the country. Some writers have drawn parallels between the CPK's program and the so-called war communism of the Soviet Union in the early 1920s; others compare DK's policies to those known as the Great Leap Forward in China in the 1950s. No material incentives were offered the Cambodian people in the plan except the bizarre promise that everyone would enjoy dessert on a daily basis—by 1980! Cambodia's newfound independence, the empowerment of the poor, and the end of exploitation were thought to be sufficient incentives and rewards.[10]

Under the plan, crops such as cotton, jute, rubber, coconuts, sugar, and kapok were also to be cultivated for export. With the money earned from exports, light industry was to be established and, eventually, heavy industry as well. Plans for the latter were particularly Utopian, for they were dependent on raw materials like iron, steel, and petroleum, which did not exist in DK. Cambodia's extensive offshore petroleum deposits were not discovered until the 1990s.

In explaining the plan to high-ranking members of the party, an unnamed spokesman, presumably Pol Pot, stated that it could be accomplished swiftly. The DK revolution, after all, was "a new experience, and an important one for the whole world, because we don't perform like others. We leap [directly to] a socialist revolution, and swiftly build socialism. We don't need a long period of time for transformation."[11]

The plan said nothing about leisure, religion, formal education, or family life. Although it was deemed crucial to "abolish illiteracy among the population," nothing was said about what people would be given or allowed to read. Some primary schools existed in base areas by 1976, but education was not extended to new people or their children until 1977 or 1978. Education above the primary level did not exist before 1978, when a belated attempt was made to establish a technical high school in Phnom Penh. In part, DK officials were making a virtue of necessity, since most men and women known to be experienced schoolteachers and hostile to the CPK were suspected of treasonous intentions and were often killed as class enemies. Former teachers who were members of the party, like Pol Pot and Ieng Sary, now had more rewarding tasks to perform.

Most Cambodians under DK had to work ten to twelve hours a day, twelve months a year to accomplish the objectives of the plan. Many of those who were unaccustomed to physical labor soon died of malnutrition and overwork, but even those who had been farmers in prerevolutionary times found themselves working longer and harder than they had before 1975, with no material rewards, limited access to their spouses and children, and very little free time. By early 1976, food was already scarce, since the surpluses from the first harvests had been gathered up to feed the army, to be stored, or to be exported. The situation deteriorated in 1977 and 1978 when much of the country was stricken with famine. Many survivors recall months of eating rice gruel without much else. One of them, now living in Australia, has said, "We looked like the Africans you see on television. Our legs were like sticks; we could barely walk."[12]

A similar famine had swept through China in the early 1960s in the wake of the Great Leap Forward. In Cambodia, news of the famine was slow to reach the leaders in Phnom Penh; when it did, starvation was seen as evidence of mismanagement and treachery by those cadres charged with distribution of food. These people, many of them loyal members of the CPK, were soon arrested, interrogated, and put to death. The DK's leaders seem to have believed that the forces they had mobilized to defeat the Americans—two weeks earlier than a similar victory had taken place in Vietnam—were sufficient for any task set by the "clear-sighted" CPK.[13]

During this second stage of the DK era, inexperienced cadres, in order to meet the targets imposed from the center, placed what were often unbearable pressures on the April 17 people and everyone else under their command. One way of achieving surpluses was to reduce the amount of rice used for seed and what had been set aside to feed the people. Rations were sufficient for survival, and in several parts of the country, people had enough to eat for most of 1976. In much of the northwest, however, rations diminished as the center's Utopian priorities came into force. Several hundred thousand more "new people" had been brought into the area in early 1976, and many of them were set to work hacking clearings out of the jungle. No Western-style medicines were available, and thousands soon died from malaria, overwork, and malnutrition.

A CRISIS IN THE PARTY

In early September 1976, Mao Zedong died shortly before the CPK was to celebrate its twenty-fifth anniversary. Pol Pot used his comments on Mao's death to state publicly for the first time that Cambodia was being governed in accordance with Marxist-Leninist ideas. He stopped short of identifying *angkar padevat* as the CPK. It seems likely that the CPK had hoped to use its anniversary on September 30 to announce its existence to the world and to launch its Four-Year Plan. As the month wore on, however, a split developed inside the CPK between those who favored the 1951 date for the foundation of the party and those who preferred 1960, when a special congress had convened in Phnom Penh and had named Pol Pot and Ieng Sary, among others, to the party's Central Committee. To those who preferred the 1960 date, the earlier one was suggestive of Vietnamese domination of the party. They viewed those who favored 1951 as people whose primary loyalties were to Vietnam. What Pol Pot later described as the putting down of a potential coup d'état against his rule was more likely a preemptive purge of several party members whose loyalties to the party (or to Vietnam) seemed to be greater than their loyalties to Pol Pot.[14]

Two prominent members of the CPK, Keo Meas and Non Suon, who both had ties to the Vietnamese-dominated phase of the party's history were arrested and accused of treason. Their confessions assert that they supported a 1951 founding date for the CPK.[15]

Overall, several thousand typed and handwritten confessions have survived from the DK interrogation center in the Phnom Penh suburb of Tuol Sleng, known in the DK period by its code name S-21. At least fourteen thousand men and women were questioned, tortured, and executed at the facility between the end of 1975 and the first few days of 1979, and over four thousand of their dossiers survive. Some of these run to hundreds of pages. The confessions are invaluable for historians, but it is impossible to tell from these documents alone whether or not a genuine conspiracy to dethrone Pol Pot and his associates had gathered momentum by September 1976. Like Sihanouk and Lon Nol, Pol Pot considered disagreements over policy to be tantamount to treason, and arguments over the party's founding date suggested to him that certain people wanted him removed from power.[16]

At the end of the month, barely four days before the anniversary of the party was to be celebrated, Pol Pot resigned as prime minister "for reasons of health" and was replaced by the second-ranking man in the CPK, Nuon Chea. Pol Pot's health had often broken down in the preceding year and a half, but he probably announced his resignation at this point to throw his enemies off balance and to draw others into the open. The resignation, in fact, may never have actually taken place. By mid-October, in any case, he was back in office. In November, after the arrest of the Gang of Four, Pol Pot and five of his colleagues traveled secretly to China to reassure themselves of continuing Chinese support. By 1978 this included two Chinese engineering regiments engaged in building a military airfield near Kompong Chhnang. It is likely that this ongoing military help was agreed upon at this time.[17]

There was still no announcement of the party's existence, however, as its leaders had decided to keep the matter secret for the time being, to postpone a formal announcement of the Four-Year Plan and to intensify the search for enemies inside the party. In the meantime, S-21 expanded its operations. Only two hundred prisoners entered the facility in 1975, but more than ten times that many (2,250) were brought there in 1976, and more than two-thirds of them were imprisoned between September and November, covering the period of unease in the CPK discussed above. Another five thousand prisoners were taken there in 1977, and approximately the same number were imprisoned in 1978. Factory workers in Phnom Penh, who knew about the center's existence but not about what went on inside its barbed-wire walls, called it a "place of entering, no leaving" (konlanh choul ot cenh). Only a dozen of the prisoners taken there for interrogation avoided being put to death.[18]

In December 1976, as the purges intensified, Pol Pot presided over a "study session" restricted to high-ranking members of the party that

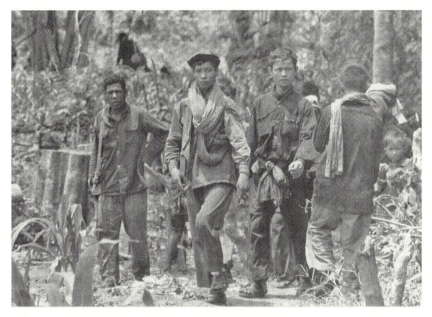

Democratic Kampuchean cadre, Thai-Cambodian border, 1979. Photo by Brian L. Stevens.

was called to examine the progress of the Cambodian revolution. The document that has survived from this meeting, a speech by Pol Pot, is darker and more pessimistic than those produced earlier in the year. In a vivid passage, Pol Pot spoke of a "sickness in the party" that had developed during 1976:

> We cannot locate it precisely. The illness must emerge to be examined. Because the heat of [previous stages of the revolution] was insufficient at the level of people's struggle and class struggle . . . we searched for the microbes within the party without success. They are buried. As our socialist revolution advances, however, seeping more strongly into every corner of the party, the army and among the people, we can locate the evil microbes. . . . Those who defend us must be truly adept. They should have practice in observing. They must observe everything, but not so that those being observed are aware of it.[19]

Who were the observers and who were the observed? People opposed to the revolution were moving targets depending on the evolving policies and priorities of the party's leadership. At different stages of DK's short history, the "evil microbes" were those with middle-class backgrounds or soldiers who had fought for Lon Nol, those who had joined the Communist movement when it was guided by Vietnam, or those who had been exposed to foreign countries. In 1977, attention shifted to the northern and northwestern zones where famines had occurred, and by 1978 victims included high-ranking members of the party, military commanders, and officials associated with the eastern zone. To be suspected, a person had only to be mentioned in the confessions of three other people. Those accused would name the people they knew, and so on. Hundreds, probably thousands of those who were taken to S-21 were completely innocent of the charges brought against them, but everyone who was interrogated was considered guilty, and nearly all those who were interrogated were killed. News of people's disappearances was used to keep their colleagues in the party in line, but the deaths themselves and the existence of the prison were not made public. The regime never expressed regret for anyone it had executed by mistake. For Pol Pot and his colleagues, too much hung in the balance for them to hesitate in attacking enemies of the party: the success of the revolution, the execution of policy, and the survival of the leaders themselves. At the end of his December 1976 speech, Pol Pot remarked that such enemies "have been entering the party continuously. . . . They remain—perhaps only one person, or two people. They remain."[20]

The effect of brutal, ambiguous threats like these on the people listening to them is impossible to gauge. Within a year many of these men and women had been arrested, interrogated, tortured, and put to death at S-21. In most cases, they were forced to admit that they had joined the "CIA" (a blanket term for counterrevolutionary activity) early in their careers. Others claimed to have worked for Soviet or Vietnamese intelligence agencies. It is unclear whether Pol Pot and the cadres at S-21 who forced people to make these confessions believed in these conspiracies or merely in the efficacy of executing anyone who was suspected by those in power.[21]

CONFLICT WITH VIETNAM

The third phase of the DK era, between the political crisis of September 1976 and a speech by Pol Pot twelve months later in which he announced the existence of the CPK, was marked by waves of purges and by a shift toward blaming Cambodia's difficulties and counterrevolutionary activity to an increasing extent on Vietnam. Open conflict with Vietnam had been a possibility ever since April 1975, when Cambodian forces had attacked several Vietnamese-held islands in the Gulf of Thailand with the hope of making territorial gains in the final stages of the Vietnam War. The Cambodian forces had been driven back and differences between the two Communist regimes had more or less been papered over, but DK's distrust of Vietnamese territorial intentions was very deep. So were Pol Pot's suspicions of the Vietnamese Communist Party, whose leaders had been patronizing toward their Cambodian counterparts for many years and had allowed Cambodia's armed struggle to flourish only in the shadow of Vietnam's. Pol Pot's suspicions deepened in July 1977 when Vietnam signed a treaty of cooperation with Laos, a move that he interpreted as part of Vietnam's plan to encircle Cambodia and to reconstitute and control what had once been French Indochina.[22]

Realizing the relative strengths of the two countries, however, Pol Pot tried at first to maintain correct relations and was unwilling to expand DK's armed forces to defend eastern Cambodia against possible Vietnamese incursions. The Vietnamese, recovering from almost thirty years of fighting, were also cautious. In 1975–76, however, their attempts to open negotiations about the frontier were rebuffed by the Cambodians, who demanded that the Vietnamese honor the verbal agreements they had reached with Sihanouk in the 1960s. Cambodians claimed parts of the Gulf of Thailand, where they hoped to profit from partially explored but unexploited offshore oil deposits, but these claims were rejected by the Vietnamese, who had similar hopes. Skirmishes along the border between heavily armed, poorly disciplined troops in 1976 led Vietnamese and Cambodian leaders to doubt each other's sincerity. The Cambodian raids were much more brutal, but the evidence for centralized control or approval for attacks on either side before the middle of 1977 is contradictory.[23]

The situation was complicated further by the fact that Pol Pot and his colleagues believed the Cambodian minorities in southern Vietnam were ready to overthrow Vietnamese rule; they wanted to attach these minorities to DK. Sihanouk and Lon Nol had also dreamt of a greater Cambodia. In fact, whatever the views of the Khmer in Vietnam might have been, they were insufficiently armed, motivated, and organized to revolt. When no uprising occurred, Pol Pot suspected treachery on the part of the agents he had dispatched to foment it. His troops were also merciless; on their cross-border raids that began in April 1977, they encountered and massacred hapless Khmer who had unwittingly failed to follow his scenario.

As so often in modern Cambodian history, what Cambodians interpreted as an internal affair or a quarrel between neighbors had unforeseen international repercussions. For several months after the death of Mao Zedong and the arrest of his radical subordinates known as the Gang of Four, the Chinese regime was in disarray. Although the four radicals were soon arrested, the new ruler, Hua Guofeng, tried to maintain Mao's momentum by opposing the Soviet Union, praising Mao's ideas and supporting third world revolutions like DK's. Many Chinese officials, including Hua's successor, Deng Xiaoping, perceived Vietnam as a pro-Soviet threat along their southern border—much as the United States at the time saw Cuba. For the Chinese, Cambodia was a convenient and conveniently radical ally. By early 1977, large quantities of arms, ammunition, and military equipment were coming into DK from China. Ironically, the Chinese were asking DK to play a role that mirrored the one played by the regime DK had overthrown, when the Khmer Republic had been "groomed" to serve the interests of the United States.[24]

This phase of the DK era ended in late September 1977 when Pol Pot, in a five-hour speech recorded for Phnom Penh radio, announced the existence of the CPK on the occasion of the seventeenth anniversary of its foundation.[25] The speech failed to explain why the party's existence had been kept a secret for so long, and the announcement may have responded to pressure from China in exchange for that country's continuing military assistance. In any case, the day after the speech was broadcast Pol Pot flew to Beijing where he was feted publicly by Hua Guofeng, whom he had met in secret a year before. The Chinese offered extensive help to DK in its confrontation with Vietnam. More realistic than DK's leaders, they did not support a full-scale war, knowing that Cambodia would lose, until they were pushed by Pol Pot and Vietnamese intransigence toward that position in 1978.[26]

Pol Pot's long speech contained some veiled warnings to Vietnam, but its main intention was to review the long trajectory of Cambodian history, culminating in the triumph of the CPK. The format was chronological, divided into a discussion of events before 1960, between 1960 and 1975, and developments in DK itself. The 1960 congress, he asserted, marked the establishment of a "correct line" for the CPK, but since armed struggle was postponed for eight more years and the party's leaders had to flee Phnom Penh in 1963, he found few benefits to mention that flowed from the party's line in terms of revolutionary practice. Benefits flowed after the anti-Sihanouk coup, to be sure, but Pol Pot failed to mention the most significant of them, Vietnamese military assistance to the Khmer Rouge. Similarly, Sihanouk himself was never mentioned.

In closing, Pol Pot noted that "with complete confidence, we rely on the powerful revolutionary spirit, experience, and creative ingenuity of our people," failing also to mention Chinese military aid. Optimistically, he predicted that Cambodia would soon have twenty million people ("Our aim is to increase the population as quickly as possible") and claimed that the average food intake had reached over three hundred kilograms (660 pounds) of rice per person per year. Many refugees later took issue with the latter statement, pointing out that by the middle of 1977 in much of the country and for the first time in Cambodian history, rice had virtually disappeared from the diet.

It is likely that Pol Pot had been encouraged to make the speech and to bring the CPK into the open by his Chinese allies and that, because of the importance of that alliance, he was happy to oblige.

In late September 1977 Pol Pot embarked on a state visit to China. At the Beijing airport, the DK delegation was met by China's premier, Hua Guofeng, and Deng Xiaoping, who was to replace Hua in 1978. The visit probably marked the high point (for Pol Pot at least) of the DK regime. The warmth of the welcome that the Cambodians received probably convinced him that the Chinese would support DK if and when hostilities broke out between Cambodia and Vietnam. In fact, while the Chinese encouraged DK's hostility toward Vietnam, they also hoped for a peaceful solution.[27]

DK CLOSES DOWN

Vietnam saw the DK-Beijing alliance that was strengthened during Pol Pot's visit to China as a provocation, and in mid-December 1977 Vietnam mounted a military offensive against Cambodia. Fourteen divisions were involved, and Vietnamese troops penetrated up to thirty-two kilometers (twenty miles) into Cambodia in some areas. In the first week of 1978, after DK had broken off diplomatic relations with Vietnam, most of the Vietnamese troops went home, taking along thousands of Cambodian villagers as hostages. The Vietnamese soon began grooming some of these hostages as a government in exile; others were given military training. One of the exiles, a DK regimental commander named Hun Sen, who had fled Cambodia in 1977, emerged as the premier of the People's Republic of Kampuchea (PRK) in 1985. Aside from the UN interregnum in 1992–93, he has remained in command of Cambodian politics ever since.

Pol Pot's response to the Vietnamese withdrawal was to claim a "total victory," while secretly purging military officers and CPK cadres in the eastern zone where the Vietnamese penetration had been the deepest. These men and women were said to have Cambodian bodies and Vietnamese minds. Several hundred of them were executed at Tuol Sleng; hundreds of others, on the spot.[28] In the confusion many DK soldiers from the eastern zone sought refuge in Vietnam. One of them, Heng Samrin, later became the chief of state of the PRK and a revered, inconsequential figure in subsequent regimes. In addition, thousands of people in the east were forcibly transferred toward the west in early 1978. Local troops in the east were massacred and replaced by troops from the southwest. The man in charge of the eastern zone, an ICP veteran named Sao Phim, committed suicide in June 1978 when summoned to Phnom Penh for consultation. The massacres in the east continued for several months.[29]

In 1978 the DK regime tried to open itself to the outside world and to improve its image with the Cambodian people. Gestures included a general amnesty offered to the population and the establishment of a technical high school in Phnom Penh. The regime welcomed visits from sympathetic journalists and foreign radicals and inaugurated diplomatic relations with non-Communist countries such as Burma and Malaysia

These actions had mixed results. For example, a Yugoslavian television crew visited DK in 1978, and the footage broadcast later in the year gave the outside world its first glimpse of life there and of Pol Pot. One of the cameramen later remarked that the only person the crew had seen smiling in Cambodia was Pol Pot. Other visitors who sympathized with DK praised everything they saw. They were taken to see places the regime was proud of, and what they saw fit their preconceptions.

Most survivors of the regime, however, remember 1978 as the harshest year of DK, when communal dining halls were introduced in many areas and rations fell below the starvation levels of 1977.

By this time also, Vietnamese attempts to reopen negotiations with DK had failed. Nearly a hundred thousand Vietnamese troops were massed along the Cambodian border by April 1978, just before Pol Pot's suppression of enemies in the eastern zone. Vietnam also signed a twenty-five-year treaty of friendship with the Soviet Union to balance the threat from China and in early December announced that a Kampuchean Front for National Salvation had been set up in "liberated Cambodian territory" to overthrow DK. The front included several leaders of later Khmer politics, such as Heng Samrin, Chea Sim, and Hun Sen.[30]

Vietnam and DK now embarked on a long and costly struggle that played into the hands of larger powers. These powers, in turn, were not prepared to take risks. There is evidence, for example, that Pol Pot requested that the Chinese provide volunteers but that the request was turned down. DK would have to face the Vietnamese (and serve Chinese interests) on its own. The parallels between the last days of DK and the last days of Lon Nol's regime in 1975 are striking, and ironic.

In December 1978 two American journalists and a Scottish Marxist academic, Malcolm Caldwell, visited Cambodia. The journalists, Elizabeth Becker and Richard Dudman, had worked in Cambodia in the early 1970s, and they were the first nonsocialist writers to visit DK.

Recalling her visit several years later, Becker wrote:

> The Phnom Penh I first glimpsed had the precise beauty of a mausoleum. . . . There was no litter on the streets, no trash, no dirt. But then there were no people either, no bicycles or buses and very few automobiles.[31]

Caldwell, who had written sympathetically about the regime, was invited to Cambodia as a friend, but Becker and Dudman were thought by DK officials to be working for the CIA, and the movements of all three were closely monitored. On their last night in the country, December 22, Caldwell was killed in his hotel room by unknown assailants perhaps connected with an anti–Pol Pot faction eager to destabilize the regime.

On Christmas Day 1978, Vietnamese forces numbering over one hundred thousand attacked DK on several fronts. Because DK forces were crowded into the eastern and southwestern zones, Vietnamese attacks in the northeast encountered little resistance, and by the end of the year several major roads to Phnom Penh were in Vietnamese hands. At this point the Vietnamese altered their strategy, which had been to occupy the eastern half of the country, and decided to capture the capital itself.

The city, by then containing perhaps fifty thousand bureaucrats, soldiers, and factory workers, was abandoned on January 7, 1979. Up to the last, DK officials had confidently claimed victory. Pol Pot, like the U.S. ambassador in 1975, escaped at the last moment in a jeep; other high officials and foreign diplomats left by train. They were followed later, on foot, by the half-starved, poorly equipped remnants of their armed forces.[32]

It was a humiliating end for the DK leaders and for their Utopian vision of Cambodia. The revolutionary organization never expressed regret for the appalling loss of life that had occurred since "liberation" in 1975. Even after DK's demise, well into the 1990s, tens of thousands of

Democratic Kampuchean killing ground near Phnom Penh, exhumed in 1979. Photo by Kelvin Rowley.

Khmer, particularly young people, were still prepared to give their lives to the first organization that had given them power and self-respect. Some of these people formed the backbone of the Khmer Rouge guerrilla army in the 1980s. Moreover, once the purges had burnt themselves out, the leaders of the CPK (despite or perhaps because of the party's official dissolution in 1981) remained in place and in command of the resistance throughout the 1980s and 1990s.[33]

Nearly everyone else welcomed the Vietnamese invasion and accepted the government that was swiftly put in place by the invaders as preferable to what had gone before. The new government called itself the People's Republic of Kampuchea (PRK) and was staffed at its upper levels by former CPK members who had defected to Vietnam in 1977–78, as well as by some Khmer who had lived in Vietnam throughout the DK period. Most Cambodians rejoiced at the disappearance of *a-Pot* ("the contemptible Pot"), as they now called the deposed prime minister. For nearly everyone the DK era had been one of unmitigated suffering, violence, and confusion. With luck, in exile, or in the PRK, most Cambodians now thought they could resume their prerevolutionary lives, which DK had held in such contempt.[34]

13

CAMBODIA SINCE 1979

THE PRK: EARLY PHASES

In early 1979 and for the first time since the 1950s, Cambodia was controlled by a foreign power. The situation was also reminiscent of the 1830s in that the power was Vietnam, but closer parallels existed with the final years of the French protectorate when the French took responsibility for Cambodia's defense, internal security, and foreign affairs, leaving less crucial areas (from their point of view) in Cambodian hands.

Almost immediately after capturing Phnom Penh, the Vietnamese helped their Cambodian protégés establish the People's Republic of Kampuchea (PRK). Its leading officials were DK military officers who had defected to Vietnam in 1978, Cambodians who had lived in Vietnam since the 1950s, and members of ethnic minorities untainted by service to DK. Several figures in this original group—Heng Samrin, Chea Sim, and Hun Sen—remained powerful through the 1980s. Hun Sen, who became prime minister in 1985 (while retaining his foreign affairs portfolio), gradually assumed more and more power on his own.

The new government promised to respect human rights, including freedom of opinion and association, but it was severe with its political opponents, as all earlier regimes had been. No elections were held until 1981, and those were not contested by opposing parties. Barely a month after declaring its existence, the PRK signed a treaty of friendship and cooperation with Vietnam. This gesture, combined with the hardships affecting all Cambodians, convinced many men and women that they might be better off outside the country.

Vietnam's occupation of Cambodia and its alliance with the Soviet Union angered the Chinese, who launched an attack on northern Vietnam in February 1979 with the tacit support of the United States. The campaign involved three hundred thousand Chinese troops and lasted for two weeks. Thousands of people were killed on both sides, and several Vietnamese cities along the border were laid waste. When the Chinese withdrew, supposedly Vietnamese policies toward Cambodia (and Chinese policies, for that matter) remained unchanged. The main effects of the attack were to encourage tens of thousands of Sino-Vietnamese to flee Vietnam and to strengthen the burgeoning U.S.-Chinese alliance. Thailand's similar alliance with China, encouraged by the United States, was beneficial to the DK military remnants filtering into Thailand and made the Vietnamese even more reluctant to withdraw from Cambodia. Like those of DK in 1978, Vietnam's leaders believed themselves surrounded by enemies.[1]

At first nearly all Cambodians welcomed the Vietnamese, not because they preferred being invaded to being autonomous but because the invasion signaled the end of DK. Almost at once, nearly everyone began moving. Throughout 1979 and for most of 1980, hundreds of thousands of Cambodians crisscrossed the country looking for relatives, returning to their homes, trading, or seeking refuge overseas. Although Vietnamese forces pursued DK armed remnants into the northwest, civil authorities did nothing to prevent this less-organized movement of people or the informal revival of trade. As the PRK struggled to its feet, many prerevolutionary institutions, including markets, Buddhism, and family farming, came back to life. Buddhist *wats* and schools reopened soon afterward. The PRK's laissez-faire policy, however, did not extend to political activity, which was monopolized by the government and the People's Revolutionary Party of Kampuchea (PRPK), a Communist grouping that shared its pre-1975 history with the discredited CPK.[2]

Amid so much disorder, most of the 1979 rice crop went untended. By the middle of the year a famine had broken out. Very few Cambodians stayed put long enough to plant the 1979–80 rice crop, and when grain stored before 1979 had been consumed or appropriated by Vietnamese forces, hundreds of thousands of Khmer had little to eat. Famine conditions were exacerbated by a drought, and it was at this point that Cambodia gained attention in the West where television audiences, already vaguely aware of the horrors perpetrated in DK, were shocked to see skeletal Khmers stumbling into Thailand or dying of starvation beside Cambodia's roads. The sufferings provoked a massive charitable response, but the delivery of food and medicine from abroad was often delayed by bureaucratic rivalries, by constraints imposed by Thailand and its allies, and to an extent by the Vietnamese themselves, who were understandably suspicious of Western motives and used some of the food and medicine to support their hard-pressed military and administrative personnel.[3]

Conditions stabilized in 1980 when the rice harvest doubled in size. In rural areas Vietnamese forces withdrew into garrisons, and local people were once again put in control of their own affairs. Rural society was a shambles. Villages had been abandoned or torn down; tools, seed, and fertilizer were nonexistent; hundreds of thousands of people had emigrated or been killed; and in most areas the survivors suffered from malaria, shock, or malnutrition. So many men had died or disappeared in DK that in some districts more than 60 percent of the families were headed by widows. Thousands of widows raised their families alone and with difficulty. In response to these conditions, as well as to collectivist ideas, the PRK instituted "solidarity groups" (*krom sammaki*) composed of several families as collective units to cultivate the land. Private ownership was not recognized, but collectives and communes, despised in DK, were not reintroduced. At the district and provincial levels, PRK officials endeavored to exert centralized control but made no effort to collect taxes or to conscript young men for military service. Schools reopened throughout Cambodia in 1979, and currency was reintroduced in 1980.[4]

For most Cambodians the reappearance of a certain amount of personal freedom, and the PRK's unrevolutionary caution, contrasted sharply with their experiences under DK. At the same time they knew

Cambodian woman and Vietnamese soldier, 1980. Photo by Grant Evans.

that the PRK owed its existence to a foreign invasion and to Vietnamese and Soviet-bloc support. Many high-ranking officials and regional cadres had served happily enough in DK, and some educated Cambodians sensed an unwholesome continuity between the successive socialist regimes. PRK officials, moreover, refused to distance themselves from Marxism-Leninism or one-party rule. Instead, they preferred to demonize the "genocidal Pol Pot–Ieng Sary clique," blaming the 1975–79 catastrophes on these two individuals rather than on the extreme but recognizably socialist policies of the CPK. The two villains were tried in absentia in Phnom Penh in August 1979. Valuable evidence about the DK period emerged at the trial, but in many respects it was a farce. No evidence was offered in Pol Pot's or Ieng Sary's defense, and the two men were condemned to death. Soon afterward, the DK interrogation center at Tuol Sleng was inaugurated by the Vietnamese as a genocidal museum. The use of the word *genocide* and comparisons of Pol Pot to Hitler suggested that as far as the PRK was concerned, DK had had a fascist rather than a Communist government.[5]

OPPOSITION TO THE PRK

The PRK was unable to engender widespread trust among what remained of Cambodia's educated elite. Most of these men and women were not prepared to entrust Cambodia to foreigners or to endure more socialism. In 1979–80 tens of thousands of them walked into exile in Thailand, eventually finding residence abroad or in the refugee camps that sprang up along the border. The loss of so many educated people, on top of the tens of thousands who had perished in DK, was a serious blow to the country,

By the end of 1979 the refugee camps sheltered several anti-Vietnamese resistance factions. One of the largest of these, led by former Prime Minister Son Sann, sought foreign support to remove the Vietnamese occupation forces and to reimpose prerevolutionary institutions, except Sihanouk, whom Son Sann had come to distrust. This faction drew many supporters from Cambodians who had been living overseas and were nostalgic, and from recent arrivals at the border who were enraged by the destruction of the 1970s and by what they saw as open-ended Vietnamese control. Son Sann was unable to establish an effective military force, however, and obtained very little material support from Vietnam's principal antagonists—China, Thailand, and the United States. In military terms these powers preferred DK.

In the meantime, DK's leadership in exile remained unchanged. The CPK continued its shadowy existence, and a DK delegation held onto Cambodia's seat at the United Nations. China and the United States supported this state of affairs so as to punish Vietnam for invading Cambodia, standing up to China, and defeating the United States. They were joined by Singapore and Thailand, both of which pursued anti-Communist, pro-Chinese policies. Supporting DK was a small price for all of these powers to pay to keep their more important alliances intact. In 1979 and 1980 the Thai military government fed, clothed, and restored to health several thousand DK soldiers who had straggled across the border, and these soldiers also received arms, ammunition, and military supplies from China, ferried through Thai ports. By 1982 the DK remnants had become a relatively effective military force. Their dependents, who were treated as political refugees, were fed and housed by agencies of the United Nations. Because of the PRK's pariah status, however, UN development agencies were prohibited from operating in Cambodia itself.[6]

In 1980 and 1981 more and more information emerged from Cambodia about the horrors of DK. Evidence from the Pol Pot–Ieng Sary trial was confirmed and amplified by refugee testimony, written memoirs, and confessions found in the archives at Tuol Sleng. The PRK inaugurated "days of hate" in 1982 that provided occasions for survivors of the DK era to tell their stories. DK spokesmen, for their part, admitted only a few mistakes and blamed the Vietnamese for executing over two million Khmer. Although PRK propaganda was often heavy-handed and inaccurate, even cautious estimates of DK-related deaths caused by overwork, starvation, mistreated diseases, and executions came close to two million Cambodians, or close to one in four then living.[7]

China and other powers, faced with the task of improving DK's image while continuing to punish Vietnam, began pressuring Prince Sihanouk, who was living in exile in Beijing, to return to political life. The prince was willing to do so only on his own terms. He did not want to renew his alliance with DK, he feared the Vietnamese, and he knew that Son Sann's faction opposed his coming back into power. At the same time, it was difficult for him to resist Chinese pressure and to remain inactive, for he still identified himself with the destiny of his country.

Maneuvers to form a coalition involving Sihanouk, Son Sann, and the DK occupied much of 1981 and 1982, while the PRK and its Vietnamese advisers worked hard to improve their image overseas. In June 1981 a constitution modeled to a large extent on Vietnam's was introduced in the PRK. The document granted a range of human rights to Cambodia's people but enjoined them to carry out the "state's political line." This document was followed by the establishment of several new ministries, the emergence from concealment of the PRPK, and elections for a National Assembly, which approved the constitution. The policies of the PRK fitted closely with Vietnamese priorities, although positions of responsibility, as the government expanded, increasingly fell to men and women without socialist credentials. Little by little the PRK became a responsive, functional government whose military, police, and foreign affairs were still subject to Vietnamese control. In this respect it resembled Cambodia in the closing years of the French protectorate. Over one hundred thousand Vietnamese troops remained on Cambodian soil.

THE CGDK

Developments in the PRK combined with DK's squalid reputation added urgency to foreign efforts to form a coalition government consistent with the Cold War policies of outside powers. In early 1981 Sihanouk met with Khieu Samphan, representing DK, to discuss how such a coalition might be formed. Son Sann was reluctant to join the talks, but in September 1981 the three factions announced that they were prepared to act together. Soon afterward, the CPK's Central Committee announced the dissolution of the party and that faction's conversion to capitalist ideas. Ieng Thirith remarked that DK had changed completely and had, among other things, restored religious beliefs. Her husband, Ieng Sary, added that Cambodia would not be subjected to socialism for "many generations." The alleged dissolution of the CPK convinced no one, but enabled the Coalition Government of Democratic Kampuchea (CGDK) to claim it was a capitalist formation. All the CPK's high officials, including Pol Pot and Ieng Sary, remained in place in the CGDK, and no non-Communists were given responsible positions. Despite their conversion to free market economics, DK-controlled camps remained much stricter than those controlled by other factions. People inside them were not allowed to leave, military commanders attended annual study sessions as they had done in the 1970s, and military aid continued to flow to the faction from China.[8]

The CGDK was unveiled in the middle of 1982. To display its territorial base, some of its followers and armed units moved a few miles across the border into Cambodia. DK representatives assumed control of the CGDK's foreign affairs (for a government in exile, the only meaningful portfolio) and stayed on at the United Nations. Its military forces were the best trained, most numerous, and most active of the three factions. Sihanouk remained in Beijng under Chinese supervision, and Son Sann soon lost even his limited freedom of maneuver. For the next ten years, the three factions continued to distrust each other, and their spokesmen made no promises about what Cambodians might expect if the coalition ever came to power. Militarily, coalition forces, some forty thousand men and women, were not particularly effective.

In 1983–85 Vietnamese and PRK troops drove the coalition's forces and their dependents back into Thailand and destroyed their encampments. The PRK then conscripted tens of thousands of workers to lay mines along the border and to block the approaches from Thailand into Cambodia. Thousands died of disease and from land mines while this work was going on.[9]

By 1983 the Vietnamese had raised and trained a PRK army, thirty thousand strong, to defend the country when they eventually withdrew. As in the past, conscription was often random, and privileged Cambodians, particularly the children of PRPK cadres, often seemed immune. Instead, they were favored for scholarships to study overseas. By 1988 some five thousand Cambodians had undergone technical or academic training abroad, principally in the Soviet Union, Cuba, and Eastern Europe.[10]

For the rest of the 1980s a military stalemate prevailed, but following the withdrawal of Vietnamese troops in 1989, coalition troops consolidated their bases inside the country, and DK troops captured the gem-producing area near Pailin in northwestern Cambodia. Their forces were unable or unwilling to follow this action up, and the resistance never controlled any major towns.

Nonetheless, in 1990–91, DK forces in particular posed a serious menace to the PRK. DK troops had occupied sparsely populated parts of Cambodia's northwest and southwest. At night they raided villages and planted antipersonnel mines along paths and in rice fields, which sooner or later killed unwary people or blew off their arms or legs. Eighty or ninety casualties caused by these mines came into Cambodia's hospitals and clinics every week, and presumably hundreds of other victims were untreated or had been killed. The war waged allegedly against the Vietnamese, like Lon Nol's in the 1970s, was now killing only Khmer. Casualties from mines continued through the 1990s, until the minefields had been cleared by international NGOs working with Khmer trainees.

THE VIETNAMESE WITHDRAWAL

Two key factors encouraged the Vietnamese to withdraw the last of their troops from Cambodia in September 1989. One was the growing self-sufficiency of the PRK, which earlier in the year had renamed itself the State of Cambodia (SOC). Another was that Soviet aid, and aid from the Soviet bloc, was sharply reduced in 1989 following crises that swept through the Soviet Union and Eastern Europe.

Prior to the withdrawal the Cambodian government announced a series of reforms that were widely popular, especially in Phnom Penh. These included revising the national anthem, changing the flag, amending the constitution to make Buddhism Cambodia's state religion, and abolishing the PRK statute that had limited monkhood to middle-aged Khmer. New laws also allowed farmers to pass title to land on to their children and householders to buy and sell real estate. The death penalty was abolished in response to criticism of Cambodia's human rights record. Although the PRPK remained in charge of Cambodia's political life, free markets and black markets flourished, traditional cultural activities revived, and collectivism was dead. The Cambodian government, on the other hand, remained unchanged. Hun Sen, who had become prime minister of the PRK in 1985, steadily consolidated his power.[11]

The new laws regarding Buddhism led to heavy expenditures, especially by émigré Khmers, on Buddhist *wats* throughout the country. Lifting restrictions on real estate produced a miniboom in speculation, restoration, and rebuilding as Phnom Penh families squatting in villas with government permission put the villas on the market inspired by rumors of peace and the hopes of renewed foreign aid that would presumably follow. During the boom, visitors to Phnom Penh noted the emergence of a small, new elite identifiable by the cars they drove, the villas they lived in, and their often-obnoxious behavior in restaurants and bars. Corruption in the SOC never reached the levels that had existed under Sihanouk or Lon Nol, but a quiet extraction of privileges had characterized PRPK cadres and high-ranking government officials over the years. Many of them had shouldered their way into business enterprises, including clandestine trading operations between Thailand and the northwest; others were assured comfortable houses, cars, and other perquisites.

Political changes in Eastern Europe and the economic boom elsewhere in Southeast Asia gave the SOC some freedom of maneuver and threatened its existence. Changes in Europe cut off aid from Communist powers, and the boom encouraged entrepreneurs and SOC officials to seek short-term returns from construction and the sale of government property and raw materials. Timber, gems, dried fish, and other products exported illicitly to Thailand and Vietnam earned little or no revenue for the SOC which, deprived of extensive foreign assistance, was almost without funds. The resistance factions, on the other hand, whose subsistence needs were met by the United Nations and foreign aid and who had few bureaucrats to pay and no services to provide, enjoyed the advantages of all guerrilla movements.

Many of Cambodia's problems were still imposed from outside the country as they had so often been. In 1989–90 most observers agreed that, without drastic changes in the foreign support that the SOC and the government in exile were receiving, their problems would remain unsolved. In July 1990, however, U.S. Secretary of State James Baker announced that the United States would cease backing the CGDK's representative at the United Nations.

Baker's move encouraged China to diminish its patronage of DK, and observers soon became optimistic about the possibility of a diplomatic breakthrough regarding Cambodia. Some hoped that the breakthrough would involve a massive intervention by the United Nations, which might establish a caretaker regime pending national elections.

THE UNTAC PERIOD AND AFTER

These hopes were fulfilled by decisions made at the international conference on Cambodia that convened in Paris in October 1991. Under the terms of agreements reached in Paris, a temporary government was established in Phnom Penh comprising representatives of the incumbent regime and delegates from the factions that had been opposing it since

1981. The four factions joined to form a Supreme National Council (SNC) presided over by Prince Sihanouk, who returned briefly to Cambodia in November 1991 after twelve years of exile and was warmly welcomed in Phnom Penh. The SNC's decisions were to be monitored by UN representatives on the spot.

The Paris agreements coincided with the end of the Cold War. They withdrew the patronage of larger powers from the Cambodian factions, reinserting them in theory into a nonaligned Cambodia where they would be free to compete for political advantage. Those in power in Phnom Penh, however, enjoyed the advantages that usually flow to political incumbents.

The arrangements envisaged in Paris were to be monitored in Cambodia by UN personnel, pending disarmament and cantonment of the factional troops, the repatriation of refugees from Thailand, and national elections for a constituent assembly. To achieve these goals, the UN established a multinational protectorate over Cambodia. During 1992 some thirteen thousand soldiers and over seven thousand civilians including detachments of police took up residence in the country. Sluggish UN procedures delayed recruitment and deployment. The United Nations Transitional Authority in Cambodia (UNTAC) arrived too late and moved too slowly to gain the respect it needed from the Cambodian factions. In May 1992 the Khmer Rouge expanded the territory under their control, refused to be monitored by the UN, and refused to disarm its forces. They were not punished or chastised. The SOC, in response, also refused to disarm and refused to allow the UN to oversee the daily operations of its powerful national police, although such oversight was a feature of the Paris agreements.[12]

UNTAC embarked on its Utopian mission slowly and with understandable foreboding. Its mandate was ambiguous, its time was limited, and most of its personnel knew nothing about Cambodia. By the time the mission ended in October 1993, UNTAC had spent over $2 billion, making it the most costly operation to date in UN history. Much of the money had gone into inflated salaries. Phnom Penh grew more crowded and more prosperous, but the rural economy remained stagnant. The country's infrastructure was still abysmal, and security was marred by a spate of politically motivated killings. Khmer Rouge forces, claiming that Vietnam remained secretly in control of the country, massacred over a hundred Vietnamese civilians in the UNTAC era. The SOC police, in turn, targeted activists belonging to opposing political parties. In 1992–93 over two hundred unarmed people were victims of politically motivated assassinations. None of the offenders was ever arrested or brought to trial.

On a positive note, the Cambodian media enjoyed unaccustomed freedom in the UNTAC period. Local human rights organizations, unthinkable in earlier times, also flourished. These organizations received Sihanouk's support and backing from the human rights component of UNTAC, which trained hundreds of Khmer human rights workers and investigated hundreds of complaints.

Other positive developments in this period, from UNTAC's point of view, were the peaceful repatriation of over three hundred thousand Cambodian refugees from Thailand and the national elections themselves, which took place on schedule in July 1993 following a massive voter-registration campaign conducted by UN workers. Contrary to the fears of many, the elections, although boycotted by the Khmer Rouge, were peaceful. Over 90 percent of the registered voters—at least 4 million people—went to the polls in Cambodia's freest, fairest, and most secret election since the colonial era. The message that the voters delivered was ambiguous. A royalist party using the acronym FUNCINPEC and led by Prince Sihanouk's eldest son, Norodom Rannaridh, won seven more seats for a constituent assembly than the Cambodian Peoples' Party (CPP), the lineal descendant of the KPRP. An anti-Communist, anti-Vietnamese party won ten of the remaining eleven seats.

For the first time in their history, a majority of Cambodians had voted against an armed, incumbent government. Unlike most Cambodian voters in the past, they had courageously rejected the status quo. What they were voting *for,* aside from peace, was much less clear.

Hun Sen and the CPP, however refused to accept defeat. By the end of 1993, a fragile compromise was reached whereby FUNCINPEC and the CPP formed a coalition government with two prime ministers, Prince Rannaridh and Hun Sen. Cabinet posts were divided among the parties represented in the assembly. Day-to-day political power in the form of provincial governorships, defense, the national police, and the entire civil service remained under CPP control. The royalist party soon lost its voice in decision making as well as its freedom of maneuver.

Cambodia's new constitution restored the monarchy and placed Sihanouk on the throne he had abandoned in 1955. Becoming king again pleased the 71-year-old monarch and his wife, who were eager to erase a personally humiliating period of history and to reestablish themselves as Cambodia's legitimate rulers. For the rest of the 1990s, however, with the monarch pleading poor health, the couple spent long periods of each year outside the country.

The losers in 1993, aside from the people who had voted against the government, were the Khmer Rouge. The movement was formally outlawed in 1994, and thousands of its followers defected to the government. Its leaders remained unrepentant, in hiding, and in good health. In the mid-1990s the Khmer Rouge still had over five thousand men and women under arms. As Thai government support for the movement faded in 1994–95, however, and as defections increased, the Khmer Rouge became more violent, massacring timber workers, kidnapping and killing a half-dozen foreigners, and mounting sporadic military attacks. Scattered evidence at the time, confirmed later, suggested that the leadership had fragmented after the elections, and that the movement was split between those willing to effect a modus vivendi with the Phnom Penh authorities and those wanting to rekindle a full-scale revolutionary conflict.

THE END OF THE KHMER ROUGE

Ieng Sary, the former DK foreign minister, defected to Phnom Penh in August 1996. He quickly received a royal pardon and was allowed to remain, with thousands of adherents, in his enclave of Pailin. Over the next few months, hundreds of Khmer Rouge soldiers were absorbed into the national army. Efforts inaugurated at the time to bring the Khmer Rouge leaders to trial for crimes against humanity, despite or perhaps partly because of foreign pressure, came to nothing.[13]

During this time the Khmer Rouge fragmented further. The effective leader of the disintegrating movement was Ta Mok, a brutal military commander. Pol Pot, suffering from poor health, was sidelined, but in June 1997, in an effort to regain control, the former dictator ordered the assassination of Son Sen, a high-ranking cadre and close associate whom he accused of treason. The assassination, which involved killing Son Sen's children and grandchildren, shocked middle-ranking Khmer Rouge cadre, who assumed they might be next. Fearing arrest, Pol Pot fled his headquarters but was soon captured and put on trial in a bizarre proceeding filmed by the American journalist Nate Thayer, who had been invited to attend. Subjected to the brutal winners' justice that had sent hundreds of thousands of Cambodians to their deaths in the DK era, Pol Pot was condemned to life imprisonment, and was led away under guard to his two-room house.[14]

THE *COUP DE FORCE* OF 1997

In the meantime the Phnom Penh regime was encountering difficulties of its own. A grenade attack against peacefully demonstrating supporters of Sam Rainsy in March 1997 claimed over twenty lives, and perennial tensions between the CCP and FUNCINPEC were exacerbated by Hun Sen's acceptance of so many Khmer Rouge defectors into the national army, and in effect into his entourage. Generals loyal to FUNCINPEC sought without success to negotiate with Khmer Rouge elements led by Ta Mok. Their efforts angered Hun Sen, and in July 1997, using troops of his personal bodyguard, he launched a preemptive coup against FUNCINPEC troops and followers in Phnom Penh. In the attack over a hundred FUNCINPEC officials and supporters were killed, several of them after being arrested and tortured. CCP casualties were minimal. Widespread looting accompanied the coup.[15]

Although the violence of the coup was not surprising, its timing from an international perspective was inept. Several donor nations suspended aid. Foreign investment dried up. Cambodia's membership in ASEAN was delayed. After consolidating his power in a manner that had seemed appropriate, Hun Sen was treated for a time as a pariah. Donor nations urged him to sponsor free and fair elections in 1998, as scheduled, for the National Assembly.

Neither the CCP nor FUNCINPEC wanted to repeat the experience of 1993. The CCP feared another defeat, while FUNCINPEC and smaller parties feared a renewal of violence. Nonetheless, as negotiations for elections crept forward, many observers believed that the CCP would gain an overwhelming victory.

The run-up to the 1998 election seemed to confirm these suspicions. Opposition parties were given no access to the electronic media and were not allowed to campaign in the countryside. Opposition party workers were harassed, and several died under suspicious circumstances. None of the perpetrators of violence in the coup was brought to justice. Prince Rannaridh returned to the country in March 1998, less than four months before the elections, and campaigned with surprising vigor. So did Sam Rainsy, who courageously attacked the CCP and drew widespread support.

The elections themselves were free and fair in the view of local and foreign electoral observers. Parties opposed to the CCP garnered 60 percent of the votes but were unwilling to form an alliance, and so arrangements were made between FUNCINPEC and the CCP to govern the country in another coalition. By the end of 1998 the new government had gotten off to a relatively good start. In April 1999 Cambodia was welcomed into ASEAN, the last country in the region to be admitted.[16]

Political, social and economic conditions in Cambodia at the end of the twentieth century were unsettling to most observers. The country suffered from the highest infant mortality rates in Southeast Asia. Less than a third of the population had access to clean water, and 2 percent of the adult population suffered from HIV/AIDS. The government, which spent only 5 percent of its funds on health, spent 40 percent on defense, largely to pay its enormous army, which by 2003 consisted of one hundred thousand soldiers, five hundred of whom were generals. Foreign donors and NGOs, despite officially expressed impatience, continued to pay for much of Cambodia's health care, education, social welfare, and rural development—all areas of the economy where there were few opportunities for people to get rich. Year after year,

Monks, Siem Reap, 2003. Photo by Douglas Niven.

anticorruption laws were drafted in the National Assembly (usually by opposition members) but died in committee. The educational system functioned so poorly that illiteracy, running at over 50 percent, was higher than it had been in the 1960s. Violent crimes, rare in prerevolutionary times, were now frequent, and unrestrained logging often carried out by military units was having disastrous ecological effects.

More positively, in 1999 Cambodia was at peace for the first time since the 1960s. For the first time in decades its government was not dependent on a predominant foreign patron. Instead, Cambodia was taking part in the affairs of Southeast Asia from which the Cold War and its own regimes had placed it at arm's length since independence. Despite Hun Sen's authoritarian style, print media in Cambodia were relatively unrestrained, and foreign human rights organizations were still free to operate in the country. Fueled by its burgeoning garment industry, which provided employment to over three hundred thousand young women, and by a boom in tourism, Cambodia's GDP grew by an a average of 6 percent a year between 1998 and 2006. The rural economy, on the other hand, grew more slowly. As a mixed blessing, Cambodia's population doubled between 1979 and 2006 when it reached 14 million, even though one baby in ten died at birth or shortly thereafter. Nearly 40 percent of the population was under sixteen.

In the first years of the new century, Hun Sen, who relished the title of strong man, astutely consolidated himself in power. He was heavily guarded and could count on the support of the army, most of the CPP, and local business interests buttressed by unconditional aid from China. He was popular in the countryside where patronage networks were largely controlled by the CPP and where his alleged personal largesse (often financed by foreign donors), like Sihanouk's in the past, produced short-term waves of adulation. So did his marathon speeches and his robust, often brutal use of language. His disdain for parliamentary procedures was as intense as Sihanouk's had been, and so was his indifference to the rule of law. Under Hun Sen, no officials have ever been convicted of corruption, and no one suspected of political assassinations has ever come to trial. In other ways Hun Sen is a new type of national leader. Unlike previous Cambodian rulers, he had spent no time as a monk. Unlike Sihanouk, Lon Nol, and Pol Pot, he has not shown much interest in Cambodia's past except as a source of revenue from tourists, over a million of whom visited Cambodia in 2005 and again in 2006. Perhaps because he owed his position to the Vietnamese, he never indulged in the racialist anti-Vietnamese rhetoric of some of his opponents. Finally, Hun Sen was to a large extent a self-made man, without ongoing obligations to foreign patrons. Arguably he has been the first genuinely modern leader of the country. His eagerness for Cambodia to become a prosperous, modern nation—like Singapore, or Malaysia, perhaps—was obviously sincere, but his inability or unwillingness to crack down on widespread corruption in the government and to divert revenue from the army and other favored bodies to the countryside impeded economic progress and discouraged long-term foreign investment.[17]

TWENTY-FIRST-CENTURY CAMBODIA

In 2002, CPP candidates captured two-thirds of the communes in national commune elections (for over ten thousand communes in the country). At the time, Hun Sen said that he would be happy to rule the country for another ten years at least. However, in the National Assembly elections of 2003—declared free and fair again by local and foreign observers—opposition to the CPP was still substantial, especially in Phnom Penh and other large towns. In these elections fewer people went to the polls than previously. The CPP gained five seats, FUNCINPEC lost seventeen, and the Sam Rainsy Party (SRP) gained nine. The CPP was unable to assemble the two-thirds parliamentary majority set out by the constitution as a mandate to govern the country. A stalemate occurred that lasted for several months, until a new CPP-FUNCINPEC coalition brokered by Hun Sen and his colleagues was formed, with Prince Rannaridh sidelined and the CPP firmly in command.[18]

Earlier in the year, riots in Phnom Penh destroyed the Thai embassy and severely damaged several Thai-owned businesses in the capital. The rioters were responding to rumors that a Thai TV actress had claimed in her program (erroneously, as things turned out) that Angkor "belonged to the Thai." It seems likely that the riots had Hun Sen's informal backing (police and firefighters were very slow to react), and that commercial rivalries between Thai and Cambodian companies of interest to those in power in Phnom Penh were involved. Using funds provided for the most part by Cambodian-owned casinos operating along the Thai border that catered to Thai gamblers, Cambodia swiftly paid the $20 million that Bangkok demanded as reparations, and diplomatic relations resumed. The riots showed that mobs could be quickly organized in the capital, especially when Cambodia's amour propre was challenged, that large sums of money could be raised quickly by the government for unexpected crises, and that Cambodian resentment, especially in Phnom Penh, about Thai domination of the Khmer economy ran deep.[19]

In October 2004, Norodom Sihanouk, in ill health and exhausted by years of verbal conflict with Hun Sen, resigned from the kingship. His youngest son, Norodom Sihamoni, a mild-mannered bachelor who had spent most of his life outside the country, succeeded him. For some time, portraits of Sihamoni joined those of his parents in public buildings without replacing them, but Sihanouk no longer took part in royal ceremonies and continued to spend almost all of his time in Beijing. Siahmoni's childlessness and Hun Sen's ongoing wariness toward the palace may foreshadow the eventual demise of monarchy as an institution in Cambodia—perhaps after Sihanouk's death.[20]

Two key developments in Cambodia since 2004 have been the discovery of massive oil deposits in parts of the Gulf of Thailand that lie in Cambodia's territorial waters and the establishment in 2006, after years of negotiations, of a tribunal in Phnom Penh to indict former leaders of the Khmer Rouge.

Offshore oil exploration, dominated by the U.S. firm Chevron-Texaco, began in 2000, following assessments made in prerevolutionary times, and cost the firm over $20 million. In 2006 Chevron announced that Cambodia had confirmed deposits of seven hundred million barrels of oil and perhaps ten million cubic feet of natural gas. Because these estimates applied only to those portions of the area already explored by the firm, the actual deposits could be much higher. The deposits should provide annual revenues of $1 billion, starting in 2009 or 2010, for at least a decade.[21] This amount is twice Cambodia's current (2006) annual budget and roughly twice the amount that the kingdom receives every year from foreign donors. Whether the deposits will turn out to be a blessing or a curse remains to be seen. The result will depend on how the revenue is spent by the government, especially in an era when foreign assistance will be significantly lower because of the deposits. Given the government's failure to account for the uses of tourist revenue—the entry fees to the Angkor park in particular—and its unwillingness to tax wealthy members of society so as to pay more for health, social welfare, infrastructure, and education, it is hard to predict that the oil revenues will be used to any great extent to pull Cambodia's rural poor out of grinding poverty or to improve the welfare of the entire population.

Negotiations between the Cambodian government and the United Nations for an international tribunal to indict leaders of the Khmer Rouge proceeded by fits and starts for almost a decade before agreement was reached at the end of 2006. Costs of the three-year effort were estimated at $60 million, nearly all of which was met by foreign donors. The Cambodian government insisted that the tribunal take place in Cambodia with the participation of local judges and lawyers as well as international ones. It did so despite the inexperience of Cambodian jurists in cases of this kind and despite fears on the part of some international observers that the Cambodians would follow instructions from Hun Sen (who would outlast the tribunal and had never shown much enthusiasm for it) instead of demonstrating their independence. Proceedings got off to a slow start in early 2007 as procedures were being ironed out.[22]

CONCLUSION

Cambodian political history since World War II, and probably for a much longer period, can be characterized in part as a chronic failure of contending groups of patrons and their clients to compromise, cooperate, or share power. These hegemonic tendencies, familiar in other Southeast Asian countries, have deep roots in Cambodia's past.

In the 1950s and 1960s, Prince Sihanouk's narcissistic style encouraged his enemies when they replaced him to be equally high-handed, uncompromising, and self-absorbed. Alternative notions of pluralism or a peaceful transfer of power did not exist then and had little traction in Cambodia thirty-five years later.

After 1970, Sihanouk, Lon Nol, Pol Pot, and to a lesser extent Hun Sen sought absolute power for themselves. Under Pol Pot this took the form of a national vendetta. The Leninist politics he favored and the purges he carried out were far worse than anything else in Cambodia's recent history, but they reflected time-honored ideas of winner-takes-all political behavior. Under the Vietnamese protectorate, Cambodian politicians were more cautious (as Sihanouk had been when the French were in control), but in the post-UNTAC era those in power reverted to form and became thin-skinned, vengeful, conspiratorial, and abrupt.

In Pol Pot's secret prison in Phnom Penh, interrogators used the phrase "doing politics" to describe the ritual of indoctrination, questioning, and torture. To many Cambodians without power before and since, politics has been synonymous with exploitation alternating with neglect. The 1993 elections, for many Khmer, were an attempt to liberate themselves from the politics that had dominated the country for so long. Subsequent elections, as we have seen, failed to alter the status quo.

Although it is fruitful to study Cambodian political history from a Cambodian perspective, as this book has tried to do, the country's location, topography, and demographic weakness have meant that its history has often been entangled with Thailand and Vietnam and the polities that preceded them. These countries, in turn and because of their size, have consistently tried to patronize or absorb their neighbor. Having Vietnam next door in the 1820s and 1830s led to a Vietnamese protectorate, and de facto Thai protectorates had been in effect at several points in the preceding centuries. In the 1860s the French loosened what had become Thai control over the Cambodian court and removed Cambodia from much of Southeast Asia by making it part of Indochina, which is to say a surrogate of Vietnam. In the 1940s and 1950s, Cambodian resistance to the French was dominated by the Vietnamese and served their interests. Later still, the fighting in Vietnam, exacerbated by U.S. intervention, reduced Cambodia's capacity to remain neutral or to control its eastern frontier. Sihanouk knew that his country would be swept into the fighting and could never emerge a victor. Unlike Lon Nol or Pol Pot, the prince had no illusions about Cambodia's military strength.

Before 1979 it was difficult for any Cambodian government to contemplate an alliance with Vietnam. The friendship cobbled together by Sihanouk and the Vietnamese Communists collapsed as soon as Sihanouk was overthrown. Spurred on by their resentments, Lon Nol and Pol Pot conducted doomed and vicious military campaigns against Vietnam. After Vietnam invaded the country at the end of 1978, it imposed a protectorate that was reminiscent in some ways of French colonialism and the 1830s.

Relations between Cambodia and Thailand have been somewhat different. Despite, or perhaps because of, cultural affinities, relations have never been marked by a sincere effort on the part of Bangkok to treat Cambodia as a sovereign nation. In the 1830s, in World War II, and again in the 1950s, 1960s, and 1980s, the Thai worked to subvert what they perceived to be hostile governments in Phnom Penh. Relations between the two countries have recently begun to mature, but the anti-Thai riots of 2003 suggest that genuine friendship between the two peoples will be difficult to achieve.

The Paris agreements, UNTAC, and the elections of 1993 thrust Cambodia into the world of Southeast Asia from which it had been isolated, by accident or design, since the eighteenth century. No longer an isolated player, a protectorate, or a component of Indochina, Cambodia became part of a region about which its people knew little and for whose modernity they were largely unprepared.

Cambodia's past greatness, as reconstructed and presented to the Cambodians by the French, is another aspect of its history that has weighed heavily on most of its leaders. In the 1950s and 1960s, Sihanouk allowed himself to be compared favorably to Jayavarman VII. Similarly, Lon Nol claimed that he had a divine mission to rescue Cambodia from "unbelievers" (*thmil*). Pol Pot, announcing that his forces had single-handedly defeated the United States, was similarly misled. In his marathon 1977 speech he remarked, "If our people can build Angkor, they are capable of anything." Hun Sen, to his credit, seems to have abandoned this kind of addictive nostalgia and sees himself as the leader of a small, modernizing country in the modern world.

The combination of personality, domineering political habits, proximity to Thailand and Vietnam, and unrealistic notions of innate greatness blended from the 1940s onward into a volatile form of nationalism which dominated the political scene for many years and which even now is occasionally called back into play by opposition politicians in Phnom Penh.

Intense and widely shared conservatism, perhaps, and the tempestuous changes in the country since 1970 have made many Cambodians reluctant to resist or even consider changing the social arrangements and political leadership that have given them so many centuries of suffering and injustice. Traditions of deference, fatalism, and hegemony enshrined in these arrangements form much of the unwritten substance of Cambodia's two thousand years of history and provide insights into the country's politics and culture that are less apt when applied to Thailand or Vietnam.

Much of Cambodia's uniqueness, I would argue, springs from deep continuities or refusals, rather than from calculated or prudent responses to the rapid and often destructive influences of modern times. Pol Pot's revolution failed in part because so many Cambodians, finding its premises painful and irrelevant, were unwilling to carry it out. Similarly, a decade of Vietnamese occupation and experiments with a far less

Boys on a bridge, Phnom Penh, 1996. Photo by Douglas Niven.

demanding form of socialism left few lasting marks. In the 1993 elections, millions of Cambodians voted for change but chose to look backward rather than ahead. This tendency has altered in recent years, especially in the towns, but deep conservatism persists among older people and in rural areas.

The so-called timelessness of Cambodia, made up to a large extent of its people's perennial, self-absorbed terms of reference, has been part of its appeal to visitors and scholars for many years. In the Pol Pot period this conservatism was a source of enormous strength; in the end it was conservatism that, at enormous human cost, defeated the DK regime. But as the country opens up to a confused and confusing world, without the promise of anyone's sustained protection, it is uncertain if this inward-looking, family-oriented conservatism, so helpful in surviving the incursions of foreign powers and foreign ideas, will be of much help if Cambodia hopes to flourish as a twenty-first-century state. It is also uncertain if notions of human rights, pluralism, and the rule of law, concepts brought into Cambodia in recent years, have taken root in a significant way among those holding power in the country, who continue to act, as previous leaders have done, as if these imported concepts had no bearing on their behavior or on how the country is governed. The predicted surge in oil revenues (discussed above) will probably reduce the leverage that foreign donors have exercised over Cambodia since 1992. Whether Cambodia's newfound economic independence will benefit ordinary Khmer more than those in power remains to be seen. With a soaring birth rate, poor health, and a government that seems to be unprepared to be genuinely responsive to people's needs, the prospects for the short and medium term appear to be very bleak. However, the resilience, talents, and desires of the Cambodian people, and their ability to defy predictions, suggest that a more optimistic assessment of their future might possibly be in order.

NOTES

Chapter 1

1. Adhémard Leclère, *Histoire du Cambodge* (Paris, 1914). See also George Coedes's critical review in *Bulletin de l'Ecole Française d'Extrême Orient (BEFEO)* 14 (1914): 47–54.

2. Subsequent surveys include Martin Herz, *A Short History of Cambodia* (New York, 1958), and David P. Chandler, *The Land and People of Cambodia* (New York, 1991). See also Ian Mabbett and David Chandler, *The Khmers* (Oxford, 1995), and John Tully, *A Short History of Cambodia* (Sydney, 2006).

3. See Lucien Hanks, "Merit and Power in the Thai Social Order," *American Anthropologist*, Vol. 64 (1962): 1247–61, and David Chandler, "The Tragedy of Cambodian History Revisited," in Chandler, *Facing the Cambodian Past: Selected Essays, 1971–1994* (Sydney and Chiangmai, 1996), pp. 310–25.

4. See Centre d'Études et de Recherches Marxistes (comp.), *Sur le "mode de production asiatique"* (Paris, 1969). See also Michael Vickery, *Society, Economics, and Politics in Pre-Angkor Cambodia: The 7th–8th Centuries* (Tokyo, 1998), pp. 7–16, 311–12.

5. See David Joel Steinberg et al. (eds.), *In Search of Southeast Asia* (Honolulu, 1987), pp. 177–244, for a discussion of the notion of "frameworks for nations." These ideas are amplified in a successor volume, written by many of the same authors: Norman G. Owen et al. (eds.), *The Emergence of Modern Southeast Asia* (Honolulu, 2005), especially pp. 161–283.

6. On Cambodian demography through the early 1970s see J. Migozzi, *Cambodge: Faits et problèmes de population* (Paris, 1973).

7. See David Chandler, *Voices from S-21: Terror and History in Pol Pot's Secret Prison* (Berkeley and Los Angeles, 1999). The number of executions in

provincial prisons was probably even higher. See Henri Locard, "Le Goulag des khmers rouges," *Communisme* (1996): 127–64.

8. For a discussion of this problem see David Chandler, "Seeing Red: Perceptions of Cambodian History in Democratic Kampuchea," in *Facing the Cambodian Past*, pp. 233–54. See also Claude Jacques, "Nouvelles orientations pour l'étude de l'histoire du pays khmer," *Asie du sudest et monde insulindien*, Vol. 14 (1982): 39–57. In more recent times, very little post-Angkorean history has been taught in Cambodian schools, and the history of the Khmer Rouge era is currently (2007) not taught at all.

Chapter 2

1. C. Mourer, "Contribution à l'étude de la préhistoire du Cambodge," *BEFEO*, Vol. 80 (1993): 143–87. See also J.P. Carbonnel, "Recent Data on the Cambodian Neolithic," in R.B. Smith and W. Watson (eds.), *Early Southeast Asia* (Oxford, 1979), pp. 223–26; Donn Bayard, "The Roots of Indo-Chinese Civilization: Recent Developments in the Pre-history of Southeast Asia," *Pacific Affairs* (*PA*), Vol. 53, No. 1 (Spring 1980): 89–114.

2. See Yashushi Kojo and Sytha Preng, "A Preliminary Investigation of a Circular Earthwork at Krek, Southeastern Cambodia," *Anthropological Science*, Vol. 106 (1998): 229–44; Charles Higham, *Early Cultures of Mainland Southeast Asia* (Bangkok, 2002), p. 185.

3. See I.W. Mabbett, "The Indianization of Southeast Asia," *Journal of Southeast Asian Studies* (*JSEAS*), Vol. 8, No. 1 (March 1977): 1–14, and Vol. 8, No. 2 (September 1977): 143–61; Paul Mus, *India Seen from the East*, trans. by I.W. Mabbett and D.P. Chandler (Clayton, Australia, 1975); and Michael Vickery, *Society, Economics, and Politics in Pre-Angkor Cambodia: The 7th–8th Centuries* (Tokyo, 1998), pp. 51–58, which emphasizes social factors. For linguistic evidence, see Judith M. Jacob, "Sanskrit Loanwords in Pre-Angkor Khmer," *Mon-Khmer Studies*, Vol. 4 (Honolulu, 1977), pp. 151–68. A good recent summary of this period is in Michael Coe, *Angkor and the Khmer Civilization* (New York, 2003) pp. 63–64.

4. G. Coedes, *The Making of Southeast Asia* (London, 1966), pp. 54–55. We will probably never know when, where, and how ancient south Indian Calukya-Pallava script arrived in Cambodia or was adapted to written Khmer.

5. See Paul Mus, *L'Angle de l'Asie* (ed. S. Thion) (Paris, 1977), especially pp. 109–21.

6. I.W. Mabbett, "*Varnas* in Angkor and the Indian Caste System," *Journal of Asian Studies* (*JAS*), Vol. 36, No. 3 (May 1977): 429–42. Coinage was another Indian practice that seems never to have been taken up by the Khmer.

7. L. Finot, "Sur quelques traditions indochinoises," *Bulletin de la Commission Archéologique de l'Indochine* (1911), pp. 20–37. See also Evéline Porée-Maspero, "Nouvelle étude sur le nagi Soma," *Journal Asiatique* (*JA*), Vol. 238

(1955), and Jacques Népote, "Mythes de fondation ET fonctionnement de l'ordre sociale dans la basse vallée du Mekong," *Péninsule* 38 (1999), pp. 33–65. See also Michael Vickery, "Funan Reviewed: Deconstructing the Ancients," *BEFEO* 90–91 (2003–4): 101–43, especially 105–9. The name Kambuja did not appear in Cambodian inscriptions until the Angkorean era.

8. K. Bhattacharya, *Les Religions brahmaniques dans l'ancien Cambodge* (Paris, 1961), p. 11n.

9. Miriam T. Stark, "The Transition to History in the Mekong Delta: A View from Cambodia," *International Journal of Historical Archaeology*, Vol. 2, No. 3 (1998): 175–203 summarizes research at Angkor Borei, which was an important urban center before, during, and after the Funan period and may well have been the capital of Funan. See also Higham, *Early Cultures of Mainland Southeast Asia*, pp. 235ff.

10. Louis Malleret, *L'Archéologie du delta du* Mekong, 4 vols. (Paris, 1959–63), especially Vols. 1 and 2. Much of the Vietnamese research at Oc-Eo and other sites has not yet been translated from Vietnamese. See P-Y Manguin, "Les cités états de l'Asie du Sud-Est cotières," *BEFEO* 87/1 (2000): 151–82.

11. See O.W. Wolters, *Early Indonesian Commerce: A Study of the Origins of Srivijaya* (Ithaca, N.Y., 1967), and Wang Gungwu, "The Nanhai Trade: A Study of the Early History of Chinese Trade in the South China Sea," *Journal of the Malay Branch of the Royal Asiatic Society (JMBRAS)*, Vol. 31, No. 2 (June 1958): 31–45.

12. Cited by G. Coedes, *The Indianized States of Southeast Asia* (Honolulu, 1968), p. 61. The capital of Funan, however, may well have been Angkor Borei. See Note 9 above.

13. Paul Wheatley, "The Mount of the Immortals: A Note on Tamil Cultural Influence in Fifth Century Indo-China," *Oriens Extremus*, Vol. 21, No. 1 (June 1974): 97–109.

14. Vickery, "Funan Reviewed," C. Jacques, "'Funan,' 'Zhenla': The Reality Concealed by These Chinese Views of Indo-China," in Smith and Watson, *Early Southeast Asia*, pp. 371–79, and O.W. Wolters, "Northwestern Cambodia in the 7th Century," *Bulletin of the School of Oriental and African Studies (BSOAS)*, Vol. 37, No. 2 (1974): 355–84.

15. Cited by L.P. Briggs, *The Ancient Khmer Empire* (Philadelphia, 1951), p. 29.

16. Ibid., p. 28.

17. See P. Paris, "Anciens canaux réconnus sur photographes aeriennes dans les provinces de Takeo et Chaudoc," *BEFEO*, Vol. 31 (1931): 221–24, and Paris, "Anciens canaux réconnus sur photographes aeriennes dans les provinces de Takeo, Chaudoc et Rach Gia," *BEFEO*, Vol. 41 (1941): 365–70. See also Paul Bishop et al., "OSL and Radiocarbon Dating of a Pre-Angkorean Canal in the Mekong Delta," *Journal of Archaeological Science* 31

(2004), pp. 319–32. Bishop argues that the canal in question, near Angkor Borei, was in use between 500 BCE and 500 CE.

18. J.D.M. Derrett, "Rajadharma," *JAS,* Vol. 35, No. 4 (August 1976): 605. The full quotation reads: "The agricultural population is fascinated with power, which is essential to its very life. The soil cannot be tilled without *protection* and *rain.*" On the subject of prowess, see Vickery, *Society, Economics, and Politics,* pp. 190–96.

19. K. Bhattacharya, "La Secte des Paçupata dans l'ancien Cambodge," *Journal Asiatique (JA),* Vol. 243 (1955): 479–87. These arguments have been overtaken by those in Vickery, *Society, Economics, and Politics,* pp. 321–417.

20. O.W. Wolters, "Khmer 'Hinduism' in the Seventh Century," in Smith and Watson, *Early Southeast Asia,* pp. 427–42.

21. See David Chandler, "Royally Sponsored Human Sacrifices in Nineteenth Century Cambodia: The Cult of *Me Sa* (Uma Mahisasuramardini) at Ba Phnom," *Facing the Cambodian Past,* pp. 119–36.

22. See Evéline Porée-Maspero, *Etude sur les rites agraires des cambodgiens,* 3 vols. (Paris, 1962–69).

23. See Institut Bouddhique (comp.), *Prachum ruong preng phak ti 8* [Collected folktales, Vol. 8] (Phnom Penh, 1971), which is concerned with *nak ta,* and my review in *JSS,* Vol. 61, No. 2 (July 1973): 219–21. See also Ang Choulean, "Le sol et l'ancêtre: L'amorphe et l'anthromorphe," *JA,* Vol. 283 (1995): 213–38, and Alain Forest, *La Culte des génies protecteurs au Cambodge* (Paris, 1993), which includes some valuable translations.

24. See Paul Lavy, "As in Heaven, so in Earth: The Politics of Vishnu, Siva and Harihara Images in pre-Angkorian Khmer Civilization," *Journal of Southeast Asian Studies (JSEAS)* 34/l (February 2003):21–36.

25. W. Solheim, "Regional Reports: Cambodia, Laos and Vietnam," *Asian Perspectives (AP),* Vol. 3 (1960): 25.

26. Paul Mus, "Cultes indiens et indigènes à Champa," *BEFEO,* Vol. 33 (1933): 367–450. See also Ashley Thompson, "Paul Mus vu de l'ouest: à propos des cultes indiens et indigènes en Asie du Sud-Est" in David Chandler and Christopher Goscha (eds.) *Paul Mus 1902–1969: L' espace d'un regard* (Paris, 2005), pp. 93–108.

27. On Lingaparvata see Claude Jacques and Philippe Lafond, *The Khmer Empire:Cities and Sanctuaries from the 5th to the 13th Century* Bangkok, 2006), pp. 65–69, and Michael Coe, *Angkor,* pp. 76–77.

28. On *kpoñ,* see Vickery, *Society, Economics and Politics,* pp. 151–55.

29. See P.N. Jenner, *A Chronological Inventory of the Inscriptions of Cambodia* (Honolulu, 1980). The earliest datable inscription found in Cambodia, K. 600, was discovered at Angkor Borei by French scholars in 1935. Intriguingly, it refers to a *kpoñ.* Vickery, *Society, Economics, and Politics,* p. 105.

30. J. Jacob, "Pre-Angkor Cambodia," in Smith and Watson, *Early Southeast Asia*, pp. 406–26. See also Jonathan Friedman, *System, Structure, and Contradiction in the Evolution of "Asiatic" Social Formations* (Ann Arbor, Mich., 1975), especially pp. 373ff., and Michael Vickery, "Some Remarks on Early State Formation in Cambodia," in Marr and Milner (eds.), *Southeast Asia in the 9th to 14th Centuries*, pp. 95–116, which draws on Friedman's work.

31. See Briggs, *Ancient Khmer Empire* (Philadelphia, 1951), pp. 38–57, for a summary of the evidence. For more recent discussions, see Michael Vickery, "Where and What Was Chenla?" in François Bizot (ed.), *Recherches nouvelles sur le Cambodge* (Paris, 1994), pp. 197–212, and Vickery, *Society, Economics, and Politics*, pp. 33–35.

32. Jacques, "'Funan,' 'Zhenla,'" p. 376.

33. Friedman, *System, Structure*, pp. 341–44. This discussion also draws on Michael Vickery, "Angkor and the Asiatic Mode of Production" (unpublished seminar paper, Monash University, November 27, 1981).

Chapter 3

1. See B.P. Groslier, *Angkor et le Cambodge au XVIe siècle* (Paris, 1958).

2. For general surveys, see Briggs, *The Ancient Khmer Empire*, and Coedes, *The Indianized States of Southeast Asia*. For syntheses of more recent research see Claude Jacques, *Angkor* (Paris, 1990), and Bruno Dagens, *Angkor: La Forêt de pierre* (Paris, 1989).

3. G. Coedes, "L'Avenir des études khmères," *Bulletin de la Société des Etudes Indochinoises (BSEI)*, Vol. 40 (1965): 205–13. The rest of this chapter, like all scholarship on Cambodia, owes a great deal to Coedes's work and that of his colleagues and pupils at the Ecole Française d'Extrême Orient.

4. G. Coedes and P. Dupont, "L'Inscription de Sdok Kak Thom," *BEFEO*, Vol. 43 (1942–43): 57–134. See also I.W. Mabbett, "Devaraja," *Journal of Southeast Asian History (JSEAH)*, Vol. 10, No. 2 (1969): 202–23; Mabbett and Chandler, *The Khmers*, pp. 88–90; and Nidhi Aeusrivognse, "The Devaraja Cult and Khmer Kingship at Angkor," in K.R. Hall and J.K. Whitmore (eds.), *Explorations in Early Southeast Asian History* (Ann Arbor, Mich., 1976), pp. 107–48. Michael Coe, *Angkor*, p. 100, notes that the Kulen ceremony occurred two years after the coronation of Charlemagne as Holy Roman Emperor.

5. K. 956, from Wat Samrong, *IC*, Vol. 7, pp. 128–29.

6. C. Jacques, "La Carrière de Jayavarman II," *BEFEO*, Vol. 59 (1972): 194–220.

7. Ibid. See also O.W. Wolters, "Jayavarman II's Military Power: The Territorial Foundation of the Angkor Empire," *Journal of the Royal Asiatic Society (JRAS)* (1973): 21–30. There is an extended discussion of Jayavarman II's

career in Vickery, *Society, Economics, and Politics* pp. 393–408, and Hiram Woodward, "Mapping the Eighth Century," unpublished paper, 2006. See also Elizabeth Moore, "The Prehistoric Habitation of Angkor," in *Southeast Asian Archaeology* (1994), pp. 27–35.

8. K. 989, stele from Prasat Ben, *IC*, Vol. 7, pp. 164–89. The place-name China probably refers to the Chinese-administered part of northern Vietnam.

9. Hermann Kulke, *The Devaraja Cult* (tr. I.W. Mabbett) (Ithaca, N.Y., 1978). See also Mabbett and Chandler, *The Khmers*, p. 90, and Hiram Woodward, "Practice and Belief in Ancient Cambodia," *JSEAS* (32 /2)(2004): 249–61.

10. G. Coedes, "Les capitales de Jayavarman II," *BEFEO*, Vol. 28 (1928): 116.

11. P. Stern, "Diversité et rhythme des fondations royales khmères," *BEFEO*, Vol. 44, No. 2 (1951): 649–85. See also Hermann Kulke, "The Early and Imperial Kingdom in Southeast Asian History," in David Marr and Antony Milner (eds.), *Southeast Asia in the 9th to 14th Centuries* (Singapore, 1989), pp. 1–22.

12. A. Bergaigne, *Les Inscriptions sanscrites du Cambodge* (Paris, 1882), p. 127.

13. For a discussion of this style see G. de Coral Remusat, "Influences javanaises dans l'art de Roluos," *JA*, Vol. 223 (1933): 190–92. See also Michael Vickery, "The Khmer Inscriptions of Roluos (Preah Ko and Lolei): Documents from a Transitional Period in Cambodian History," *Seksa Khmer* (new series, 1999): 47–92. Vickery notes: "These inscriptions indicate that the polity centered at Roluos was dominant over a wide area of northern Cambodia extending from the present northwestern border to Katie and including Kompong Cham and Kompong Thom. On the other hand, there is no sign of any authority over the heartland of pre-Angkor Cambodia, what is now the center and the south" (p. 84).

14. K. 713, stele from Preah Ko, *IC*, Vol. 1, pp. 18–31. On the notion of "three worlds" shared by Hinduism and Buddhism, see G. Coedes and C. Archaimbault, *Les Trois mondes* (Paris, 1973).

15. K. 809, from Prasat Kandol Dom, *IC*, Vol. 1, p. 43.

16. Cited in S. Sahai, *Institutions politiques et organisation administrative du Cambodge* (Paris, 1970), p. 42n. The early eighth-century temple of Ak Yum, in the Angkor region, seems to have been a rudimentary temple-mountain. See Bruno Brugier, "Le prasat Ak Yom: Etat des connaissances" (Paris, 1994); Vickery, *Society, Economics, and Politics*, p. 391; and Helen Jessup, *Art and Architecture of Cambodia* (London, 2004), pp. 60–61.

17. See Eleanor Mannika, *Angkor Wat: Time, Space and Kingship* (Honolulu, 1996); and R. Stencel and Eleanor Moron, "Astronomy and Cosmology at Angkor Wat," *Science*, Vol. 193 (July 23, 1978): 281–87.

18. See G. Coedes, "A la recherche du Yasodharasrama," *BEFEO*, Vol. 32 (1932): 84–112, and Bergaigne, *Inscriptions sanscrites*, pp. 166–211.

19. On the importance of the northeast, see P. Paris, "L'importance rituelle du nord-est et ses applications en Indochine," *BEFEO*, Vol. 41 (1941): 301–33.

20. See B.P. Groslier, *Inscriptions du Bayon* (Paris, 1973), p. 156, and David Chandler, "Maps for the Ancestors: Sacralized Topography and Echoes of Angkor in Two Cambodian Texts," in *Facing the Cambodian Past*, pp. 25–42, especially note 28.

21. See V. Goloubew, "Le Phnom Bakheng et la ville de Yasovarman," *BEFEO*, Vol. 33 (1933): 319–44, and V. Goloubew, "Nouvelles recherches autour de Phnom Bakheng," *BEFEO*, Vol. 34 (1934): 576–600. See also Christophe Pottier, "A la recherche de Gouloupura," *BEFEO* 87 (2000): 79–107, which argues that Yasodharapura, unlike the city of the same name constructed under Jayavarman VII, discussed below, was open, without gates or walls.

22. J. Filliozat, "Le Symbolisme du monument du Phnom Bakheng," *BEFEO*, Vol. 44, No. 2 (1954): 527–54.

23. See John Black, *The Lofty Sanctuary of Khao Prah Vihar* (Bangkok, 1976).

24. Bergaigne, *Inscriptions sanscrites*, p. 322. For similar passages see pp. 227, 376.

25. See G. Coedes, "Le Véritable fondateur du culte de la royauté divine au Cambodge," in H.B. Sarkar (ed.), *R. C. Majumdar Felicitation Volume* (Calcutta, 1970), pp. 56–66. See also Sahai, *Institutions*, p. 46n. For a helpful discussion of Koh Ker, see Jacques and Lafond, *Khmer Empire*, pp. 107–33.

26. G. Coedes, "Les Inscriptions de Bat Chum," *JA*, Vol. 10, No. 8 (1908): 213–54. See also Michael Freeman, *A Guide to Khmer Temples in Thailand and Laos* (Bangkok, 1996), pp. 58–60.

27. K. 806, Pre Rup stele, *IC*, Vol. 1, pp. 73–142. For a fine-grained study of two of Rajendravarman's temples see Alexandra Haendel, "The Divine in the Human World: Sculpture at Two Tenth-Century Temples at Angkor," *Artibus Asiae*, Vol. LXV, No. 2 (2005): 213–52.

28. See L. Finot and V. Goloubew, *Le Temple d'Içvarapura* (Paris, 1926).

29. K. 111, stele from Wat Sithor, *IC*, Vol. 6, p. 196, where Senart's comment is cited by G. Coedes.

30. G. Coedes, "L'Inscription de Toul Komnap Ta Kin (K. 125)," *BEFEO*, Vol. XXVIII (1928): 140–44.

31. Michael Vickery, "The Reign of Suryavarman I and Royal Factionalism at Angkor," *JSEAS*, Vol. 16, No. 2 (1985): 226–44.

32. M. De Coral Remusat, "La Date de Takev," *BEFEO*, Vol. 34 (1934): 425.

33. G. Coedes, "Le serment des fonctionnaires de Suryavarman I," *BEFEO,* Vol. 13, No. 6 (1913): 11–17. For a similar oath sworn by Cambodian officials in the nineteenth and twentieth centuries, see Chandler, "Maps for the Ancestors," passim.

34. H. de Mestrier du Bourg, "La première moitié du XIe siècle au Cambodge," *JA,* Vol. 258 (1970): 281–314.

35. Kenneth Hall, "Eleventh-Century Commercial Development in Angkor and Champa," *JSEAS,* Vol. 10, No. 2 (September 1979): 420–34, and Hall, "Khmer Commercial Development and Foreign Contacts Under Suryavarman I," *Journal of Economic and Social History of the Orient (JESHO),* Vol. 18, No. 3 (1975): 318–33. See also Claude Jacques, "Sources on Economic Activities in Khmer and Cham Lands," in Marr and Milner, *Southeast Asia in the 9th to 14th Centuries,* pp. 327–34. Eileen Lustig's forthcoming thesis at the University of Sydney on units of value at Angkor (which, tantalizingly, never used money) will greatly enhance our knowledge of Angkorean economics.

36. A. Barth, *Inscriptions sanscrites du Cambodge* (Paris, 1885), p. 139.

37. Paul Mus, *India Seen from the East,* passim.

38. I.W. Mabbett, "Kingship at Angkor," *JSS,* Vol. 66, No. 2 (July 1978): 1–58. See also Mabbett and Chandler, *The Khmers,* pp. 34–106.

39. See M.C. Ricklefs, "Land and the Law in the Epigraphy of Tenth Century Cambodia," *JAS* 26/3 (1967): 411–20.

40. I.W. Mabbett, "Some Remarks on the Present State of Knowledge About Slavery at Angkor," in Anthony Reid (ed.), *Slavery, Bondage, and Dependency in Southeast Asia* (St. Lucia, Australia, 1983); Y. Bongert, "Note sur l'esclavage en droit khmer ancien," in *Etudes d'histoire du droit privé offertes à Paul Pettiot* (Paris, 1959), pp. 27–44. For a discussion of the pre-Angkorean phenomenon see Vickery, *Society, Economics and Politics,* pp. 239 ff.

41. I.W. Mabbett, "*Varnas* in Angkor and the Indian Caste System," *JAS,* Vol. 36, No. 3 (May 1977): 429–42.

42. Institut Bouddhique, Phnom Penh, Commission des Moeurs et Coutumes Cambodgiennes (CMCC), Archive number 94.004. The disappearance of this archive in the 1970s was a serious blow to scholarship, although some portions collected before 1950 have survived on microfilm.

43. L. Finot, "L'Inscription de Ban Theat (K. 364)," *BEFEO,* Vol. 12 (1912): 1–27, stanzas 33–34.

44. See Mannika, *Angkor Wat,* passim.

45. For a summary of this debate see G. Coedes, *Angkor* (Oxford, 1963), pp. 34–38.

46. Eleanor Moron (later, Mannika), "Configuration of Time and Space at Angkor Wat," *Studies in Indo-Asian Art and Culture,* Vol. 5 (1977): 217–67.

47. See Mannika, *Angkor Wat,* pp. 42–44.

48. Groslier, *Inscriptions du Bayon*, p. 50. See B.P. Groslier, "La Cité hydraulique angkorienne. Exploitation ou surexploitation du sol?" *BEFEO*, Vol. 66 (1979): 161–202. See also Groslier, "Agriculture et religion dans l'empire angkorien," *Etudes rurales*, Nos. 53–56 (January–December 1974): 95–117. Groslier's arguments are expanded in Jacques Dumarçay and Pascal Royère, *Cambodian Architecture, Eighth to Thirteenth Century* (Leiden, 2001), pp. xvii–xxix. For a contrary argument see W.J. Van Liere, "Traditional Water Management in the Lower Mekong Basin," *World Archaeology*, Vol. 11, No. 3 (Fall 1980): 265–80. Van Liere suggests that the artificial lakes at Angkor had no distributive function but served merely as adjuncts to the metaphysical worldview of Angkorean kings. The farming of the shores of the Tonle Sap when the lake receded, however, was quite advanced and may well have been able to support the sizable populations needed to build the temples and serve in them. See also Robert Acker, "New Geographical Tests of the Hydraulic Thesis at Angkor," *Southeast Asia Research*, Vol. 6, No. 1 (March 1998): 5–47; Charles Higham, *The Civilization of Angkor* (Oxford, 2001) pp. 56ff; and Greater Angkor Project, "Redefining Angkor: Structure and Environment in the Largest Low Density Urban Complex of the Pre-Industrial World," *Udaya* 4 (2003), pp. 107–23, especially 112–13, which argue that the symbolic significance of the *baray* should not be underestimated, nor should their practical uses. The hydraulic infrastructure at Angkor was enormous and sophisticated, but responded poorly to ecological pressures to change.

49. Briggs, *Ancient Khmer Empire*, p. 206.

50. For a useful summary of arguments see Olivier de Bernon, "Note sur l'hydraulique theocratique angkorienne" *BEFEO* 84 (1997): 340–8.

51. See Leigh Dayton, "The Lost City," *New Scientist* (January 13, 2001), pp. 30–33. The Angkor region as mapped from the air covered one thousand square kilometers.

52. Groslier, "La Cite hydraulique angkorienne." See also Rhoads Murphey, "The Ruin of Ancient Ceylon," *JAS*, Vol. 16, No. 1 (February 1957): 181–200.

53. Michael Coe, "The Khmer Settlement Pattern: A Possible Analogy with That of the Maya," *American Antiquity*, Vol. 22 (1957): 409–10, and Coe, "Social Typology and Tropical Forest Civilizations," *Comparative Studies in Society and History (CSSH)*, Vol. 4 (1961–62): 65–85, who suggests that Angkor was not so much a city as a ceremonial site. See also Victor Lieberman, *Strange Parallels: Southeast Asia in Global Context, c.800–1830* (Cambridge, 2003), esp. pp. 236–42, a perceptive comparative account.

54. Coe, *Angkor*, p. 150.

55. See Greater Angkor Project, "Redefining Angkor: Structure and Environment in the Largest Low Density Urban Complex of the Pre-Industrial World" *Udaya* 4 (2003): 107–23, passim, and Roland Fletcher, "Seeing

Angkor: New Views on an Old City," *Journal of Oriental Society of Australia*, Vol. 320 (2001): 1–27.

Chapter 4

1. G. Coedes, *Angkoran Introduction* (Hong Kong, 1963), pp. 84–107.

2. B.P. Groslier, *Inscriptions du Bayon* (Paris, 1973), p. 141.

3. This statue was discovered in 1958. See G. Coedes, "Le Portrait dans l'art khmer," *Arts Asiatiques (AA)*, Vol. 7, No. 3 (1960): 179–88, and Claude Jacques, "The Historical Development of Khmer Culture from the Death of Suryavarman II to the XIVth Century," in Joyce Clark and Michael Vickery (eds.), *The Bayon: New Perspectives* (Bangkok, 2007), which argues that Jayavarman VII was raised as a Buddhist in Jayadityapura.

4. See J. Boisselier, "Réflexions sur l'art du Jayavarman VII," *BSEI*, Vol. 27, No. 3 (1952): 261–73; Paul Mus, "Angkor at the Time of Jayavarman VII," *Indian Arts and Letters*, Vol. 11 (1937): 65–75; and Mus, "Angkor vu du Japon," *France Asie (FA)*, Nos. 175–76 (1962): 521–38. See also Philippe Stern, *Les monuments khmers du style du Bayon et Jayavarman VII* (Paris, 1965), pp. 177–98.

5. See Mus, "Angkor at the Time of Jayavarman VII"; Mus, "Angkor vu du Japon"; and Boisselier, "Réflexions."

6. Groslier, *Les inscriptions du Bayon*, p. 152.

7. G. Maspero, *Le Royaume de Champa* (Paris, 1928), p. 164.

8. K. 485, stele from Phimeanakas, *IC*, Vol. 2, p. 171.

9. Ibid., p. 175.

10. Coedes, "Le Portrait." Groslier, *Inscriptions du Bayon*, p. 194, however, claims that Coedes's inventory of portrait statues is incomplete. See also Son Soubert, "Head of Jayavarman VII," in Helen Ibbetson Jessup and Thierry Zephir (eds.), *Sculpture of Angkor and Ancient Cambodia: Millennium of Glory* (New York, 1997), pp. 300–1, and Ashley Thompson, "The Suffering of Kings: Substitute Bodies, Healing, and Justice in Cambodia," in John Marston and Elizabeth Guthrie (eds.) *History, Buddhism, and New Religious Movements in Cambodia* (Honolulu, 2004), pp. 91–112.

11. L. Finot, "L'Inscription sanscrite de Say-Fong," *BEFEO*, Vol. 3, No. 2 (1903): 18–33. See also G. Coedes, "Les Hôpitaux de Jayavarman VII," *BEFEO*, Vol. 40 (1940): 344–47. Claude Jacques kindly provided this translation of the passage, amending that of Finot (personal communication). See also Kieth Rethy Chhem, "*Bhaisajyaguru* and Tantric Medicine in Jayavarman VII Hospitals," *Siksacak* 7 (2005), pp. 9–17.

12. Boisselier, "Réflexions," p. 263.

13. Michael Vickery, "Introduction" to Clark and Vickery, *The Bayon* (2007).

14. J. Auboyer, "Aspects de l'art bouddhique au pays khmer au temps de Jayavarman VII," in W. Watson (ed.), *Mahayanist Art After A.D. 900* (London, 1977), pp. 66–74.

15. K. 273, Ta Prohm inscription, *BEFEO,* Vol. 6, No. 2 (1906): 44–81.

16. G. Coedes, "Les gîtes d'étape à la fin du XIIIe siècle," *BEFEO,* Vol. 40 (1940): 347–49. On "fire shrines," as Claude Jacques has redefined these structures, see Jacques and Lafond, *The Khmer Empire,* pp. 263–64.

17. See G. Coedes, "Le Stèle de Preah Khan," *BEFEO,* Vol. 41 (1941): 256–301. The passage quoted appears on p. 287.

18. Groslier, *Inscriptions du Bayon,* p. 167.

19. This passage derives in large part from arguments advanced by Hiram Woodward, in private communications. See also his "Preface" to Clark and Vickery, *The Bayon.*

20. See Ta Prohm inscription.

21. See L. Finot and V. Goloubew, "Le Symbolisme de Nak Pean," *BEFEO,* Vol. 23 (1923): 401–5, and V. Goloubew, "Le Cheval Balaha," *BEFEO,* Vol. 27 (1927): 223–38.

22. J. Boisselier, "Pouvoir royal et symbolisme architectural: Neak Pean et son importance pour la royauté angkorienne," *AA,* Vol. 21 (1970): 91–107.

23. See G. Groslier, *A l'ombre d'Angkor* (Paris, 1916), pp. 148–82.

24. See Jacques Dumarçay, *Le Bayon, histoire architectural du temple* (Paris, 1973), especially pp. 57–64. For an interesting explanation of changes in the iconography of the Bayon, see Hiram W. Woodward Jr., "Tantric Buddhism at Angkor Thom," *Ars Orientalis,* Vol. 12 (1981): 57–68; J. Boisselier, "The Meaning of Angkor Thom," in Jessup and Zephir, *Sculpture of Angkor and Ancient Cambodia,* pp. 117–121; Claude Jacques, "Les Derniers siècles d'Angkor," in *Comptes Rendus de l'Académie des Inscriptions et Belles-Lettres* (Paris, 1999), pp. 367–90; and the chapters by Claude Jacques and Olivier Cunin in Clark and Vickery, *The Bayon.*

25. K. 287, stele from Prasat Chrung, *IC,* Vol. 4, p. 250.

26. On the meaning of the name, see Vickery, "Introduction" to Clark and Vickery, *The Bayon,* which notes that in the nineteenth century local people called several Angkorian temples by this name citing Etienne Aymonier, *Le Cambodge,* Vol. 3 (Paris, 1904), pp. 143–44. See also Saveros Pou, "From Old Khmer Epigraphy to Popular Tradition: A Study of the Names of Cambodian Monuments," in S. Pou, *Selected Papers in Khmerology* (Phnom Penh, 2003), p. xxx.

27. See Jean Boisselier and David Snellgrove (eds.), *The Image of the Buddha* (Paris, 1978), p. 410.

28. See Michael Vickery, "Introduction" to Clark and Vickery, *The Bayon.*

29. On Banteay Chhmar see Christophe Pottier, "A propos du temple de Banteay Chhmar," *Aséanie* 13 (June 2004): 132–49.

30. For a detailed discussion of this religious shift see G. Coedes, "Documents sur l'histoire politique et religieuse du Laos occidental," *BEFEO*, Vol. 25 (1925): 1–202. See also A. Leclère, *Le Bouddhisme au Cambodge* (Paris, 1989), pp. 1–34; Daniel M. Veidlinger, *Speaking the Dharma: Writing Orality and Textual Transmission in Buddhist Northern Thailand* (Honolulu, 2006); and David K. Wyatt, "Relics, Oaths and Politics in Thirteenth Century Siam," *JSEAS* 34 (2003): 21–39.

31. Briggs, *The Ancient Khmer Empire*, pp. 242 and 259.

32. Zhou Daguan, *Cambodia: The Land and Its People* (ed. and tr. Peter Harris) (Chiangmai, 2007), a fresh translation from the Chinese that supplements P. Pelliot (ed.), *Mémoires sur les coutumes du Cambodge de Tcheou Ta Kuan* (Paris, 1951).

33. K. 287, stele from Prasat Chrung, *IC*, Vol. 4, p. 208.

34. Ashley Thompson, "Changing Perspectives: Cambodia After Angkor," in Jessup and Zephir, *Sculpture of Angkor and Ancient Cambodia*, pp. 22–32 at 23.

35. G. Coedes, "Une période critique dans l'Asie du Sud Est: Le XIIIe siècle," *BSEI*, Vol. 33 (1958): 387–400.

36. Daguan, *Cambodia: The Land and Its People*, passim.

37. Interestingly, although Cambodian classical literature makes almost no mention of slaves, a popular folktale cycle in Cambodia is concerned with the triumphs of a wily, unscrupulous slave, Tmenh Chey, who outwits everyone he meets, including the emperor of China. See Pierre Bitard (tr.), *La Merveilleuse histoire de Thmenh Chey l'astucieux* (Saigon, 1956).

38. M.C. Ricklefs, "Land and Law in the Epigraphy of Tenth Century Cambodia," *JAS*, Vol. 26, No. 3 (May 1967): 411–20.

39. L. Finot and V. Goloubew, *Le Temple d'Içvarapura* (Paris, 1926), p. 83.

40. L. Finot, "Temple de Mangalatha à Angkor Thom," *BEFEO*, Vol. 25 (1925): 393–406; C. Jacques, "Les Derniers siècles d'Angkor"; and Jacques, "The Historical Development of Khmer Culture" in Clark and Vickery (eds.), *The Bayon*.

Chapter 5

1. For a discussion of Thai and Khmer chronicle histories for this period, see Michael Vickery, *Cambodia and Its Neighbors in the 15th Century*, and M. Vickery, "The Composition and Transmission of Ayudhya and Cambodian Chronicles," in Anthony Reid and David Marr (eds.), *Perceptions of the Past in Southeast Asia* (Singapore, 1979), pp. 130–54.

2. O.W. Wolters, "The Khmer King at Basan," *Asia Major*, Vol. 12, No. 1 (1966): 86. On Chinese relations, see Wang Gungwu, "China and Southeast Asia 1402–1424," in his *Community and Nation* (Singapore, 1981), pp. 58–80. The volume of trade with China in the fourteenth century was often substantial. In 1387, for example, Cambodia exported fifty-nine elephants

and sixty thousand catties of incense to China (Ibid., p. 56). See also Michael Vickery, *Cambodia and its Neighbors in the 15th Century* (Singapore, 2004), especially pp. 9–10, 25–16, and 42–50.

3. Michael Vickery, "The 2/k 125 Fragment: A Lost Chronicle of Ayudhya," *JSS*, Vol. 65, No. 1 (January 1977): 1–80. See also Vickery, *Cambodia After Angkor: The Chronicular Evidence for the Fourteenth to Sixteenth Centuries* (Ann Arbor, Mich., 1977), pp. 500ff, and A. Thompson, "*Changing Perspectives: Cambodia After Angkor,*" in Helen Ibbetson Jessup and Thierry Zephir (eds.), *Sculpture of Angkor and Ancient Cambodia: Millennium of Glory* (New York, 1997), passim. See also Victor Lieberman, *Strange Parallels* (Cambridge, 2003), especially pp. 236–42.

4. G. Coedes, "La Fondation du Phnom Penh," *BEFEO*, Vol. 13, No. 3 (1913): 6–11. The region, of clear commercial importance, had been settled long before then. See Olivier de Bernon, "Le plus ancien edifice subsistant du Phnom Penh: une tour angkorienne sise dans l'enceinte du Vatt Unalom," *BEFEO* 88 (2001): 249–60. For pre-Angkorian inscriptions discovered near Phnom Penh, see Vickery, *Society, Economics and Politics*, pp. 153, 295, and 360. See also Ashley Thompson, "Lost and Found: The Four Faced Buddha, and the Seat of Power in Middle Cambodia," *Southeast Asian Archaeology 1998* (Hull, 2000), pp. 245–64.

5. See M.M. Gullick, *Indigenous Political Systems of Western Malaya* (London, 1958), especially pp. 125–43.

6. Vickery, "The 2/k 125 Fragment," pp. 60–62.

7. Vickery suspects that this story, which has entered Khmer folklore, is legendary. See his review of Mak Phoeun, *Histoire du Cambodge de la fin du XVIe siècle au debut de XVIIIe, BEFEO* 83 (1996): 405–15.

8. See Yoneo Ishii (ed. and tr.), *The Junk Trade from Southeast Asia: Translations from the Tosen Fusetsu-gaki 1674–1723* (Singapore, 1998), pp. 153–93 and especially 166. Ishii's documents show that Cambodia was a "two-headed bird" (see Chapter 8), paying homage to what are now Thailand and Vietnam well before the nineteenth century, when the term appears in contemporary documents.

9. See Chapter 12.

10. See B.P. Groslier, *Le Cambodge au XVIe siècle* (Paris, 1958), pp. 142–44.

11. This and the quotation in the preceding paragraph are taken from C.R. Boxer (ed.), *South China in the Sixteenth Century* (London, 1953), p. 63. A Chinese trader quoted by Ishii, *The Junk Trade*, p. 32, writing in the 1680s: "The land's produce is not plentiful, the people are not obedient and there are very few products available."

12. Groslier, *Le Cambodge au XVIe siècle*, p. 69. See also J. Dumarçay, "Le Prasat prei près d'Angkor Wat," *BEFEO*, Vol. 59 (1970): 189–92, and G.

Coedes, "La Date d'exécution des deux bas-reliefs tardifs d'Angkor Wat," *JA,* Vol. 250 (1962): 235–43. See also Saveros Lewitz, "Les inscriptions modernes d'Angkor Vat" *JA* (1972): 107–29. See also Jacques Dumarcay, *The Site of Angkor* (Oxford, 1995), p. 64, which suggests that three other temples at Angkor—Bakheng, the Bapuon, and Banteai Kdei—were also "profoundly altered" at this time.

13. Khin Sok, "Deux inscriptions tardifs du Phnom Bakheng," *BEFEO,* Vol. 65, No. 1 (1978): 271–80. See also S. Pou, "Inscription du Phnom Bakheng" in Pou (ed.), *Nouvelles inscriptions du Cambodge* (Paris, 1989), pp. 20–27.

14. Khin Sok, "L'Inscription de Vatta Romlock," *BEFEO,* Vol. 67 (1980): 125–31, and Saveros Pou, "Inscription du Vat Romlok," *BEFEO,* Vol. 70 (1981): 126–30.

15. See G. Janneau, *Manuel pratique pour le cambodgien* (Saigon, 1876), pp. 87–88, and Evéline Porée-Maspero, *Etude sur les rites agraires des cambodgiens,* 3 vols., (Paris, 1962–69), p. 111. In 1971 Cambodia's chief of state, Lon Nol, related the legend to the U.S. ambassador as a way of explaining how Cambodia's superiority to its neighbors had been depleted. See David Chandler, *The Tragedy of Cambodian History: Politics, War, and Revolution Since 1945* (New Haven, 1991), p. 213. For a spirited retelling of the legend see Ang Choulean, "Nandin and His Avatars," in Jessup and Zephir, *Sculpture of Angkor and Ancient Cambodia,* pp. 62–70. In 2005 the myth was alive and well. See Alexandra Kent's chapter in Alexandra Kent and David Chandler (eds.), *People of Virtue: Reconfiguring Religion, Power and Moral Order in Cambodia Today* (Copenhagen, 2007).

16. Ang Choulean, "Nandin and His Avatars."

17. See A. Cabaton (ed. and tr.), *Brève et véridique relation des évènements du Cambodge par Gabriel Quiroga de San Antonio* (Paris, 1941). See also L.P. Briggs, "Spanish Intervention in Cambodia," *T'oung Pao* (1949), pp. 132–60.

18. See W.J.M. Buch, "La Compagnie des Indes et l'Indochine," *BEFEO,* Vol. 36 (1936): 97–196, Vol. 37 (1937): 121–237, and D.K. Basset, "The Trade of the English East India Company in Cambodia, 1651–1656," *JRAS* (1962): 35–62. See also Jean-Claude Lejosne, "Historiographie du Cambodge aux XVIe et XVIIe siècles: Les Sources portugaises et hollondaises," in Pierre L. Lamant (ed.), *Bilan et Perspectives des Etudes Khmeres (Langue et Culture)* (Paris, 1997), pp. 179–208.

19. Cabaton, *Brève et véridique relation,* p. 100.

20. Jean Delvert, *Le Paysan cambodgien* (The Hague, 1961), especially pp. 371ff. In *Cambodia After Angkor,* pp. 513–20, Vickery argues that trade and communication in the Angkor period were primarily over roads built and maintained by corvée labor. Riverine traffic, carried out by individuals, both foreigners and local entrepreneurs, on the other hand, linked the country to-

gether and Cambodia to the outside world after the shift of the government to the south. Vickery amplifies these arguments in *Cambodia and its Neighbors*.

21. Cabaton, *Brève et véridique relation*, p. 208.

22. See the nineteenth-century prose chronicle numbered P. 6 in the Fonds Phnom Penh collection of the Ecole Française d'Extrême Orient in Paris. Several post-Angkorean inscriptions at Angkor testify to the persistence of an elite. For a discussion of this period, see May Ebihara, "Societal Organization in Sixteenth and Seventeenth Century Cambodia," *JSEAS* 15(1) (September 1984): 280–95.

23. See Carool Kersten, "Cambodia's Muslim King: Khmer and Dutch Sources on the Conversion of Reameathipdei I (1642–1658)," *JSEAS* 37(1) (February 2006): 1–22.

24. Ishii, *Junk Trade*, p. 123.

25. S. Pou, *Etudes sur le Ramakerti* (Paris, 1977), pp. 48–49.

26. See Saveros Pou and K. Haksrea, "Liste d'ouvrages de *Cpap*," *JA*, Vol. 269 (1981): 467–83, and David Chandler, "Narrative Poems (*Chbap*) and Pre-Colonial Cambodian Society," *Facing the Cambodian Past*, pp. 45–60. For the Cambodian texts of these poems, and an elegant French translation, see Saveros Pou, *Guirlande de cpap*, 2 vols., (Paris, 1988).

27. Clifford Geertz, *The Religion of Java* (New York, 1960), pp. 248–60. A campaign to dismantle the hierarchy of pronouns occurred in the revolutionary era; see John Marston, "Language Reform in Democratic Kampuchea" (M.A. thesis, University of Minnesota, 1985). By 2006, and indeed well before then, the pre-1970 linguistic hierarchy had broken down, especially among urban Khmer.

28. Saveros Pou's three-volume edition and critique of the *Ramakerti* was published by *BEFEO* in Paris in 1977–79. The volumes include a Cambodian text, a French translation, and a volume of commentary, *Etudes sur le Ramakerti*. See also Judith Jacob (tr.), *The Reamker* (London, 1987). In the early 1820s, Malay speakers in southern Vietnam referred to the Tonle Sap as the "Lake of Sri Rama." See John Crawfurd, *Journal of an Embassy to the Courts of Siam and Cochin-China* (London, 1828, repr. Oxford 1967), p. 466.

29. Porée-Maspero, *Etude sur les rites*, Vol. 3, p. 528.

30. F. Bizot (ed.), *Histoire de Reamker* (Phnom Penh, 1973). According to Thong Thel (personal communication), this Khmer text resembles Thai-language versions more closely than it does the seventeenth-century Cambodian text.

31. See David Chandler, "Songs at the Edge of the Forest: Perceptions of Order in Three Cambodian Texts," in *Facing the Cambodian Past*, pp. 76–99, and Peter Carey, *The Cultural Ecology of Early Nineteenth Century Java* (Singapore, 1974), p. 4. See also Penny Edwards, "Between a Song and a *Priy*: Tracking Cambodian Cosmologies and Histories through the Forest," in Anne Hansen and Judy Ledgerwood (eds). *At the Edge of the Forest: Essays in Honor of David Chandler* (Ithaca, N.Y., 2007).

32. See F. Martini, "Quelques notes sur le Reamker," *Artibus Asiae (AA)*, Vol. 24, Nos. 3–4 (1961): 351–62, and Martini, *La Gloire de Rama* (Paris, 1978), pp. 19–30.

33. I am grateful to Barbara Hatly for this insight into *wayang*.

34. A. Leclère, *Les Codes cambodgiens*, 2 vols. (Paris, 1898), Vol. 1, pp. 123–75.

35. On Vietnam's "march south" and early relations with Cambodia, see Michael Cotter, "Toward a Social History of the Vietnamese Southward Movement," *JSEAH*, Vol. 9, No. 1 (March 1968): 12–24, and Mak Phoeun and Po Dharma, "La Deuxième intervention militaire vietnamienne au Cambodge," *BEFEO*, Vol. 77 (1988): 229–62.

36. E. Gaspardone, "Un chinois des mers du sud," *JA,* Vol. 240, No. 3 (1952): 361–85. On Cambodian relations with Siam in this period, see Dhiravat na Pembejra, "Seventeenth Century Ayutthaya: A Shift to Isolation?" in Anthony Reid (ed.), *Southeast Asia in the Early Modern Era: Trade, Power and Belief* (New Haven, 1997). See also Ishii, *The Junk Trade*, pp. 153–93.

37. See Saveros Pou, "Les Inscriptions modernes d'Angkor," *JA,* Vol. 260, No. 242 (1972): 107–29, and David Chandler, "An Eighteenth Century Inscription from Angkor Wat," in *Facing the Cambodian Past*, pp. 15–24.

38. On Taksin's reign, see C.J. Reynolds, "Religious Historical Writing and the Legitimation of the First Bangkok Reign," in Anthony Reid and David Marr (eds.), *Perceptions of the Past in Southeast Asia* (Singapore, 1979), pp. 90–107, and Lorraine Gesick, "The Rise and Fall of King Taksin: A Drama of Buddhist Kingship," in Lorraine Gesick (ed.), *Centers, Symbols, and Hierarchies: Essays on the Classical States of Southeast Asia* (New Haven, 1983), pp. 90–105.

39. See Clifford Geertz, *Negara: The Theater State in Nineteenth Century Bali* (Princeton, N.J., 1980), especially pp. 110–27, and Tony Day, *Fluid Iron: State Formation in Southeast Asia* (Honolulu, 2002), pp. 7–8, 175.

Chapter 6

1. For a discussion of Asian maps see David P. Chandler, "Maps for the Ancestors: Sacralized Topography and Echoes of Angkor in Two Cambodian Texts," in *Facing the Cambodian Past* (Chiangmai, 1996), pp. 25–42, and E.R. Leach, "The Frontiers of 'Burma,'" *CSSH*, Vol. 3 (1960–61): 49–68. See also Thongchai Winichakul, *Siam Mapped: A History of the Geo-Body of a Nation* (Honolulu, 1989). According to Adhémard Leclère, *Recherches sur le droit publique des cambodgiens* (Paris, 1894), p. 221, the boundaries of a *sruk* in traditional Cambodia were "those of the rice fields belonging to it." These varied from year to year. Dawn Rooney, *Angkor* (Bangkok, 2006), p. 454, shows an eighteenth-century European map in which Cambodia is almost entirely unmapped.

2. National Library, Bangkok, *Chotmai Het* (*CMH* [Official correspondence]) 1203/1 *kho* 41 mentions a Thai map of Cambodia. Democratic Republic of Vietnam, Bureau of Historical Research (comp.), *Dai nam thuc luc chinh bien* [Primary compilation of the veritable records of imperial Vietnam] (*DNTL*), Vol. 19, p. 240, mentions a Vietnamese one, but these have apparently not survived.

3. Eng Sut, *Akkasar mahaboros khmaer* [Documents about Khmer heroes], (Phnom Penh, 1969), p. 1148.

4. *DNTL*, Vol. 15, p. 115, and Vol. 22, p. 157.

5. E. Aymonier, *Géographie du Cambodge* (Paris, 1876), pp. 31–59.

6. Ibid., p. 49.

7. *CMH* 3/1192/4/1, and 3/1204/1 *ko* /2.

8. See W.E. Willmott, "History and Sociology of the Chinese in Cambodia Prior to the French Protectorate," *JSEAH*, Vol. 7, No. 1 (March 1966): 15–38.

9. C.E. Bouillevaux, *Voyage en Indochine* (Paris, 1858), p. 168. See also Alexander Hamilton, *A New Account of the East Indies* (London, 1727, repr. 1930), p. 106: "There are about two hundred *Topasses,* or *Indian Portugeze,* settled and married in *Cambodia,* and some of them have pretty good posts in the Government, and live great after the Fashion of that Country."

10. On the ethnography of nineteenth-century Cambodia, see Wolfgang Vollman, "Notes sur les relations inter-ethniques au Cambodge du XIXe siècle," *Asie du Sud-Est et Monde Insulindien,* Vol. 4, No. 2 (1973): 172–207.

11. *DNTL*, Vol. 15, p. 171.

12. *DNTL*, Vol. 3, p. 385. See also C. Flood (tr.), *The Dynastic Chronicles, Bangkok Era, the Fourth Reign,* 3 vols. (Tokyo, 1965–67), Vol. 1, p. 171, which quotes King Duang of Cambodia as writing the French in 1858: "Cambodia wanted to build ships, put masts on them and sail them in order to trade with other countries, but Vietnam would not permit Cambodia to sail in and out."

13. William Milburn, *Oriental Commerce* (London, 1813), pp. 449–50.

14. See Ishii, *The Junk Trade from Southeast Asia,* pp. 153–93.

15. Saveros Lewitz, "La Toponymie khmère," *BEFEO* 53/2, No. 2 (1967): 467–500.

16. For a description of Cambodian rice-growing villages in the 1950s, see Jean Delvert, *Le Paysan cambodgien* (Paris, 1962), pp. 322–70.

17. See Khin Sok, *L'annexation du Cambodge par les Vietnamiens au XIXe Siecle* (Paris 2002), pp. 281–359, providing the Khmer text and French translation of a vivid nineteenth-century verse chronicle discussed below (see note 19).

18. See David Chandler (tr.), "The Origin of the Kounlok Bird," in Frank Stewart and Sharon May (eds.), *In the Shadow of Angkor: Contemporary Writing from Cambodia* (Honolulu, 2004), pp. 36–41.

19. These two texts are dealt with in detail in Chandler, "Songs at the Edge of the Forest," in *Facing the Cambodian Past,* pp. 76–99. On the significance of the forest see Charles Malamoud, "Village et foret dans l'ideologie de l'Inde brahmanique," *Archives europeenes de sociologie* XVI (1976): 3–20. Also see Penny Edwards, "Between a Song and a *Priy*: Tracking Cambodian Cosmologies and Histories Through the Forest," in Anne Hansen and Judy Legerwood (eds.), *At the Edge of the Forest: Essays in Honor of David Chandler* (Ithaca, N.Y., 2007).

20. France, Archives l'outremer, Aix-en-Provence (hereafter cited as AOM), Fonds Indochinois A–30 (22), "Rapport confidentiel sur le Cambodge," August 1874.

21. Truong Buu Lam, "L'Autorité dans les villages vietnamiens du XIXe siècle," in G. Wijawardene (ed.), *Leadership and Authority* (Singapore 1968), pp. 65–74.

22. G. Janneau, "Le Cambodge d'autrefois," *Revue Indochinoise (RI),* Vol. 17, No. 3 (March 1914): 266. The article draws on observations that Janneau made in the 1860s, i.e., in the earliest years of French protection.

23. See H.D. Evers (ed.), *Loosely Structured Social Systems: Thailand in Comparative Perspective* (New Haven, 1969), and Robert Textor, "The 'Loose Structure' of Thai Society: A Paradigm Under Pressure," *PA,* Vol. 50, No. 3 (Fall 1977): 467–73. See May Ebihara, "Societal Organization in Sixteenth- and Seventeenth-Century Cambodia," *JSEAS,* 15(1) (September 1984): 280–95, at 295: "Various discussions in the past regarding the nature of Southeast Asian societies (e.g. debates over "loose structure") have . . . assumed that a society must necessarily be one thing or another. Obviously societies are bundles of many 'things,' which are not always neatly integrated or consistent with one another."

24. See Eric Wolf, "Kinship, Friendship, and Patron-Client Relations," in M. Banton (ed.), *The Social Anthropology of Complex Societies* (London, 1966), pp. 1–22, and Wolf, *Europe and the People Without History* (Berkeley, 1982), pp. 79–88.

25. Louis Finot, "Proverbes cambodgiens," *RI,* Vol. 7, No. 2 (January 1904): 74.

26. Thiounn, "Cérémonial cambodgien concernant la prise des fonctions des mandarins nouveaux promus," *RI,* Vol. 10, No. 1 (January 1907): 75. See also P. Bitard, "Les songes et leurs interprétations chez les cambodgiens," in *Sources orientales II: Les songes et leur interprétations* (Paris, 1959), p. 258, which reports that to dream of eating human flesh or a freshly severed head means that one will become a provincial governor. As recently as 2004, a rural Khmer told an American anthropologist that officials "will eat anything— land, or people, or anything!" (Eve Zucker, personal communication).

27. See Chapter 7 and Ian Harris, *Cambodian Buddhism: History and Practice* (Honolulu, 2005), Chapter 4.

28. J. Gonda, *Ancient Indian Kingship from a Religious Point of View* (Leiden, 1966), p. 91.

29. The Thai system is discussed in A. Rabibhadana, *Organization of Thai Society in the Early Bangkok Period* (Ithaca, N.Y., 1969), pp. 98–104.

30. See manuscript chronicle P–6, Fonds Phnom Penh collection, Ecole Française d'Extrême Orient, pp. 11–12.

31. Rabibhadana, *Organization of Thai Society,* p. 44.

32. See A. Leclère, "*Sdach tranh,*" *RI,* Vol. 7 (1905): 1378–84, and Chandler, "Royally Sponsored Human Sacrifices in Nineteenth Century Cambodia," in Chandler, *Facing the Cambodian Past* (Chiangmai, 1996), pp. 119–35. See also Vickery, *Society, Economics and Politics,* p. 154.

33. Gonda, *Ancient Indian Kingship,* p. 36.

34. A. Leclère, *Les Codes cambodgiens* (Paris, 1898), Vol. 1, p. 216.

35. For an analysis of the Chinese system, see John K. Fairbank (ed.), *The Chinese World Order* (Cambridge, Mass., 1968), especially pp. 1–19 and 63–89.

36. See P. Boudet and A. Masson (eds.), *Iconographie historique de l'Indochine française* (Paris, 1931), plates 128–29.

37. See D.G. Deveria, *Histoire des relations de la Chine avec Annam du XVIe au XIXe siècles* (Paris, 1880), pp. 52–54.

38. See W. Vella, *Siam Under Rama III* (Locust Valley, N.Y., 1957), p. 60.

39. Crawfurd, *Journal of an Embassy to the Courts of Siam and Cochin-China* (London, 1828), p. 146: "The Cochin-Chinese Ambassadors were yesterday presented to the King. They were received, I am told, without much ceremony, the intercourse being considered of so friendly and familiar a nature as not to call for extraordinary formalities."

40. AOM, Fonds Indochinois A–30 (6), Carton 10.

41. Institut Bouddhique, manuscript chronicle from Wat Srolauv, p. 23.

42. Rama III, *Collected Writings* (Bangkok, 1967), p. 140.

Chapter 7

1. Eng Sut, *Akkasar mahaboros khmaer* [Documents about Khmer heroes] (Phnom Penh, 1969), p. 1013.

2. AOM, Fonds Indochinois A–30 (12), Carton 11. Letter from Doudart de Lagrée to the governor of Cochin China, January 8, 1866.

3. Quoted in C. Wilson, *State and Society in the Reign of Mongkut, 1851–1867* (Ann Arbor, Mich., 1971), p. 983. Similarly, in 1945, Charles de Gaulle told the French scholar Paul Mus, "We'll return to Indochina because we are the stronger ones" ("*Nous rentrons en Indochine parce que nous*

sommes les plus forts"). See Chandler and Goscha (eds.), *L'espace d'un regard: Paul Mus 1902–1969* (Paris, 2006), p. 33.

4. For Thai evidence, see David Chandler, *Cambodia Before the French: Politics in a Tributary Kingdom 1794–1847* (Ann Arbor, Mich., 1974), pp. 83–84. See also Khin Sok, *Le Cambodge entre le Siam et le Vietnam* (Paris, 1991).

5. *CMH* 2/1173/19 *ko*. See also *DNTL*, Vol. 3, pp. 146–47.

6. For a discussion of the rebellion see David P. Chandler, "An Anti-Vietnamese Rebellion in Early Nineteenth Century Cambodia," in *Facing the Cambodian Past: Selected Essays, 1971–1994* (Sydney and Chiangmai, 1996), pp. 61–75. See also *DNTL*, Vol. 5, pp. 85ff., *DNTL*, Vol. 6, p. 107, and L. Malleret, *Archéologie du delta de Mekong*, 4 vols. (Paris, 1959–63), Vol. 1, pp. 27–33.

7. Institut Bouddhique, manuscript chronicle from Wat Prek Kuy (1874), p. 27.

8. See David P. Chandler, "Royally Sponsored Human Sacrifices in Nineteenth Century Cambodia."

9. See Chapter 9.

10. Manuscript chronicle from Wat Prek Kuy, p. 58.

11. A. Leclère, *Recherches sur le droit publique des cambodgiens* (Paris 1894), p. 151.

12. *DNTL*, Vol. 7, p. 79.

13. *DNTL*, Vol. 14, p. 123.

14. See Choi Byung Wook, *Southern Vietnam Under the Reign of Minh Mang (1820–1841): Central Policies and Local Response* (Ithaca, N.Y., 2004), p. 95.

15. Rama III, *Collected Writings* (Bangkok, 1967), p. 142.

16. The campaign is discussed in Chandler, *Cambodia Before the French*, pp. 113–18.

17. Chronicle from Wat Prek Kuy, p. 61.

18. *DNTL*, Vol. 14, pp. 53–54. The practice of kidnapping urban populations was a feature of precolonial Southeast Asian wars and resurfaced with a vengeance when the Cambodian Communists drove over two million urban Cambodians into the countryside in April 1975; see Chapter 12.

19. *DNTL*, Vol. 15, p. 113.

20. Ibid., p. 232.

21. *DNTL*, Vol. 16, pp. 21–22, 106.

22. On Queen Mei see Trudy Jacobsen, *Lost Goddesses:The Denial of Female Power in Cambodian History* (Copenhagen, 2007), Chapter 5.

23. *DNTL*, Vol. 18, pp. 249–50. See also *DNTL*, Vol. 19, p. 55, which discusses some shortcomings of the system. Choi Byung Wook, *Southern*

Vietnam, p. 96, refers to 1835 as "the year when Cambodia became part of Vietnam."

24. *DNTL,* Vol. 17, p. 30.

25. Ibid., p. 230.

26. *DNTL,* Vol. 19, p. 238.

27. Ibid., p. 329.

28. G. Aubaret (tr.), *Gia Dinh Thung Chi* [History and description of lower Cochin China] (Paris, 1867), p. 131.

29. See David Chandler, *The Tragedy of Cambodian History: Politics, War, and Revolution Since 1945* (New Haven, 1991), pp. 203–4. Although anti-Vietnamese racism waned in the 1990s, politicians in the 1998 election campaign stirred up anti-Vietnamese sentiment by accusing Cambodia's ruling party of being a puppet of Vietnam. Anti-Thai riots, encouraged by the government, broke out in Phnom Penh in January 2003. See Chapter 13.

30. *DNTL,* Vol. 19, p. 310.

31. *DNTL,* Vol. 18, p. 225. In 1839 Minh Mang ordered a survey of Cambodia's raw materials: *DNTL,* Vol. 21, pp. 239–40.

32. *DNTL,* Vol. 21, pp. 173, 235.

33. *DNTL,* Vol. 19, pp. 88–89; see also *DNTL,* Vol. 16, p. 109.

34. Thipakarawong, *Phraratchapongsawadan Chaophraya* [Royal chronicle] (Bangkok, repr. 1961), Vol. 2, p. 9. In 1838 one of Minh Mang's advisers suggested that "indigenous people be allowed to rule themselves and collect taxes" so as to save the Vietnamese money. The emperor told him to stop making suggestions of this sort.

35. See, for example, Nguyen Khac Vien and Françoise Corrèze, *Kampuchea 1981: Témoignages* (Hanoi, 1981).

36. *DNTL,* Vol. 21, pp. 269–72.

37. Chandler, *Cambodia Before the French,* pp. 140–41.

38. *DNTL,* Vol. 20, p. 263.

39. *DNTL,* Vol. 22, p. 157.

40. *DNTL,* Vol. 20, p. 7.

41. See Chandler, *Cambodia Before the French,* p. 25, note 37.

42. Thailand, Royal Institute, *Chotmaihet ruang thap yuan khrang ratchakan thi 3* [Correspondence about the Vietnamese army in the third reign] (Bangkok, 1933), p. 17.

43. *DNTL,* Vol. 23, p. 112.

44. *DNTL,* Vol. 22, p. 228.

45. *DNTL,* Vol. 23, p. 155.

46. Ibid., p. 114.

47. Thailand, Royal Institute, *Chotmaihet,* p. 38.

48. Thailand, Royal Institute, *Chotmaihet,* p. 33, and *CMH,* 3/1202/40.

49. Chandler, *Cambodia Before the French,* pp. 156–58.

50. K.S.R. Kulap (pseud.), *Sayam Anam yut* [Siam's wars with Vietnam] (Bangkok, 1906, repr. 1971), p. 916.

51. *DNTL*, Vol. 23, p. 351.

52. Chandler, *Cambodia Before the French*, p. 155.

53. *CMH*, 3/1206/6.

54. Chandler, *Cambodia Before the French*, pp. 179–81.

55. See David Chandler, "Going Through the Motions: Ritual Aspects of the Reign of King Duang of Cambodia," in *Facing the Cambodian Past*, pp. 100–8, and Ian Harris, *Cambodian Buddhism: History and Practice* (Honolulu, 2005), pp. 45–47.

56. Eng Sut, *Akkasar mahaboros*, p. 1027. Jacobsen, *Lost Goddesses*, Chapter 5, drawing on Duang's written works, accuses him persuasively of misogyny.

57. Inscription K. 142, from Wat Baray, translated in E. Aymonier, *Le Cambodge* (Paris, 1904), pp. 349–51.

58. For a discussion of these chronicle histories see Chandler, "Going Through the Motions," passim. For a political history of Duang's reign see Bun Srun Theam, "Cambodia in the Mid-Nineteenth Century: A Quest for Survival, 1840–1863" (M.A. thesis, Asian Studies, Australian National University, 1981), especially pp. 104–68. For an insightful European description of Duang's court, see L.V. Helms, "Overland Journey from Kampot to the Royal Residence," first published in 1851 and reprinted in *Aséanie* 16 (December 2005): 157–62.

59. Many of these letters are contained in Thailand, Office of the Prime Minister (comp.), *Thai sathapana kasat khamen* [The Thai establish the Khmer kingdom] (Bangkok, 1971), especially pp. 49–65. I'm grateful to David Wyatt for providing this reference.

60. Charles Meyniard, *Le Second empire en Indochine* (Paris, 1891), p. 461. Minh Mang had noted in 1822 that "Cambodia is in the midst of powerful neighbors, and the fear of being invaded is great." Bun Srun Theam, "Cambodia in the Mid-Nineteenth Century," pp. 138–67, discusses the mission in some detail.

Chapter 8

1. Jean Delvert, *Le Paysan cambodgien* (The Hague, 1961), pp. 425–28.

2. Charles Meyniard, *Le Second empire en Indochine* (Paris, 1891), pp. 403–8.

3. Henri Mouhot, *Voyage dans les royaumes de Siam, du Cambodge, et de Laos* (Paris, 1972), pp. 174–76.

4. See G. Taboulet (ed.), *La Geste française en Indochine*, 2 vols. (Paris, 1955), p. 334, and Milton Osborne, *The French Presence in Cochinchina and Cambodia: Rule and Response (1859–1905)* (Ithaca, N.Y., 1969), p. 27.

5. F. Julien, *Lettres d'un précurseur* (Paris, 1885), p. 46.

6. See Taboulet, *La Geste,* pp. 621–29, and R.S. Thomson, "Establishment of the French Protectorate over Cambodia," *Far Eastern Quarterly (FEQ),* Vol. 4 (1945): 313–40.

7. Taboulet, *La Geste,* pp. 630–35. See also Eng Sut, *Akkasar mahaboros khmaer* [Documents about Khmer heroes] (Phnom Penh, 1969), p. 1113.

8. For a stirring treatment of this expedition, see Milton Osborne, *River Road to China* (London, 1975).

9. Gregor Muller, *Cambodia's "Bad Frenchmen": The Rise of Colonial Rule and the Life of Thomas Caraman, 1840–1887* (New York and London, 2006).

10. Osborne, *French Presence,* pp. 211–14, and Eng Sut, *Akkasar mahaboras,* p. 1172.

11. For the full text of the treaty see Taboulet, *La Geste,* pp. 67–72. See also Khing Hoc Dy, "Santhor MOK, poète et chroniqueur du XIXe siècle," *Seksa Khmer,* Vol. 3, Nos. 3–4 (December 1981): 142. Mok, a courtier, tried to keep Thomson from entering Norodom's quarters. Thomson kicked him out of the way, and Mok later composed a poem about the incident, beginning, "Oh Frenchman, you miserable robber, you dared to lift your foot and kick the secretary to the king."

12. For a discussion of the rebellion see Osborne, *French Presence,* pp. 206–28, and John Tully, *France on the Mekong* (Lanham, Md., 2002), pp. 83–110.

13. Luc Durtain, *Dieux blancs, hommes jaunes* (Paris, 1930), p. 261. See also Paul Collard, *Cambodge et Cambodgiens* (Paris, 1926), p. 115, for the comment that "the people showed their repugnance toward the freedoms we had unexpectedly provided."

14. L. Henry, *Promenade au Cambodge et au Laos* (Paris, 1894), p. 64n.

15. Osborne, *French Presence,* p. 237.

16. *AOM* 3E 3(i), report from Kandal, May 1898.

17. Jean Hess, *L'Affaire Yukanthor* (Paris, 1900), p. 77. For discussions of this crisis see P. Doumer, *L'Indochine française* (Paris, 1905), pp. 230–31; Osborne, *French Presence,* pp. 243–46; and Alain Forest, *Le Cambodge et la colonisation française: Histoire d'une colonisation sans heurts* (Paris, 1980), pp. 59–78. See also Pierre Lamant, *L'Affaire Yukhanthor* (Paris, 1985).

18. AOM, 3 E–10 (2), second trimester report from Stung Treng, 1923.

19. Manuscript chronicle of Sisowath's reign, formerly in the library of the royal palace, microfilmed by Centre for East Asian Studies, Tokyo (hereafter, Sisowath chronicle), p. 1025. See also John Tully, *Cambodia Under the Tricolour: The Sisowath Years, 1904–1927* (Clayton, Australia, 1996).

20. Ibid., pp. 103–4.

21. See Harry Franck, *East of Siam* (New York, 1926), pp. 24–25. A. Pannetier, *Notes cambodgiennes* (Paris, 1921), p. 140, asserted that opium addiction was widespread among the Cambodian militia. See also Roland Meyer, *Saramani* (Paris, 1922), pp. 122–23. Collard, *Cambodge et cambodgiens*, p. 277, mentions Sisowath's addiction to opium but adds that the drug is "not harmful to Asiatics."

22. A. Leclère, *Cambodge: Fêtes civiles* (Paris, 1916), pp. 30–31. See also Sisowath chronicle, pp. 1068–74.

23. See Meyer, *Saramani*, pp. 132–51; Jean Ajalbert, *Ces phénomènes, artisans de l'Empire* (Paris, 1941), pp. 189–92; Forest, *Le Cambodge*, pp. v–vii; and Okna Veang Thiounn, *Voyage en France du roi Sisowath* (ed. and tr. Olivier de Bernon) (Paris, 2006), which is a previously unpublished narrative of the trip written by a palace official who accompanied the king.

24. Sisowath chronicle, pp. 1077–86. See also Jean Ajalber, *L'Indochine en péril* (Paris, 1906), pp. 87–111, and Thiounn, *Voyage en France*, pp. 101–1477.

25. The Cambodian dancers participated in the colonial exhibition of 1931 and also performed at the New York World's Fair in 1939–40. See Bruno Dagens, *Angkor: La Forêt de pierre* (Paris, 1989), pp. 110ff.

26. For a discussion of the retrocession, see L.P. Briggs, "The Treaty of March 23, 1907, Between France and Siam," *FEQ*, Vol. 5 (1946): 439–54.

27. Sisowath chronicle, pp. 1107–10.

28. See C. Wilson, "The *Nai Kong* of Battambang, 1824–1868," in C. Wilson et al. (eds.), *Royalty and Commoners, Contributions to Asian Studies*, Vol. 15 (Leiden, 1980), pp. 66–72, and *Phongsawadan muang phratabong* [Chronicle of the region of Battambang] No. 16 of series, *Prachum Phongsawadan* [Collected chronicles] (Bangkok, 1969), pp. 94–106.

29. The unusual frequency of landlordism, sharecropping, and outsiders in these two regions was extrapolated by radical theorists in the 1970s to characterize rural society throughout the country. According to Pol Pot, landlordism, which was rare on a national scale, was the "major problem" in prerevolutionary Cambodia. Communist Party favoritism toward landless peasants flowed from this faulty analysis and partly from a felt need to imitate time-honored Chinese social categories. See William Willmott, "Analytical Errors of the Kampuchean Communist Party," *PA*, Vol. 54, No. 2 (Summer 1981): 209–27.

Chapter 9

1. Sisowath chronicle, pp. 1166–67. See also John Tully, *Cambodia Under the Tricolour: The Sisowath Years, 1904–1927* (Clayton, Australia, 1996). On the 1916 Affair see Milton Osborne, "Peasant Politics in Cambodia: The 1916 Affair," *Modern Asian Studies* (MAS) 12 (1978): 217–43.

2. AOM 3 E12 (2), report from Svay Rieng, 1915.

3. For a discussion of developments in Cambodia in the 1920s, see F. Baudouin, *Le Cambodge pendant et après la grande guerre* (Paris, 1927), and A. Silvestre, *Le Cambodge administratif* (Phnom Penh, 1924). See also Réné Morizon, *Monographie sur le Cambodge* (Paris, 1930).

4. See A. Souyris-Rolland, "Les Pirates au Cambodge," *BSEI*, Vol. 25, No. 4 (1950): 307–13. The rubric *piraterie* follows immediately after *situation politique* in the format of monthly French reports from the *résidences*, where banditry is seen in terms of security rather than ideological dissidence. AOM 3 E12(2), a report from Svay Rieng in 1921, asserts that "a life of raiding others, full of the unexpected, composed of tricks, pursuits and ambushes, all without great physical danger, is one of the sports to which Cambodians are addicted." See also Alain Forest, *Le Cambodge et la colonisation française: Histoire d'une colonisation sans heurts* (Paris, 1980), pp. 373–412. David Johnston, "Bandit, *Nakleng*, and Peasant in Rural Thai Society," in C. Wilson et al. (eds.), *Royalty and Commoners, Contributions to Asian Studies*, Vol. 15 (Leiden, 1980), pp. 90–101, provides a comparable Thai perspective.

5. A. Pannetier, *Notes cambodgiennes* (Paris, 1921, repr. 1986), p. 75.

6. The sculpture was carved by Louis Bottinelly. For a study of the influence of Indochina on French imaginative writers, see L. Malleret, *L'Exotisme indochinois dans la littérature française depuis 1860* (Paris, 1934), especially pp. 183–92, 216–44. Novels set in Cambodia dating from this period include Charles Bellan, *Fleur de lotus* (Paris, 1924); Pierre Benoit, *Le Roi lépreux* (Paris, 1927); Jean Dorsenne, *Sous le soleil des bonzes* (Paris, 1934); George Groslier, *La route du plus fort* (Paris, 1935); André Malraux, *La Voie royale* (Paris, 1930); and Marguerite Duras, *Un barrage contre la Pacifique* (Paris, 1952). See also Penny Edwards, *Cambodge: The Cultivation of a Nation (1963–1945)* (Honolulu, 2007). Edwards argues that Cambodge, which became the independent kingdom of Cambodia after 1954, was a cooperative, only partially conscious construction, in colonial times, by the French and members of the Cambodian elite.

7. AOM 3E 8(3), report from Prey Veng, 1924. Félix Louis Bardez, born in Paris in 1882, had served in Indochina, largely in Cambodia, since 1908.

8. For a detailed account of these incidents, see David P. Chandler, "The Assassination of *Résident* Bardez (1925)," *JSS*, Vol. 72, No. 2 (1982): 35–49. See also Walter Langlois, *André Malraux: The Indo-China Adventure* (New York, 1966), pp. 185–88, and Durtain, *Dieux blancs, hommes jaunes* (Paris, 1930), pp. 264–65.

9. For the French text of this ordinance, see Dik Keam, *Phum Direchan* [Bestiality Village] (Phnom Penh, 1971), pp. 154–59.

10. Ben Kiernan kindly leant me his recorded interview with one of the assailants, Sok Bith, which took place in September 1980. Bith served a fifteen-year sentence for the assault.

11. AOM 3E 7(6), annual reports from Kratie, 1925–26.

12. This paper has finally received the scholarly attention it deserves in Edwards, *"Cambodge."* See also Bunchhan Muul, *Kuk Niyobay* [Political prison] (Phnom Penh, 1971), pp. 8–14.

13. Like *Nagara Vatta,* the colonial issues of *Kambuja Surya,* which effectively published Cambodian-language literature for the first time, deserve detailed attention. See Jacques Népote and Khing Hoc Dy, "Literature and Society in Modern Cambodia," in Tham Seong Che (ed.), *Essays on Literature and Society in Southeast Asia* (Singapore, 1981), pp. 56–81.

14. For a discussion of these two texts, see David Chandler, "Cambodian Royal Chronicles (*Rajabangsavatar*), 1927–1949: Kingship and Historiography in the Colonial Era," in *Facing the Cambodian Past,* pp. 189–205, and Chandler, "Instructions for the Corps of Royal Scribes: An Undated Cambodian Manuscript from the Colonial Era," Ibid., pp. 159–64.

15. William E. Willmott, *The Chinese in Cambodia* (Vancouver, 1967), and Willmott, "History and Sociology of the Chinese in Cambodia Before the French Protectorate," *JSEAH,* Vol. 7, No. 1 (March 1966): 15–38.

16. On education see Forest, *Le Cambodge,* pp. 143–65, and Jacques Nepote, "Education et développement dans le Cambodge moderne," *Mondes et développement,* No. 28 (1974): 767–92. On women in colonial Cambodia, see Jacobsen, *Lost Goddesses,* Chapter 7, and Penny Edwards, "Womanizing Indochina: Fiction, Nation and Co-Habitation in Colonial Cambodia, 1890–1930," in Judith Clancy-Smith and Frances Gouda (eds.), *Domesticating the Empire: Race, Gender and Family Life in French and Dutch Colonialism* (Charlottesville, Va., 1998), pp. 108–30, and P. Edwards, "Propa-Gender: Marianne, Joan of Arc, and the Export of French Gender Ideology to Cambodia," in T. Chafer and Amanda Sakur (eds.), *Promoting the Colonial Idea: Propaganda and Visions of Empire in France* (New York, 2002), pp. 116–32.

17. For reports on the Depression on Cambodia, see AOM 3E 15 (8), annual reports from Kampot; AOM 3 (5), from Kandal; and AOM 3E 10 (4), from Stung Treng. Alert to positive developments, a French administrator reported in 1933 that the crash had led to the collapse of private fortunes in Takeo, adding that "a powerful form of solidarity was born in shared poverty, making a *table rase* of ancient antagonisms of class and even of race"; AOM 3E 7 (6), report from Takeo.

18. Norodom Sihanouk, *L'Indochine vue de Pékin* (Paris, 1972), pp. 27–28.

19. See H. de Grauclade, *Le Réveil du peuple khmer* (Hanoi, 1935). For a less optimistic view, see G. de Pourtales, *Nous, à qui rien n'appartient* (Paris, 1931), pp. 115ff.

20. See, for example, Ben Kiernan, "Origins of Khmer Communism," in *Southeast Asian Affairs 1981* (Singapore, 1980), pp. 161–80. See also Ben Kiernan, *How Pol Pot Came to Power* (London, 1985), pp. 8ff.

21. A description of Thanh's activities during and after World War II can be found in the present chapter. See also David Chandler, "The Kingdom of Kampuchea, March-October 1945," in *Facing the Cambodian Past*, pp. 165–88.

22. See, for example, AOM 3E 8 (12), 1923, annual report of the governor of Prey Veng.

23. *L'Écho du Cambodge*, July 19, 1933.

24. A helpful study of this period, although it says very little about Cambodia, is A.W. McCoy (ed.), *Southeast Asia Under Japanese Occupation* (New Haven: Yale University Southeast Asian Studies, Monograph Series No. 22, 1980).

25. Decoux has discussed this period in his memoirs, *A la barre de l'Indochine* (Paris, 1949). See also N. Sihanouk, *Souvenirs doux et amers* (Paris, 1981), pp. 59–114.

26. For a discussion of the war see John Tully, *France on the Mekong*, pp. 333–39.

27. Charles Robequain, *The Economic Development of French Indo-China* (Oxford, 1944), p. 366.

28. See Milton Osborne, "King-making in Cambodia: From Sisowath to Sihanouk," *JSEAS*, Vol. 4, No. 3 (September 1973): 169–85.

29. Sihanouk, *L'Indochine vue de Pékin*, pp. 19–30, and Sihanouk, *Souvenirs doux et amers*, pp. 35–50.

30. Sihanouk chronicle, pp. 136–40.

31. See V.M. Reddi, *A History of the Cambodian Independence Movement 1863–1955* (Tirupati, 1971), pp. 82–84; Bunchhan Muul, *Kuk niyobay* [Political prison] (Phnom Penh, 1971); and Kong Somkar, *Achar Hem Chieu* [Venerable Hem Chieu] (Phnom Penh, 1971).

32. This information is drawn from unpublished correspondence between Son Ngoc Thanh, in exile in 1943, and his nationalist colleagues in Cambodia. The letters are housed in the Monash University Library.

33. Interestingly, Sok Bith, the illiterate farmer implicated in Bardez's assassination (see Note 10 above), knew about Hem Chieu but about few other nationalist figures.

34. G. Gautier, *Jeune Cambodge* (Phnom Penh, 1943), p. 4. See also *Indochine*, No. 153 (August 5, 1943) and No. 210 (August 10, 1944). AOM E 11 (7), note from Pursat, 1944, states that romanized Khmer was being taught at

that time in all Cambodian schools. Romanization had mixed, not necessarily unhappy, results (Eveline Porée-Maspero, letter of August 27, 1982).

35. Robert Ollivier, "Le Protectorat français au Cambodge" (Ph.D. diss., University of Paris, 1969), p. 213.

36. Sihanouk chronicle, p. 399.

37. Ollivier, "Le Protectorat français," p. 198. Cambodia's declaration of independence, ironically, was written in French (author's interview with Nhek Tioulong, September 1981). The French name for the kingdom became Cambodge again in 1946 .

38. Lt. Tadakame, attached as a political adviser to the palace, remained in Cambodia after the war and joined an Issarak band.

39. Sihanouk chronicle, p. 493.

40. See Charles Meyer, *Derrière le sourire khmer* (Paris, 1971), pp. 115–16; Reddi, *History of the Cambodian Independence Movement,* pp. 105–9; and *Realités cambodgiennes,* July 9 and 16, 1967.

Chapter 10

1. Chandler, *The Tragedy of Cambodian History: Politics, War and Revolution since 1945* (New Haven, 1991), Chapter l.

2. V.M. Reddi, *A History of the Cambodian Independence Movement 1863-1955* (Tirupati, 1971), p. 124.

3. The material in this paragraph is drawn from Ben Kiernan, "Origins of Khmer Communism," in *Southeast Asian Affairs 1981* (Singapore, 1980), pp. 161–80; Bunchhan Muul, *Charet Khmer* [Khmer mores] (Phnom Penh, 1974); and Wilfred Burchett, *Mekong Upstream* (Hanoi, 1957). See also John Tully, *France on the Mekong,* pp. 457–70.

4. P. Preschez, *Essai sur la démocratie au Cambodge* (Paris, 1961), pp. 17–19; Reddi, *History of the Cambodian Independence Movement,* pp. 124–26; and AOM, Cambodge, 7 F 29 (4), "Etude sur l'évolution de la politique intérieure et les partis politiques khmers" (1951), passim. See also Chandler, *The Tragedy of Cambodian History,* Chapters 2 and 3, and Michael Vickery, "Looking Back at Cambodia," in Ben Kiernan and Chanthou Boua (eds.), *Peasants and Politics in Kampuchea, 1942–1981* (London, 1982), pp. 89–113.

5. AOM, Cambodge 7F 29 (7), "Etude sur les mouvements rebelles au Cambodge, 1942–1952" (hereafter "Etude sur les mouvements"), pp. 9–10.

6. Reddi, *History of the Cambodian Independence Movement,* p. 129. There were additional colonial elections in 1947 and 1951. Women were not allowed to vote nationally until the 1958 elections. Arguably, the 1947 and 1951 elections were the last to be free and fair in Cambodia until those sponsored by the United Nations in 1993. They were in any case the first elections of any kind in Cambodian history.

7. See also Kiernan, "Origins of Khmer Communism," pp. 163–67, and Reddi, *History of the Cambodian Independence Movement,* pp. 151–54.

8. Prince Yuthevong has not yet received any scholarly attention. When he died while undergoing treatment for tuberculosis in a French hospital in Phnom Penh in 1947, rumors spread that he had been assassinated by the French. See Reddi, *History of the Cambodian Independence Movement,* p. 137n., and Chandler, *The Tragedy of Cambodian History,* p. 37. No evidence has emerged that this was really the case.

9. Sihanouk, *Souvenirs,* pp. 158–168; Reddi, *History of the Cambodian Independence Movement,* pp. 165–73.

10. Vickery, "Looking Back at Cambodia," p. 97. See also Martin Herz, *A Short History of Cambodia* (New York and London, 1958), p. 83.

11. U.S. Foreign Broadcast Information Service (FBIS), *Broadcasts from the Far East,* November 7, 1951.

12. Quoted in Reddi, *History of the Cambodian Independence Movement,* p. 183.

13. Author's interviews with Channa Samudvanija, Chiangmai, September 1981, and Bangkok, May 1988.

14. See Chandler, *The Tragedy of Cambodian History,* pp. 59–61; Donald Lancaster, *The Emancipation of French Indo-China* (Oxford, 1961), p. 272; and M. Laurent, *L'Armée au Cambodge et dans les pays en voie de développement en Sud Est Asiatique* (Paris, 1968), especially pp. 283–91.

15. "Etude sur les mouvements," p. 64ff. See also Steve Heder's magisterial study, *Cambodian Communism and the Vietnamese Model. Vol 1: Imitation and Independence* (Bangkok, 2004).

16. Kiernan, "Origin of Khmer Communism," p. 168.

17. See "Etude sur les mouvements," pp. 84, 87. The second citation notes that some "autarchic collective farms, like *kholkozes,* have been noted . . . in Kompong Cham" in 1952. Interestingly, this region was a stronghold of radical activity in the 1950s and the 1960s and a seedbed in the 1970s for cadres in Democratic Kampuchea.

18. FBIS, November 28, 1951.

19. FBIS, April 4, 1979. Phnom Penh may well be the only city outside of China that boasts a boulevard named after Sihanouk's former patron, Mao Zedong.

20. For further details, see Chandler, *The Tragedy of Cambodian History,* pp. 61–67.

21. "Lettre de l'Association des Etudiants Khmers en France à sa Majesté Norodom Sihanouk," Paris, July 6, 1952. According to Ben Kiernan, this document was the work of Hou Yuon, a Cambodian radical purged in 1975. The manifesto appeared in Khmer in *Khmer Nisut* [Khmer student], No. 14 (August 1952). In the same issue, writing as Khmer Daom [Original Khmer],

Saloth Sar, later known as Pol Pot, contributed two essays. One of these ("Monarchy or Democracy?") appears as an appendix to Ben Kiernan and Serge Thion, *Khmers Rouges!* (Paris, 1981), pp. 357–60. The other, entitled "The Royal Trip to European Countries," closes with a poem claiming that "royal edicts are dishonest" and seek to destroy the "solidarity of students." Interestingly, none of the articles in the periodical takes an internationalist view of the Indochina war. The antimonarchic, pro-assembly position that they all assume suggests that Pol Pot and his colleagues, at this stage, supported Son Ngoc Thanh's form of dissidence rather than the Vietnamese-sponsored KPRP.

22. Reddi, *History of the Cambodian Independence Movement,* p. 205. See also Norodom Sihanouk, *La Monarchie cambodgienne et la croisade royale pour l'indépendence* (Phnom Penh, c. 1957), passim; Chandler, *The Tragedy of Cambodian History,* pp. 67–72; and John Tully, *France on the Mekong,* pp. 475–81.

23. Norodom Sihanouk and Wilfred Burchett, *My War with the CIA* (Harmondsworth, 1973), p. 153, and Reddi, *History of the Cambodian Independence Movement,* p. 20.

24. Ollivier, "Le Protectorat français," pp. 344–46.

25. Ibid., p. 358ff., conveys the impression of approaching anarchy in Phnom Penh. Such an atmosphere may well have accelerated French willingness to negotiate with the king.

26. Sihanouk, *Souvenirs,* pp. 209–12.

27. Kiernan, "Origins of Khmer Communism," p. 179.

28. In 1981 Nhek Tioulong stated that in the mid-1950s, when he served in Sihanouk's cabinet, it soon became almost impossible for the newly independent regime to collect taxes levied on land and harvests. To Cambodian peasants, it seems, independence meant being relieved of these particular levies (author's interview with Nhek Tioulong, August 1981).

29. *Cambodge,* April 14, 1955.

30. On the 1955 election see Chandler, *The Tragedy of Cambodian History,* pp. 81–84, and Philip Short, *Pol Pot: The History of a Nightmare* (London, 2004), pp. 110–12.

Chapter 11

1. For details of this confrontation, see Chandler, *The Tragedy of Cambodian History: Politics, War and Revolution Since 1945* (New Haven, 1991), Chapter 4, and Michael Vickery, "Looking Back at Cambodia," in Ben Kiernan and Chanthou Boua (eds.), *Peasants and Politics in Kampuchea, 1942–1981* (London, 1982).

2. U.S. intelligence agencies were involved in both the Sam Sary plot of 1958–59 and the Dap Chhuon plot of February 1959. Sam Sary, a high offi-

cial formerly favored by Sihanouk, became a dissident and fled to Thailand, perhaps with U.S. encouragement, in early 1959. Hoping to overthrow Sihanouk, Thai officials unsuccessfully tried to forge an alliance between Sary and the dissident exile Son Ngoc Thanh. In February, Dap Chhuon, the warlord of Cambodia's northwest, encouraged by the Thai, threatened to revolt. He had been provided with gold bullion, arms, and radio equipment by the Saigon regime and perhaps by the Thai as well. The U.S. Central Intelligence Agency (CIA) was aware of the plot but failed to inform Sihanouk about it. For a detailed discussion see Chandler, *The Tragedy of Cambodian History*, pp. 99–107. Sam Sary's son, Sam Rainsy, became a prominent Cambodian politician, opposed to the ruling party, in the 1990s.

3. Robert Shaplen, *The Lost Revolution: Vietnam 1945–1965* (New York, 1966) pp. 367ff.; Simone Lacouture, *Cambodge* (Lausanne, 1964), pp. 133–52. For a biographical overview, see also Milton Osborne, *Sihanouk: Prince of Light, Prince of Darkness* (Sydney, 1995). Julio Jeldres, formerly Sihanouk's personal secretary, is working on an official biography of the prince. Sihanouk's own memoirs for this period, *Souvenirs doux et amers* (Paris, 1981), make lively reading but should be used with caution.

4. Two astute analyses of Sihanouk's foreign policy are Roger Smith, *Cambodia's Foreign Policy* (Ithaca, N.Y., 1965), and Nasir Abdoul Carime, "Mise en perspective de la diplomatie sihanoukienne," *Péninsule*, Vol. 36 (1998): 175–91. See also Kenton Clymer, *United States and Cambodia, 1870–2000* (New York, 2004).

5. See Ben Kiernan, *How Pol Pot Came to Power* (London, 1985), pp. 202ff., based largely on interviews conducted between 1979 and 1982. See also David Chandler, *Brother Number One: A Political Biography of Pol Pot*, 2nd ed. (Boulder, Colo., 1999), pp. 64–71, and Philip Short, *Pol Pot*, pp. 143–44.

6. For an absorbing analysis of arts and culture in the Sihanouk era see Ly Daravudh and Ingrid Muan (eds.), *Cultures of Independence* (Phnom Penh, 2001).

7. See Kenton J. Clymer, "The Perils of Neutrality: The Break in US-Cambodian Relations, 1965," *Diplomatic History*, Vol. 23, No. 4 (Fall 1999): 609–31. See also George McT. Kahin, *Southeast Asia: A Testament* (London, 2003), pp. 249–60, an account that is more critical of the United States.

8. For analyses of Sihanouk's reaction to Samlaut, see Kiernan, *How Pol Pot Came to Power*, pp. 249ff.; Elizabeth Becker, *When the War Was Over* (New York, 1986), pp. 119–22; and Chandler, *The Tragedy of Cambodian History*, Chapter 5. Perhaps because the rebellion failed, the Khmer Communists never claimed any responsibility for it.

9. On Saloth Sar's visit to Vietnam see Thomas Engelbert and Christopher Goscha, *Falling Out of Touch: A Study of Vietnamese Communist Policy Toward an Emerging Cambodian Communist Movement, 1930–1975* (Clayton, Australia, 1995), which draws on Vietnamese documentation. See also Chandler, *Brother Number One: A Political Biography of Pol Pot*, 2nd ed. (Boulder, Colo. 1999), pp. 69–73, and Philip Short, *Pol Pot*, pp. 156–58. For a discussion of political conditions in China at this time, see Roderick MacFarquhar and Michael Schoenhals, *Mao's Last Revolution* (Cambridge, Mass., 2006), pp. 15–34.

10. For contemporary treatments of this period that are hostile to the prince, see Charles Meyer, *Derrière le sourire khmer* (Paris, 1971), and J.C. Pomonti and Serge Thion, *Des courtisans aux partisans: La crise cambodgienne* (Paris, 1971). See also Laura Summers, "The Sources of Economic Grievance in Sihanouk's Cambodia," *Southeast Asian Journal of Social Science,* Vol. 14, No. 1 (1986), and Remy Prud'homme, *L'Économie du Cambodge* (Paris, 1969). Summers and Prud'homme eloquently describe the economic malaise that affected Cambodia in the late 1960s.

11. On the coup see Chandler, *The Tragedy of Cambodian History,* pp. 197–99. See also Pomonti and Thion, *Des courtisans aux partisans;* Justin Corfield, *Khmers Stand Up!* (Clayton, Australia, 1994); and William Shawcross, *Sideshow: Nixon, Kissinger, and the Destruction of Cambodia* (New York, 1979). Kahin, *Southeast Asia,* pp 279–99, makes a strong case for U.S. involvement, especially from Saigon, to support the coup. Evidence that the coup was planned in Washington is less persuasive, but Washington accepted the result almost immediately.

12. For a stirring evocation of this period see Robert Sam Anson, *War News* (New York, 1989).

13. For accounts of the U.S. bombing, see Shawcross, *Sideshow,* pp. 209–19, and Ben Kiernan, "The American Bombardment of Kampuchea, 1969–1973," *Vietnam Generation,* Vol. 1, No. 1 (Winter 1989): 4–42.

14. For accounts of the Communist entry into Phnom Penh see, among others, François Ponchaud, *Cambodia Year Zero* (New York, 1978), pp. 1–22, and Someth May, *Cambodian Witness* (London, 1986), pp. 100–5. The Khmer Rouge did not use "year zero" or "year one" in their propaganda, but they spoke often of Cambodian history having ended and begun on April 17.

Chapter 12

1. See David P. Chandler, "Seeing Red: Perceptions of History in Democratic Kampuchea," in David P. Chandler and Ben Kiernan (eds.), *Revolution and Its Aftermath in Kampuchea: Eight Essays* (New Haven, 1983); Serge Thion, "The Pattern of Cambodian Politics," in David Ablin and Marlowe Hood (eds.), *The Cambodian Agony* (Armonk, N.Y., 1988), pp. 149–64;

François Ponchaud, "Social Change in the Vortex of Revolution," in Karl Jackson (ed.), *Cambodia 1975–1978: Rendezvous with Death* (Princeton, N.J., 1989), pp. 151–78; Ben Kiernan, *The Pol Pot Regime: Politics, Race, and Genocide Under the Khmer Rouge* (New Haven, 1995); and Steve Heder, "Racism, Marxism, Labeling and Genocide in Ben Kiernan's *The Pol Pot Regime*," *Southeast Asian Research*, No. 5 (1997): 101–53, which takes issue with some of Kiernan's findings.

2. For vivid, early accounts of the evacuation see François Ponchaud, *Cambodia Year Zero* (New York, 1978), pp. 1–51, and Pin Yathay, *L'Utopie meurtrière* (Paris, 1980), pp. 39–56. See also Kevin McIntyre, "Geography as Destiny: Cities, Villages and Khmer Rouge Orientalism," *Comparative Studies in Society and History*, Vol. 35 (1996): 730–58. The move may also have been made in an effort to outpace the more cautious revolutions in China and Vietnam. Philip Short, *Pol Pot: The History of a Nightmare* (London, 2004), pp. 300–1. The Chinese had carried out partial, forced rustification campaigns in the 1960s, known as *xiafong*. See John Bryan Starr, *Understanding China* (London, 2003), p. 127.

3. Author's interview with a former civil engineer, April 1987. See also David Chandler, Muy Hong Lim, and Ben Kiernan, *The Early Phases of Liberation in Cambodia: Conversations with Peang Sophy* (Clayton, Australia, 1976).

4. See Michael Vickery, *Cambodia 1975–1982* (Boston, 1983), pp. 64–188. Vickery's findings about temporal and spatial variations in the DK era have been corroborated by several scholars and by my own interviews in the 1980s and 1990s.

5. See Timothy Carney, "The Organization of Power," in Jackson, *Cambodia 1975–1978*, pp. 79–107, and John Marston, "Khmer Rouge Songs," *Crossroads* 16/1 (2002): 100–12.

6. See Ben Kiernan (ed.), *Genocide and Democracy in Cambodia: The Khmer Rouge, the United Nations, and the International Community* (New Haven, 1993), and Patrick Heuveline, "'Between One and Three Million': Towards the Demographic Reconstruction of a Decade of Cambodian History (1970–1979)," *Population Studies*, Vol. 52 (1998): 49–65. See also Steve Heder, "Racism, Marxism, Labeling and Genocide in Ben Kiernan's *The Pol Pot Regime*."

7. See Henri Locard (ed. and tr.), *Pol Pot's Little Red Book: The Sayings of Angkar* (Chiangmai, 2004), p. 210.

8. Norodom Sihanouk, *Prisonnier des khmers rouges* (Paris, 1986), pp. 87–110.

9. For the text of the constitution see Ponchaud, *Cambodia Year Zero*, pp. 199–206. See also David P. Chandler, "The Constitution of Democratic Kampuchea: The Semantics of Revolutionary Change," *PA*, Vol. 49, No. 3 (Fall 1976): 506–15.

10. For the text of the Four-Year Plan see Chandler, Kiernan, and Chanthou Boua, *Pol Pot Plans the Future* (New Haven, 1988), pp. 36–118. On the DK economy see Charles Twining, "The Economy," in Jackson, *Cambodia 1975–1978*, pp. 109–50, and Marie Martin, *Le mal cambodgien* (Paris, 1989), pp. 156–202.

11. Chandler, Kiernan, and Boua, *Pol Pot Plans the Future*, p. 36.

12. Author's interview with former Buddhist monk, Melbourne, March 1988.

13. DK officials called their economic plan the great leap forward [*maha lout ploh*], borrowing Chinese terminology without acknowledgment. It will probably never be known whether Pol Pot and his colleagues were aware in the 1970s that China's Great Leap Forward had failed; see William Joseph, "A Tragedy of Good Intentions: Post-Mao Views of the Great Leap Forward," *Modern China*, Vol. 12, No. 4 (October 1986): 419–57.

14. On the 1951/1960 controversy, see Chandler, Kiernan, and Boua, *Pol Pot Plans the Future*, pp. 164–76, and David Chandler, "Revising the Past in Democratic Kampuchea: When was the Birthday of the Party?" in David Chandler, *Facing the Cambodian Past* (Chiangmai, 1996), pp. 215–32.

15. See David Chandler, *Voices from S-21: Terror and History in Pol Pot's Secret Prison* (Berkeley, 1999), pp. 57–62.

16. On the facility see Chandler, *Voices from S-21*, passim, and Anthony Barnett, Ben Kiernan, and Chanthou Boua, "Bureaucracy of Death: Documents from Inside Pol Pot's Torture Machine," *New Statesman*, May 2, 1980. See also Douglas Niven and Chris Riley (eds.), *Killing Fields* (Santa Fe, N.M., 1996), and Rachel Hughes, "The Abject Artifacts of Memory: Photographs from the Cambodian Genocide," *Media, Culture and Society* 25 (2003): 123–44.

17. Chandler, *Voices from S-21*, p. 57. On Pol Pot's China visit, unreported elsewhere, see Short, *Pol Pot*, p. 362. The never-completed airfield, ironically, was near the village where Bardez was assassinated in 1925. Hundreds of Khmer workers died at the site from mismanaged explosions and overwork (Henri Locard, personal communication).

18. Ibid., pp. 35–36. See also Vann Nath, *A Cambodian Prison Portrait: One Year in the Khmer Rouge's S-21* (Bangkok, 1998).

19. See Chandler, Kiernan, and Boua, *Pol Pot Plans the Future*, p. 183.

20. Ibid., p. 185.

21. "The Last Plan," in Jackson, *Cambodia 1975–1978*, pp. 299–314. The text, with its ideas of a continuous postrevolutionary class warfare, echoed the views of the Cultural Revolution's leaders in China. See Andrew Walder, "Cultural Revolution Radicalism: Variations on a Stalinist Theme," in William Joseph et al. (eds.), *New Perspectives on the Cultural Revolution* (Cambridge, Mass., 1991), pp. 41–62. See also Chandler, *Voices from S-21*, pp. 44–76.

22. See Nayan Chanda, *Brother Enemy* (New York, 1986), pp. 109–10. On Cambodia's recently confirmed oil deposits, see Chapter 13

23. On the conflict see Chanda, *Brother Enemy,* and Grant Evans, Kelvin Rowley, *Red Brotherhood at War* (London, 1984; rev. ed., 1990).

24. See Chanda, *Brother Enemy*, pp. 255ff., and Evans and Rowley, *Rea Brotherhood at War*, pp. 115ff.

25. Pol Pot, "Long Live the 17th Anniversary of the Communist Party of Kampuchea," a speech delivered at the Olympic Stadium in Phnom Penh on September 27, 1977, and broadcast two days later on FBIS, October 4, 1977.

26. On the China visit see Chandler, *Brother Number One*, pp. 137–38, drawing on Chanda, *Brother Enemy*, pp. 100–2. See also Short, *Pol Pot*, pp. 375–76.

27. On Hun Sen see Harsh and Julie Mehta, *Hun Sen: Strong Man of Cambodia* (Singapore, 1999), a somewhat hagiographic study.

28. On the eastern zone purges see Kiernan, *The Pol Pot Regime,* pp. 369–75, 405–11. An aborted uprising in Siem Reap province in April 1977 is ably treated by Margaret Slocomb, "Chikreng Rebellion: Coup and Its Aftermath in Democratic Kampuchea" *Journal of the Royal Asiatic Society* 16/1 (April 2006): 59–72, which includes interviews with survivors.

29. Elizabeth Becker, *When the War Was Over* (New York, 1986), p. 389

30. Evan Gottesman, *Cambodia after the Khmer Rouge* (New Haven, 2003), pp. 7–8.

31. On this visit see Becker, *When the War Was Over*, pp. 387–435, and Chandler, *Brother Number One*, pp. 153–55. Short, *Pol Pot*, pp. 394–95, writes that Pol Pot believed that Dudman, "a CIA agent," had killed Caldwell. Short himself thinks that the most likely killers were a Vietnamese commando team.

32. On the final days of the regime see Short, *Pol Pot,* pp. 396–400.

33. For Khmer Rouge activity in the 1980s see Christophe Peschoux, *Les 'nouveaux' khmers rouges: Enquête 1979–1990* (Paris, 1992).

34. See Kate Frieson, *The Impact of the Revolution on Khmer Peasants: 1970–1975* (Ann Arbor, Mich., 1992), which records the indifference of most rural Cambodians to revolutionary pressures in the early 1970s. See also Frank Smith, *Interpretive Accounts of the Khmer Rouge Years: Personal Experience in Cambodian Peasant World View* (Madison, Wis., 1989).

Chapter 13

1. The first detailed study of this period was by Michael Vickery, *Kampuchea* (London, 1986). A full-scale analysis, less sympathetic to the regime, is Evan Gottesman, *Cambodia after the Khmer Rouge* (New Haven, 2003). See also Margaret Slocomb, *The Peoples' Republic of Kampuchea: The Revo-*

lution after Pol Pot (Chiangmai, 2004). On Hun Sen, see Harsh and Julie Mehta, *Hun Sen: Strong Man of Cambodia* (Singapore, 1999).

2. See the vivid accounts of Denise Affonço, *La digue des veuves* (Paris, 2005), and U Sam Oeur, *Crossing Three Wildernesses* (Minneapolis, 2005), pp. 281–302.

3. For contrasting treatments of this period, see William Shawcross, *The Quality of Mercy* (New York, 1984) passim; Michael Vickery, *Cambodia 1975–1982* (Boston, 1983), pp. 218ff.; and Stephen Morris, *Why Vietnam Invaded Cambodia* (Stanford, 1999).

4. Gottesman, *Cambodia after the Khmer Rouge,* pp. 79–101.

5. On the trial see Gottesman, *Cambodia after the Khmer Rouge,* pp. 60–65; Tom Fawthrop and Helen Jarvis, *Getting Away with Genocide?* (Sydney, 2005) pp. 40–52; and Affonço, *Digue des veuves,* pp. 221–44. Affonço was an eloquent witness at the trial. The lawyer named by the court to defend Ieng Sary and Pol Pot, an African-American Communist, said at the trial, "I did not come half way round the world to give approval to a monstrous crime. . . . It is now clear that Pol Pot and Ieng Sary were criminally insane monsters." Howard J. de Nike et al. (eds.), *Genocide in Cambodia: Documents from the Trial of Pol Pot and Ieng Sary* (Philadelphia, 2000), p. 504. See also David Chandler, *Voices from S-21* (Berkeley, 1999), pp. 4–10, and Charles McDermid, "Looking Back at the 1979 People's Revolutionary Tribunal," *Phnom Penh Post,* January 16–February 28, 2007, which contains interviews with scholars and several witnesses at the trial.

6. On Western indifference to the PRK, see Eva Mysliwiec, *Punishing the Poor: The International Isolation of Kampuchea* (Oxford, 1988).

7. The most recent attempt to assess the number of deaths under DK is P. Heuveline, "'Between One and Three Million': Towards the Demographic Reconstruction of a Decade of Cambodian History (1970–1979)," *Population Studies,* Vol. 52 (1998): 49. See also Craig Etcheson, *After the Killing Fields: Lessons of the Cambodian Genocide* (Westport, Conn., 2005), pp. 118–19.

8. Chinese aid to the DK faction has been estimated at approximately $30 million per year, but no figures have ever been published. China has given substantial aid to all Cambodian governments since 1956, except the years 1970–75 and 1979–93, when it supported resistance movements.

9. See Margaret Slocomb, "The K-5 Gamble: National Defense and Nation Building under the Peoples' Republic of Kampuchea," *JSEAS* 32/2, (June 2001): 195–210, and Gottesman, *Cambodia after the Khmer Rouge,* pp. 223–37.

10. Gottesman, *Cambodia after the Khmer Rouge,* pp. 336–50. For an interesting collection of essays about Cambodian culture in the early 1990s, see May Ebihara, Carol Mortland, and Judy Ledgerwood (eds.), *Cambodian Culture Since 1975: Homeland and Exile* (Ithaca, N.Y., 1994).

11. Gottesman, *Cambodia after the Khmer Rouge,* pp. 316–35.

12. On the UNTAC period see Peter Bartu, "The 'Fifth Faction': The United Nations Intervention in Cambodia 1991–1993" (Ph.D. diss., Monash University, 1998); Michael Doyle et al. (eds.), *Keeping the Peace: Multi-Dimensional UN Operations in Cambodia and El Salvador* (Cambridge, 1997); Trevor Findlay, *Cambodia: The Legacy and Lessons of UNTAC* (New York, 1995); and Steve Heder and Judy Ledgerwood (eds.), *Propaganda, Politics, and Violence in Cambodia in the UNTAC Period* (Armonk, N.Y., 1996).

13. On the run-up to the tribunal see David Chandler, "Will There Be a Trial for the Khmer Rouge?" *Ethics & International Affairs,* 14 (1) (2000): 67–82, and Tom Fawthrop and Helen Jarvis, *Getting Away with Genocide: Elusive Justice and the Khmer Rouge Tribunal* (Sydney, 2004), pp. 155–88.

14. On Pol Pot's closing years see Chandler, *Brother Number One: A Political Biography of Pol Pot* (Boulder, Colo., 1999), pp. 178–88 and Philip Short, *Pol Pot: The History of a Nightmare* (London, 2004), pp. 435–42.

15. See Nick Cummins, *The 1997 Coup in Cambodia: The Prince, the Comrade and the Revolutionary* (Clayton, Australia, 2007), a fresh and definitive treatment. Over nine years of asking questions about the coup, I have never heard anyone mention CPP casualties. There may have been almost none. In 2001, denying that he had ordered anyone killed, Hun Sen told a journalist, "If I really gave the order for killing FUNCINPEC officials . . . there would be no FUNCINPEC today." Nayan Chanda, "The Ruler's Rules," *Far Eastern Economic Review,* 10 May 2001.

16. On the 1998 elections see Sophie Richardson, *The July 1998 Cambodian National Election* (Washington, D.C., 1999); Caroline Hughes and Kim Sedara, *The Evolution of Democratic Process and Conflict Management in Cambodia: A Comparative Study of Three Cambodian Elections* (Phnom Penh, 2004); and Caroline Hughes, *The Political Economy of Cambodia's Transition, 1991–2001* (London, 2003), pp. 67–76.

17. For a harsh assessment see Steve Heder, "Hun Sen's Consolidation: Death or the Beginning of Reform?" *Southeast Asian Affairs 2005,* pp. 113–30. Heder calls Cambodia (from a political perspective) "a maze of patronage, corruption and repression" (p. 114). See also Kheang Un, "Patronage Politics and Hybrid Democracy: Political Change in Cambodia, 1993–2003" *Asian Perspective* 29/2 (2005): 203–30.

18. Hughes and Sedara, *The Evolution of Democratic Process,* pp. 25–32. On the postelection maneuvers see Heder, "Hun Sen's Consolidation," pp. 115ff.

19. Tin Maung Maung Tan, "Cambodia: Strong Man, Terrible Man, Invisible Man," *Southeast Asian Affairs 2004,* pp. 73–89, and Alexander Hinton, "Khmerness and the Thai 'Other': Violence, Discourse and Symbolism in the 2003 Anti-Thai Riots in Cambodia," *JSEAS* 37/5 (October 2006): 445–68.

20. Heder, "Hun Sen's Consolidation," pp. 120ff.

21. On the oil deposits see Adam Piore, "Crash Strapped Cambodia Eyes Black Gold," *Christian Science Monitor,* August 30, 2006.

22. The tribunal is called the Extraordinary Chambers of the Courts of Cambodia (ECCC). See Seth Mydans, "Proceedings to Open on Aged Chiefs of Khmer Rouge," *International Herald Tribune,* August 4, 2006. See also Tom Fawthrop and Helen Jarvis, *Getting Away with Genocide? Elusive Justice and the Khmer Rouge Tribunal* (Sydney, 2005); Steve Heder and Brian Tittemore, *Seven Candidates for Prosecution,* 2nd ed. (Phnom Penh, 2004); and John C. Ciorciari (ed.), *The Khmer Rouge Tribunal* (Phnom Penh, 2006).

BIBLIOGRAPHIC ESSAY

This essay selects and evaluates major primary and secondary sources for Cambodian history that are available in French and English. A reading knowledge of French is essential for people interested in Cambodian history before 1954.

General Works

An excellent bibliographic introduction to Cambodia is Helen Jarvis, *Cambodia* (Santa Barbara, Calif., 1997), which provides astute commentary for its numerous citations. See also Justin Corfield and Laura Summers, *Historical Dictionary of Cambodia* (Lanham Md., 2003), a valuable research tool, and Bruno Brugier (ed.), *Bibliographie du Cambodge Ancien* (Paris, 1998), a thorough compilation.

An early attempt to synthesize Cambodian history, relying heavily on chronicle histories, is Adhémard Leclère's *Histoire du Cambodge* (Paris, 1914; reprinted 1975). Unfortunately, Leclère is cavalier in his use of sources and is difficult to verify. A more recent synthesis, emphasizing early history, is Ian Mabbett and David Chandler, *The Khmers* (Oxford, 1995). See also John Tully, *A Short History of Cambodia: From Empire to Survival* (Sydney, 2005), a skillful, up-to-date overview. The best short study of traditional Cambodian culture is still Solange Thierry's *Les Khmers* (Paris, 1964). David Chandler, *Facing the Cambodian Past: Selected Essays 1971–1994* (Sydney and Chiangmai, 1996), is a collection about Cambodia that is largely historical. See also Saveros Pou, *Selected Papers on Khmerology* (Phnom Penh, 2003), which collects some of her invaluable work published in French and English over the last forty years. In *Lost Goddesses: The Denial of Female Power in Cambodian History* (Copenhagen, 2007), Trudy Jacobsen has perceptively traced the roles, activities, and persecutions of women through the *longue durèe* of Cambodian history.

There are no serious studies of Cambodian urban life, although work in progress on Phnom Penh by Milton Osborne and Paul Reeve promises to close this gap. Michel Igout, *Phnom Penh Then and Now* (Bangkok, 1993), has pleasing illustrations. Rural studies are still dominated by Jean Delvert's magisterial *Le paysan cambodgien* (Paris and The Hague, 1961); see also E. Porée-Maspéro's three-volume study, *Etude sur les rites agraires des cambodgiens* (Paris and The Hague, 1962–69). Ang Choulean, *Les Etres surnaturels dans la religion populaire khmère* (Paris, 1986), and Alain Forest, *Le culte des génies protecteurs au Cambodge* (Paris, 1992), are also valuable. Two good monographic studies of village life in the Sihanouk era are May Ebihara, *Svay* (Ann Arbor, Mich., 1971), and G. Martel, *Lovea* (Paris, 1975), complemented by Eve Zucker's insightful work in progress, which deals with an ethnic Khmer upland village in the early 2000s. On Cambodian Buddhism, excellent recent studies include Ian Harris, *Cambodian Buddhism: History and Practice* (Honolulu, 2005); John Marston and Elizabeth Guthrie (eds.), *History, Buddhism, and New Religious Movements in Cambodia* (Honolulu, 2004); and Anne Hansen's *How to Behave: Buddhism and Modernity in Colonial Cambodia* (Honolulu, 2007). For a helpful analysis of more recent history see Caroline Hughes, *The Political Economy of Cambodia's Transition, 1991–2000* (London, 2003).

From Prehistory to the Decline of Angkor

Work on prehistory is not yet as advanced in Cambodia as it is in Vietnam and Thailand although there has been some exciting progress in recent years. A good, brief introduction to the subject is Donn Bayard, "The Roots of Indo-Chinese Civilization," *Pacific Affairs*, Vol. 53, No. 1 (Spring 1980):89–114. See also Charles Higham's invaluable *Early Cultures of Mainland Southeast Asia* (Bangkok, 2002) and his earlier synthesis, *The Archaeology of Mainland Southeast Asia* (Cambridge, 1989). For recent scholarly developments see Miriam T. Stark, "The

Transition to History in the Mekong Delta: A View from Cambodia," *International Journal of Historical Anthropology* 2/3 (1998): 175–203, which discusses the ongoing excavations at Angkor Borei in southwestern Cambodia, now believed by many to have been the capital of Funan. See also J. Nepote, "Mythes de fondation et fonctionnement de l'ordre sociale dans la basse vallée du Mékong," *Peninsule* 38 (1999): 33–64.

The historiography of the pre-Angkorean period has been revolutionized by Michael Vickery's masterly study, *Society, Economics, and Politics in Pre-Angkor Cambodia* (Tokyo, 1998), the fruit of decades of research. See also M. Vickery, "Funan Reviewed: Deconstructing the Ancients," *BEFEO* 90–91 (2003–4), pp. 101–43. On the vexed issue of Indianization see Vickery, *Society*, pp. 51–58, and I.W. Mabbett, "The 'Indianization' of Mainland Southeast Asia: A Reappraisal" in Natasha Eilenberg et al. (eds.), *Living a Life According to the Dharma: Papers in Honor of Professor Jean Boisselier's 80th Birthday* (Bangkok, 1997), pp. 342–53.

On Angkor, L.P. Briggs's classic work, *The Ancient Khmer Empire* (Philadelphia, 1951), is still useful. A superb recent overview is Michael D. Coe, *Angkor and the Khmer Civilization* (New York, 2003). See also Mabbett and Chandler, *The Khmers*; Charles Higham, *The Civilization of Angkor* (London, 2001); and Claude Jacques and Philippe Lafond, *The Khmer Empire: Cities and Sanctuaries from the 5th to the 13th Century* (Bangkok, 2006).

Students wishing to examine Angkorean inscriptions may consult A. Barth and A. Bergaigne, *Inscriptions sanscrites du Cambodge*, 2 vols., (Paris 1885, 1893), and G. Coedes, *Les inscriptions du Cambodge*, 8 vols. (Hanoi and Paris, 1937–66). The eighth volume of Coedes's compilation is an index of the entire corpus. Coedes's work has been extended by Saveros Pou, *Nouvelles inscriptions du Cambodge* (Vol.1, Paris, 1980; Vols. II and III, Paris 2001).

Monographic studies of Angkorean culture and institutions include S. Sahai, *Les institutions politiques et l'organisation administrative du Cambodge ancien* (Paris, 1970); Jean Boisselier, *Le Cambodge* (Paris, 1966), an archaeological handbook; K. Bhattacharya, *Les religions brahmaniques dans l'ancien Cambodge*, (Paris, 1961); and B.P. Groslier and Jacques Arthaud, *Angkor: Art and Civilization* (New York, 1966).

See also Alexis Sanderson, "The Shaivite Religion among the Khmers" BEFEO 90–91 (2003–4): 345–462, a wide-ranging study. Bruno Dagens, *Angkor: La Forêt de pierre* (Paris, 1989), traces the role of Angkor in later history, while Michael Freeman and Claude Jacques, *Angkor* (Bangkok, 2003), is a beautifully illustrated text that draws on recent research. See also Jacques and Lafond, *The Khmer Empire,* and Helen Ibbetson Jessup and Thierry Zephir (eds.), *Sculpture of Angkor and Ancient Cambodia: Millennium of Glory* (New York, 1997), the catalogue for a stunning exhibition of Khmer art. Travelers to Cambodia should consult Dawn Rooney, *Angkor: Cambodia's Wondrous Temples* (Bangkok, 2007).

Two important studies of kingship at Angkor are H. Kulke, *The Devaraja Cult* (Ithaca, N.Y., 1978), and Ian Mabbett, "Kingship in Angkor," *Journal of the Siam Society,* Vol. 66, No. 2 (July 1978): 1–58. Another stimulating study, stressing the measurements of Angkor Wat and its astronomical aspects is Eleanor Mannika, *Angkor Wat: Time, Space, and Kingship* (Honolulu,1996).

The most detailed study of the reign of Jayavarman VII is B.P. Groslier, *Les inscriptions du Bayon* (Paris, 1973), which has a good bibliography. Students should also consult Phillipe Stern, *Les monuments khmers du style du Bayon et Jayavarman VII* (Paris, 1965). Joyce Clark and Michael Vickery (eds.), *The Bayon: New Perspectives* (Bangkok, 2007), is a superb and partly revisionist collection of essays. An absorbing eyewitness report on everyday life at Angkor in the late thirteenth century is by the Chinese diplomat Zhou Daguan, who visited Cambodia for several months in 1296–97. See Zhou Daguan's *Cambodia: The Land and its People* (ed. and tr. Peter Harris) (Chiangmai, 2007), a fresh translation from the Chinese that is preferable to earlier versions.

Cambodia After Angkor

This crucial period of Cambodian history is attracting increased scholarly attention. For the fifteenth century see Michael Vickery's pathbreaking essay, *Cambodia and Its Neighbors in the 15th Century* (Singapore, Asia Research Institute, Working Paper 27, 2004). See also Claude Jacques, "Les derniers siècles d'Angkor," *Comptes rendus de l'Academie des Inscriptions et belles-Lettres* (2001), which extends the life span of Angkor into the fifteenth century, and his chapter in Clark and Vickery, *The Bayon*. See also Ashley Thompson, "Changing Perspectives: Cambodia After Angkor" in Jessup and Zephir, *Sculpture of Angkor*, pp. 22–33, and her absorbing essay, "Introductory Remarks Between the Lines: Writing Histories of Middle Cambodia," in Barbara Watson Andaya (ed.), *Other Pasts: Women, Gender and History in Early Modern Southeast Asia* (Honolulu, 2000), pp. 47–68. One reason for the ongoing neglect of this period is that the Cambodian chronicle texts are so unreliable, as Michael Vickery has shown in *Cambodia After Angkor: The Chronicular Evidence for the Fourteenth to Sixteenth Centuries* (Ann Arbor, Mich., 1977). Vickery's closing chapter is a valiant attempt to make sense of the period as a whole. For the sixteenth century, B.P. Groslier, *Angkor et le Cambodge au XVIe siècle d'après les sources portugaises et espagnoles* (Paris, 1958), is helpful. Post-Angkorian inscriptions have been edited by Saveros Pou in *Bulletin de l'Ecole Française d'Extrême Orient*, Vol. 59 (1972) and Vol. 62 (1975). Dr. Pou has also edited and translated the chef d'oeuvre of classical Cambodian literature, the *Reamker*, 3 vols. (Paris, 1977–79), as well as the normative poems, or *chbab*, that have been so influential in Cambodian cultural life: see Saveros Pou (ed. and tr.), *Une guirland de chbab* (Paris, 1988). See also Judith Jacob, *The Traditional Literature of Cambodia* (Oxford, 1996). For a valuable synthesis on Cambodia see May Ebihara, "Societal Organization in Sixteenth and Seventeenth Century Cambodia," *Journal of Southeast Asian Studies*, Vol. 15, No. 2 (September 1984): 280–95; see also Khin Sok (ed. and tr.), *Chroniques royales du Cambodge: De Bana Yat à la prise de Lanvek* (Paris, 1988), and the next volume Mak Phoeun (ed. and tr.), *Chroniques royales du Cambodge (de 1594 à 1677)* (Paris, 1981) pp. 179–208. Mak Phoeun, "Essai d'un tableau chronologique des rois de Cambodge de la période post-angkorien," *Journal Asiatique* 290 (2002): 101–61, is a helpful guide for students of the period.

On Europeans in Cambodia in the sixteenth and seventeenth centuries see Jean-Claude Lejosne, "Historiographie du Cambodge aux XVIe et XVIIe siècles," in Pierre L. Lamant (ed.), *Bilan et perspectives des Ètudes khmères (Langue et Culture)* (Paris, 1997); Carool Kersten (ed. and tr.), *Strange Events in the Kingdoms of Cambodia and Laos*

(1635–1644) (Bangkok, 2003); and Gabriel Quiroga de San Antonio, *A Brief and Truthful Relation of Events in the Kingdom of Cambodia* (Bangkok, 1998). Gregory Mikaelian, "La gestion administrative du royaume khmère d'aprés un code institutionel du XVIIe siècle," *Peninsule 35* (1998): 65–168, is a valuable translation of a key administrative text. Insights on trade between Japan and Cambodia in the seventeenth and eighteenth centuries (using Chinese junks) is Yoneo Ishii (ed.), *The Junk Trade from Southeast Asia: Translations from the Tosen Fusetsu-gaki 1674–1723* (Singapore 1998), pp. 153–93.

For the first half of the nineteenth century, see David P. Chandler, *Cambodia Before the French: Politics in a Tributary Kingdom, 1794–1847* (Ann Arbor, Mich., 1974); Khin Sok, *Le Cambodge entre le Siam et le Vietnam (de 1775 a 1860)* (Paris, 1991); and Khin Sok, *L'annexation du Cambodge par les Vietnamiens au XIXe Siècle* (Paris, 2002), a critical edition of two Khmer verse chronicles written in the 1850s.

The French Protectorate, 1863–1954

For a critical overview of the colonial period see John Tully's absorbing *France on the Mekong: A History of the Protectorate in Cambodia* (Lanham, Md., 2002), and Penny Edwards, *Cambodge: The Cultivation of a Nation, 1860–1945* (Honolulu, 2007), a pathbreaking analysis of Khmer nationalism in the colonial era. For the early colonial period, G. Taboulet (ed.), *La geste française en Indochine*, 2 vols. (Paris, 1955), a collection of documents, is useful and so is Milton Osborne's, *The French Presence in Cochinchina and Cambodia: Rule and Response (1859–1905)* (Ithaca, N.Y., 1969). For the early twentieth century, see Alain Forest, *Le Cambodge et la colonisation française: Histoire d'une colonisation sans heurts (1897–1920)* (Paris, 1980), and John Tully, *Cambodia under the Tricolour: The Sisowath Years* (Clayton, Australia 1996). For the closing years of the colonial era see Philippe Preschez, *Essai sur la démocratie au Cambodge* (Paris, 1961), which is especially good on the political scene in Cambodia after World War II.

For the early phases of Cambodian radicalism, see Ben Kiernan, *How Pol Pot Came to Power*, 2nd ed. (New Haven, 2005); Philip Short, *Pol Pot: The Anatomy of a Nightmare* (New York, 2005), pp. 47–144; and

J.C. Pomonti and Serge Thion, *Des courtesans aux partisans: La crise cambodgienne* (Paris, 1971). See also Steve Heder, *Cambodian Communism and the Vietnamese Model. Vol 1: Imitation and Independence* (Bangkok, 2004). Ben Kiernan and Chanthou Boua (eds.), *Peasants and Politics in Kampuchea, 1942–1981* (London, 1982), contains valuable primary material. For a discussion of decolonization in Cambodia see Donald Lancaster, *The Emancipation of French Indo-China* (New York, 1961). Norodom Sihanouk's memoirs, *L'Indochine vue de Pékin* (Paris, 1972) and *Souvenirs doux et amers* (Paris, 1981), both fascinating, may be used with caution.

Cambodian History 1955–75

For an overview of events in this period see Chandler, *The Tragedy of Cambodian History: Politics, War, and Revolution Since 1945* (New Haven, 1991), Chapters 3 through 6. See also Kiernan and Boua (eds.), *Peasants and Politics in Kampuchea, 1942–1981*. Kenton Clymer, *United States and Cambodia, 1870–2000*, 2 vols. (New York, 2004), is a helpful survey. See Milton Osborne's insightful *Before Kampuchea* (London, 1979), which deals with Cambodia in the mid-1960s. A hostile treatment of the Sihanouk era that has stood up well is Charles Meyer, *Derrière le sourire khmer* (Paris, 1971). For an enlightening cultural overview of the Sihanouk years drawing on extensive interviews, see Ly Daravuth and Ingrid Muan (eds.), *Cultures of Independence: An Introduction to Cambodian Arts and Culture in the 1950s and 1960s* (Phnom Penh, 2001). A lively, authoritative memoir that traverses five decades of Cambodian history from the 1940s is U Sam Oeur, *Crossing Three Wildernesses* (Minneapolis, 2005).

For the Lon Nol era, William Shawcross, *Sideshow: Nixon, Kissinger, and the Destruction of Cambodia* (New York, 1979), is a withering attack on U.S. policies toward Cambodia in 1970–75, and Justin Corfield, *Khmers Stand Up!* (Clayton, Australia, 1994), is a judicious political history. For a history of Cambodian-Vietnamese Communist relations see Thomas Engelbert and Christopher Goscha, *Falling Out of Touch: A Study of Vietnamese Communist Policy toward an Emerging Cambodian Communist Movement, 1930–1975* (Clayton, Australia, 1995), which is a fascinating collection of previously unpublished Vietnamese texts.

The Pol Pot Era

There are many readable accounts of the Pol Pot era, some of them written by survivors. An early analysis of the revolution and still one of the best, is François Ponchaud, *Cambodia Year Zero* (New York, 1978). Two fine-grained studies are Michael Vickery's *Cambodia 1975–1982* (Boston, 1983, repr. Bangkok, 2004), and R.A. Burgler, *The Eyes of the Pineapple: Revolutionary Intellectuals and Terror in Democratic Kampuchea* (Saarbrücken, 1990). Elizabeth Becker, *When the War Was Over* (New York, 1986), reviews the era perceptively, and two helpful collections of essays are David Chandler and Ben Kiernan (eds.), *Revolution and Its Aftermath in Kampuchea: Eight Essays* (New Haven, 1983), and Karl Jackson (ed.), *Cambodia 1975–1978: Rendezvous with Death* (Princeton, N.J., 1989). Kiernan's *The Pol Pot Regime: Politics, Race, and Genocide* (New Haven, 1996) uses valuable oral evidence gathered in the early 1980s. Chandler, Kiernan, and Chanthou Boua (eds. and trs.), *Pol Pot Plans the Future: Confidential Leadership Documents from Democratic Kampuchea 1976–1977* (New Haven, 1988) is a compilation of primary documents. See also Timothy Carney, *Communist Party Power in Kampuchea (Cambodia): Documents and Discussion* (Ithaca, N.Y., 1977).

David Chandler, *Voices from S-21: Terror and History in Pol Pot's Secret Prison* (Berkeley and Los Angeles, 1999) examines a key Khmer Rouge facility, drawing on its voluminous archives. For an anthropological perspective on the period see Alexander Hinton, *Why Did They Kill? Cambodia in the Shadow of Genocide* (Berkeley and Los Angeles, 2005). Henri Locard (ed. and tr.), *Pol Pot's Little Red Book: The Sayings of Angkar* (Chiangmai, 2005), is a disturbing collection of Khmer Rouge slogans. For an insightful collection of essays about Cambodian politics see Serge Thion, *Watching Cambodia* (Bangkok, 1993). The demography of the mass killings in Cambodia is dealt with in Marek Sliwinski, *Une analyse demographique du genocide des Khmer rouges* (Paris, 1995).

The best survivors' accounts are probably Pin Yathay, *Stay Alive, My Son* (Ithaca, N.Y., 2000); Someth May, *Cambodian Witness* (London, 1986); Haing Ngor, *A Cambodian Odyssey* (New York, 1987); and Ung

Bunheang and Martin Stuart Fox, *The Murderous Revolution* (Sydney, 1984). See also Dith Pran (ed.), *Children of Cambodia's Killing Fields* (New Haven, 1997), a poignant collection of memoirs. Laurence Picq's vivid memoir, *Beyond the Horizon* (New York, 1989), recounts the experiences of a Frenchwoman who was married to a DK official and who worked in the DK Ministry of Foreign Affairs. See also Wynne Cougill (ed.), *Stilled Lives: Photographs from the Cambodian Genocide* (Phnom Penh, 2004), a moving collection of photographs of youthful Khmer Rouge cadre with biographical data.

On Pol Pot see Chandler, *Brother Number One: A Political Biography of Pol Pot*, 2nd ed. (Boulder, Colo., 1999), and Philip Short's more detailed *Pol Pot: The Anatomy of a Nightmare* (New York, 2004). Material collected and published in English and Khmer by the Cambodian Genocide Program sponsored by Yale University and housed in the Documentation Center-Cambodia in Phnom Penh (DC-Cam) is invaluable for students of this period. Many new documents are bound to appear in the lifetime of the tribunal to try leaders of the Khmer Rouge, which convened in 2006.

Cambodia since 1979

For early assessments of events since 1979 see Grant Evans and Kelvin Rowley, *Red Brotherhood at War* (London, 1984; rev. ed., 1990); Nayan Chanda, *Brother Enemy* (New York, 1986); and William Shawcross, *The Quality of Mercy* (New York, 1984). The best scholarly overview of the PRK regime is Evan Gottesman, *Cambodia after the Khmer Rouge: Inside the Politics of Nation Building* (New Haven, 2003), which supplements Michael Vickery's *Kampuchea* (London, 1986) and can be read alongside Margaret Slocomb's more sympathetic account, *The Peoples' Republic of Kampuchea, 1979–1989: The Revolution after Pol Pot* (Chiangmai, 2003). Eva Mysliwiec, *Punishing the Poor: The International Isolation of Kampuchea* (Oxford, 1988), attacks international indifference to Cambodia in the 1980s.

Grant Curtis, *Cambodia Reborn?* (Washington D.C., 1999), deals with the UNTAC and post-UNTAC periods. Two worthwhile recent collections include Kiernan (ed.), *Genocide and Democracy in Cambodia: The Khmer Rouge, the United Nations, and the International Community*

(New Haven, 1993), and Steve Heder and Judy Ledgerwood (eds.), *Politics, Violence, and Propaganda in Cambodia in the UNTAC Period* (Armonk, N.Y., 1995). The UNTAC period is covered perceptively by Michael W. Doyle, *UN Peacekeeping in Cambodia: UNTAC's Civil Mandate* (Boulder, Colo., 1995).

For developments in the mid-1990s, see Frederick Z. Brown and David G. Timberman (eds.), *Cambodia and the International Community* (Singapore, 1998). Judy Ledgerwood (ed.), *Cambodia Emerges from the Past: Eight Essays* (De Kalb, Ill., 2002), and MacAlister Brown and Joseph Zasloff, *Cambodia Confounds the Peace-Makers, 1979–1998* (Ithaca, N.Y., 1998). For astute, pessimistic readings of the current political scene see Caroline Hughes, *The Political Economy of Cambodia's Transition, 1991–2001* (New York and London, 2003), and Sorpong Peou, *Intervention and Change in Cambodia: Towards Democracy?* (New York and Singapore, 2000). A stimulating study of Cambodian women workers is Anniksa Dirks, *Khmer Women on the Move: Migration and Global Experiences in Cambodia* (Honolulu, 2007). Karen J. Cooke, *Cambodia Now* (Jefferson, N.C., 2005), vividly conveys the feel of contemporary life.

On cultural matters in recent years, see May Ebihara, Judy Ledgerwood, and Carol Mortland (eds.), *Cambodian Culture Since 1975: Homeland and Exile* (Ithaca, N.Y., 1994), and Toni Samantha Phim and Ashley Thompson, *Cambodian Dance* (New York, 1999). See also Alexandra Kent and David Chandler (eds.), *People of Virtue: Reconfiguring Religion, Power and Moral Order in Cambodia Today* (Copenhagen, 2007). Cambodian literature is treated in detail in Khing Hoc Dy, *Contribution à l'histoire de la littérature khmère*, 2 vols. (Paris, 1990, 1993), while a good survey of twenty-first-century Cambodian cultural politics is Leakthina Chau-Pech Ollier and Tim Winter (eds.), *Expressions of Cambodia: The Politics of Tradition, Identity and Change* (London and New York, 2006). See also the *Journal of Southeast Asian Studies,* Vol. 37, No. 3 (October 2006), which devotes several articles to the theme "Reassessing Tradition in Times of Change: Post War Cambodia Reconsidered."

Books about the tribunal to indict leaders of the Khmer Rouge for crimes against humanity include Tom Fawthrop and Helen Jarvis, *Get-*

ting Away with Genocide? Elusive Justice and the Khmer Rouge Tribunal (Sydney, 2005); Steve Heder and Brian Tittemore, *Seven Candidates for Prosecution*, 2nd ed. (Phnom Penh, 2004); and John C. Ciorciari (ed.), *The Khmer Rouge Tribunal* (Phnom Penh, 2006).

INDEX

351